A Kingdom of Priests

The Stories of Revelation

Brenda Weltner

Preface

- When will the rapture take place?
- When will the 7 Seals be opened?
- Who will kill the Antichrist?
- When will the temple be rebuilt in Jerusalem?
- When will Christ return to earth?

I know the answers to all these questions, and soon you will, too.

I could have called this book, <u>The Revelation Code</u>, because Revelation was given to us in coded form. Once you know how to crack the code, you can know the story of the End, and, like all codes, everything is as plain as day once you know the secret.

Not everyone can say that they have cracked the code of Revelation—but I can, and I'm confident that I can tell you the stories of the people who will be living during the time of The End.

You're one of them...

A Kingdom of Priests   1

Introduction

At its most basic, Revelation is a prophetic message about the end times. The Apostle John received the prophecies through a series of visions given to him by God, which he then recorded in the book known as Revelation. Detailed in the visions were the events which would take place on the earth prior to Christ's 2nd Coming. That much is plain.

What's not so plain, however, is how to understand the prophecy God has given us? Contained within its pages are visions of mystical creatures, dragons with seven heads, and beasts coming up from the sea. What does all this mean? The story in Revelation is not like other Bible stories: Noah and the flood, the birth of Christ, or the miracle of the loaves and fishes. These stories are relatively easy to understand, but how are we meant to decipher the story of *Revelation*?

In my experience, most people who have a willingness to tackle the book of Revelation at all, begin studying the book the way most books are read and understood: with the assumption that the beginning of the story is recorded in the beginning of the book, and the end of the story is at the end of the book—but that doesn't seem to be the case with Revelation. Chapters begin and end with little or no obvious connection to the events in previous or succeeding chapters. New characters arrive out of thin air. Random events are strung together like so many beads on a string. The book is illogical and confusing. Many a sincere believer has walked away, more baffled about end time events than when they began, concluding that the book is basically indecipherable and unknowable.

Is Revelation Chronological?

Reading Revelation is like viewing a tapestry from the backside. Threads of the story line weave in and out among the various visions. Characters disappear and then reappear again in unexpected places. Threads are left dangling in the middle of nowhere as visions leave us hanging. The chronology is complex and broken up, even within chapters. The story—if indeed there *is* a story—is hard to follow, and it's nearly impossible to know where the various threads begin and where they end. Trying to visualize the picture being woven on the other side of the tapestry feels like an effort in futility.

Much of the confusion surrounding how to interpret Revelation stems from a seeming lack of a coherent chronology within the book. The 'end' of the story—the return of Christ and the setting up of His millennial reign—is clearly seen in the last few chapters of Revelation. The 'beginning' seems to start somewhere around the time the Lamb takes the scroll in the opening chapters of the book;

but there is no chapter and verse that we can point to and say *this is where the story starts.*

Most scholars would readily agree that the events depicted in Revelation are not placed in chronological order in the book. Nevertheless, there still is a tendency to interpret the book as though it *were* chronological. Bible teachers start with the underlying assumption that the book is telling *only one story*. Their study begins with chapter one, and then advances on to chapter 2, and so on, moving through the book chapter by chapter, in an attempt to string together a coherent narrative *based on the way the chapters are laid out in the book*. In the long run, this method of interpretation is doomed to failure, because Revelation is not one story—it's *many* stories, with bits and pieces of each of the stories interspersed among the various visions. It's the reader's job to gather up the individual pieces which lie scattered throughout the book, and assemble each one of the stories, one 'puzzle piece' at a time.

A series of visions...

In giving us the book of Revelation, God has placed in our hands the *whole story*—the Big Story—of the last days, but the end time narrative is so big, so complex, and involves so many people, that *no one story is capable of communicating everything* that God wanted to tell us. So God chose to reveal the Big Story through a series of smaller stories—in the form of visions—with each vision communicating some aspect or portion of the larger story. Through the visions of Revelation, God has provided us with all the details necessary to create a unified and comprehensive description and chronology of the last days.

The visions of Revelation chronicle the stories of the people who will be living at the time of the end. More than being a prophetic recounting of the various Seal, Trumpet and Bowl judgments, Revelation is primarily a book *about people*: the 24 Elders, the 144,000 of Israel, the 'saints', the martyrs and so on. And rather than focusing on the disasters that will overtake the earth during the last days, the purpose of Revelation is to bring hope, encouragement and blessing to the individuals who will be a part of the end time story, by *revealing to them in advance what is going to take place*. Ultimately, if you can tell the individual stories of the different characters in Revelation, you will understand the Big Story as well.

Similar to the way filmmakers move from scene to scene in a movie, with each scene containing some vital piece of information intended to move the plot forward, Revelation also moves the story forward through multiple scenes which John received as visions. Like scenes in a movie, the visions tell the stories of people and how their lives will intersect during the end times; and like a good detective film which must be viewed more than once to catch all the clues, Revelation must be read, and reread, in order to identify all the pieces of the various stories which lie hidden in the visions—pieces cleverly disguised as seemingly insignificant details.

These often overlooked details are vitally important components of the story, and no detail in *any* of the visions is random—but carefully placed in a particular vision *for a reason*. Employing an economy of language and restraint that could only originate from God, we have been provided with enough clues, and exactly the *right* clues, to be able to construct a deep and meaningful narrative of the end of days.

Working through Revelation is somewhat like putting together several different puzzles at one time with all the pieces of the different puzzles jumbled in the same box. Once we sort through the various pieces in the box we call "Revelation", and have laid the pieces out in front of us, we can then discover similarities between the pieces which help us know which pieces go with which puzzle. After putting together each of the smaller stories—the individual puzzles—we can then go about constructing the larger chronology of Revelation. We do this by 'deconstructing' the smaller visions and then, using the same puzzle pieces, we can reconfigure them to create the Big Story of the last days. Or, to use another analogy, Revelation is more like a Rubik's Cube than Monopoly—you have to keep moving things around until everything is in the right place, something you can't do when playing a board game—or when you attempt to interpret Revelation chapter by chapter!

Visions can be Topical

When we examine the visions of Revelation, we discover that some of the visions are topical in nature, as opposed to visions which tell a story. For instance, the 7 Seals that are opened in Revelation chapter 6, are all part of one vision we could call 'The Seal Vision". The events portrayed when the seals are opened, take place sequentially, beginning with the events associated with the opening of the first Seal and ending with the events associated with the Lamb opening the 7th Seal. Even though we know the *order* that Christ will open the seals, we still don't know exactly *when* each associated event will take place in the larger timeline of Revelation.

The Four Horsemen will 'ride' as the first four seals are opened, followed by the 5th Seal Martyrs, the 6th Seal wrath of God and the 7th Seal of silence in heaven. All of this may seem obvious, but it's important to understand that, even though Revelation is not chronological, there *is* an order to the events. We also need to understand that just knowing the *order* that events will unfold, doesn't tell us exactly *when* the events will take place. When will the 'Horsemen' ride? When are the martyrs killed? When does the wrath take place? When—and why—the silence in heaven at the opening of the 7th Seal? All these are mysteries which cannot be solved just by reading the Seal vision. In order to understand *when* each of the Seals will be opened, we need more information; information that can be found in one or more of the *other* visions of Revelation.

Revelation is a collection of many stories, most of which are set in the timeframe of the seven years before the return of Christ. God chose to tell the story indirectly and symbolically, through layering the various visions over one another. If we 'reverse engineer' the book *using the same process and peeling back the layers*, we can unlock the identity of the various characters and get to know them well enough to be able to tell their stories. Being able to tell their stories is important because some of the characters we see on the pages of Revelation are actually you and me! In the book of Revelation, God is telling us *our* story.

Before we can interpret the actual stories in Revelation, we need to understand the context and setting of the book itself, which is God's temple in heaven.

Chapter 1: Flowing from the Source

> "God has put all things under His feet, and has appointed Him universal and supreme Head of the Church, which is His Body." Ephesians 1:22 (Weymouth)

> "...the Father is greater than I." John 14:28b

The Divine Hierarchy

There is a hierarchy within the Godhead of the Father, Son and Holy Spirit. The Father is the ultimate Source of all things within the Divine Community; and His Son is the Source of all things pertaining to the Church, which is His Body. All that the Father possesses, He has granted to His Son, and the Father shares all things with His Son.

Much of our understanding of the attributes of the triune God are actually found within the pages of Revelation. The majesty of Almighty God, Christ's divine nature, and the fellowship and cooperation of the Spirit, are portrayed in the symbolism and imagery contained in the visions. The characteristics of the Persons who make up the Divine Community, and their interactions with each other, is as much a part of the end time story as anything else we read about in Revelation.

Jesus is the Divine Son

1. God shared the prophetic word concerning the end times with the Son:

> "This is the Revelation of Jesus Christ, which God gave him to show to his servants the things which must happen soon." Revelation 1:1a

The prophecy contained within the pages of Revelation reveals the unfolding of the Almighty's plan concerning the end of days; a plan which, until the time of John, had been hidden away in the heart of God. The Father took it upon Himself to reveal His end time plan to Jesus, and He described to His Son *how and when believers would be brought into the throne room of heaven.* The source of the book of Revelation is the Father; and this makes the prophecies of Revelation unique in all of Scripture. Every other prophecy in the Bible was given by the inspiration of the Holy Spirit to ordinary men, but Revelation was given directly from Almighty God to His Son.

"Knowing this first, that no prophecy of Scripture is of private interpretation. 21 For no prophecy ever came by the will of man, but holy men of
God spoke, being moved by the Holy Spirit." 2 Peter 1:20,21

The Holy Spirit was not the source of the visions given to John. Rather the Father
Himself revealed the details of the end time story to His Son, Jesus, who then re-
layed the message given to Him, to an angel. The angel told John, who wrote an
account of all he saw and heard. Christ, the angel and John all claimed that their
testimony was accurate and that they faithfully communicated the message exactly as they received it.

"This is the Revelation of Jesus Christ, which God gave him to show to his
servants the things which must happen soon, which he sent and made
known by his angel to his servant, John, 2 *who testified to God's word and
of the testimony of Jesus Christ, about everything that he saw.*" Revelation 1:1,2 *(italics mine)*

"He said to me, "Write, 'Blessed are those who are invited to the wedding
supper of the Lamb.' " He said to me, *"These are true words of God."*"
Revelation 19:9

"John, to the seven assemblies that are in Asia: Grace to you and peace
from God, who is and who was and who is to come; and from the seven
Spirits who are before his throne; 5 and from Jesus Christ, the *faithful
witness.*" Revelation 1:4, 5a

"To the angel of the assembly in Laodicea write:
'The Amen, the *Faithful and True Witness*, the Beginning† of God's
creation, " Revelation 3:14

"I, Jesus, have sent my angel *to testify these things to you* for the assemblies." Revelation 22:16a

Were it not for the book of Revelation, we would have very few details concerning
the events connected with the close of the age, and especially how those days
would impact *believers*; but God in His mercy has given His people a prophetic
book to prepare them for the rapid unfolding of events which will soon overtake
the world.

Though Revelation is a relatively short book—containing only 22 chapters—it is a
very deep book and it's in its depth (not length) that the story is told. Through the
use of symbols and images, end time events are layered over various allusions

found elsewhere in both the Old and New Testaments. Revelation tells the story of the end *indirectly*, pointing the reader to specific biblical stories, types and shadows, from which we learn the rest of the story.

This very last book of the Bible incorporates the high-points of the whole of scripture, and is the most concise, dense and meaty of all prophetic books, encapsulating the richness of Old Testament patterns, the nuances of Pauline doctrine and the passionate echos of Christ's first coming as recounted in gospel of John the Beloved disciple. It's as though God gathered up all of His favorite scripture passages and lovingly crafted them into this one prophecy for His end time saints.

The bottom line is that Revelation is a gift from the Father to those of us who find ourselves at the close of history.

2. God declares that He is the Alpha and the Omega and His Son shares this title of divinity as well:

> "I am the Alpha and the Omega," says the Lord God, "who is and who was and who is to come, the Almighty." Revelation 1:8 (About the Father.)

> "I am the Alpha and the Omega, the First and the Last, the Beginning and the End." Revelation 22:13 (Applied to Christ.)

'Alpha' is the first letter in the Greek alphabet and 'omega' is the last letter. These two letters encapsulate the eternal nature of both the Father and the Son. They are the "A to Z", the 'first and the last'...and everything in between. Christ and the Father declare their eternal existence through the metaphor of two Greek letters. Neither the Father nor the Son were created—They have always been. The divine Son has been in fellowship with the Father from eternity past and, together with the Holy Spirit, they comprise the triune community of God. The fact that both the Father and the Son share this title should lay to rest any thought that Christ is less than divine or that He is a created being.

3. God shares His power over the nations with Christ:

> "He who overcomes, and he who keeps my works to the end, to him I will give authority over the nations. 27 He will rule them with a rod of iron, shattering them like clay pots, as I also have received of my Father. " Revelation 2:26, 27

God has given all authority to His Son, and Christ will rule over the nations of the earth. During the Millennium, any challenge to Christ's authority on the part of the nations of the earth will met with force: He will rule with a 'rod of iron'. Obedience will be required of all mankind, and Christ will have the power and authority to enforce His will.

4. God shares His throne with His Son:

> "He who overcomes, I will give to him to sit down with me on my throne, as I also overcame and *sat down with my Father on his throne.*" Revelation 3:21

> "He showed me a river of water of life, clear as crystal, proceeding out of the *throne of God and of the Lamb*...3 There will be no curse any more. The *throne of God and of the Lamb* will be in it, and his servants will serve him." Revelation 22:1,3

A throne is a symbol of authority, power, control and honor. God's throne is an eternal throne and He shares His power and right to rule with His Son, the Lamb. Decrees are issued from the throne, and those seated on the throne must be obeyed.

5. The Father and the Lamb execute 'wrath':

> "They told the mountains and the rocks, "Fall on us, and hide us from the face of him who sits on the throne, and from the wrath of the Lamb!" Revelation 6:16

When the Day of the Lord comes, the righteous judgment of God will fall upon rebellious, mortal men. The Lamb will execute the wrath that God has prepared for the rebels of the Antichrist kingdom.

6. The Father and the Lamb both receive worship:

> "After these things I looked, and behold, a great multitude which no man could count, out of every nation and of all tribes, peoples, and languages, standing before the throne and before the Lamb, dressed in white robes, with palm branches in their hands. 10 They cried with a loud voice, saying, "Salvation be to our God, *who sits on the throne, and to the Lamb!*" Revelation 7:9, 10

Both the One seated on the throne and the Lamb are worshiped and adored by men and angels. Only God is worthy of the worship of all of creation; and the Lamb, being God, is also worshiped by angels and redeemed, glorified humanity. There is no jealousy between the Father and the Son, and they are worshiped individually and together.

7. The Father shares the kingdoms of the world with His Son:

> "The seventh angel sounded, and great voices in heaven followed, saying, "The kingdom of the world has become the Kingdom of our *Lord and of his Christ*. He will reign forever and ever!" Revelation 11:15

At the end of the wrath of God, the surviving nations on the earth will belong to the Lord and His Christ—His anointed One. The conquered nations will be the spoils of war and Christ and His Father will rule over mankind forever.

8. The Father and the Son are the temple of New Jerusalem:

> " I saw no temple in it, for the Lord God the Almighty and the Lamb are its temple." Revelation 21:22

A temple is the place where God and men meet together. It is the intersection of earth and heaven and the place where mortals encounter the Divine Presence. In some ways, a temple is a kind of 'no man's land', a place belonging neither solely to God or to man, but the location where a 'truce' is called between them, where atonement is made and where prayers are offered.

There is, however, no temple in the New Jerusalem, the heavenly City which will come down from heaven at the end of the Millennium. At that time, sin and death will be done away with and there will no longer be the necessity of a priest to offer sacrifices, acting as a 'go-between' between a holy God and sinful man. Heaven and earth will unite as God and man find common ground in the Holy City. The Almighty and the Lamb, along with glorified saints, will live on earth with re-deemed men and women, the blood of the Lamb having made everlasting peace between God and man.

9. Both Christ and His Father possess radiant glory:

> "The city had no need of the sun or of the moon to shine in it, for the glory of God illuminated it. The Lamb is its light." Revelation 21:23

The splendor of God is often depicted as light. The glory of God is present in Christ, and the splendor of their glory radiates from both Father and Son.
In the pages of Revelation, God has told us a little something about Himself and his relationship with His Son. The relationship between the Father and the Son is one of love and extravagant giving. These two attributes—of love and generosity— are also revealed in the Son's relationship with His people. The same riches which we see the Father bestowing on His Son, the Son then lavishes upon His people.

Many of the same divine blessings that the Father shares with Christ, Christ will share with His glorified saints.

1. Christ shares the message of the end times given to Him by the Father:

> "This is the Revelation of Jesus Christ, which God gave him to show to his servants the things which must happen soon, which he sent and made known by his angel to his servant, John." Revelation 1:1

The 'revelation of Jesus Christ' is the prophetic message which the Father communicated to Jesus, which Jesus, in turn, gave to an angel to give to John. The fact that Jesus used an intermediary to deliver the prophecy to John is highly significant. The Father gave the revelation to Christ; and He in turn delivered the message to John via an angel. This recalls the giving of the Law on Mount Sinai, when God used an angel to deliver the Law to Moses; and then Moses took the law he was given and mediated the covenant with the children of Israel. The fact that Christ also used an angelic intermediary—rather than delivering the message Himself—is indicative of His divine rank.

Because the book of Revelation is a divine oracle, delivered through a mediator, it needs to be received by God's people with the same reverence as was the giving of the Law in the Old Testament. Those for whom the book of Revelation was written are advised to give heed to the words of God contained in this prophecy, and to keep them, as the prophecy of Revelation contains the *new commandments* of God for His end time servants.

2. Our Great High Priest has made us kings and priests through His blood:

> "...and from Jesus Christ, the faithful witness, the firstborn of the dead, and the ruler of the kings of the earth. To him who loves us, and washed us from our sins by his blood— 6 and he made us to be a Kingdom, priests to his God and Father—to him be the glory and the dominion forever and ever. Amen." Revelation 1:5,6

This passage contains the key to understanding the identity of the various groups of believers who appear before God's throne in the heavenly temple, and is our starting place for decoding the book of Revelation. *Christ has made us kings and priests to His God and Father.* In describing believers as priests, God is not just using a nice spiritual sounding metaphor, He is using *THE* metaphor that will be used throughout the book to describe our relationship with God, and how believers arrive in heaven! The Father does not refer to us as the Bride, or even as His children. We are His *priests*, people who are qualified to enter into the heavenly Holy of Holies and serve in His presence.

Much of the prophecy in Revelation is devoted to detailing how the priesthood of believers enters the Holy of Holies—God's throne room in the heavenly temple. In this short verse in Revelation 1:6, we are told that believers have been made priests; and one of the main plot lines in Revelation is the story of *how and when priests enter into God's service*. The only way that believers can serve as priests in the heavenly temple is to actually be brought into heaven.

In chapters 4 & 5 of Revelation, we are introduced to the 24 Elders, who are seated on thrones in God's throne room, wearing golden crowns on their heads.

> "Immediately I was in the Spirit. Behold, there was a throne set in heaven, and one sitting on the throne 3 that looked like a jasper stone and a sardius. There was a rainbow around the throne, like an emerald to look at. 4 Around the throne were twenty-four thrones. On the thrones were twenty-four elders sitting, dressed in white garments, with crowns of gold on their heads." Revelation 4:2-4

In chapter 5, the Elders hold golden bowls of incense with which they offer up the prayers of the saints on earth. They are presented as royalty, as kings—who also act as priests. The 24 Elders are glorified saints—the kings and priests mentioned in Revelation 1.

Numbers are often used symbolically in the scriptures. The numbers '7' and '12' are common symbolic numbers representing 'completion and divinity' (7) and 'divine government' (12). The number '24', however, is seldom used in the Bible and most people attempting to decode the number '24' in this passage about the 24 Elders, assume that the symbolic meaning of the number '24', is actually the product of 2 x 12. The 24 Elders then seem to represent the 12 apostles plus the 12 patriarchs of Israel.

However, the number '24' is actually used in a prophetically significant way in 1 Chronicles 24. King David, who set up the administration for the temple which his son, Solomon, would later build, divided the priests into 24 divisions or courses. Each division of priests was assigned a tour of duty in the temple, during which time they would minister to God.

The idea of the members of the priesthood being divided into groups, is carried over into the book of Revelation, as we see various groups of priest/kings arriving in the heavenly throne room over the course of seven years. First, the 24 Elders appear in chapters 4 & 5, later the 5th Seal Martyrs (Revelation 6 & 7), and then the 144,000 of Israel (Revelation 14), the "Over-comers" (Revelation 15) and finally the Martyrs of the Beast who are resurrected at the return of Christ (Revelation 20).

The number '24', which is connected with the Elders, who are symbolically represented as priest/kings seated in God's presence, provides a clue that perhaps the different groups of believers seen in heaven at different times, are *priestly divisions*, each group having been brought into God's presence at a specific time relative to their tour of duty. This implies the likelihood that there may be more than one rapture/resurrection that will take place during the course of the seven years prior to the return of Christ.

The passage concerning believers being made into priests, also broadly hints that the end time events will be described in the context of 'temple' imagery. The layout of the temple, its furnishings, the appointed feast days and the various priestly functions—all of which are present in Revelation—tell us in symbolic fashion, when the various divisions of priests will arrive in the temple, and the circumstances which will precede their arrival. The only way to really understand Revelation is to interpret it through the filter of the Hebraic temple rites and rituals.

Because temple imagery is such an important key to arriving at a precise and comprehensive interpretation of Revelation, we'll be taking a much closer look at the Temple, the Feast days, etc., later in this book.

3. Christ shares His power over the nations:

> "He who overcomes, and he who keeps my works to the end, to him I will give authority over the nations. 27 He will rule them with a rod of iron, shattering them like clay pots, as I also have received of my Father'" Revelation 2:26,27

Christ has not only qualified believers to be God's priests in heaven, He has also declared that they will rule with Him as kings on earth. Christ, who has been given authority from God to rule over the kingdoms of the world, will also grant authority for *glorified believers* to rule over the nations. Believers will rule on earth during the thousand year reign of Christ on earth (a time also referred to as the Millennium).

4. Christ shares His royal throne:

> "He who overcomes, I will give to him to sit down with me on my throne, as I also overcame and sat down with my Father on his throne." Revelation 3:21

The 24 Elders, who represent believers in heaven, will be the first to appear in the throne room of God, with each Elder seated on his own throne. A throne represents authority, power and the right to rule. The individual thrones on which each

Elder is seated, represent the believer's reward for faithful service on earth. The fact that each Elder has his own throne indicates that every believer will rule in his own right, exercising the dominion given to him as a reward for faithful service here on earth. In addition, believers will be granted the privilege of being seated with Christ on *His* throne, exercising the power and authority of Christ on His behalf on the earth. To be seated with Christ on His throne is to share all the authority and honor of the One to whom the throne belongs. Christ shares His royal authority with His glorified saints.

5. He places His name on us:

> "There will be no curse any more. The throne of God and of the Lamb will be in it, and his servants will serve him. 4 They will see his face, and his name will be on their foreheads." Revelation 22:3,4

Just as a wife takes the name of her husband, and in so doing identifies her life with his; in like manner, the saints of God will be known as those who belong to Christ and are a part of the family of God, sharing His identity, character and resources. To share one's name is to share everything that goes with that name. The name encapsulates the Person and also declares ownership. Christ places His name on His people because they belong to Him, and they will have a share in His inheritance.

6. Christ shares His reign with us:

> " I saw thrones, and they sat on them, and judgment was given to them. I saw the souls of those who had been beheaded for the testimony of Jesus and for the word of God, and such as didn't worship the beast nor his image, and didn't receive the mark on their forehead and on their hand. They lived and reigned with Christ for a thousand years." Revelation 20:4

All believers will rule and reign with Christ as kings on the earth. The believers martyred by the Beast will be resurrected to rule with Christ at His glorious appearing and they, too, will be priests to God. They will be the last division of priest/kings to arrive in the heavenly Holy of Holies, and they will reign with Christ on earth.

7. Believers share in the tribulation (persecution) of Christ:

> "I John, your brother and partner with you in the oppression, Kingdom, and perseverance in Christ Jesus, was on the isle that is called Patmos because of God's Word and the testimony of Jesus Christ. " Revelation 1:9

Tribulation simply means persecution, suffering and oppression. Believers, especially end time believers, can expect to share in the same kind of persecution which Christ experienced at His first coming. His tribulation resulted in His sacrificial death on a cross. Multitudes of believers during the last days will be compelled to lay down their lives because of their testimony of Jesus.

7. Christ shares His glory with us:

> "The Spirit himself testifies with our spirit that we are children of God; [17] and if children, then heirs—heirs of God and joint heirs with Christ, if indeed we suffer with him, that *we may also be glorified with him.*[18] For I consider that the sufferings of this present time are not worthy to be compared with the glory which will be revealed toward us." Romans 8:16-18

Though Revelation does not speak specifically about the glory which the saints will possess, the theme of the believer's ultimate glorification appears throughout the New Testament, and especially in the writings of the Apostle Paul. To be 'glorified' is to share in Christ's glory. One day we will be like Him and His glory will be revealed in and through us. Tribulation, persecution and suffering for the sake of Christ, precede glorification.

8. Believers will accompany Christ when He judges the wicked:

> "These will war against the Lamb, and the Lamb will overcome them, for he is Lord of lords and King of kings; and those who are with him are called, chosen, and faithful."" Revelation 17:14

> "The armies which are in heaven, clothed in white, pure, fine linen, followed him on white horses." Revelation 19:14

The Old Testament scriptures tell us that Christ will execute the wrath of God *alone*, as He tramples out the winepress of God's fury, but we will accompany Him when He comes to judge the wicked and we will partake in the spoils of war gained by the Lord's defeat of His enemies.

There is one thing which Christ and His Father will NOT share with us: they will not share their right to be worshiped, which is an acknowledgement on the part of created beings of the essential, intrinsic worthiness of God. We never see the angels worshiping the glorified saints. Angelic worship is directed toward God and the Lamb, extolling *their* worthiness. However, mortal people who enter the Millennium will do obeisance to glorified believers:

> "Behold, I make some of the synagogue of Satan, of those who say they are Jews, and they are not, but lie—behold, I will make them to come and worship before your feet, and to know that I have loved you." Revelation 3:9

This kind of worship is an acknowledgement of another's worth. Christ will insist that the mortal people who enter the Millennial Kingdom do obeisance to His glorified saints. This is not because of who we are as individuals or because we are deserving of worship, but because He loves us! Christ's love for His people will be expressed in that He will require mortal people to honor us in the coming kingdom.

In the hierarchy of God, the flow of authority moves from the Father to the Son. It then proceeds from both the Father and the Son to the Spirit, and from there to the Body of Christ.

1. The ministry of the Spirit flows from both the Father and the Son.

> " I saw in the middle of the throne and of the four living creatures, and in the middle of the elders, a Lamb standing, as though it had been slain, having seven horns and seven eyes, which are the seven Spirits of God, sent out into all the earth." Revelation 5:6

In Revelation, the Holy Spirit is often referred to as the 'seven Spirits'. Seven is the number associated with divinity and fullness. The Holy Spirit is a part of the divine community of God and He manifests the fullness of the Divine nature. He is not a 'force', but a Person who is intimately involved in the carrying out of the plans and purposes of both the Father and the Son. The seven horns on the Lamb represent the omnipotence of the Spirit of God and the seven eyes speak of His omniscience. Omnipotence and omniscience are attributes which belong to God; they are resident in the Lamb, and expressed through the Spirit. The Lamb will send the Spirit out into the world during the last days, much as He did in the first century, when, at the feast of Pentecost, the early disciples were empowered by the Holy Spirit, whom Christ sent from heaven to indwell believers.

In addition to being associated with the number '7', the Spirit is intimately connected to the throne of God. The Spirit is not seated on the throne as are Almighty God and the Lamb, but He dwells in the immediate presence of the throne of God, ready to act on behalf of the Godhead.

> "John, to the seven assemblies that are in Asia: Grace to you and peace from God, who is and who was and who is to come; and from the seven Spirits who are before his throne;" Revelation 1:4

The lightening flashes, sounds and thunder which proceeds from the throne is, I believe, a manifestation of the groans of the Spirit in response to the judgments of God which are about to be initiated upon the earth.

The Spirit is also depicted as 7 torches or lamps which burn before the throne. In the earthly temple, the seven branched menorah, which gave light to the interior of the Holy Place, represents the torches of fire in the presence of the heavenly throne.

> "Out of the throne proceed lightnings, sounds, and thunders. There were seven lamps of fire burning before his throne, which are the seven Spirits of God." Revelation 4:5

In Revelation, the number seven is particularly associated with the Spirit. The Holy Spirit is represented by 7 torches or lamps of fire which burn before the throne, and by the 7 horns and 7 eyes on the Lamb. He is associated with the Thunders, rumblings and voices which emanate from the throne. Because the number 7 is connected with the Spirit and the throne in heaven, I believe that the 7 'Thunders' of Revelation 10:3 are also a depiction of the seven-fold Spirit:

> " He cried with a loud voice, as a lion roars. When he cried, the seven thunders uttered their voices. " Revelation 10:3

John was told to seal up the words of the 7 Thunders; and even though we can only speculate as to what the Thunders said, we can be fairly certain that the words John heard came from the voice of the Spirit in response to the roar of the Lion, who is Christ.

After the Second Coming of Christ, after His millennial reign and after the final judgment at the Great White Throne, God will create a new heaven and a new earth. God will do away with His temple in heaven, and His Presence will dwell in His new throne room—the new Holy of Holies—represented by the New Jerusalem, the city which lies four-square. There will be no Holy Place, no menorah, altar of incense or table of showbread, because there will be no darkness, no need for prayer and everyone will fellowship in the Presence of God.
At that time the River of Life will flow from the throne of God. The life-giving ministry of the Spirit will be represented by the waters of Life flowing from God's throne, the life-giving waters being made available to all who desire to drink. In John 7:37-39, Jesus used the analogy of rivers of life when referring to the Spirit:

> "Now on the last and greatest day of the feast, Jesus stood and cried out, "If anyone is thirsty, let him come to me and drink! 38 He who believes in me, as the Scripture has said, from within him will flow rivers of living

water." 39 But he said this about the Spirit, which those believing in him were to receive. For the Holy Spirit was not yet given, because Jesus wasn't yet glorified." John 7:37-39

"He showed me a river of water of life, clear as crystal, proceeding out of the throne of God and of the Lamb." Revelation 22:1

The Spirit and the Bride will grant men and women access to the New Jerusalem where they can drink from the River of Life which flows from the throne of God in the Holy City. They will invite individuals who came out of the Millennium, as well as those who were resurrected at the Great White Throne judgment, whose names were written in the book of Life of the Lamb, to partake of the River of Life:

"The Spirit and the bride say, "Come!" He who hears, let him say, "Come!" He who is thirsty, let him come. He who desires, let him take the water of life freely." Revelation 22:17

The Thunders, lightenings and voices of the Spirit which, even now, emanate from the throne of God, will be transformed from expressions of grief, angst, and judgment, to the joyful sounds of the beautiful River of Life in the Paradise of God. The fruit and leaves of the Tree of Life on either side of the River will bring healing to the nations. The Holy Spirit, who expresses the heart, mind and will of God and the Lamb, will make the life of God available to all who desire to partake.

2. The Son 'seals' believers in the Holy Spirit:

" I saw another angel ascend from the sunrise, having the seal of the living God. He cried with a loud voice to the four angels to whom it was given to harm the earth and the sea, 3 saying, "Don't harm the earth, the sea, or the trees, until we have sealed the bondservants of our God on their foreheads." Revelation 7:2,3

" Now he who establishes us with you in Christ and anointed us is God, 22 who also sealed us and gave us the down payment of the Spirit in our hearts." 2 Corinthians 1:21,22

Paul tells us that all believers are sealed in the Holy Spirit. The presence of the Spirit in our lives assures us that we belong to God and that He will make good on His promises to us. One of God's promises is that one day soon we will serve as priests in His presence.

Chapter 2: The Angel of the Lord

The 'Angel of the Lord' was a manifestation of the pre-incarnate Son of God who appeared in the Old Testament scriptures at spiritual inflection points. The Angel of the Lord was sent by God to deliver the children of Israel at the time of their Exodus from Egypt. He manifested as the pillar of cloud by day and the pillar of fire by night, guiding and protecting Israel during their wilderness wanderings. The scriptures tell us that God's 'Name' was in Him. He is also called the Angel of the Presence. It's apparent that this angel was no ordinary angel:

1. God declared that this Angel must be obeyed because "My Name is in Him":

> " Behold, I send an angel before you, to keep you by the way, and to bring you into the place which I have prepared. 21 Pay attention to him, and listen to his voice. Don't provoke him, for he will not pardon your disobedience, for my name is in him. 22 But if you indeed listen to his voice, and do all that I speak, then I will be an enemy to your enemies, and an adversary to your adversaries. 23 For my angel shall go before you, and bring you in to the Amorite, the Hittite, the Perizzite, the Canaanite, the Hivite, and the Jebusite; and I will cut them off." Exodus 23:20-23

> " In all their affliction he was afflicted,
> and the angel of his presence saved them.
> In his love and in his pity he redeemed them.
> He bore them, and carried them all the days of old" Isaiah 63:9

Christ also appears several times as the Angel of the Lord in the book of Revelation. He is depicted as the Messenger of God, the One who will guide and protect His people in a future deliverance just as He did during Israel's first exodus from Egypt. In the book of Exodus, the Angel of the Lord manifested as the glory which appeared over the tabernacle in the pillar of cloud and fire. The Angel of the Lord was an integral part of the Exodus story and, symbolically, He will also play a role in the end times.

2. In Exodus, the Angel of the Lord (Christ) was the member of the Godhead who appeared in the pillar of cloud and fire to guide God's people:

> " Yet in this thing you didn't believe Yahweh your God, 33 who went before you on the way, to seek out a place for you to pitch your tents in: in fire by night, to show you by what way you should go, and in the cloud by day." Deuteronomy 1:32,33

3. In Revelation, the Angel of the Lord acts as God's messenger and representative, in a variety of capacities. He seals God's servants (Revelation 7), raises the dead and changes the living (Revelation 10), oversees the destruction of the Harlot (Revelation 18), and leads the remnant of Israel into the wilderness (Zechariah 14). The Angel of the Lord is equated with God Himself:

> " In that day Yahweh will defend the inhabitants of Jerusalem. He who is feeble among them at that day will be like David, and David's house will be like God, like Yahweh's angel before them." Zechariah 12:8

4. At the time of the first exodus from Egypt, Christ—appearing as the Angel of the Lord—manifested in the pillar of cloud and fire which rested over the tabernacle; thus He is also intimately connected with the temple/tabernacle imagery of Revelation.

> " On the day that the tabernacle was raised up, the cloud covered the tabernacle, even the Tent of the Testimony. At evening it was over the tabernacle, as it were the appearance of fire, until morning. [16] So it was continually. The cloud covered it, and the appearance of fire by night. [17] Whenever the cloud was taken up from over the Tent, then after that the children of Israel traveled; and in the place where the cloud remained, there the children of Israel encamped. " Numbers 9:15-17

The pillar of fire and cloud reminds us of the presence of God where the brightness of His glory is enveloped by clouds and smoke. Whenever we read about an angel who is concealed by a cloud or who manifests the glory of God in the book of Revelation, we can assume that this is an appearance of the Angel of the Lord, who is Christ.

5. The Angel of the Lord comes from the place of the rising sun to seal the servants of God. A little known title for Jesus is "Sunrise" as we see in Zechariah's song:

> "Because of the tender mercy of our God, with which the Sunrise from on high will visit us." Luke 1:78

> "But to you who fear my name shall the Sun of Righteousness arise with healing in its wings. You will go out and leap like calves of the stall." Malachi 4:2

> "Arise, shine; for your light has come, and Yahweh's glory has risen on you!" Isaiah 60:1

" I saw another angel ascend from the sunrise, having the seal of the living God. He cried with a loud voice to the four angels to whom it was given to harm the earth and the sea." Revelation 7:2

Those who are sealed, will receive the healing mercy of God and walk in the light of the Spirit, for the Angel of the Lord will bestow upon His servants the gift of the Holy Spirit. The Apostle Paul uses the metaphor of sealing when describing how all believers are sealed by the Spirit:

"In him you also, having heard the word of the truth, the Good News of your salvation—in whom, having also believed, you were sealed with the promised Holy Spirit, 14 who is a pledge of our inheritance, to the redemption of God's own possession, to the praise of his glory." Ephesians 1:13,14

"For however many are the promises of God, in him is the "Yes." Therefore also through him is the "Amen", to the glory of God through us.
21 Now he who establishes us with you in Christ and anointed us is God,
22 who also sealed us and gave us the down payment of the Spirit in our hearts." 2 Corinthians 1:20-22

The seal of the Spirit is the guarantee that God will make good on all of His promises to us. The Holy Spirit anoints believers, setting them apart for service. He will anoint the 144,000 of Israel by sealing them in the Holy Spirit. The Holy Spirit is 'sent out into all the earth', by the Lamb with seven horns and seven eyes, which represents the Spirit of God.

Summary:

Unlike other prophetic books which were authored by men inspired by the Holy Spirit, the book of Revelation was given directly from God to Christ. Christ then delivered the message to His angel, who conveyed the message to John, who then recorded the book we know of as "Revelation". Christ, the angel and John all affirmed the truth of the testimony which they gave.

Echoes of Exodus show up in Revelation: the giving of commandments, the pattern of the tabernacle, the priesthood, the appointed times, the Angel of the Lord and the glory of God. All of these suggest that Revelation is to be interpreted in the context of the Exodus of the children of Israel from Egypt, and that the story will lean heavily on 'temple' imagery.

The number 'seven'—the number symbolizing divinity and completion—is connected to the Holy Spirit. The number '24' is connected to the divisions of the priesthood which are described in 1 Chronicles 24. Believers, as priests and kings, are represented by the 24 Elders, who will be brought into the heavenly throne room at their appointed time, according to their 'division'.

Chapter 3: The Structure of the Temple in Heaven

When God met with Moses on the top of Mount Sinai, Moses was shown the pattern for the tabernacle that God wanted him to build. The tabernacle was to be a shadow of God's temple in heaven:

> "...who serve a copy and shadow of the heavenly things, even as Moses was warned by God when he was about to make the tabernacle, for he said, 'See, you shall make everything according to the pattern that was shown to you on the mountain.'" Hebrews 8:5

The earthly tabernacle was a symbolic replica of the heavenly temple. The earthly tabernacle reflected the spiritual architecture of heaven, the place of God's throne, and the way for sinful man to approach a holy God. The plan of salvation, including the Person and work of the Lord Jesus, was depicted in the various feast days connected with temple/tabernacle worship. The book of Hebrews describes some of the ways that Jesus fulfilled the types and shadows hidden in the tabernacle, the priesthood and the sacrificial system. The inner glory of the tabernacle was hidden from view, covered in ordinary animal skins, illustrating the hidden glory of Christ in His humanity. The tabernacle was the focal point of the encampment of the children of Israel in the wilderness. Spiritually speaking, the glorified, risen Christ is the center and focus of Christian love and worship in this present day.

The earthly tabernacle consisted of a tent with two compartments and an outer court. The smaller of the two compartments was called the Holy of Holies and it was the place where the presence of God dwelt over the mercy seat which was on top of the ark of the covenant. The Holy of Holies was separated from the larger compartment, the Holy Place, by means of a thickly woven curtain. In front of the curtain which separated the Holy of Holies and the Holy Place, and facing the Holy of Holies on the west, stood the golden altar of incense. The golden seven branched menorah shed its light from the south side of the Holy Place, and the golden table of showbread was on the north side. To the east, directly opposite the altar of incense, the ark and the curtain, was the sole entrance to the tent of meeting. The tabernacle was designed to be disassembled and transported as the children of Israel traveled, following the the Angel of the Lord in the pillar of cloud and fire.

Only qualified priests were allowed to enter the tabernacle. God chose the tribe of Levi to be His priests. They represented the 'first born' of Israel, and the priests belonged to God as His possession. They ministered before the Lord continually, day and night, offering incense and prayers on the golden altar. Once a year, on the Day of Atonement, the high priest entered into the Holy of Holies and performed the rituals associated with that most sacred day of the year.

The tabernacle, its furniture, the priests and the holy days are all patterns describing the process of redemption, and how man could be delivered from the penalty of sin and brought near into the very presence of God through the sprinkled blood on the mercy seat. Layer upon layer of meaning was concealed, and later revealed, in the imagery of the tabernacle, particularly in the book of Hebrews. The ministry, life, death and resurrection of Christ, and the subsequent giving of the Holy Spirit to those who believed in Him, were all prefigured in the tabernacle and the rituals connected with temple worship. When the children of Israel came into the land of promise, Solomon constructed a permanent temple that was based on the pattern of the tabernacle. Solomons' temple, though, was larger and grander than the tabernacle, and was established on Mt Zion, in Jerusalem, the Holy City.

When God wanted to describe how His people would gain access into His presence in heaven, He chose to use tabernacle-temple imagery to tell the story.

Chapter 4: God's Temple and the Nature of Time

"One generation goes, and another generation comes; but the earth remains forever. 5 The sun also rises, and the sun goes down, and hurries to its place where it rises. 6 The wind goes toward the south, and turns around to the north. It turns around continually as it goes, and the wind returns again to its courses. 7 All the rivers run into the sea, yet the sea is not full. To the place where the rivers flow, there they flow again.

8 All things are full of weariness beyond uttering. The eye is not satisfied with seeing, nor the ear filled with hearing. 9 That which has been is that which shall be, and that which has been done is that which shall be done; and there is no new thing under the sun.

10 Is there a thing of which it may be said, "Behold, this is new?" It has been long ago, in the ages which were before us." Ecclesiastes 1:4-10

A baby is born, grows into maturity, then dies. Another baby is born, and the cycle repeats. The sun rises day after day. The things you have seen, you will see again. Through the words of Solomon, God has told us that there is nothing new under the sun! For those of us who are waiting for the return of Christ, this recycling of time hints at the possibility that we may be able understand future events by examining the cycles and patterns of the past. The scriptures seem to indicate that all future events have been foreshadowed in the templates of history. *"Is there anything of which one might say, "'See this, it is new?' Already it has existed for ages which were before us.'"*

> "Remember the former things of old;
> for I am God, and there is no other.
> I am God, and there is none like me.
> 10 I declare the end from the beginning,
> and from ancient times things that are not yet done.
> I say: My counsel will stand,
> and I will do all that I please." Isaiah 46:9,10

God plainly states that He has already told us what will happen at the end of time. He has given us His prophetic Word as contained in the Bible and He has told us that He operates according to well-defined patterns, templates and cycles. He is a God of order and precision and planning.

Cycles of Time

At the very beginning of creation, when God divided the day from the night, He established the means for tracking time. Each sunrise would mark a new day. Seven days would comprise a week. The weeks were further divided into months according to the cyclical phases of the moon. The constellations would cycle through the ecliptic plane, returning to their starting point at the end of the year, initiating a new year and a new cycle. Time was charted in cycles: cycles of the moon, the constellations cycling through the ecliptic and the yearly festival cycle. In Isaiah, we read that the feasts 'cycle' around.

> "Woe to Ariel! Ariel, the city where David encamped! Add year to year; let the feasts come around." Isaiah 29:1

To God, time is not linear, but cyclical. *Linear* time can be compared to horse walking down a road, headed into town: he starts his journey at the barn, ambles down the road and ends up in town. *Cycles* of time can be compared to the wheels attached to the cart being drawn by the horse. The cart wheels *roll* down the road, with each point on the wheel's circumference touching the road, over and over again. Both the horse and the cart with its wheels, move forward from the same place, traverse the same road and end at the same place—but their journey to the destination is not the same. The horse moves forward in a straight line, but the wheels on the cart cycle 'round and 'round.

Because God's concept of time is cyclical instead of linear, we can assume that the experiences and the events which take place in the world, are never truly 'new', but only a variation on a theme, consisting of patterns which emerge over and over again with unerring predictability. The life cycles of plants, people, nations are examples of predictable patterns.

God has placed demarcations in the cycle of time using several different means. He employs the regularly occurring signs in the heavens, and He uses His appointed times—His feasts and festivals—to let us know *where* we are in the journey of redemption. God uses the cycle of His appointed times—the Feasts of the Lord—to help us understand the on-going progression of His plan of salvation. Even in our western world we talk about economic cycles, solar cycles, political and social cycles. The cyclical nature of time has been hard-wired into the human soul.

Time can also be thought of as a 'fractal' of sorts. A fractal is a never-ending pattern based on a simple mathematical equation. A spiral is an example of a fractal pattern found in nature, which can manifest as something as immense as a galaxy, or as minute as a shell that can be held in one's hand.
As we have already seen, the number '7' is often used symbolically in the scriptures to represent things which are divine, complete, perfect or whole. The divine

stamp of God's view of time was first seen in the scriptures in the period of time we call a week: 6 days of work and one day to rest. The cyclical, 7 day week has been a part of human civilization since the very beginning. Seven is a 'time fractal' that God established at creation.

God's appointed times—the Feast days—are also in patterns of '7'. There are seven feasts of the Lord. There are 7 weeks from First Fruits to Pentecost. The land 'rests' every 7th year. There are 7 x 7= 49 years, in the Jubilee cycle. There are 70 'weeks' of years in the prophecy of Daniel 9. There are 70 years in the average human life span. At the end of 7,000 years of human history, this 'age' will conclude. The Millennial reign of Christ—where His 'day' is as a thousand years, will comprise the 7th and final 'day' in the 'week' of human history.

Another number which relates to time is the number '12'. There are 12 hours in a day, 12 months in a year, and once every 12 years Jupiter cycles through the ecliptic plane, having spent one year in each of the 12 constellations.

In the book of Judges, we read about the cycles of Israel's spiritual rebellion, which resulted in their enslavement to their enemies. When they cried out to God, He delivered them through a judge. Once the judge was dead, Israel would rebel again, repeating the cycle of rebellion, judgment and deliverance.

> " Yahweh raised up judges, who saved them out of the hand of those who plundered them. [17] Yet they didn't listen to their judges; for they prostituted themselves to other gods, and bowed themselves down to them. They quickly turned away from the way in which their fathers walked, obeying Yahweh's commandments. They didn't do so.
>
> [18] When Yahweh raised up judges for them, then Yahweh was with the judge, and saved them out of the hand of their enemies all the days of the judge; for it grieved Yahweh because of their groaning by reason of those who oppressed them and troubled them. [19] But when the judge was dead, they turned back, and dealt more corruptly than their fathers in following other gods to serve them and to bow down to them. They didn't cease what they were doing, or give up their stubborn ways. " Judges 2:16-19

One of the reasons that God will not excuse mankind's ignorance and willful rebellion in the end times, is that He has made His mercy and justice evident through cyclical patterns of divine patience followed by divine judgment. The consequences of mankind's rebellion—which will be manifested in the wrath of God during the last days—has already been foreshadowed in the stories of the judgment of Sodom and Gomorrah, as well as in the story of Noah and the flood.

The memory of the flood is embedded in all cultures of the world and legends of a world-wide flood are to be found among all people groups on earth.

Though God's mercy was evident through the preaching of Noah during the time when Noah constructed the ark; God's judgment could not be averted forever. When Noah's message of repentance toward God was scorned and refused, God's mercy was replaced by indignation, resulting in the judgment of the flood. The judgment that came upon the antediluvian world, was immediately preceded by the rescue of Noah and his family before judgment fell. This is a pattern that will take place once again before the 2nd Coming of the Lord: God will deliver His people before He pours out His judgments on the wicked.

This understanding—that God sees time as a cycle—is crucial if you want to know how—and when—end time events will play out. God revealed the story of the last days using the very same cyclical patterns that we find elsewhere in scripture. God communicated the end times through a series of visions; and the visions layer over one another, like the minute hand of a clock which goes 'round and 'round over the same face. The various events described in the different visions of Revelation will run concurrently. An event that was covered in one vision will overlay the events in another vision. The stories of Revelation are told via cycles, using patterns already found in the Bible—especially the patterns of the appointed times.

Because God views time as cyclical and not linear, we need to understand that Revelation cannot be interpreted as though the visions contained in the book were linear or chronological, with the events unfolding in a 'straight line'. We can expect to see the events portrayed in Revelation as layered, repeating cycles, where the sun, moon and stars mark time, and where the types and shadows of the Feast Days—God's appointed times—reveal the actual dates when the events we read about will finally take place. The cyclical patterns, as well as the types and shadows of Scripture, provide the framework upon which we can construct a multi-dimensional interpretation of the prophecy given to us by God in this final book of the Bible.

While the tabernacle, and later, the temple, were standing on earth, they were the center and focal point of life for the nation of Israel. Everything revolved around the temple: the commandments which guided their daily lives, the appointed pilgrimages, the offerings and sacrifices. The appointed times determined when Israel would appear before God, and how they could achieve right standing before Him. The earthly appointed times follow the pattern of spiritual, heavenly realities—realities which manifested in the life, death and resurrection of Christ. The starry host, as well as the Lord's appointed times, were the clock and calendar of the temple, and they still provide the method for calculating future 'temple' events as depicted in Revelation. And since we have already seen how the book of

Revelation is a 'temple' story, the timing of end time events will employ 'temple time' utilizing the cyclical Feast Days of the Lord.

Chapter 5: Priests and Kings: The Believer's Destiny

What is the Christian's eternal destiny? What future awaits those of us who trust in Christ? Simply put, our destiny is to exist in everlasting fellowship with God—fellowship which begins in the 'here and now' as a result of being 'born from above' via the agency of the Holy Spirit. This fellowship will continue upon our arrival in heaven and on into eternity. As God's *'ekklesia'*, we have been called 'out of the world' and 'to' God; and wherever He is, that is where we will be as well. Christ died that He might bring us to God:

> "Because Christ also suffered for sins once, the righteous for the unrighteous, that he might bring you to God..." 1 Peter 3:18a

Our eternal fellowship with the Father is symbolized in many different ways in the Bible. Our communion has been represented by a family, where we have been adopted as God's 'sons' and heirs. Believers are also likened to a 'bride—the 'wife' of His Son, the Lord Jesus. We are also pictured as God's 'house' and His temple:

> " For through him we both have our access in one Spirit to the Father. 19 So then you are no longer strangers and foreigners, but you are fellow citizens with the saints and of the household of God, 20 being built on the foundation of the apostles and prophets, Christ Jesus himself being the chief cornerstone; 21 in whom the whole building, fitted together, grows into a holy temple in the Lord; 22 in whom you also are built together for a habitation of God in the Spirit." Ephesians 2:18-22

However, the symbol that most aptly represents our eternal destiny as presented *in the book of Revelation*, is summed up in the phrase: "a kingdom of priests":

> "...and he made us to be a Kingdom, priests to his God and Father." Revelation 1:6a

God originally chose Israel out of all the nations of the world to be His nation of 'priests and kings':

> "Now therefore, if you will indeed obey my voice and keep my covenant, then you shall be my own possession from among all peoples; for all the earth is mine; 6 and you shall be to me a kingdom of priests and a holy nation.' These are the words which you shall speak to the children of Israel." Exodus 19:5,6

When Israel rejected her Messiah, the honor and privilege of being God's priests and kings was transferred to Christians...to believers. The apostle Peter tells us that we have been chosen as God's 'royal priesthood':

> "But you are a chosen race, a royal priesthood, a holy nation, a people for God's own possession, that you may proclaim the excellence of him who called you out of darkness into his marvelous light." 1 Peter 2:9

The Law, the tabernacle and the priesthood—along with the associated temple rites, appointed times, sacrifices and offerings—were given to the nation of Israel while they were in the wilderness at Sinai. Over the next few centuries, every day, year after year, the priests would offer sacrifices to God and preside over the yearly festivals, but they were only role-playing the various aspects of the redemptive plan of God. The priests—and the rituals they performed—were merely shadows and 'place holders' until such a time as Christ would come, and, through His life and atoning death on the cross, become the substance and fulfillment of those shadowy place holders.

The earthly priesthood was a prophetic picture of Christ *and His Body*—all those who would be called to serve God as priests in the actual temple in heaven. Early on in Revelation, in the very first chapter, believers are described as a "kingdom and priests to God" through the blood of Christ:

> "...To him who loves us, and washed us from our sins by his blood— 6 and he made us to be a Kingdom, priests to his God and Father—to him be the glory and the dominion forever and ever. Amen." Revelation 1:5b, 6

This is how God, the Source of Revelation, chose to depict believers: as priests and kings. In the opening pages of the book, *He lets us know how He wants us to think about ourselves*. The importance of understanding how God views our destiny in the end time scenario—the destiny which is best summed up in how believers are depicted in Revelation—cannot be over-emphasized: God intends for us to use the *image and pattern of the priesthood*—not the Body or Bride or any other type—when decoding the end time prophecies in Revelation.

God's 'throne room' is the prototype for the 'Holy of Holies' in the earthly temple; the most holy place where the ark of the covenant—the 'throne' of God—was located. This ultra-holy compartment of the temple was off-limits to the people of Israel, and even the high priest could not enter anytime he wished, but only on the Day of Atonement. This was the one day during the course of the year, when a mortal man could enter into God's presence in the earthly temple and live to tell about it:

> "Yahweh said to Moses, 'Tell Aaron your brother not to come at just any time into the Most Holy Place within the veil, before the mercy seat which is on the ark; lest he die; for I will appear in the cloud on the mercy seat.'" Leviticus 16:2

> "This shall be an everlasting statute for you, to make atonement for the children of Israel once in the year because of all their sins." Leviticus 16:34

Believers who 'overcome' and stand victorious during the time of tribulation, will reign with Christ as kings during the Millennium. They will be given 'power over the nations' as promised to the church of Thyatira:

> "He who overcomes, and he who keeps my works to the end, to him I will give authority over the nations. 27 He will rule them with a rod of iron, shattering them like clay pots, as I also have received of my Father." Revelation 2:26,27

To the church of Philadelphia, Christ promises that they will be an integral part of the temple of God:

> "He who overcomes, I will make him a pillar in the temple of my God." Revelation 3:12a

In Revelation 4, John is called to come up to heaven and see what's taking place there. He sees God's throne, the seven Spirits of God before the throne, the four Living Creatures and 24 Elders wearing white robes with golden crowns on their heads. They are seated on thrones in the very presence of God:

> "Around the throne were twenty-four thrones. On the thrones were twenty-four elders sitting, dressed in white garments, with crowns of gold on their heads." Revelation 4:4

These 'Elders' are kings as evidenced by the 24 thrones on which they are seated, as well as the golden crowns upon their heads. They are seated in God's presence—in His throne room, the heavenly equivalent of the Holy of Holies in the temple. This indicates that, in addition to being kings, they are also priests.

Revelation 5:8 confirms the priestly calling of the 24 Elders, for each of them are holding a golden bowl of incense, interceding for the saints on earth:

> "Now when he had taken the book, the four living creatures and the twenty-four elders fell down before the Lamb, each one having a harp, and

golden bowls full of incense, which are the prayers of the saints.." Revelation 5:8

The 24 Elders in chapter 5 represent the 'new arrivals' in God's heavenly throne room. They sing a song, and the song they sing is a new song. The song is 'new' because no living creature or angel will have ever sung this particular song before. The song is 'new' because the 24 Elders are the only beings in heaven who know *first hand* the truth of the 'lyrics' of the song—a song which gives praise and honor to Christ for purchasing their redemption with His blood:

> "They sang a new song, saying,
> 'You are worthy to take the book
> and to open its seals,
> for you were killed,
> and bought us for God with your blood
> out of every tribe, language, people, and nation,
> 10 and made us kings and priests to our God;
> and we will reign on the earth.' " Revelation 5:9, 10

They rejoice in the fact that they have been redeemed to God, and that God has ordained them to be His kings and priests, and that they, along with other believers, will minister in heaven's temple, and rule and reign with Christ on the earth.

The Numbers

Numbers are a very important part of the symbolism used in Revelation. The numbers that appear in Revelation are almost always used symbolically—not literally. Numbers are incorporated into the symbolism, providing 'clues' which help us identify who, or what, is being 'numbered'. The numbers give us information that Revelation does not actually tell us in so many words, information which is hidden in the symbolic meaning of the specific number that is being used.

The 144,000 of Israel—12,000 people from each of the 12 tribes of Israel—are a good example of how numbers are used as symbols. The number '12' represents 'divine government' as well as 'those who are chosen'. The number '1,000' represents the 'fullest possible amount'. So, symbolically speaking, the 144,000 are the 'full complement of God's chosen people, who will also be rulers in His divine government'. Many people teach that the number, 144,000, is a literal number, describing a literal 144,000 *men*, who are chosen from among the 12 tribes of Israel. They do not realize that the number, 144,000, is a part of a coded message which uses numbers as a part of the code; and that the numbers help us to identify God's end time chosen people who will rule with Christ on earth.

40

- *The numbers that appear in Revelation are meant to be understood symbolically. The only exception to this rule is when numbers are associated with time: as in 1260 days, 42 months, 5 months, 3.5 days, etc.; or to describe a sequence of numbered events such as the 7 Seals, 7 Trumpets, etc.*

Aside from a couple of references to giants with six fingers and six toes (24 digits altogether), the number '24' is sited very few times in scripture. Because the number '24' is not used in a way that is familiar to most people, there is a tendency to not see the number 24 as its own clue; but to interpret it by its factors: 12 and 2; and then assume that the 24 Elders represent 2 entities with 12 members in each 'set', such as the 12 tribes of Israel *plus* the 12 apostles. When the number '24' is interpreted as the sum of its parts, the true meaning of the symbol is lost.

Revelation tells us that there are 24 Elders seated before God in His throne room, the heavenly temple. Though the number '24' is used very infrequently in the Bible, in the passage where we *do* see it used, 1 Chronicles 24, we discover that there is a strong connection between the number '24' and the priesthood.

When King David's son, Solomon, was chosen to be his successor, David bequeathed to Solomon the plans and wherewithal to build the first Temple in Jerusalem. David drew up the plans for the temple, which his son was then tasked with constructing. In addition to providing Solomon with the building plans and the real estate on which the temple would be erected, David also set up the system of administration for those who would later serve in the temple.

In chapter 24 of 1 Chronicles, we are told that David divided the priests into 24 different 'divisions' or 'courses'. Each 'course' of priests was assigned a specific period of time in which to minister in the house of the Lord. The number '24' has a strong association with the priesthood as evidenced by how the 24 divisions of priests rotated their days of service in the temple according to their administrative order. The gospel of Luke tells us that Zechariah—the father of John the Baptist—was a member of the priestly division of Abijah, one of the the 24 divisions that was serving in the temple when Zechariah was visited by the angel, Gabriel:

> "There was in the days of Herod, the king of Judea, a certain priest named Zacharias, of the *priestly division of Abijah*. He had a wife of the daughters of Aaron, and her name was Elizabeth. " Luke 1:5

The number '24' is used multiple times in chapters 23-27 of 1 Chronicles, and the number '24', is one of the most frequently reoccurring numbers in those chapters. For example, the Levites number 24,000 men over the age of 30; the priests were divided into 24 groups. The singers, musicians and those who prophesy—both men and women—were divided into 24 groups as well. Chapter 26 tells us about the 24 'watches' for the gatekeepers, and chapter 27 records that the military and civil officials were to oversee divisions consisting of 24,000 people each. The number '24' is, therefore, associated with those who serve in the temple, and with the priests in particular; and when used in Revelation, the number '24' is pointing us directly to this passage in 1 Chronicles 24.

Since the number '24' is connected to the rotation of different divisions of the earthly priesthood, we can expect that Revelation will also describe the rotations of different divisions of priests who will be coming into the heavenly Holy of Holies, with each group arriving in the order in which they are assigned.

More 'priests'

Revelation connects the 24 Elders with those who have been made into a 'kingdom of priests'. We know that God has made us priests and kings through the blood of Christ:

> "To him who loves us, and washed us from our sins by his blood— 6 and he made us to be a Kingdom, priests to his God and Father—to him be the glory and the dominion forever and ever. Amen." Revelation 1:5b, 6

Christ is our faithful High Priest, and He set the example for what it means for us to be priests to God. Even now, Christ is interceding for us before the throne of God in heaven:

> "Therefore he is also able to save to the uttermost those who draw near to God through him, seeing that he lives forever to make intercession for them." Hebrews 7:25

Once Christ takes the scroll from His Father (Revelation 5), He will no longer be interceding for believers on earth as their heavenly High Priest. He will be stepping into His new role as the heir of David and the coming *King*. And who will take His place before the altar of incense, interceding for the new believers on earth? That will be the role of the raptured and resurrected body of Christ—the 24 Elders.

Just as Jesus, having lived as a man in a fallen world, could be a faithful and compassionate High priest for us, so we, too, as priestly Elders in heaven, will be sympathetic and effective 'prayer warriors' for our new brethren on earth. We will begin to exercise our role as priests in heaven *before* we rule as kings on the earth.

The 24 Elders represent the *first group*—the first 'division'—of priests who will enter God's throne room in the heavenly Holy of Holies. I believe that the 24 Elders are also represented by the 'child' who is 'caught up' in Revelation 12:5. The 'child' is brought to the throne of God—the very place where we first see the 24 Elders in chapter 4:

> "She gave birth to a son, a male child, who is to rule all the nations with a rod of iron. Her child was caught up to God and *to his throne*." Revelation 12:5

> " Immediately I was in the Spirit. Behold, there was a throne set in heaven, and one sitting on the throne 3 that looked like a jasper stone and a sardius. There was a rainbow around the throne, like an emerald to look at. 4 Around the throne were twenty-four thrones. On the thrones were twenty-four elders sitting, dressed in white garments, with crowns of gold on their heads." Revelation 4:2-4

The next 'priestly' division seen in heaven after the appearance of the 24 Elders, are the 5th Seal martyrs, people from every tribe, tongue, people and nation who stand before the throne of God:

> "They washed their robes and made them white in the Lamb's blood. 15 Therefore they are before the throne of God, and they serve him day and night in his temple. He who sits on the throne will spread his tabernacle over them." Revelation 7:14b-15

These saints, who were martyred by the Harlot and the earth dwellers, were also brought into the heavenly Holy of Holies, where the Elders are seated. They stand before the throne of God in heaven and their role is to serve God day and night *in His temple*. Remember that in the earthly temple, the *priests* were the only ones allowed access to the Holy of Holies—a shadow of God's throne room in heaven. Like the earthly temple where only the priests could enter to serve God, only God's priests have the privilege of entering the heavenly temple. The martyrs of the Harlot, who will appear in heaven just prior to the midpoint, the time when Satan is cast out of heaven, represent a second group or 'course' of priests seen ministering in God's temple.

The next group to appear in heaven will be the 144K of Israel: a representative 12,000 people from each of the 12 tribes. These believers are 'sealed' on their foreheads:

> "Don't harm the earth, the sea, or the trees, until we have sealed the bondservants of our God on their foreheads!" 4 I heard the number of

those who were sealed, one hundred forty-four thousand, sealed out of every tribe of the children of Israel. " Revelation 7:3,4

In Revelation 14, the 'seal' is gone...and is replace by writing:

"I saw, and behold, the Lamb standing on Mount Zion, and with him a number, one hundred forty-four thousand, having his name and the name of his Father *written on their foreheads*. " Revelation 14:1

The believers of the church of Philadelphia will also have God's name written on them, and they will dwell in the temple of God:

"He who overcomes, I will make him a pillar in the temple of my God, and he will go out from there no more. I will write on him the name of my God and the name of the city of my God, the new Jerusalem, which comes down out of heaven from my God, and my own new name." Revelation 3:12

The church of Philadelphia represents the 'over-coming' first fruits of Israel, the 144K, who are promised that they will be removed from the earth before the 'hour of trial':

"Because you kept my command to endure, I also will keep you from the hour of testing which is to come on the whole world, to test those who dwell on the earth. " Revelation 3:10

(I'll be going into much more detail about the identity of the 144, 000 (144K) of Israel, the letters to the seven churches, the Harlot, etc, later in this book. Right now I'm only providing the identities of the various divisions of the priesthood who will eventually arrive before God's throne, at the time they begin their priestly duties.)

Sometime before the destruction of the Harlot at the 6th Trumpet—the time referred to in Revelation 3:10 as the 'hour of trial which comes on the whole earth'—the 144K will have already been received into heaven. (More on this later!)

The 144,000 of Israel are the third division of priests to arrive in heaven. They begin their rotation in the throne room of God before the 'hour of trial', and again, they sing a song which only they can sing...a song which reflects their personal experience of redemption:

> "3 They sing a new song before the throne and before the four living creatures and the elders. No one could learn the song except the one hundred forty-four thousand, those who had been redeemed out of the earth. " Revelation 14:3

Because the 144K appear before God's throne in the heavenly temple, we know they are priests as well, along with the 24 Elders and the great multitude standing before God's throne.

Shortly after the 144K will have arrived in heaven, the Two Witnesses will 'ascend into heaven', having been resurrected at the midpoint which will coincide with the 6th Trumpet/2nd Woe. No doubt they, too, will be numbered among the heavenly priesthood.

> " I heard a loud voice from heaven saying to them, 'Come up here!' They went up into heaven in a cloud, and their enemies saw them. 13 In that day there was a great earthquake, and a tenth of the city fell. Seven thousand people were killed in the earthquake, and the rest were terrified and gave glory to the God of heaven.

> 14 The second woe is past. Behold, the third woe comes quickly." Revelation 11:12-14

The next group or 'company' of priests to appear in heaven will be the 'Over-comers', believers who were victorious over the Beast:

> "I saw something like a sea of glass mixed with fire, and those who overcame the beast, his image,* and the number of his name, standing on the sea of glass, having harps of God. 3 They sang the song of Moses, the servant of God, and the song of the Lamb, saying,
> 'Great and marvelous are your works, Lord God, the Almighty! Righteous and true are your ways, you King of the nations.' " Revelation 15:2,3

This 4th division of priests will be taken into heaven sometime during the reign of the Beast, during the last 42 months of the 7 years before the visible return of Christ to the earth. The priests who are a part of the Overcomer rapture will be living believers who will have refused to take the mark of the Beast or worship the Beast or its image or take the number of his name. Because the mark of the Beast will not be instituted until after the midpoint, we know that there will be overcoming believers on the earth *after* the midpoint, after the Beast has begun his 42 month reign. Once these believers are raptured into heaven, they will worship and praise God, singing *their* song, standing beside the sea of glass which is before God's throne.

There is one last group of priests among the priestly divisions who won't appear in heaven until *after* the second coming of Christ: they are the believers who will be martyred—beheaded—by the Beast:

> "The rest of the dead didn't live until the thousand years were finished. This is the first resurrection. 6 Blessed and holy is he who has part in the first resurrection. Over these, the second death has no power, but they will be priests of God and of Christ, and will reign with him one thousand years." Revelation 20:5,6

The martyrs of the Beast are specifically named priests and kings in this passage. If there was any doubt that 'tribulation' saints share the same destiny as believers—as priests and kings—this one passage should lay that to rest. Not until this last group appears in heaven, will the complete Body of Christ—the full complement of priests—finally be in heaven with God. With the resurrection of this last group of martyrs, the 'Bride' will have made herself ready, and she will then live in the New Jerusalem with her Bridegroom, the Lord Jesus Christ:

> "I heard something like the voice of a great multitude, and like the voice of many waters, and like the voice of mighty thunders, saying, 'Hallelujah! For the Lord our God, the Almighty, reigns! 7 Let's rejoice and be exceedingly glad, and let's give the glory to him. For the wedding of the Lamb has come, and his wife has made herself ready.' " Revelation 19:6,7

In summary, Revelation depicts the following groups, or 'divisions', of priests who comprise the heavenly 'priesthood'. The divisions are as follows:

1) Christ, who is our High Priest and the first to go 'behind the veil'.
2) The 24 Elders, consisting of the resurrected 'dead in Christ' and raptured believers.
3) The 5th Seal martyrs
4) The 144K of Israel.
5) The Two Witnesses.
6) The 'Over-comers'.
7) The martyrs who will be beheaded by the Beast/Antichrist.

Chapter 6: Understanding The Rapture in Revelation

The term, "rapture", is not actually found in our English Bibles. It's taken from Latin version of the Bible, (the Vulgate) and the Latin word, '*rapiemur*', meaning "we are caught up". The Greek word, '*harpazo*', is translated in our Bibles as 'caught up', and this is what Christians mean by the rapture. Believers will be 'caught up' to meet the Lord in the air in their new, glorified bodies. This 'catching away' is often referred to as the rapture.

In dispensational circles, the rapture of the church is described as an event whereby Christ returns to the earth—suddenly and unexpectedly—to meet His Church/Bride/Body in the clouds. This event then sets into motion a 7 year 'tribulation', a time when the wrath of God over-whelms a God-hating world. The raptured Church—now present in heaven—enjoys a seven year marriage supper while the saints on earth are subjected to persecution, various Seal, Trumpet and Bowl judgments and the horrors associated with the reign of the Beast. Dispensationalists also believe that there is *only one* rapture of believers.

Understanding the 'Revelation' Given to Christ

Chapter one, verse one of Revelation says this:

> "This is the Revelation of Jesus Christ, which God gave him to show to his servants the things which must happen soon." Revelation 1:1a

When Christ walked this earth as a man, He had limited knowledge of end time events. He only knew what His Father revealed to Him through the Spirit, and what He discerned through meditating on the prophecies in the Old Testament scriptures. After Jesus ascended into heaven, His Father disclosed to Him additional, *new information* about the end time events.

The book of Revelation is that new information, most of which was not revealed to the Old Testament prophets, the apostle Paul or *any other* New Testament writer. Revelation gives us a wealth of *new* information concerning the last days, detailing for us how the various divisions of 'priests' arrive in heaven.

If we have received any teaching on eschatology at all, we need to understand that, to one extent or another, we have been 'indoctrinated'. That's not necessarily a bad thing, but what we may think constitutes 'orthodox' biblical doctrine may not be what the Bible actually teaches at all. There is something to be said for personally examining the scriptures and arriving at ones' own conclusions, especially concerning end time events. Even the most well-meaning, intelligent and spiritually minded teacher or pastor could be wrong in their eschatology, *especially* if they are not using the book of Revelation as their *primary source material* when they teach on end time events.

Much of what I am sharing may sound rather unorthodox, but I believe my views to be scripturally sound. My goal is to accurately reflect what the scripture says and I'm using as my primary source the 'premier' end time authority on the subject—the book of Revelation.

Types and Shadows of the Rapture

There are several principles of Bible interpretation that will help guide the earnest seeker in their efforts to 'decode' Revelation:

1. Revelation uses *symbols and imagery* to 'veil' the story. This means that the rapture of believers in Revelation will be depicted via imagery and symbols, in the same way that other events of the end time story are represented using symbols.
2. Revelation tells the end time story utilizing the Hebraic style of interpretation, which is *indirect and multi-layered*, as opposed to the more straightforward, linear, rational and chronological Greek style of interpretation. The rapture(s) will be referred to *indirectly*, hidden beneath layers of symbolism.
3. Revelation uses symbolic imagery to *draw attention to other passages* of scripture, particularly Old Testament passages, which then provide additional details allowing us to uncover the rest of the story. Revelation alludes to various Old (and New) Testament passages that are vitally important in helping us understand the complete story.
4. Revelation is not chronological, nor is it one long vision; rather it is composed of *many discreet visions*, and the different visions layer over one another, presenting different aspects of the same period of time. The visions of Revelation reveal multiple timelines: each character in the story will have their own vision(s) and timeline. Thus, we can expect that the rapture(s) may be addressed in more than one vision.

The "Elijah/Elisha" Template

Revelation 12:5 tells us that the 'child' will be 'caught up' to God and to his throne' in heaven. As we have already seen, the Greek word for 'caught up' is the word '*harpazo*', meaning to "snatch quickly by force". Christians commonly refer to the '*harpazo*' as the 'rapture'. This is the same word Paul used to describe believers being taken into heaven:

"Then we who are alive, who are left, will be caught up together with them in the clouds to meet the Lord in the air. So we will be with the Lord forever." 1 Thessalonians 4:17

Are there any other places in the Bible where we read about someone being taken into heaven quickly and forcefully? The answer to that is, yes...Elijah.

The story of Elijah's translation into heaven provides a very detailed template for how God will bring some of the various 'courses' of 'priest/kings' into His presence; and how the 'baton' will be passed from one group of priests to another. The story is found in 2 Kings, chapter 2:

"1 When Yahweh was about to take Elijah up by a whirlwind into heaven, Elijah went with Elisha from Gilgal. 2 Elijah said to Elisha, "Please wait here, for Yahweh has sent me as far as Bethel."
Elisha said, "As Yahweh lives, and as your soul lives, I will not leave you." So they went down to Bethel.
3 The sons of the prophets who were at Bethel came out to Elisha, and said to him, "Do you know that Yahweh will take away your master from over you today?"
He said, "Yes, I know it. Hold your peace."
4 Elijah said to him, "Elisha, please wait here, for Yahweh has sent me to Jericho."
He said, "As Yahweh lives, and as your soul lives, I will not leave you." So they came to Jericho.
5 The sons of the prophets who were at Jericho came near to Elisha, and said to him, "Do you know that Yahweh will take away your master from over you today?"
He answered, "Yes, I know it. Hold your peace."

6 Elijah said to him, "Please wait here, for Yahweh has sent me to the Jordan."
He said, "As Yahweh lives, and as your soul lives, I will not leave you." Then they both went on. 7 Fifty men of the sons of the prophets went and stood opposite them at a distance; and they both stood by the Jordan. 8 Elijah took his mantle, and rolled it up, and struck the waters; and they were divided here and there, so that they both went over on dry ground. 9 When they had gone over, Elijah said to Elisha, "Ask what I shall do for you, before I am taken from you."
Elisha said, "Please let a double portion of your spirit be on me."

10 He said, "You have asked a hard thing. If you see me when I am taken from you, it will be so for you; but if not, it will not be so."

11 As they continued on and talked, behold, a chariot of fire and horses of fire separated them; and Elijah went up by a whirlwind into heaven. 12 Elisha saw it, and he cried, "My father, my father, the chariots of Israel and its horsemen!"

He saw him no more. Then he took hold of his own clothes and tore them in two pieces. 13 He also took up Elijah's mantle that fell from him, and went back and stood by the bank of the Jordan. 14 He took Elijah's mantle that fell from him, and struck the waters, and said, "Where is Yahweh, the God of Elijah?" When he also had struck the waters, they were divided apart, and Elisha went over." 2 Kings 2:1-14

There are three main 'characters' in this story: Elijah, his servant, Elisha, and the 'sons of the prophets'. Elijah went on a 'farewell tour' to say good-bye to the sons of the prophets. Elijah, Elisha and the sons of the prophets *all knew* that Elijah was going to be taken away that day. As Elijah went from town to town, his servant, Elisha, followed him, not wanting to leave Elijah. Finally Elijah asked Elisha what he wanted and Elisha replied that he wanted a 'double portion of Elijah's spirit'. Elisha wanted to 'inherit' the double portion as Elijah's 'son' and heir.

Elijah replied that if Elisha *saw* Elijah leave, he would have what he requested. Elijah was taken up in a fiery chariot while Elisha looked on. As the whirlwind whisked Elijah into heaven, his mantle fell on the ground and Elisha picked it up and, using Elijah's mantle, was able to perform the same miracle that Elijah had performed, that of parting the Jordan River. Elisha then knew that he had received what he requested—a double portion of the Spirit which was on Elijah.

• *Incidents in the lives of various Bible characters provide 'templates' to help us decode Revelation.*

The 'Elijah-Elisha' pattern provides a template to help us 'decode' how and when the various 'divisions' of priests will enter the heavenly temple, as well as when the next group will have the 'baton' passed to them:

1. Each group *will know when* they are about to be taken into heaven. The exception to this will be believers who will be taken on a day 'no man knows the day or hour.' More on this later...
2. People who are *not* being taken will also know when these believers are going to leave.
3. The 144K of Israel—the group of people that will come to Christ following the departure of raptured 'priests'—will, like Elisha, receive a 'double portion' of the Spirit, because they will be present, and watching, when the previous group was taken.

Christ's Ascension and the "Elijah-Elisha' Rapture Template

Christ's ascension into heaven also followed the 'Elijah-Elisha' rapture template. Like Elijah, Jesus knew when He was going to depart into heaven and He told His disciples to meet Him on the Mount of Olives:

> "Being assembled together with them, he commanded them, 'Don't depart from Jerusalem, but wait for the promise of the Father, which you heard from me. 5 For John indeed baptized in water, but you will be baptized in the Holy Spirit not many days from now.'
>
> "But you will receive power when the Holy Spirit has come upon you. You will be witnesses to me in Jerusalem, in all Judea and Samaria, and to the uttermost parts of the earth. 9 When he had said these things, as they were looking, he was taken up, and a cloud received him out of their sight." Acts 1:4,5, 8–9

On the day when Jesus knew He would be leaving, and His disciples were gathered together with Him, He gave them some final instructions before His departure. After telling them to remain in Jerusalem to await the promised Holy Spirit, Jesus ascended into heaven in full view of His disciples. Ten days later, on Pentecost, those who watched Him go into heaven were granted the Holy Spirit. The disciples received the 'inheritance'...the double portion of the Spirit.

Christ is our great High Priest and He is the first glorified Priest to have entered into God's temple. His presence in the heavenly temple guarantees that we ourselves will one day have access to heaven, through the substitutionary sacrificial death of Christ:

> "He has made us a kingdom of priests *through His blood.*"

'Rapture, ascension, translation': these are all words that describe the different ways people have been taken into heaven. The word 'rapture or 'caught up', implies a sudden, forceful snatching away. Elijah was 'caught up' in a fiery chariot and disappeared in a whirlwind. The 'fiery chariot' and the 'whirlwind' tell us that Elijah needed 'transportation' to get to heaven as he did not possess the power or the authority to enter heaven apart from God's will and enablement. And, for reasons not disclosed in the story, his departure was swift and sudden.

Jesus, however, was not 'caught up', rather He was 'taken up'. The phrase 'taken up' comes from the Greek word, "*epairó*", meaning 'to lift up' or 'raise'. This word doesn't imply haste, force, speed, or the idea that the individual who was being raised was being 'acted upon' by another entity. Jesus simply raised Himself slowly into the clouds and disappeared from view.

Even though Jesus had the authority and power to ascend into heaven at any time after His resurrection, His ascension on the Mount of Olives followed the pattern God outlined for us in the story of Elijah. Jesus' ascension took place: *1)* on a known date; 2) His disciples watched Him go; and 3) the disciples who saw Him depart received the 'double portion' of the Spirit shortly thereafter. (The 'double portion' refers to the inheritance which is promised to the first born son. More on this later!)

The 'Enoch' Template:

Enoch was another person who was taken into heaven in his mortal body, but the Bible doesn't tell us how he was taken, or if he knew the details surrounding his translation beforehand; we only are told that it happened. There's no record that anyone saw Enoch leave, either. One day he was walking on the earth in fellowship with God and then...he was gone: "He was not...for God took him."

> "By faith Enoch was taken away, so that he wouldn't see death, and he was not found, because God translated him. For he has had testimony given to him that before his translation he had been well pleasing to God." Hebrews 11:5

Enoch lived during the time prior to the flood, during a time of ever increasing evil and violence in the world. When the evil in the world finally reached the breaking point, God sent the flood, preserving Noah in an ark. Before Enoch was taken into heaven, people knew that he was a personal friend of God.

Sometime before the flood came, God removed Enoch from the world, taking him into heaven, "that he should not see death'. The promise God made to Enoch was that he would never die; and because of this, he is an type of those who will be granted access to heaven without dying, a preview of coming attractions for believers who will be alive during the days preceding the next world-wide judgment of God during the time of His wrath at the end of the age.

Out of all the priests and kings—believers in Jesus—who will be going to heaven when their division is called up, there is one group that will not know the day or hour of their departure—that being the division of priests I call the "Over-comers". Whereas both Jesus' departure and Elijah's departure were 'advertised' ahead of time, we know that Enoch's translation was quiet and secretive. No one knew ahead of time that he would be leaving or when he departed. One day he was there...and the next day, he was gone. He did, however, leave a 'note' for those left behind—the testimony of a life that pleased God. The same will hold true for the faithful Over-comers, who will be taken at a time known only to God, after which God's judgment and wrath will descend on the earth.

If the pattern illustrated in the 'Elijah-Elisha' template holds true, present day believers will know when they will be taken into heaven. The 144K and the 5th Seal martyrs will know the day when they will be going into heaven, too. The Two Witnesses will know their day of departure as well, but the 'Over-comers'—those saints who are on earth after the Beast begins to reign—will *not know* the day or hour of their departure. This group of priests will be waiting for the only rapture that is referred to as the secret, 'thief in the night' rapture. Because they will not know the day when they will be raptured, they will need to be watching and be ready to leave at any time. This is the rapture that Jesus referred to in the Olivet discourse:

> " 'But no one knows of that day and hour, not even the angels of heaven, but my Father only. 37 As the days of Noah were, so will the coming of the Son of Man be. 38 For as in those days which were before the flood they were eating and drinking, marrying and giving in marriage, until the day that Noah entered into the ship, 39 and they didn't know until the flood came and took them all away, so will the coming of the Son of Man be. 40 Then two men will be in the field: one will be taken and one will be left. 41 Two women will be grinding at the mill: one will be taken and one will be left. 42 Watch therefore, for you don't know in what hour your Lord comes. 43 But know this, that if the master of the house had known in what watch of the night the thief was coming, he would have watched, and would not have allowed his house to be broken into. 44 Therefore also be ready, for in an hour that you don't expect, the Son of Man will come.' " Matthew 24:36-44

Jesus compared this particular coming for His people to the days of Noah; the days just before God's judgment came on the earth in the form of a flood. Men, women and the *nephilim* were living their lives just like every other day until the day Noah entered the ark. Once Noah was safely in the ark, the trap was sprung, and the wicked were destroyed. Normal life came to an end for everyone.

Jesus also compared His coming to a thief sneaking into a house in order to steal items of value. A thief does not make an appointment with the owner of the house in order to steal from him! The thief pries open the window, takes what he came for, and quietly leaves. That's the picture that Jesus gave us in this passage: He is going to 'sneak' into the Beast's domain and steal away believers—people whom the Beast has claimed as his own—before the wrath of God is poured out on the world.

Later in this book I will explain more about how the various divisions of the priesthood will arrive in heaven on 'appointed days'. The Feasts of the Lord, also referred to as the appointed days—prefigure the times when the people of God, His priests, will appear in heaven. The Feasts of the Lord occur on known days and that's one of the reasons why believers will know the day when they will be leaving.

The Day of the Lord/wrath of God coincides with the secret, 'thief in the night' rapture of believers. The day when these believers are raptured, will be the same day that the wrath of God comes on the world. If Satan and the Beast/Antichrist could *prevent or delay* this final rapture, they could theoretically delay or prevent the judgment of God upon their kingdom! Satan knows that believers are not destined for wrath—that God will not pour His wrath on His people—but instead God must remove them before judgment falls. The Lord will come unexpectedly for this last group of believers, so as to avoid satanic interference and a delay in the out-pouring of judgment.

The apostle Paul also refers to this same 'thief in the night' rapture, which he says will take place just before "sudden destruction"—also known as the 'wrath of God'—descends on the Beast kingdom:

> "But concerning the times and the seasons, brothers, you have no need that anything be written to you. 2 For you yourselves know well that the day of the Lord comes like a thief in the night. 3 For when they are saying, 'Peace and safety,' then sudden destruction will come on them, like birth pains on a pregnant woman. Then they will in no way escape. 4 But you, brothers, aren't in darkness, that the day should overtake you like a thief.
>
> 5 You are all children of light and children of the day. We don't belong to the night, nor to darkness, 6 so then let's not sleep, as the rest do, but let's watch and be sober. 7 For those who sleep, sleep in the night; and those who are drunk are drunk in the night. 8 But since we belong to the day, let's be sober, putting on the breastplate of faith and love, and for a helmet, the hope of salvation. 9 For God didn't appoint us to wrath, but to the obtaining of salvation through our Lord Jesus Christ, 10 who died for us, that, whether we wake or sleep, we should live together with him." 1 Thessalonians 5:1-10

We know that there will be a group of believer/priests who will be living during the reign of the Beast. These people will need to 'keep the commandments' of God by refusing the mark of the Beast which, if taken, would incorporate them into the Beast's kingdom and spell their eternal doom. Believers who are alive at that time will *not know* the day that Christ will return for them, but they are assured that sometime during a 42 month 'window' of time, Christ *will* come for them—

that His return is 'imminent' and 'at the door'. They will need to be awake and sober and not give up hope that Christ will preserve them from the wrath to come.

The 42 month 'window' of departure for the Over-comers will be sometime *after* the midpoint/abomination of desolation, but before the end of 42 months, at which time Christ will return at His visible Second Coming. Paul describes this particular rapture of believers in the following passage:

> " Now, brothers, concerning the coming of our Lord Jesus Christ and our gathering together to him, we ask you ² not to be quickly shaken in your mind or troubled, either by spirit or by word or by letter as if from us, saying that the day of Christ has already come. ³ Let no one deceive you in any way. *For it will not be unless the rebellion comes first, and the man of sin is revealed, the son of destruction.* ⁴ He opposes and exalts himself against all that is called God or that is worshiped, so that he sits as God in the temple of God, setting himself up as God.*"* 2 Thessalonians 2:1-4

These believers are not destined for wrath. They will not be present on earth during the time of wrath; they will be removed by Christ before God judges the world.

The "Over-comers"—the last group of priests to be raptured—will be taken into heaven secretly, without earthly fanfare or warning. Once the world notices that believers are no longer present on earth, and God's wrath begins to rain down, they will understand—but too late—that God knows how to separate the righteous from the wicked before He pours out His vengeance on an unrepentant world.

Chapter 7: The Feasts of the Lord: Timing the Rapture(s)

If the destiny and dwelling place of believers is in heaven as God's priests, there must come a time when believers are transferred from the earth to their home in heaven. We know that when believers die, their souls go to be with the Lord. Though their spirits and souls are in God's presence, they still lack their permanent 'home'—their glorified bodies. The details of when and how people are glorified follows the 'harvest pattern' which is also laid out in scripture.

The Harvest Pattern

The Lord commanded that the children of Israel gather before Him three times a year. Those three compulsory gatherings coincided with the three main harvest times in Israel. At each harvest festival, the people were required to bring the 'first fruits' of their harvest to the Lord. The first fruits were given to God as His portion of the crops and they were the guarantee of a greater harvest to come.

In biblical times, every harvest consisted of three parts: the first fruits offering which belonged to God, the main harvest, and the gleanings. The first fruits were brought to the temple and presented to the Lord. After the first fruits offering was made, the main harvest was then reaped. The left-overs—the gleanings—were left in the field for the poor and the stranger to gather. The owner of the field (or orchard or vineyard) was not allowed to harvest the gleanings:

> " You shall observe a feast to me three times a year. 15 You shall observe the feast of unleavened bread. Seven days you shall eat unleavened bread, as I commanded you, at the time appointed in the month Abib (for in it you came out of Egypt), and no one shall appear before me empty. 16 And the feast of harvest, the first fruits of your labors, which you sow in the field; and the feast of ingathering, at the end of the year, when you gather in your labors out of the field.

> 17 Three times in the year all your males shall appear before the Lord Yahweh. " Exodus 23:14-17

> " When you reap the harvest of your land, you shall not wholly reap the corners of your field, neither shall you gather the gleanings of your harvest. 10 You shall not glean your vineyard, neither shall you gather the fallen grapes of your vineyard. You shall leave them for the poor and for the foreigner. I am Yahweh your God. " Leviticus 19:9,10

In the New Testament, Jesus used 'harvest' imagery to describe God's 'crop' of souls:

> "The enemy who sowed them is the devil. The harvest is the end of the age, and the reapers are angels." Matthew 13:39

Jesus' death on Passover and His resurrection on First Fruits, identified one of the reasons the Lord established His 'appointed times'—or feast days—in the Old Testament. *The seven Feasts of the Lord symbolically portray how God would redeem mankind, and they also provide a pattern for how God would go about gathering His people to Himself.* The story of redemption would include the substitutionary sacrifice of the perfect Lamb of God on Passover. Just as on the first Passover during the days of Moses, when all who placed the blood of the lamb on the door posts of their house were saved from the death angel; even now, all those who trust in the shed blood of the Lamb to cover their sin, have passed from death to life—the 'death angel' has passed over them.

In similar ways, hidden beneath the rites and rituals that are memorialized in the various feasts of the Lord, some aspect of God's plan of salvation of mankind will find fulfillment. Because the Feast days are cyclical, and were celebrated year after year, different aspects of any one Feast may be emphasized during the course of God's unfolding plan of salvation. *Multiple fulfillments* of the feast days may occur over the course of prophetic history. The only exception to this that I have found, is the feast of Passover, which has only one fulfillment, that being the day that Christ, the perfect Lamb of God was crucified. Jesus fulfilled every aspect of the Passover feast once and for all on the day He died.

As we move through the cycle of feast days, we can see how from their inception, God imbedded His secret plans into each of the feasts. Many of the feast days have yet to find their final fulfillment, and this is especially true of the fall feast days. Most of the fulfillments of the spring/summer feasts have already taken place at Christ's His first coming. The fall feast days, however, still await their complete and final fulfillments.

In Bible times, Israel's agricultural season began with the barley harvest in the spring. The first fruits the barley were brought to the Lord at the time of Unleavened Bread/Passover/First Fruits.

The next crop to be harvested was the wheat, which began in the early summer. Pentecost (Shavuot or the Feast of the Harvest) was the appointed time when the first fruits of the wheat harvest were brought to the Temple.

The Feast of Tabernacles, which took place in the fall, coincided with the ripening olives, grapes, and other fruits, which were harvested at the end of the summer.

The harvest pattern shows us how and when God 'harvests' His crop *of people;* and also when He receives and sanctifies the *first fruits* of each harvest. Jesus died on Passover (as the Lamb of God) and was raised on First Fruits, at the time of the ingathering of the first fruits of the barley harvest. Christ was the Passover Lamb who was sacrificed for our sins, and He is also the First Fruits of the 'barley' harvest. His death and resurrection satisfied the 'type' for both the Passover and the first fruits offering on the feast of First Fruits:

> "Most certainly I tell you, unless a grain of wheat falls into the earth and dies, it remains by itself alone. But if it dies, it bears much fruit." John 12:24

Christ was the initial 'grain of wheat' who died. Like the seed planted in the earth which must 'die' to allow a fresh crop to spring forth, Christ died and was buried and then sprang forth from the grave, the source of new life for all who would believe in Him.

In addition to the three 'first fruits' festivals of First Fruits, Pentecost and Tabernacles, there are four additional feasts, seven in total. The seven feasts are:

1. The Feast of Passover
2. The seven days of Unleavened Bread
3. The Feast of First Fruits
4. The Feast of Pentecost fifty days after First Fruits, taking place in the early summer.
5. The Feast of Trumpets, which begins the fall feasts.
6. The Day of Atonement, the one day of the year when the high priest could enter the Holy of Holies in the temple. This feast takes place 10 days after the Feast of Trumpets.
7. The Feast of Tabernacles, lasting 7 days with an "8th day" of assembly added at the end of the feast.

The Barley Harvest: Departed Souls

Unlike wheat, which has a hard outer layer called the chaff, barley is a grain that has a soft chaff or no outer layer at all. Spiritually speaking, barley—which has no chaff—represents souls who have no bodies; while wheat, which *does* have a hard outer layer, represents souls *with* bodies—living people.

After His crucifixion, Christ descended into Sheol, the place of the dead. He took the keys of death and Hades, and then He gathered ALL the righteous Old Testament saints who trusted in Him in prior generations, and transferred them from the place of the dead, into heaven. These souls represent the main 'barley' harvest, which typifies believers without bodies being transferred from the domain of the dead into heaven:

> " But to each one of us, the grace was given according to the measure of the gift of Christ. 8 Therefore he says,
> "When he ascended on high,
> he led captivity captive,
> and gave gifts to people."✧
> 9 Now this, "He ascended", what is it but that he also first descended into the lower parts of the earth? 10 He who descended is the one who also ascended far above all the heavens, that he might fill all things." Ephesians 4:7-9

Paul tells us that Christ descended into the lower parts of the earth, and from that place, from Sheol, He gathered those who had been held captive in the realm of the dead, and led them into God's presence in heaven.

But remember—the owner of the field (the Lord) was not permitted to gather the entire 'crop' of righteous souls who were in Sheol. He had to leave some of the 'gleanings' behind. That meant that not all the righteous dead in Sheol could accompany Christ and their brethren into Paradise! Christ was compelled to leave some souls behind. Not wanting to leave them in Sheol, Christ *resurrected them back into their mortal bodies*. Thus the compartment of Sheol where the 'righteous dead in Christ' were being held captive, was no longer in business, and the gleanings—newly resurrected souls—went back to the land of the living on earth, being resurrected back into their previous mortal bodies:

> " Jesus cried again with a loud voice, and yielded up his spirit. 51 Behold, the veil of the temple was torn in two from the top to the bottom. The earth quaked and the rocks were split. 52 The tombs were opened, and many bodies of the saints who had fallen asleep were raised; 53 and coming out of the tombs after his resurrection, they entered into the holy city and appeared to many. " Matthew 27:50-53

Those who were resurrected at that time, no doubt testified to what they had just witnessed in Sheol, including Jesus' victory over death, and how He single-handedly emptied Sheol of the souls of faithful dead believers. The newly resurrected saints were then resurrected into back their mortal bodies, just as Lazarus went

60

back into his mortal body when Jesus raised him from the dead. All these newly resurrected believers who had just been released from Sheol would die again, after which they would go—not to Sheol—but to heaven to be with the Lord.

The barley harvest represents the transfer of the spirits of the righteous from Sheol into the presence of God. The three parts of the spiritual barley harvest are as follows: Christ, the first fruits, who was made alive in the Spirit prior to His bodily resurrection; the Old Testament believers held in Sheol who represent the main harvest of souls; and the resurrected saints who appeared in Jerusalem at the time of Christ's resurrection, who were the gleanings of the spirits of the righteous, believing dead which had been in Sheol. (Matthew 27:50-53)

The 'Wheat' Harvest: from Pentecost to the Day of Atonement

The next harvest in the yearly agricultural cycle of Israel, was the wheat harvest. Wheat has a hard outer layer called the chaff. Wheat typifies those who are still alive, who will be taken bodily into heaven. Pentecost is the celebration of the first fruits of the wheat harvest. We know from Acts chapters 1 & 2, that the Holy Spirit descended from God on the day of Pentecost. The 120 disciples (including the 12 disciples minus Judas) upon whom the Spirit descended that day, fulfilled the first fruits aspect of the wheat harvest. These disciples were offered by Christ to His Father, and God accepted Christ's first fruits offering as evidenced by the tongues of fire resting on the believer's heads. Whereas the type of the barley harvest dealt with the souls of people who had died, Pentecost, the first fruits feast of the 'wheat' harvest, was about how believers were offered as *living sacrifices*. On the day of Pentecost, the 12 disciples, plus the rest of the 120 believers, PLUS 3,000 new converts were all filled with the Spirit. The first fruits festivals are when God receives the very first people who believe in Christ and then sanctifies them for service. All these Spirit-filled people were sent out by God and turned the world up-side down for Christ.

The main 'wheat' harvest has not yet taken place, but will be reaped when living, present day believers are glorified and raptured into God's presence. The ingathering of the main wheat harvest is symbolized by the rapture of the 'child' of Revelation 12, who is "caught up to God and to His throne"; and by the 24 Elders present in the throne room of God. They are seated in heaven, in the very presence of God. There, in the throne room of heaven, the 24 Elders act as priests, seated before the golden altar.

If the 'Elijah-Elisha' template holds true—the pattern established in 2 Kings 2 whereby those who 'watch' one group of believers go into heaven, who then receive the 'double portion' of the Holy Spirit shortly thereafter; *and* if the 144K of Israel are sealed at the *only first fruits feast **not** to have been fulfilled,* which is the feast of Tabernacles (more on this later), we can assume that the 'child' of Revelation 12 will have had to have been 'caught up' shortly before the 144K are to be sealed. Is there a feast day which comes directly before the Feast of Tabernacles (the feast when the 144K will be sealed) that may be a likely candidate for the day the 'child' is raptured into the heavenly temple?

Fulfillments of the Fall Feasts

There are two feasts which immediately precede the feast of Tabernacles: the Feast of Trumpets and the Day of Atonement. I believe that the dead in Christ will be resurrected on the Feast of Trumpets and that living believers will be 'changed'—glorified—on that day as well. Paul tells us that the living will be changed at the same time that the dead in Christ are raised, at the 'last trumpet' However, the day that *living* believers are changed into their immortal bodies *may not be the same day that they are raptured*. There are 15 days between the Feast of Trumpets and the Feast of Tabernacles; and sandwiched in between those two feasts is the Day of Atonement.

In ancient Israel, there was only *one day* when the priest could enter the Holy of Holies, and that was on the Day of Atonement. This day then, is the most likely day for believers to begin their priestly ministry in the heavenly Holy of Holies, which is the spiritual reality upon which the earthly priesthood is based.

In the second vision of Revelation 12, the 'child' is 'born' and then the Dragon attempts to devour him:

> "Another sign was seen in heaven. Behold, a great red dragon, having seven heads and ten horns, and on his heads seven crowns. 4 His tail drew one third of the stars of the sky, and threw them to the earth. The dragon stood before the woman who was about to give birth, so that when she gave birth he might devour her child. 5 She gave birth to a son, a male child, who is to rule all the nations with a rod of iron. Her child was caught up to God and to his throne." Revelation 12:3-5

The *birth* of the child has often been equated with the *rapture* itself, but I'm of the opinion that there are actually two different events which are taking place in this passage concerning the child: first the child is 'born' and then, shortly afterward, it's 'caught up'. The 'birth' of the child is distinct from the 'catching away'. The birth and the rapture appear as two separate events, taking place at two different times, *separated by a brief period* when the Dragon will seek to devour the child. If the rapture and the 'change' are indeed, two different events, then the child's birth may be equated with believers being 'born' into new, glorified bodies. Just as we have been 'born again' spiritually, we will be born again physically as

62

well. Immediately upon receiving our glorified bodies here on earth, the Dragon—Satan—will attempt to 'devour' the newly glorified saints in order to prevent their departure to the throne room.

Spiritual warfare is real; and Satan and his angels wield power in both the spiritual and earthly dimensions. Satan will have already brought his 'back up' forces to the earth as we read in Revelation 12, when he casts a third of his 'stars'—angels—to the earth, leaving the other two-thirds of his angels in heaven. Why would Satan go to such great lengths to prevent the child from entering the throne room of heaven?

In Revelation 5, we read that a call went out for someone who was 'worthy', who was qualified to open the scroll and break its seals. A search was undertaken—in heaven, the earth and even under the earth. No one was found worthy to open the scroll until the Lamb—Jesus—came out from the midst of the Elders.

The Lamb, along with the Elders, had been engaging in the priestly service of intercession for the saints on earth. Even now Jesus' role in heaven is that of our great High Priest who makes intercession for us before the throne of God. Would Jesus leave His priestly role as intercessor if there were no priests to take His place interceding on His behalf? Would He step into His role as the 'Lion of the tribe of Judah' if that meant abandoning His ministry as our faithful High Priest?

Without the presence of the next 'rotation' of priests in heaven—as represented by the 24 Elders—Jesus would not be in a position to take the scroll. Jesus could not leave the altar, take the scroll and still remain faithful to be the advocate for His people on earth. If Jesus could be prevented from taking the scroll of judgment because there was no one to relieve Him of His priestly duties, this would result in a spiritual 'stand-off' between the Christ and Satan, with Satan having the upper hand. Jesus would be 'blocked' from stepping into His role as King and Judge; and Satan could theoretically stall his impending doom. This is the reason why I believe that Satan will attempt to prevent the new priests from accessing the throne room of God.

The possibility of evil entities preventing other spiritual beings from traversing between heaven and earth is not new, and an example is recorded for us in the scriptures, in the book of Daniel:

> "Then he said to me, ' Don't be afraid, Daniel; for from the first day that you set your heart to understand, and to humble yourself before your God, your words were heard. I have come for your words' sake. 13 But the prince of the kingdom of Persia withstood me twenty-one days; but, behold,

Michael, one of the chief princes, came to help me because I remained there with the kings of Persia.' " Daniel 10:12,13

The angel, Gabriel, had a message to deliver to the prophet, Daniel, but because of heavy warfare in the spirit realm, he was delayed in delivering his message to Daniel for 21 days. Not until Michael came to assist him with back-up support, was Gabriel able to get through the enemy lines and deliver the message. What was the message that the angel was carrying? It was the '70 Week' prophecy of Daniel 9:25-27!

There are no extra words in Revelation, there is no unnecessary language. If the book tells us that the child is 'born' and that it is subsequently 'caught up', then that is exactly what will take place, with the Dragon attempting to devour the child in between the two events. The 'birth' and the 'catching away' are two distinct events.

Ten days after the Feast of Trumpets is the Day of Atonement; and five days after the Day of Atonement, the Feast of Tabernacles begins.

Just as the first three spring feasts of Passover, Unleavened Bread and First Fruits were fulfilled in rapid succession two thousand years ago at the death, burial and resurrection of Christ; some aspects of the three fall feasts will be fulfilled in rapid succession as well, in the resurrection and glorification of believers on the Feast of Trumpets; the rapture of living believers on the Day of Atonement, followed by the sealing of the 144K of Israel, and the Gentile believers at Tabernacles. Those who watch the 'child' depart will be filled with the 'double portion' inheritance reserved for the 'first born'. The Day of Atonement will be fulfilled at least one more time, when the Lord returns at His 2nd Coming which will also on the Day of Atonement.

Harvesting the gleanings of the 'Wheat'

The gleanings of the spiritual barley harvest were not taken into Paradise with the Lord when He emptied Sheol of the Old Testament dead in Christ. The owner of the field must always leave some of the crop behind. This holds true for the end time harvest, and the gleanings of the wheat as well. The 'gleanings' in this case are people who will come to Christ after the main harvest (present day believers) have been glorified. The 'gleanings' must always be left behind. These left behind saints will die for their faith during the persecution of the Harlot and the Scarlet Beast. (The persecution being referred to here is instigated before the midpoint by the Harlot, and should not be confused with the persecution instigated by the Beast during the last 3.5 years before the visible return of Christ. The Harlot religion and the Beast religion are two different and opposing religions—much more

64

on this later in the book.) Once the martyrs have arrived in heaven, they will receive their 'white robes'—their glorified bodies.

The Fall Crops: Olives, Grapes and Other Fruit

The last harvest of the year is the harvest of the olives, other fruits and grapes. The olive tree is a symbol of spiritual Israel (Romans 11), and represents those of Israel who will come to Christ and be baptized/sealed in the Spirit at the Feast of Tabernacles. The 'other fruits' are Gentiles who will come to Christ after the first rapture, and the 'grapes' represent the wicked who will be trodden in the winepress of God's fury.

In Israel, the first fruits of the olive harvest were offered at the Feast of Tabernacles in the fall. The 144K of Israel are called 'first fruits' in Revelation 14 because they will be the first to come to Christ out of the nation of Israel once present day believers are gone. If the 144K are the *first fruits* of the 'olive' harvest, the *main* harvest of olives would be those who come to Christ from Israel before the actual visible return of Christ to earth. The 'first fruits' will be taken into heaven before the 'hour of trial' and the 'main harvest' will be brought in at the 'Over-comer' rapture of Revelation 14:14 and 15:2, along with believing Gentiles represented by the 'other fruit'. The 'gleanings' of the fall harvest will be those beheaded by the Beast who will be resurrected after Christ's visible return at His Second Coming.

In addition to the transfer/resurrection/rapture events already mentioned above, the Two Witnesses will be resurrected and taken into heaven at the midpoint. Every resurrection/rapture/ascension *is on a known date* with the exception of the 'Over-comer' rapture, which will take place on an unknown, unspecified day and hour, pictured as Christ coming as a thief in the night. The *timeframe* of that final rapture, though, *is* known, taking place *after* the abomination of desolation but *before* the visible return of Christ to the earth 1260 days later. (See 2 Thessalonians 2:1,2.)

The 'grapes' represent the wicked who will also be 'harvested' at the time of the end. The Beast and the False Prophet represent the 'first fruits' and they will be cast alive into the Lake of Fire at Christ's visible return to earth:

> "The beast was taken, and with him the false prophet who worked the signs in his sight, with which he deceived those who had received the mark of the beast and those who worshiped his image. These two were thrown alive into the lake of fire that burns with sulfur." Revelation 19:20

The Beast and the False Prophet will be taken in a 'reverse rapture' where they enter their eternal destiny in the Lake of Fire apart from dying. The 'main harvest' of the wicked will be those who oppose Christ, who are killed by the Lord at Armageddon. They will await their resurrection at the Great White Throne judgment along with the rest of the wicked dead throughout time:

> "21 The rest were killed with the sword of him who sat on the horse, the sword which came out of his mouth. So all the birds were filled with their flesh. " Revelation 19:21

> "Another angel came out of the temple which is in heaven. He also had a sharp sickle. 18 Another angel came out from the altar, he who has power over fire, and he called with a great voice to him who had the sharp sickle, saying, 'Send your sharp sickle and gather the clusters of the vine of the earth, for the earth's grapes are fully ripe!' 19 The angel thrust his sickle into the earth, and gathered the vintage of the earth and threw it into the great wine press of the wrath of God. 20 The wine press was trodden outside of the city, and blood came out of the wine press, up to the bridles of the horses, as far as one thousand six hundred stadia." Revelation 14:17-20

Satan represents the 'gleanings' of the grape harvest. He will be cast into the pit, bound in chains, awaiting his release after the thousand year reign of Christ. Because Christ cannot 'harvest' the gleanings, He will not judge Satan until the thousand years are over:

> "I saw an angel coming down out of heaven, having the key of the abyss and a great chain in his hand. 2 He seized the dragon, the old serpent, who is the devil and Satan, who deceives the whole inhabited earth, and bound him for a thousand years, 3 and cast him into the abyss, and shut it and sealed it over him, that he should deceive the nations no more until the thousand years were finished. After this, he must be freed for a short time." Revelation 20:1-3

> "The devil who deceived them was thrown into the lake of fire and sulfur, where the beast and the false prophet are also. They will be tormented day and night forever and ever." Revelation 20:10

God gives us patterns in His Word which reveal His plans and purposes for His people. He uses types and shadows, symbols and metaphors, parables and allegory—to reveal spiritual truth. God's three part harvest pattern—of the first fruits, main harvest and gleanings—is the pattern He has established for gathering His harvest of souls into His barn, as well as how He disposes of the wicked. Any end time scenario which does not take into consideration when, how and why people arrive in heaven, (or the Lake of Fire), will be incomplete and misleading.

In summary: God uses the three part harvest pattern as a type of how He gathers His people. The seven Feasts of the Lord—which are connected with the harvest pattern—describe God's plan for bringing people to Himself through the death and resurrection of Christ, through the giving of the Holy Spirit, as well as the various resurrection and rapture/transfer events.

The timing of the harvest of souls can be summarized as follows:

Barley Harvest:

Passover, Unleavened Bread and First Fruits take place in the spring during the time of the barley harvest. Barley is a grain without a hard outer layer and represents souls who have died and no longer possess a body.

Christ was the First Fruits of the barley harvest, the first to be made alive in the Spirit. The righteous dead in Sheol, who represent the 'main' harvest, were transferred from Sheol into heaven; and the 'gleanings' were the resurrected saints who appeared to many people in Jerusalem after Jesus' resurrection. These people would to die again, and then appear in their spirits in the heavenly throne room to await their reunification with their resurrected and glorified bodies.

Wheat Harvest:

The first fruits of the wheat harvest were offered at Pentecost. The first 120 disciples, upon whom the Holy Spirit came, represented the first fruits of the 'wheat' harvest. The 'main' harvest will be represented by all believers—both living and dead—who have trusted in Christ—from the very first Old Testament saints—through present day believers. All these will either be 'changed' from mortal to immortal (if they are living) or will be resurrected (if they have died), with both transformations taking place on the Feast of Trumpets, the first of the three fall feasts of the Lord. The 'dead in Christ' will receive their new bodies in heaven. The changed and glorified living believers will remain on earth until the Day of Atonement, ten days later.

Believers, who will be martyred by the earth dwellers and the Harlot during the 10 days of persecution which will begin in the spring, ten days before the Feast of First Fruits in 2021, comprise the 'gleanings' of the 'wheat harvest'. (More on this later...) They will appear before the Lord in heaven on First Fruits, during the time of the barley harvest, when souls without bodies will again enter the throne room of God. These souls will receive their 'white robes', representing their glorified bodies, while they are in heaven.

Chapter 8: Puzzle Pieces

Understanding how and when the events depicted in the various visions in the book of Revelation will actually unfold can pose a bit of a challenge. Sometimes, though, we see similar 'puzzle pieces' showing up in two or more visions: this is an indication that the events and characters in the visions may be connected in some way, and that the visions may actually overlay one another at the place where we see the similarities. The 'Seal' vision may, in fact, overlay the 'Trumpet' vision, which in turn, may overlay the 'Bowl' vision. We can use the similarities between these visions as 'registration marks', similarities which tell us that these 'puzzle pieces' are connected.

When Revelation depicts almost identical events taking place in multiple visions, then we need to examine these passage carefully to see if these events might actually be taking place at, or around, the same time. This is particularly true of events associated with the wrath of God and the return of Christ to earth. A large earthquake connects several visions together as we see in the 6th Seal, the 7th Bowl and the 7th Trumpet:

The 6th Seal:

> " I saw when he opened the sixth seal, and there was a great earthquake. The sun became black as sackcloth made of hair, and the whole moon became as blood. 16 They told the mountains and the rocks, "Fall on us, and hide us from the face of him who sits on the throne, and from the wrath of the Lamb, 17 for the great day of his wrath has come, and who is able to stand?" Revelation 6:12,16, 17

The 7th Bowl:

> "The seventh poured out his bowl into the air. A loud voice came out of the temple of heaven, from the throne, saying, 'It is done!' 18 There were lightnings, sounds, and thunders; and there was a great earthquake such as has not happened since there were men on the earth—so great an earthquake and so mighty. 19 The great city was divided into three parts, and the cities of the nations fell. Babylon the great was remembered in the sight of God, to give to her the cup of the wine of the fierceness of his wrath." Revelation 16:17-19

The 7th Trumpet:

> " The seventh angel sounded, and great voices in heaven followed, saying,
> ' The kingdom of the world has become the Kingdom of our Lord and of his Christ. He will reign forever and ever!' 16 The twenty-four elders, who sit on

their thrones before God's throne, fell on their faces and worshiped God, [17] saying: 'We give you thanks, Lord God, the Almighty, the one who is and who was, because you have taken your great power and reigned. [18] The nations were angry, and your wrath came, as did the time for the dead to be judged, and to give your bondservants the prophets, their reward, as well as to the saints and those who fear your name, to the small and the great, and to destroy those who destroy the earth.'

> [19] God's temple that is in heaven was opened, and the ark of the Lord's covenant was seen in his temple. Lightnings, sounds, thunders, an earthquake, and great hail followed." Revelation 11:15-19

I've highlighted the common thread running through these three separate visions: a great earthquake, hail, lightning, thunder; mountains and islands disappearing and the wrath of God. All of this sounds like events which are associated with the Day of the Lord, the wrath of God and the Second Coming of Christ.

Each of these three visions also provided us with additional details not mentioned the other visions. The 6th Seal provides us with the following information not mentioned in the 7th Bowl or the 7th Trumpet:

> "The sun became black as sackcloth made of hair, and the whole moon became as blood. [13] The stars of the sky fell to the earth, like a fig tree dropping its unripe figs when it is shaken by a great wind. [14] The sky was removed like a scroll when it is rolled up. Every mountain and island was moved out of its place."

We learn that everyone, regardless of rank or station, tries to hide from the Lord:

> "Then the kings of the earth and the great ones and the generals and the rich and the powerful, and everyone, slave and free, hid themselves in the caves and among the rocks of the mountains, calling to the mountains and rocks, 'Fall on us and hide us from the face of him who is seated on the throne.' "

The 7th Bowl tells us that, upon the out-pouring of this final bowl, the wrath is finished:

> "The seventh angel poured out his bowl into the air, and a loud voice came out of the temple, from the throne, saying, 'It is done!' "

We also learn that the 'great city' was split and that all the cities of the nations fell:

> "The great city was split into three parts, and the cities of the nations fell."

The 7th Trumpet uses the phrase, "your wrath *came*" written in the past tense, informing us that the wrath of God was completed by the time the 7th angel blew his Trumpet:

> "The nations raged,
> but your wrath came,
> and the time for the dead to be judged.."

Another passage in Revelation gives us more details about the 7th Trumpet. We are told that the 7th Trumpet will signal the end of the 'mystery of God' that was announced to His servants:

> "...but that in the days of the trumpet call to be sounded by the seventh angel the mystery of God, as he announced to his servants the prophets, should be fulfilled." Revelation 10:7

The 'mystery of God' is the actual unveiling of the end time events as described in the whole book of Revelation. The book of Revelation is the 'mystery of God' which is being referred to in this passage. The 7th Trumpet sounds when *all the events* of the seven years have already taken place and the wrath is complete. In other places, we learn that the 'wrath of God' is associated with the destruction of the Beast system, Armageddon and the return of Christ.

The 6th Seal, the 7th Bowl and the 7th Trumpet are three different 'puzzle pieces' connected with the same event: the wrath of God and the 2nd Coming of Christ. We can infer then, that since these events are associated with the return of Christ, that the actual out-pouring of the wrath of God and the Lamb must take place towards *the end of the seven years*—the time immediately preceding Christ's visible return to earth. The wrath of God cannot start at the beginning of the seven years, or in the middle of the 'tribulation' because *the wrath depicted in the 6th Seal, 7th Bowl and 7th Trumpet is associated with the sudden appearance of Christ to judge the world*, and we know that the 2nd Coming of Christ doesn't happen until the end. The wrath is complete (as indicated by the writer using the past tense 'thy wrath *came*') at the sounding of the 7th Trumpet, when Christ's victory over His enemies is conclusive. Included in the Seal, Trumpet and Bowl visions, are a great earthquake and the wrath of God being—or having been—poured out.

If the events described in these three visions are indeed giving us different aspects of the same basic event, we can assume that the *visions of the Trumpets, Seals and Bowls overlay one another in other parts of the timeline as well.* **If this is true for these three visions, then it applies to all the visions of Revelation as well.**

The 6th and 7th Seals, the 7th Trumpet and 7 Bowls depict different aspects of the wrath of God and the Second Coming of Christ. If we were to search throughout the book of Revelation, we would find even more passages that deal with the 'wrath of God' and 'The End'.

The 'End'...over and over again...

Even though the wrath of God is something that takes place at the *end* of the story, the 'pieces' of the puzzle that deal with God's wrath, and 'The End' are strewn throughout the book. There are many other passages in Revelation that refer to The End, beginning in the very first chapter:

> "Behold, he is coming with the clouds, and every eye will see him, including those who pierced him. All the tribes of the earth will mourn over him. Even so, Amen" Revelation 1:7

This passage describes Jesus' visible return to the earth at the close of the age informing us that everyone will see Him when He returns.

The next time we see events associated with The End, and the victorious return of Christ to earth, is found in chapter 5, when ALL creation—including fallen angels and Satan himself—will worship Christ:

> "^{1} I looked, and I heard something like a voice of many angels around the throne, the living creatures, and the elders. The number of them was ten thousands of ten thousands, and thousands of thousands, ^{12} saying with a loud voice, 'Worthy is the Lamb who has been killed to receive the power, wealth, wisdom, strength, honor, glory, and blessing!'
>
> ^{13} I heard every created thing which is in heaven, on the earth, under the earth, on the sea, and everything in them, saying, ' To him who sits on the throne and to the Lamb be the blessing, the honor, the glory, and the dominion, forever and ever! Amen!' " Revelation 5:11-13

The apostle Paul also concurs with this testimony, that at the end, every created being will bow the knee before Christ:

> "^{9} Therefore God also highly exalted him, and gave to him the name which is above every name, ^{10} that at the name of Jesus every knee should bow, of those in heaven, those on earth, and those under the earth, ^{11} and that every

tongue should confess that Jesus Christ is Lord, to the glory of God the Father." Philippians 2:9-11

The first part of the vision in Revelation 5:1-10, describes a mighty angel crying out 'Who is worthy to take the scroll and open its seals?" A search is conducted throughout all creation to find someone who is worthy, but no one is found...until the Lamb—Christ—comes forward and takes the scroll from His Father. We know that this scene does not happen at The End, as it is not associated with the second coming of Christ or the wrath of God. Christ is taking the scroll, and this happens toward the beginning of the Big Story. The last part of the vision, though, omits *all the other events of the seven years*, jumping directly to what I call the 'happy ending', at which time all creation will acknowledge Christs' worthiness to reign.

The theme of the vision in Revelation 5, is the *worthiness* of Christ, and we are informed that of all created beings, everywhere, only Jesus is worthy to take the scroll and open its seals. By the time the wrath is over, and the Lamb has set up His millennial kingdom, ALL creatures will acknowledge His worth—even the fallen beings whose fate will be eternal suffering in the Lake of Fire.

In addition to various events associated with The End which appear in Revelation chapters 1 and 5; The End appears elsewhere in Revelation: in chapter 14:14-20; all of chapters 15 and 16; chapter 17:14; and all of chapter 19, for a total of at least 8 different places in the book. Each of these passages provide us with information that can be used to construct a chronology of the larger story of Revelation, and will give us more details about how the story ends.

By incorporating various aspects of The End in multiple visions, God is making a point: **Christ *will* return and He *will* be victorious over all His enemies. Believers can be assured that they are not forgotten and that they will participate in His triumph.**

In addition to themes pertaining to the worthiness of Christ, the wrath of God and The End in general; there are other themes which will cycle through the book, appearing in a number of different visions: themes involving Christ, the martyrs, the Beast and so on. Vision will layer over vision, adding ever deeper complexity and dimensionality to the narrative. We should not underestimate the importance of this method for interpreting Revelation, for now when we notice common threads and similarities between the visions, we can match the characters and events of one vision, with the same or similar characters and events in another vision. This ability to layer the visions over one another is one of the little known keys for decoding the book. This is where the small often over-looked details in the visions help us to create a timeline: the details provide 'registration-marks' so we know where to match up the characters with their story as it develops in other visions.

Just as the past tense verb, 'Thy wrath *came*', indicated to us that the 7th Trumpet will be the very last thing that will take place before the rule of Christ begins, there are other timing clues that indicate where to place the various elements of the visions in a storyline. We can piece together the larger puzzle—the Big Story— by matching the symbolic connections between the smaller 'little stories', the visions which make up Revelation.

So here's what we've discovered about interpreting Revelation thus far:

1) Revelation is not one long vision, but is comprised of many small, but related, visions. Many 'little stories' make up the Big Story of the end time narrative.
2) The order in which the visions appear in Revelation does not give us an accurate portrayal of the actual chronology of the Big Story.
3) Revelation is not linear, and does not tell the story in a 'straight line'. The visions 'layer' over one another and there are actually multiple story lines interwoven throughout the book, where different threads follow each of the different character's story lines.
4) The commonalities present between the various visions are clues informing us that the people and events may be connected in the context of the larger story.

The wrath of God will end at the return of Christ to the earth, at Armageddon, and will take place sometime just prior to the close of the 7 year timeframe commonly known as 'the tribulation'.

Chapter 9: Finding Common Threads & Constructing a Chronology

In the previous example, I demonstrated how the 6th Seal, the 7th Bowl and the 7th Trumpet all seem to be pointing to a time when the wrath of God will be poured out on the world and the return of Christ to the earth. They all reference a great earthquake and the out-pouring of the wrath of God. The 'earthquake' and the 'wrath' are what link these visions to one another.

The same or similar *characters* also seem to appear in different visions. Like the 'earthquakes' and the 'wrath' which appear in the Seal, Trumpet and Bowl visions—indicators that elements of these visions take place around the same time —we can trace characters (like the martyrs) who show up in several different visions and learn their stories. The actions and dialogue of these characters will differ from vision to vision, and it's what we see them *doing and saying* in each vision, and *who* they are interacting with, that will enable us to follow their stories throughout the 7 year timeframe. The events associated with the characters in the visions are what actually moves the Big Story forward.

The 24 Elders, the martyrs, the earth dwellers and the Harlot are some of the characters who have roles to play in the visions. Also included within those visions are *time indicators*. We can observe the actions of the characters and deduce from the surrounding verses, approximately when during the course of the 7 years the action is taking place, which enables us to construct a timeline of events.

The Martyrs

There are a number of visions where we read about people who are martyred for their faith. In Revelation 6:9-11, at the opening of the 5th Seal, we see 'souls under the altar' who are crying out for their blood to be avenged. They are given a 'white robe' (a resurrection body) and told to rest a little longer:

> "9 When he opened the fifth seal, I saw underneath the altar the souls of those who had been killed for the Word of God, and for the testimony of the Lamb which they had. 10 They cried with a loud voice, saying, "How long, Master, the holy and true, until you judge and avenge our blood on those who dwell on the earth?" 11 A long white robe was given to each of them. They were told that
>
> they should rest yet for a while, until their fellow servants and their brothers, who would also be killed even as they were, should complete their course." Revelation 6:9-11

In the next chapter—Revelation 7:9-17—we see people from "every tribe, tongue, people and nation" appearing in heaven having washed their robes, making them 'white in the blood of the Lamb'. These people were killed during a time known as the 'great tribulation' and their 'robes' were washed in the 'blood of the Lamb':

> "9 After these things I looked, and behold, a great multitude which no man could count, out of every nation and of all tribes, peoples, and languages, standing before the throne and before the Lamb, dressed in white robes, with palm branches in their hands. 10 They cried with a loud voice, saying, "Salvation be to our God, who sits on the throne, and to the Lamb!"

> 11 All the angels were standing around the throne, the elders, and the four living creatures; and they fell on their faces before his throne, and worshiped God, 12 saying, "Amen! Blessing, glory, wisdom, thanksgiving, honor, power, and might, be to our God forever and ever! Amen."

> 13 One of the elders answered, saying to me, "These who are arrayed in the white robes, who are they, and where did they come from?" 14 I told him, "My lord, you know."He said to me, "These are those who came out of the great suffering *(tribulation)*.They washed their robes and made them white in the Lamb's blood.

> 15 Therefore they are before the throne of God, and they serve him day and night in his temple. He who sits on the throne will spread his tabernacle over them. 16 They will never be hungry or thirsty any more. The sun won't beat on them, nor any heat; 17 for the Lamb who is in the middle of the throne shepherds them and leads them to springs of life-giving waters. And God will wipe away every tear from their eyes." Revelation 7:9-17

The Elder tells John that these people who keep appearing in heaven, came out of a time of intense persecution on earth. They appear *bodily* in heaven. In other words, they are *not* disembodied spirits. If they were only spirits they would not be wearing white robes, standing or holding palm branches in their hands. Disembodied spirits have no need of clothing, neither can they 'hold' anything, for they have no hands.

The Elder tells John that these people keep 'coming' out of the great persecution.

"These are the ones coming out of the great tribulation."

The martyrs don't arrive all at once. The tense of the Greek verb translated as "coming" indicates a continual arrival of martyrs into heaven. If this group of people had been taken in a rapture event, they wouldn't 'keep coming' into heaven; they would have arrived all at once.

The 5th Seal martyrs in Revelation 6 were told to rest until the full number of their 'fellow servants who were to be killed as they were', arrived in heaven. This is the passage which confirms that the martyred saints will be arriving in heaven, not all at once, but one by one, as they are put to death. Finally, the whole group will be assembled before the throne of God, in their resurrection bodies which are represented by their 'white robes'.

Symbols and Imagery (Part One)

Before moving on to other passages which speak of the martyrs, I would like to point out the meaning of the some of the symbolism used in these passages of Revelation. The 'robes' that were 'washed in the blood of the Lamb' refer to the slain bodies of the people of God. The passage is not talking about how these martyrs were saved through the blood of Christ, but about the fact of their martyrdom. The martyrs died for their testimony of Jesus and for His sake, and that's why Christ sees the blood of the martyrs *as though it were His own blood.*

Revelation tells the end time story via symbols and imagery. The robes 'washed in blood'—the slain bodies of the martyrs—were transformed into the 'white robes' of the martyr's resurrected bodies. The multitudes who come out of the 'great tribulation' are seen standing before God in their resurrected and glorified bodies, 'wearing white robes'.

We see the martyred saints in yet another vision, this time in Revelation 12:11. They are those who 'loved not their lives even unto death' and they appear in heaven around the time that war breaks out between Michael and the Dragon, when the Dragon—Satan—is cast out of heaven, permanently.

> " I heard a loud voice in heaven, saying, "Now the salvation, the power, and the Kingdom of our God, and the authority of his Christ has come; for the accuser of our brothers has been thrown down, who accuses them before our God day and night. 11 They overcame him because of the Lamb's blood, and because of the word of their testimony. They didn't love their life, even to death. 12 Therefore rejoice, heavens, and you who dwell in them. Woe to the earth and to the sea, because the devil has gone down to you, having great wrath, knowing that he has but a short time."" Revelation 12:10, 11

Not long after the Dragon is cast out of heaven, he will begin to pursue the woman of Revelation 12 (more on her later). This marks the beginning of the last half of the 7 years, a point in time commonly known as the midpoint, the time of the 'abomination of desolation' and the time when Israel—represented by the 'woman'— must flee into the wilderness for 1260 days or 'time, times and half a time'. (In this book, I will usually refer to the day of the 'abomination of desolation' as the '*midpoint*'—the middle of the group of 7 years commonly known as 'the tribulation'.)

> "13 When the dragon saw that he was thrown down to the earth, he persecuted the woman who gave birth to the male child. 14 Two wings of the great eagle were given to the woman, that she might fly into the wilderness to her place, so that she might be nourished for a time, times, and half a time, from the face of the serpent." Revelation 12:13, 14

Shortly before the Dragon/Satan is cast out of heaven, *martyrs will have already begun arriving in heaven*. Believers who died for the sake of Christ appear before the throne of God *prior to the midpoint*, before the abomination of desolation, before the beginning of the reign of the Beast/Antichrist. Because they are in heaven *before* the midpoint, and we know from other passages that the Antichrist/Beast does not begin his reign until *at* the midpoint, the Antichrist/Beast *cannot be responsible for the death of these believers*. If the Antichrist didn't kill these people...who did?

The Harlot, the Earth Dwellers and the Martyrs

Enter the Harlot. The Harlot and the earth dwellers are responsible for the death of the martyrs. They are the great persecutors of believers during the first half of the seven years. The Harlot—"Mystery Babylon"—is described as being "drunk with the blood of the saints":

> "I saw the woman drunken with the blood of the saints and with the blood of the martyrs of Jesus. When I saw her, I wondered with great amazement." Revelation 17:6

In order to get 'drunk' one must drink a lot of alcohol in a short period of time. The same holds true for the Harlot—a lot of blood will be spilled during a brief time period and she will revel in the death of the martyrs.

Revelation 17:1,2 tells us that the Harlot incites the 'earth dwellers' to persecute and kill believers, along with the kings of the earth:

> "One of the seven angels who had the seven bowls came and spoke with me, saying, 'Come here. I will show you the judgment of the great prostitute who sits on many waters, 2 with whom the kings of the earth committed sexual

immorality. Those who dwell in the earth were made drunken with the wine of her sexual immorality.' " Revelation 17:1,2

The 'dwellers on earth' (or 'earth dwellers') do not refer to *all* people who live on earth, but only to those people whose hearts, minds and affections are set on earthly things. The earth dwellers—people who will be influenced by the Harlot—will participate along side the Harlot in this 'drunken' orgy of death.

The 5th Seal martyrs will cry out to God for their blood to be avenged on those who 'dwell on earth':

> "They cried with a loud voice, saying, 'How long, Master, the holy and true, until you judge and avenge our blood on those who dwell on the earth?' " Revelation 6:10

The martyrs who appear before the throne of God in Revelation 7, *and* the 5th Seal martyrs of Revelation 6, *plus* the martyrs of Revelation 12, who 'loved not their lives', *are the same group of martyred saints*. They will be put to death by the Harlot and the earth dwellers. They will be resurrected and appear before God's throne *prior to the midpoint* of the seven years.

What 'Great Tribulation'?

Could these groups of martyred saints in chapters 6, 7 and 12, be the same group of people martyred during the same purge? My investigation indicates that they are, indeed, one and the same group of people.

But now we run into a problem: we are told the martyrs in Revelation 7 come out of a time of persecution referred to as the 'great tribulation'. Most Bible teachers believe that the 'great tribulation' that these martyrs are 'coming out of' is the same 'great tribulation' that Jesus described in Matthew 24:

> "'When, therefore, you see the abomination of desolation, which was spoken of through Daniel the prophet, standing in the holy place (let the reader understand), 16 then let those who are in Judea flee to the mountains. 17 Let him who is on the housetop not go down to take out the things that are in his house. 18 Let him who is in the field not return back to get his clothes. 19 But woe to those who are with child and to nursing mothers in those days! 20 Pray that your flight will not be in the winter nor on a Sabbath, 21 for then there will be great suffering *(tribulation)*, such as has not been from the beginning of the world until now, no, nor ever will be." Matthew 24:15-21

The general understanding of *when* the 'great tribulation' takes place is not where Revelation 12 seems to indicate it actually occurs! Most pre-tribulation dispensationalists believe that the 'great tribulation' occurs during the *second half* of the 7 years, not during the first half, as seems to be indicated in Revelation 12. Remember—some of the martyrs are *already present* in heaven as war breaks out between Michael and the Dragon and we know this battle takes place PRIOR to the midpoint of the 7 years.

But in Matthew, Jesus seems to be telling us that the 'great tribulation' will take place AFTER the midpoint—after the 'abomination of desolation'. Which interpretation is correct?

A closer look at 'whose' tribulation is taking place will help us understand what's really going on, and that the Bible actually makes reference to (at least) two different events called the 'great tribulation'. When we examine the details in Revelation 7, we read that the people who are martyred are believers from 'every tribe, tongue, people and nation'; in other words, they are gentiles—non-Jews—and they die for their faith:

> "After these things I looked, and behold, a great multitude which no man could count, *out of every nation and of all tribes, peoples, and languages,* standing before the throne and before the Lamb, dressed in white robes, with palm branches in their hands." Revelation 7:9

The 'great tribulation' spoken of by Jesus in Matthew 24, is the great tribulation for *the Jews*—the remnant of Israel—most of whom will not die, but will escape with their lives into the wilderness.

In *Revelation,* the 'great tribulation' applies to gentile believers who are killed before the midpoint of the 7 years. The 'great tribulation' in *Matthew* applies to the Jewish remnant, who will escape into the wilderness. Each of these 'great tribulations' takes place at different times during the 7 years, and involves different groups of people. For the martyrs of the Harlot and the earth dwellers, their great tribulation will take place sometime during the first 3.5 years; and for Israel, the 'great tribulation' will occur after the abomination of desolation, during the last 3.5 years.

The same 'great tribulation' Jesus described in Matthew, is actually referred to in Revelation as well, but the story in Revelation is told via symbolic imagery. In Revelation 12, we read about the woman who birthed the Man-child who must flee into the wilderness for 'time, times and half a time' or 1260 days. This is the same event as the 'great tribulation' Jesus described in Matthew 24.

Ten Days of Persecution

In the letter to the church of Smyrna (Revelation 2:8-11), Jesus describes a ten day period of intense persecution which will result in the death of many believers:

> "Don't be afraid of the things which you are about to suffer. Behold, the devil is about to throw some of you into prison, that you may be tested; and you will have oppression for ten days. Be faithful to death, and I will give you the crown of life." Revelation 2:10

Could the '10 days' of 'tribulation' be associated with the death of the martyrs at the hands of the Harlot and the earth dwellers? Could this passage be referring to the time of 'great tribulation' described in Revelation 7? To find out, we'll need to examine the letters to the seven churches.

Chapter 10: A Unified Book

From beginning to end, Revelation *is prophecy* given to end time believers so that they will know the things that will take place prior to the return of Christ:

> " He said to me, ' These words are faithful and true. The Lord God of the spirits of the prophets sent his angel to show to his bondservants the things which must happen soon.'"

> 7 "Behold, I am coming soon! Blessed is he who keeps the words of the prophecy of this book." Revelation 22:6,7

The whole of Revelation pertains to the time of the end, and thus the *entire book* applies to the generation of people who will be living when the events described in the prophecy take place.

Some Bible scholars believe the information contained in the letters to the seven churches applies exclusively to the seven actual churches present on the earth during the first century, churches that were in existence during John's lifetime. Some believe that the seven churches represent different 'church ages' or eras of Christianity. The triumphs and perils of each 'age,' are represented by one of the seven churches, and that together, the seven churches encompass two thousand years of church history—from the persecution endured by the early believers at the time of the apostles—to the lukewarm church of Laodicea and the 'raptured' church of Philadelphia during the time of the end.

Because most Bible teachers view the visions of Revelation as being 'linear' and chronological rather than 'cyclical' and layered, the events described in the first 3 chapters of Revelation (which include the letters to the seven churches) are interpreted as having already taken place sometime in the past. The linear, Western view of Revelation tends to leave scholars with no reasonable option *except* a historical interpretation of some kind.

When the letters to the seven churches are viewed as history, rather than as end time prophecy, the information contained in letters to the seven churches becomes disconnected from the rest of the book of Revelation, with the letters have no particular relevance for end time 'tribulation' saints. According to this method of interpretation, the letters do not provide any details regarding the narrative presented in the rest of the book. "Move along...nothing to see here!"

However, within the book of Revelation itself, there is *no indication* that we are to apply the content of the letters to *anyone other than end time saints—believ-*

ers who will be alive when the events of Revelation unfold. Revelation represents itself as being *prophecy of the last days*. It is not history...at least not until the events described therein have taken place!

> "For the *testimony of Jesus is the spirit of prophecy*." Revelation 19:10

> "This is the Revelation of Jesus Christ, which God gave him to show to his servants the things which must happen soon *(or 'quickly')*, which he sent and made known by his angel to his servant, John." Revelation 1:1

The 'testimony' of Jesus is the prophetic word contained in the book of Revelation. This prophecy was given for the benefit of those who would be living during the last days—the very people who would need to know the sequence of events which will take place, so that they can be prepared to persevere during tribulation and persecution. The whole book is a *unified prophetic narrative* that necessarily *must include* the information contained in the letters to the seven churches. The story cannot move forward without the details they provide.

Seven Prophetic Churches

The seven churches are symbolic, as are most things in Revelation. The meaning of the names of the churches corresponds with the situation being described. The letter to the church of Smyrna provides an example:

The name 'Smyrna' means 'myrrh'. Myrrh is a resin used as a component of incense, holy anointing oil, and perfumes, as well as to embalm the dead. The church of Smyrna is told that some of them will die for the Lord. The 5th Seal martyrs—the martyrs about whom this letter speaks—are depicted in Revelation 6 as being 'under the altar'—the altar of incense—the very place where their brethren, the 24 Elders, have been offering their prayers as incense in golden bowls. Myrrh is symbolic of suffering, death, prayers and sanctification; and as such, the name, Smyrna, is an apt symbolic name for those who will lay down their lives for Christ and appear under the altar of incense. Because myrrh is also connected with the priestly anointing oil, we can conclude that the martyrs will also be priests in God's temple.

Sometimes the historical background of one of the seven churches will be prophetic. The location of Laodicea is an example. The city of Laodicea did not have a natural source of water and had to pipe their water in from other locations. Two different sources of water, from two separate towns, delivered water to the people of Laodicea: one water source provided cool, refreshing water, but by the time it traveled the few miles to Laodicea, the water was tepid. The second water source was from a hot spring, but it, too, was lukewarm upon arrival. The water was neither cool and refreshing or warm and medicinal. Jesus told this church that because they were 'lukewarm' He would spew them out of His mouth...unless they repented.

Every one of the seven churches makes use of either a symbolic name ("Smyrna") or a characteristic of the actual church bearing the same name, as in the church of Laodicea. We'll see how these seven symbolic churches represent God's end time assemblies as we move through the book.

Jesus is Coming...

Almost every one of the seven letters either alludes to, or explicitly states, the fact that Jesus is *coming* for them:

Ephesus: "Remember therefore from where you have fallen, and repent and do the first works; or else *I am coming to you swiftly*, and will move your lamp stand out of its place, unless you repent." Revelation 2:5

Pergamum: "15 So also you likewise have some who hold to the teaching of the Nicolaitans. 16 Repent therefore, or else *I am coming to you quickly* and I will make war against them with the sword of my mouth." Revelation 2: 15, 16

Thyatira: "25 Nevertheless, hold that which you have firmly *until I come*. 26 He who overcomes, and he who keeps my works to the end, to him I will give authority over the nations." Revelation 2:25, 26

Sardis: "Remember therefore how you have received and heard. Keep it and repent. If therefore you won't watch, *I will come as a thief*, and you won't know what hour I will come upon you." Revelation 3:3

Philadelphia: "10 Because you kept my command to endure, I also will keep you from the hour of testing which is to come on the whole world, to test those who dwell on the earth. 11 *I am coming quickly!* Hold firmly that which you have, so that no one takes your crown. " Revelation 3:10, 11

Laodicea: "19 As many as I love, I reprove and chasten. Be zealous therefore, and repent. 20 Behold, I stand at the door and knock. If anyone hears my voice and opens the door, then *I will come in to him* and will dine with him, and he with me. " Revelation 3:19, 20

Most people who hold to a pre-tribulation rapture, think that the church of Philadelphia represents present day believers, and that Christ will come for them in a rapture event before the 'hour of trial'. They interpret the 'hour of trial' as the seven year 'tribulation'. If that is so, why does Jesus say that He is coming to the other churches as well? How is He 'coming' to them? Is there more than one rapture? If Jesus said He was coming for the church of Philadelphia, He must also be coming for the other churches in a similar way. In other words, Jesus' 'coming' is not a reference to His visible return at the Second Coming when every eye will see Him, but to a personal 'coming' for His people.

We'll examine all of this in more detail later on.

The Persecuted Church and the Destruction of the Persecutors

Because the letters are actually prophecies written to assemblies of end time believers, we can assume that the letter to the church of Smyrna—and all the information it contains—will pertain to end time believers as well.

In the letter to the church at Smyrna, we read that though the devil instigates the persecution of God's people, that it will be "Mystery" Babylon—the Harlot religious system—and the 'earth dwellers', who will actually carry out his plan. (Revelation 17:1-6)

In Revelation 17:6, we see that the woman (the Harlot) is "drunk with the blood of the saints and the blood of the martyrs of Jesus".

> "And on her forehead a name was written, 'MYSTERY, BABYLON THE GREAT, THE MOTHER OF THE PROSTITUTES AND OF THE ABOMINATIONS OF THE EARTH.' 6 I saw the woman drunken with the blood of the saints and with the blood of the martyrs of Jesus. When I saw her, I wondered with great amazement." Revelation 17:5,6

Shortly after this intense ten days period of persecution, the Harlot *is herself* destroyed by the Beast and the Ten Kings who hate her:

> "16 The ten horns which you saw, they and the beast will hate the prostitute, will make her desolate, will strip her naked, will eat her flesh, and will burn her utterly with fire. 17 For God has put in their hearts to do what he has in mind, to be of one mind, and to give their kingdom to the beast, until the words of God should be accomplished." Revelation 17:16,17

"Mystery"Babylon—the Harlot— is destroyed in one hour, on a single day, by fire.

8 Therefore in one day her plagues will come: death, mourning, and famine; and she will be utterly burned with fire, for the Lord God who has judged her is strong.

9 The kings of the earth who committed sexual immorality and lived wantonly with her will weep and wail over her, when they look at the smoke of her burning, 10 standing far away for the fear of her torment, saying, 'Woe, woe, the great city, Babylon, the strong city! For your judgment has come in one hour.' " Revelation 18:8-10

"For in a single hour all this wealth has been laid waste." Revelation 18:17

"For in a single hour she has been laid waste." Revelation 18:19

The destruction of Babylon—the Harlot—will take place at the 6th Trumpet (the 2nd Woe, Revelation 8:13; 9:13-21).

"13 The sixth angel sounded. I heard a voice from the horns of the golden altar which is before God, 14 saying to the sixth angel who had the trumpet, "Free the four angels who are bound at the great river Euphrates!"

15 The four angels were freed who had been prepared for that hour and day and month and year, so that they might kill one third of mankind. 16 The number of the armies of the horsemen was two hundred million. I heard the number of them. 17 Thus I saw the horses in the vision and those who sat on them, having breastplates of fiery red, hyacinth blue, and sulfur yellow; and the horses' heads resembled lions' heads. Out of their mouths proceed fire, smoke, and sulfur. 18 By these three plagues, one third of mankind was killed: by the fire, the smoke, and the sulfur, which proceeded out of their mouths. 19 For the power of the horses is in their mouths and in their tails. For their tails are like serpents, and have heads; and with them they harm." Revelation 9:13-19

A Single Hour

The destruction of the Harlot is described as taking place in a 'single hour', on a predetermined day, by fire, smoke and sulphur. In Revelation, this 'hour' is not a metaphorical or symbolic hour, but an actual hour of 60 minutes, taking place on a very specific day, a day which has been predetermined by God from ages past. Though Revelation often employs the use of symbols to tell the story, references to *time* are meant to be taken literally: 1260 days, 'time, times and half a time'... and one hour, are all meant to be taken at face value. Whenever we see 'one hour' in Revelation, we know we are looking at the destruction of the Harlot at the 6th

Trumpet/2nd Woe. The phrase 'one hour' first appears in Revelation 3, in the promise to the church of Philadelphia:

> "Because you kept my command to endure, I also will keep you from the hour of testing which is to come on the whole world, to test those who dwell on the earth." Revelation 3:10

There are several common interpretations about what constitutes the 'hour of testing/trial'. Some believe that the 'hour of trial' refers to the whole 7 years of the end times (commonly referred to as the 'tribulation'). Others see the 'hour of trial' as the 42 month reign of the Beast/Antichrist during the last half of the 'tribulation'. In both of these cases, the 'hour of trial' is assumed to be a metaphorical 'hour', and not a literal hour of 60 minutes. As has already been pointed out, every other measurement of time in Revelation is interpreted as being literal by most teachers.

When attempting to interpret any passage of scripture, it's important that we have a method that governs how we're going to interpret the passage. These rules —our 'hermeneutic'—keep us consistent in our interpretation. If we're going to interpret 1260 days as 1260 literal days, and 42 months as 42 literal months, then whenever a unit of time is mentioned, we'll need to assume it's referring to a literal measurement of time, and not a metaphor, unless there is a superseding consideration. As a result of my study in Revelation, I have concluded that Revelation is very consistent in its use of time, and that any time measurement—be it days, months, or hours—is meant to be taken literally.

The 'hour' is referred to in Revelation 9, at the 6th Trumpet:

> "So the four angels, who had been prepared for the hour, the day, the month, and the year, were released to kill a third of mankind."

...and in reference to the destruction of the Harlot:

> For in a single hour your judgment has come." Revelation 18:10

> "For in a single hour all this wealth has been laid waste." Revelation 18:17

> "For in a single hour she has been laid waste." Revelation 18:19

...in reference to the 10 Kings who will be a part of this destruction:

"¹² The ten horns that you saw are ten kings who have received no kingdom as yet, but they receive authority as kings with the beast for one hour." Revelation 17:12

This hour takes place at the same time the Two Witnesses are resurrected:

"¹³ In that hour there was a great earthquake, and a tenth of the city fell. Seven thousand people were killed in the earthquake, and the rest were terrified and gave glory to the God of heaven." Revelation 11:13

The 2nd 'gospel' angel proclaims the hour of the judgment of the Harlot, which will take place at the midpoint:

"⁷ He said with a loud voice, "Fear the Lord, and give him glory, for the hour of his judgment has come. Worship him who made the heaven, the earth, the sea, and the springs of waters!"" Revelation 14:7

The only exception to how the word 'hour' is used is when Christ comes to 'reap' the harvest of the earth (a rapture event), which will take place on a day and hour known only to God:

"And another angel came out of the temple, crying out with a loud voice to Him who sat on the cloud, 'Put in your sickle and reap, for the hour to reap has come, because the harvest of the earth is ripe.' " Revelation 14:15

The 'hour' of Babylon's destruction is a big deal in Revelation. In fact, the destruction/judgment of the Harlot is a bigger deal than the reign of the Beast! More verses are dedicated to the Harlot and her demise then are dedicated to the reign of the Beast and his ultimate destruction. Why is that? It's because Revelation was written to believers, not to Israel; and what the 'Anti-messiah' is to the Jews, the 'Anti-church'—the Harlot—is to believers. The false religious system—which will include 'faux' Christianity—will be the biggest persecutor of real Christians the world has ever seen. More believers will die at the hands of the Harlot and the earth dwellers than will die during the reign of the Beast, and many of their persecutors will call themselves 'Christians'. That is the reason why John 'marveled' when he saw the Harlot:

"⁶ I saw the woman drunken with the blood of the saints and with the blood of the martyrs of Jesus. When I saw her, I wondered with great amazement." Revelation 17:6

So-called 'Christians' who actually are a part the Harlot system, will be 'drunk with the blood of the saints'. The Harlot will be a greater threat to believers during the first 3.5 years—than the Antichrist will be to them during the last 3.5 years. I'll be going into more detail about the identity of the Harlot—Mystery, Babylon—her origins and how she has deceived the world through sorcery, later in the book.

As a result of the Harlot's treatment of God's people, the Lord has already predetermined the hour for her destruction. On one day, at a specific hour, the Harlot and all those associated with her, will be destroyed by four angels and 200 million man army, with 'fire, smoke and sulphur'. God will take 'vengeance' on the Harlot and those who massacred the 5th Seal martyrs: the same martyrs who appeared under the altar, who were told to 'rest a little while' until the full number of their brethren who were to be killed as they were, joined them in heaven. Once the full complement of martyrs is present and accounted for in heaven, their blood will be avenged at the 6th Trumpet.

The persecution of believers during the 'great tribulation' has a precise beginning and a pre-determined end date. After exactly 10 days of persecution, shortly after the last martyr is present in heaven, God will take His vengeance on the Harlot and her associates, using the Beast and the ten Kings as His agents. A third of mankind will be swept up in her destruction, by plagues of fire, smoke and sulphur. Believers who were not martyred by the Harlot, some of whom may have taken refuge in 'Babylon' during the 10 day purge of believers, will need to 'come out of her' lest they be killed in her plagues.

> "4 I heard another voice from heaven, saying, 'Come out of her, my people, that you have no participation in her sins, and that you don't receive of her plagues, 5 for her sins have reached to the sky, and God has remembered her iniquities.' " Revelation 18:4,5

At least a third of mankind—the majority of those who align themselves with the Harlot religious system—will be destroyed. When the Harlot is destroyed, those who are a part of that system will be destroyed as well.

The Destruction of the Harlot at the Midpoint

According to Revelation 11:14, the destruction of the Harlot, will take place around the same time that the Two Witnesses resurrect and ascend into heaven—at the "2nd Woe". The 2nd Woe is associated with the 6th Trumpet:

> "I saw, and I heard an eagle, flying in mid heaven, saying with a loud voice, 'Woe! Woe! Woe to those who dwell on the earth, because of the other

blasts of the trumpets of the three angels, who are yet to sound!' " Revelation 8:13

"Mystery"Babylon will be destroyed shortly after her ten day persecution of believers:

> "When he opened the fifth seal, I saw underneath the altar the souls of those who had been killed for the Word of God, and for the testimony of the Lamb which they had. 10 They cried with a loud voice, saying, 'How long, Master, the holy and true, until you judge and avenge our blood on those who dwell on the earth?' 11 A long white robe was given to each of them. They were told that they should rest yet for a while, until their fellow servants and their brothers, who would also be killed even as they were, should complete their course." Revelation 6:9-11

> "11 After the three and a half days, the breath of life from God entered into them, and they stood on their feet. Great fear fell on those who saw them. 12 I heard a loud voice from heaven saying to them, 'Come up here!' They went up into heaven in a cloud, and their enemies saw them. 13 In that day there was a great earthquake, and a tenth of the city fell. Seven thousand people were killed in the earthquake, and the rest were terrified and gave glory to the God of heaven.

> 14 The second woe is past. Behold, the third woe comes quickly." Revelation 11:11-14

Babylon falls to make way for 'Beast Religion'. God judges the Harlot system before He judges the Beast, the False Prophet, or anything else on earth. The final 3.5 years will be a 'show down' between only two contenders : the One True God and His Son; versus the forces of darkness led by the Beast, the False Prophet and Satan. While vestiges of the Harlot religious system will remain during the reign of the Beast, the system as a whole will not be left to operate as a 'third' system, neither will it coexist with the religious system of the Beast, False Prophet and Dragon (which is often referred to as the 'one world' religion). Once the Harlot's dominant influence is eliminated, the Beast and his agents will quickly fill the void left by the Harlot.

Revelation tells us that the Harlot religious system will continue to exist during the reign of the Beast in some form. Even after 1/3 of the earth's population is destroyed in God's judgment of Mystery, Babylon, many people will still refuse to give up their idolatry:

"20 The rest of mankind, who were not killed with these plagues, didn't repent of the works of their hands, that they wouldn't worship demons, and the idols of gold, and of silver, and of brass, and of stone, and of wood, which can't see, hear, or walk." Revelation 9:20

God will 'remember' this group of Harlot 'devotees' who refused to repent of their idolatry when He pours out His wrath at the end of the 7 years:

"19 The great city was divided into three parts, and the cities of the nations fell. Babylon the great was remembered in the sight of God, to give to her the cup of the wine of the fierceness of his wrath. " Revelation 16:19

Revelation is a unified book, and the whole book—including the letters to the seven churches, provides us with clues about the "who, when, where and how" of the end time events. The ten day period of trial mentioned in the letter to the church of Smyrna, as well as the 'hour' during which the Harlot will be destroyed, are meant to be taken as a literal hour, and a literal 10 days. We've also followed the thematic thread of the relationship between the martyrs and the Harlot.

What do we know about the end-time story thus far?

1. Believers will be present on earth during the last 7 years. Some will be killed during a ten day persecution, instigated by the Harlot/Babylonian religious system. This will be the 'great tribulation' for believers.
2. The martyrs will receive their glorified bodies as they arrive in heaven.
3. Satan will be cast out of heaven the same time the martyrs appear in heaven.
4. Once the Dragon is cast to the earth, he will persecute the woman/Israel, who will then flee to a prepared place for 1,260 days. (According to the gospel of Matthew, this takes place on the heels of the abomination of desolation. This is the 'great tribulation' for Israel.)
5. The Harlot will be destroyed by the Beast and the 10 Kings on the same day that the Two Witnesses ascend. (2nd Woe/6th Trumpet)
6. The number who will be killed at the 6th Trumpet, by 'fire, smoke and sulphur, amounts to a third of mankind.

Chapter 11: Some Principles of Interpretation

Revelation is a story of hope, deliverance and judgment.

It is the story of God's ultimate plan in Christ to procure a people for Himself.

It is the story of the crushing of Satan and the defeat of his minions, including the Antichrist.

It is the story of how God will judge this current evil, misaligned world system; a system manipulated by dark entities who derive power and control over humanity via deception.

It is the story of *the culmination of all things* in the end times.

Typically, discussions surrounding the end times tends to focus on the rapture of believers, the identity of the Antichrist, the nature of the 'mark' of the Beast and the coming one world government. Though all of these are legitimate topics for our consideration, Revelation actually contains more details and warnings for believers concerning the 'Harlot'—also known as 'Mystery, Babylon'—than it does the Antichrist!

Who or what is the Harlot? Why is she a such a prominent figure in the end time narrative? What is her role and how will people recognize her? In what way does she pose a threat to believers? Why should we care?

Symbols and Imagery (Part 2)

Revelation is a tightly woven, intertwined and multi-dimensional story, in which the detailed symbolic descriptions of the people, places and events that comprise the end time narrative, are provided for our consideration. Perhaps the most important principle, *the one* guiding principle that needs to be kept in the forefront of our minds, is that almost everything in Revelation is communicated via symbols and imagery. Even a casual reading of the book of Revelation suggests that the book uses symbols and symbolic language to tell its rather complex and dramatic story.

Like the writings of the Old Testament prophets, who also utilized symbolism to foretell future events, Revelation makes use of prophetic symbolism to tell the story of events concerning the last days. The 'truth' of the story is disguised—hidden beneath a *layer of symbolism*.

No one reading the Revelation would interpret "the Lamb" as being a literal baby sheep! We intuitively know that the Lamb represents the Eternal Son of God who gave His life as a substitutionary payment for our sins. The "Dragon" doesn't really have 7 heads and 10 horns; instead the 7 heads and 10 horns symbolically portray how Satan manifests himself through 7 kings/kingdoms and 10 kings on the earth. Nearly everything in Revelation is veiled in symbolism, and in order to arrive at the plain meaning of the story, one must first crack the code of the symbols.

- *Revelation uses imagery and symbolic language to describe and identify people, places and events during the end times.*

Deciphering the actual meaning of the symbols can be a bit challenging, but it's not as difficult as one may think. We can decode the meaning of many of the symbols by examining how the same symbol is used in other places in the Bible, especially as it's used in the Old Testament. There are numerous examples of how Revelation takes Old Testament symbols, and transfers them into the end time narrative in a way that is congruent and harmonizes with the whole of scripture.

Common symbols—such as numbers—are pretty straightforward as to their symbolic meanings. For example, the number '7', represents 'completion or fulness', ie: the 7 days of creation equals 1 complete week. 'Seven' is also the number associated with God and with His divine attributes. Whenever we see the number '7' used in Revelation, we can assume that the number will either be associated with God, ie: "the 7 Spirits before the throne"; or the 'fulness' of whatever is being described, ie: the 7 churches.

In the case of other imagery and symbolism, Revelation itself will often decode the significance of a particular symbol: the seven "stars" are angels; the seven "lampstands" are the seven churches of Asia Minor; the "Dragon" is Satan.

Greek or Hebrew??

Revelation is a peculiar book. Although originally written in the Greek language, Revelation's perspective and 'flavor' is not Greek at all, but Hebraic, reflecting the worldview of the ancient Hebrews. This 'Greek/Hebrew' dichotomy poses a real problem for those of us who attempt to interpret Revelation, mostly because we live in a society which is heavily influenced by the Greek/western concepts of logic, science and rational discourse. We are decidedly unfamiliar with the 'language' of the ancient nation of Israel, and how the Jews perceived and interpreted spiritual realities. Revelation defies conventional interpretive methods, and unashamedly presents itself as a seemingly incomprehensible mash-mash of disjointed and irrational, fantastical visions, with no discernible rhyme or reason—at least not from a 'western/Greek' point of view.

The prevailing 'western'/Greek perspective is 'left-brained'—rational, orderly, and sequential. Viewing time as 'linear', the Greek way of thinking seeks to communicate important spiritual truths by systematically laying an irrefutable foundation and then building upon that foundation, one concept at a time. In our western understanding of how prophecy *should* be interpreted, the end time narrative would be solidly laid out in the opening chapters of the book and move forward smoothly and logically, with the events in each chapter taking place, one after another in perfect chronological order. The story would start at the 'beginning', and the end of the story would, of course, be at 'the end'.

So what happens when we run Revelation through our Greek mental filter? Well, we attempt to 'outline' the book and title the various chapters. We talk about the historical context of the book. We *do* know that there is a 'happy ending' for believers when Christ returns, and we know that His return is preceded by catastrophic events taking place on the earth. It's also plain that the devil is defeated and that all who love Jesus will live happily ever after. And that, my friends, is about all that we can know for sure about the story in Revelation when we run the book through our Greek 'filter' of logic, reason and linear thinking.

Revelation, however, is decidedly 'right-brained'. Written from the more picturesque Hebrew mind-set, the Hebraic style seeks to inculcate spiritual truths *indirectly* through the use of pictures, symbols, rituals and the like. Time is viewed as being cyclical. Similar events repeat themselves over and over again, in ever expanding and profound ways. To the Hebrew mind, spiritual truths unroll like a scroll. As the cycles repeat, deeper truths emerge, exposing more detail and richness as the story progresses.

Rather than taking the more direct Greek approach—which appeals to men's reason and intellect—the Hebraic style 'emotes' the truth of things. By comparing deep spiritual truths to common, earthy things—often wildly disparate things—Jesus Himself used symbolism and imagery in the parables, to both reveal, and conceal, spiritual truth in the traditional Hebrew manner.

In the parable of the sower, Jesus compared men's hearts to soil. The Word of God was a seed. Birds were agents of Satan. This style of communication demands that the hearer reflect on the words and contemplate their underlying meaning. A certain amount of curiosity helps, too, in order to understand the deeper implications of the story. There's a reason why God veils the truth beneath stories, symbols and pictures: it's so that spiritual truth will find a home in our hearts before it finds a place in our heads.

- *Revelation is not logical...or chronological...or rational. The symbolic, multi-layered and indirect Hebraic style of interpreting spiritual truths must be employed in order to properly interpret Revelation.*

Bible colleges and seminaries generally teach the Bible in a systematic, orderly way, utilizing the familiar western/Greek rational style of investigative study. Revelation, which was written from the Hebraic perspective, is the 'square peg' that must fit, somehow into the 'round hole' of systematic theology. The problem, as we have discovered, is that Revelation doesn't lend itself to the Greek interpretive system. It is not logical, orderly or rational. Furthermore, we can expect that, for the most part, pastors and teachers who have been equipped under the formal "Greek-style" Bible training, may find themselves in unfamiliar and uncharted waters when they attempt to interpret Revelation.

The 'one size fits all' method of understanding the Bible which currently prevails in our seminaries and Bible colleges, may be the primary reason why very few pastors teach prophecy or address issues concerning the end times. Seminary did not equip them with the perspective necessary to tackle Revelation!

Like a stone skipping over a pond, the familiar 'Greek method' can only hope to offer a cursory understanding of Revelation—a quick skim over the surface of the book. The Greek method can describe what it sees in Revelation, and outline the chapters, but it cannot *tell you the story*. When trained theologians teach Revelation, they teach facts about Revelation, but they do not tell the story. Deep in our hearts, we know there is a thrilling and spellbinding story that has yet to be told. We know there is more to be discovered, more that lies hidden beneath the surface of Revelation, just waiting to be brought to the surface.

Chapter 12: More Principles for Interpreting the Visions of Revelation

We know that Revelation was written as a series of visions. Closer examination reveals that there are three main *types* of visions, and that there is a *pattern* which most of the visions follow that enables us to know when a vision begins and when it ends. The three main types of visions are:

- "Event" visions: These visions describe a *series of events* which will take place in the story. The visions of the Seals, the Trumpets and the Bowls are examples of event visions. All that takes place within each vision is sequential; that is, the seals are opened in order, and the first seal is followed by the 2nd seal and so on. When placing the events associated with each seal on a timeline, the correct sequence must be maintained. Seal #7 will not take place before seal #6, and so on.
- "Character/Plot" visions: These visions introduce us to the various characters and tell their story. Characters include the 144,000 of Israel, the Martyrs, the Two Witnesses, the Beast(s), the Harlot and the False Prophet. Character/plot visions often include 'day counts', which help us to correctly insert the story-line into its proper place within the chronological framework of the book. Sometimes a character/plot vision takes place within the context of a larger vision, creating a 'vision within a vision'. In the Trumpet vision, there are two additional visions that take place *within* the Trumpet vision: the story of the 'Mighty Angel' of chapter 10; and the vision of the Two Witnesses. (More on this later...)
- "Flashback" visions: These visions tell the story 'after the fact'. The story of the Harlot, the Scarlet Beast and the fall of Babylon is an example of a 'flashback' vision. (Revelation chapters 17-19)

Since Revelation was written as a series of visions, we need know when a vision begins and when it ends. So, how do we to know when a vision begins and when it ends? This is a very important question. If we can't correctly identify the beginning and ending points, we will not be able determine where to place the events in the vision on a timeline. An example of this is in Revelation 8:

> "¹ When he opened the seventh seal, there was silence in heaven for about half an hour. ² I saw the seven angels who stand before God, and seven trumpets were given to them." Revelation 8:1,2

The seventh seal is opened by the Lamb in verse one. This is the 7th and last seal of the Seal vision, which began in Revelation chapter 6. *The seventh seal is part of the Seal vision.* In verse 2, we read about the seven angels who are going to blow seven trumpets. The chapter and verse numbers seems to indicate that the action of the 7th Seal (verse 1) somehow immediately precedes the appearance of the 7 Trumpet angels (verse 2). Many people then assume that the Trumpets 'come out of' the Seal judgements, because verse 2 'follows' verse 1; and the trumpets 'follow' the 7th Seal.

Actually, the seventh seal is *the end* of the Seal vision, and Revelation 8:2 begins the Trumpet vision, which is its own story, with a whole new series of events and its *own timeline*.

So, one way to know when a vision ends, is when the next verse appears to start a whole *new topic*. In the example above, once we get to the opening of the 7th and last seal, which signals that we may be at the end of that particular vision, and we see something *new*—like angels getting ready to blow trumpets, we know that we have just left the Seal vision and have now started a new vision, the Trumpet vision.

When I was attempting to find the beginning and end points of the various visions, I discovered a pattern: a vision would begin...the story would unfold...and then there would be an event that seemed out of place chronologically—an event that was often, but not always, associated with the wrath of God and the return of Christ.

In the very beginning of this book, we saw how the 6th and 7th Seal, the 6th and 7th Bowls and the 7th Trumpet all appeared to take place on or around the same time. In the Seal vision, there are seven seals which the Lord opens one by one. Seals 1-4 describe what is commonly known as "the four horsemen of the apocalypse". The 5th seal describes the 'martyrs under the altar' in heaven. Both the 6th seal (earthquakes, moon to blood, men hiding from the wrath of the Lamb) and the 7th seal (silence in heaven), depict events associated with the wrath of God and the return of Christ to the earth.

In the Trumpet vision, Trumpets 1-6 describe events which will take place *just prior to the midpoint of the seven year timeframe*. The 7th and final trumpet most certainly takes place at 'the end', when 'the mystery of God is fulfilled' (Revelation 10:7), and the "kingdom of the world has become the kingdom of our Lord and of his Christ..." (Revelation 11:15) If one didn't understand this pattern, one would think that the 7th Trumpet was blown immediately after the Two Witnesses were resurrected and brought to heaven!

> "11 After the three and a half days, the breath of life from God entered into them, and they stood on their feet. Great fear fell on those who saw them. 12 I heard a loud voice from heaven saying to them, 'Come up here!' They

went up into heaven in a cloud, and their enemies saw them. 13 In that day there was a great earthquake, and a tenth of the city fell. Seven thousand people were killed in the earthquake, and the rest were terrified and gave glory to the God of heaven.

14 The *second woe* is past. Behold, the third woe comes quickly.

15 The *seventh angel sounded,* and great voices in heaven followed, saying, 'The kingdom of the world *has become* the Kingdom of our Lord and of his Christ. He will reign forever and ever!' " Revelation 11:11-15

This pattern, whereby the last event in a vision is a depiction of an event which will take place *at the end of the seven years,* holds true in several other visions as well.

In chapter 5, we see God's throne room in heaven and the Lamb receiving the scroll. The 24 Elders fall down and worship the Lamb (5:8), and then we see **ALL** creation worshiping the Lamb, including "every creature in heaven, on the earth, under the earth and in the sea." All are praising God and the Lamb! (5:13)

"6 I saw in the middle of the throne and of the four living creatures, and in the middle of the elders, a Lamb standing, as though it had been slain, having seven horns and seven eyes, which are the seven Spirits of God, sent out into all the earth. 7 Then he came, and he took it out of the right hand of him who sat on the throne. 8 Now when he had taken the book, the four living creatures and the twenty-four elders fell down before the Lamb, each one having a harp, and golden bowls full of incense, which are the prayers of the saints."

This all-inclusive worship *does not occur during the seven years,* when much of God's creation will be in open rebellion to Him, but it *will* occur at the end, when 'every knee shall bow and every tongue confess that He is Lord to the glory of God the Father." (Philippians 2:9-11)

One of the ways we know we have come to the end of a vision, is when we see events associated with the wrath of God, the 2nd Coming of Christ and the declaration of all creation (including every fallen person or entity) that Jesus is Lord. sang a new song, saying,

> " 'You are worthy to take the book
> and to open its seals,
> for you were killed,
> and bought us for God with your blood

out of every tribe, language, people, and nation,
¹⁰ and made us kings and priests to our God;
and we will reign on the earth.'

¹¹ I looked, and I heard something like a voice of many angels around the throne, the living creatures, and the elders. The number of them was ten thousands of ten thousands, and thousands of thousands, ¹² saying with a loud voice, 'Worthy is the Lamb who has been killed to receive the power, wealth, wisdom, strength, honor, glory, and blessing!'

¹³ I heard every created thing which is in heaven, on the earth, under the earth, on the sea, and everything in them, saying, 'To him who sits on the throne and to the Lamb be the blessing, the honor, the glory, and the dominion, forever and ever! Amen!'

¹⁴ The four living creatures said, 'Amen!' Then the⁺ elders fell down and worshiped." Revelation 5:6-14

Chapter 13: Starting Over

The standard interpretation of Revelation usually consists of a 'chronological' narrative of Seal, Trumpet and Bowl judgments (in that order); with an 'interlude' or two, a few Beasts and various groups of people arriving in heaven. Revelation has been taught as though it were one, long vision with a couple of out-of-place parenthesis type visions thrown in for good measure.

We need to begin afresh. We need to exchange our western/Greek 'filter' for a Hebraic one and start using the more unfamiliar Hebraic interpretive methods. We need to look at Revelation with new eyes.

A Scrapbook of Visions

I have already mentioned that, rather than Revelation being one long vision, it is actually a series of many small, discreet but related, visions; something more akin to pages in a photo album or a scrapbook. If we were to use the analogy of a 'scrapbook' as a model for understanding the visions, each vision would have its own 'page' in the album: there would be a 'Seal' page depicting all the seal events; there would be a 'Trumpet' page depicting all the trumpet events, and so on.

The seven 'Seals' would be arranged in order—one through seven—on the page. Likewise the seven 'Trumpets' would also be arranged on the 'Trumpet' page in order, from one to seven. Every vision would have its own page and the page would be placed in the book where it made the most sense to the one who composed the book. We should not assume that all the Seal events will take place before all the Trumpet events just because the 'Seal' page comes before the 'Trumpet' page in the book. Revelation uses the individual visions—the various 'pages' in the scrapbook—to tell us bits and pieces of many stories, giving us snapshots of the characters as they move forward through the end times.

The Whole and the Sum of the Parts

Revelation is the only book of the Bible that has a special blessing attached to the reading, hearing and obeying of its message. There is also a dire warning: no one is to add anything to its pages or subtract anything from it. Revelation is written in 'code'; and every word and verse and placement of words and verses is a crucial part of the coded message.

Revelation is best understood as a 'whole' before it is dissected and understood as the sum of its parts. When one looks at a painting, for example, the first thing one sees is the painting itself—*as a whole*. The individual brushstrokes, the subtle nuances of color and shading, the minute details are a part of the whole, and, upon first glance, do not appear as separate and distinct from the whole of the painting.

How this 'whole view' applies to Revelation manifests in how we go about studying the book. We need to 'see' the whole book, all at once, before we can understand how the details fit in. *This means reading and re-reading the book until we can mentally remember what is in each chapter and understand the basic contents of the book.* We need to be familiar with what we see happening at the end of the book, because those events are also a part of the beginning of the book. It's not enough to read through the book once or twice. Discerning where the various visions end, and another vision begins and being able to recall details presented throughout the whole book is crucial. We need to observe what we're reading...really look at it—all of it— as though we were seeing it for the first time.

This 'whole' view of Revelation is absent from most treatments of eschatology, where the prophecy teacher assumes that the interpretation of the book is built on a foundation laid in the early chapters of the book. The interpretation of Revelation is then anchored to the beginning chapters and verses, and all the visions relate somehow to the 'foundation' laid in the beginning. The reality is, that there is no 'foundation' laid in Revelation, nothing anchoring the 'beginning' chapters, nothing in Revelation 1 which establishes a framework for understanding the story, except for one thing: *that Christ has made us kings and priests to His God.* The early chapters of the book are no more foundational than chapters 5, 10, 12, 15 or any other chapter! Each chapter is an equal part of the whole: each vision is a portion of the one body of revelation.

The only way I know of to have a 'whole' view of Revelation is to read and reread the book. Only after we have a grasp of the whole, can we start looking at the individual parts. We can begin anywhere, in any chapter, to observe the details. In studying Revelation, there is nothing right about starting with chapter one, verse one. Or to put it another way, there is nothing wrong with starting our investigation in chapter 12. This method of study is permissible because, as we have already seen in our discussion of the Greek vs Hebraic styles of interpretation, the narrative in Revelation does not travel in a straight line.

- *Becoming familiar with the whole book of Revelation is necessary before attempting to interpret it.*

Towards the beginning of this book, you'll notice that I didn't begin my commentary at Revelation chapter one, verse one. First, I established the idea that Revelation is a 'temple' story, and that temple imagery will be used to tell the story. Next, we examined the similarities between the 6th Seal, the 7th Bowl and the 7th

Trumpet. We saw that all of these were associated with a great earthquake and the wrath of God, and we were able to determine that they will take place toward the very end of the story. Next we followed the thread of the martyrs. The martyrs then connected us to the Harlot, the 'great tribulation' and the 6th Trumpet judgment of the Harlot system. I could have started with the martyrs, or the Beast/Antichrist. Like a puzzle, Revelation is constructed by starting some-where—anywhere—and seeing where the pieces fit. And, like any puzzle, each piece will fit in *only one place*.

We can open the book of Revelation anywhere...in the 'middle' if we like... and observe whatever we see on that particular page, chapter or vision. As we move through the book, we might notice that a character that appeared on the 'Seal' page also shows up on the 'Trumpet' page: that's probably an important connec-tion. The more we study the various pages/visions of the 'scrapbook' the more connections we will make. Eventually a story line will emerge and a chronology will start to crystalize; not in the normal way, where we start at the beginning, at chapter one and work our way to the end, but in a way that requires us to focus on the amazing *details* of each vision. To understand, we must observe...intent-ly...and connect the dots between the various visions. To use yet another analogy, we must engage ourselves in spiritual detective work, searching for clues in the visions in order to put together a timeline of events which will fit together per-fectly, having no internal contradictions.

When exploring the details surrounding the martyrs, we discovered that several visions contained information about those who were killed for their faith. We learned that they were persecuted by the Harlot and the earth dwellers sometime before the midpoint of the seven years. Then, shortly after the martyrs appeared in heaven in their resurrected, glorified bodies, the Harlot was judged. The Beast and the 10 Kings were used as God's agents to destroy the Harlot in a single hour on a predetermined day, by fire, smoke and sulphur at the 6th Trumpet, 2nd Woe, midpoint. All this information came from different visions in several differ-ent chapters. We were able to pull out the various relevant details from the differ-ent visions, and place them in a way that makes sense on a larger timeline of events.

Art...not Science

In some ways, the study of Revelation is 'art'...not science. Like a beautifully pieced quilt or the 'Mona Lisa', there are no real rules about where to start look-ing in order to appreciate the artistry. Once one is drawn in by any aspect of the book, all the rest of the book will begin to unfold and reveal its secrets as well.

This is not to say that Revelation is devoid of order; but rather that its order is that of the craftsman or artist instead of the sterile system of the mathematician or scientist. Yet nothing in Revelation is random: every word in every vision—the exact placements of each vision within the book—the symbols and imagery that are used the book—all is perfection and artistry of the highest order.

Though it may not be apparent at first, there is a reason for every brushstroke on the canvas, every word in the book; a reason which is found in the heart of the Artist and waiting to be discovered by the diligent and 'unconventional' student.

Chapter 14: Back to the Harlot...

A major theme in Revelation is the Harlot system and how she will operate during the end times, especially her influence on Christianity and her ultimate destruction in a single hour. Revelation tells us that the Harlot system is the very first enemy God will judge on earth during the time of the end. The instruments God will use to bring about her destruction are none other than the Beast and the 10 Kings—the 10 Kings being symbolized by 10 horns—who align themselves with the Antichrist. (In Revelation, the Antichrist is known as the "Beast".)

> [15] "He said to me, ' The waters which you saw, where the prostitute sits, are peoples, multitudes, nations, and languages. [16] The ten horns which you saw, they and the beast will hate the prostitute, will make her desolate, will strip her naked, will eat her flesh, and will burn her utterly with fire. [17] For God has put in their hearts to do what he has in mind, to be of one mind, and to give their kingdom to the beast, until the words of God should be accomplished.' " Revelation 17:15-17

Most Christians are unaware of the dangers associated with the Harlot system, and how this 'system' will come to the fore during the last days; igniting the *greatest persecution of Christians in human history.*

> [24] "In her was found the blood of prophets and of saints, and of all who have been slain on the earth." Revelation 18:24

Those who teach the book of Revelation—and the prophetic events leading up to the 'last days'—often do not distinguish between the 'Beast' religious system and the 'Harlot' religious system, and believe that these two systems will operate as one religious system during the end. They do not understand that because the Harlot system 'rides the Beast'—that *she* controls him and that she will be the one calling the shots, and not the Beast. The Beast will not take kindly to being controlled by the Harlot, and, like all prostitutes, she will be 'used' for a short time by the Beast to destroy true Christians, and then when her usefulness is over, she will be disposed of in one hour of conflagration. The Harlot will not be destroyed until she, along with the 'earth dwellers', put into motion a systematic, 10 day pogrom of world-wide persecution and bloodshed during which the lives of untold millions of Christians will be snuffed out. Never again in the history of the world will believers endure such persecution; not even during the reign of the Beast.

Living in the 'Matrix'...

Very few people are aware of how the Harlot's very ancient system of control has paved the way for the reign of the Beast...the Antichrist.

A popular science fiction movie, 'The Matrix', depicts life under a similar control system, a system so pervasive and ubiquitous that it is almost impossible to detect or describe:

> *"The Matrix is everywhere. It is all around us. Even now, in this very room. You can see it when you look out your window, or when you turn on your television. You can feel it when you go to work, when you go to church, when you pay your taxes. It is the world that has been pulled over your eyes to blind you from the truth." Morpheus in "The Matrix"*

The system—the Matrix—is described as being in the air we breath, the water we drink and the thoughts we think. It's in our schools, hospitals, courts of law, churches, governments and economic systems. Because it's everywhere and in everything, its existence is invisible, and virtually undetectable to most people.

Another quote from the movie:

> *"The Matrix is a system, Neo. That system is our enemy. But when you're inside, you look around, what do you see? Businessmen, teachers, lawyers, carpenters. The very minds of the people we are trying to save... You have to understand, most of these people are not ready to be unplugged. And many of them are so inured, so hopelessly dependent on the system, that they will fight to protect it."*

Even though the movie depicts the matrix as a futuristic computer simulation run by evil, non-human entities, the system itself is real and quite ancient: its genesis going back to the Tower of Babel.

The Origins of 'Mystery' Babylon

In Revelation, the ubiquitous nature of the Babylonian religious system is symbolized by a prostitute who "sits on many waters."

> "[1] One of the seven angels who had the seven bowls came and spoke with me, saying, "Come here. I will show you the judgment of the great prostitute who sits on many waters, [2] with whom the kings of the earth committed sexual immorality. Those who dwell in the earth were made drunken with the wine of her sexual immorality." [3] He carried me away in the Spirit into a wilderness. I saw a woman sitting on a scarlet-colored beast, full of

blasphemous names, having seven heads and ten horns. 4 The woman was dressed in purple and scarlet, and decked with gold and precious stones and pearls, having in her hand a golden cup full of abominations and the impurities of the sexual immorality of the earth. 5 And on her forehead a name was written, "MYSTERY, BABYLON THE GREAT, THE MOTHER OF THE PROSTITUTES AND OF THE ABOMINATIONS OF THE EARTH." Revelation 17:1,15

The Harlot is everywhere. Her control is world-wide, encompassing multitudes and nations. The name written on her forehead, "Mystery, Babylon", indicates that her nefarious roots go back to the very dawn of civilization, all the way back to Babel/Babylon. Her other names indicate the nature of her 'trade': the "Prostitute", the "Harlot" and the 'mother of harlots':

"MYSTERY, BABYLON THE GREAT, THE MOTHER OF THE PROSTITUTES AND OF THE ABOMINATIONS OF THE EARTH." Revelation 17:5

In the scriptures those who go after false gods are said to 'play the harlot':

"17 Yet they didn't listen to their judges; for they prostituted themselves to other gods, and bowed themselves down to them. They quickly turned away from the way in which their fathers walked, obeying Yahweh's commandments. They didn't do so." Judges 2:17

"15 Don't make a covenant with the inhabitants of the land, lest they play the prostitute after their gods, and sacrifice to their gods, and one call you and you eat of his sacrifice; 16 and you take of their daughters to your sons, and their daughters play the prostitute after their gods, and make your sons play the prostitute after their gods." Exodus 34:15, 16

The Harlot seduces the world through promises of wealth, prestige and influence. People curry her favor. They depend on her wealth and influence to get a leg up in the world.

"4 The woman was dressed in purple and scarlet, and decked with gold and precious stones and pearls, having in her hand a golden cup full of abominations and the impurities of the sexual immorality of the earth." Revelation 17:4

The Harlot's Family Tree

In order to understand how the Harlot came to be so powerful and influential, we will need to trace her roots back to her origins; back to Babel.

> 1 "The whole earth was of one language and of one speech. 2 As they traveled east, they found a plain in the land of Shinar, and they lived there. 3 They said to one another, 'Come, let's make bricks, and burn them thoroughly.' They had brick for stone, and they used tar for mortar. 4 They said, 'Come, let's build ourselves a city, and a tower whose top reaches to the sky, and let's make a name for ourselves, lest we be scattered abroad on the surface of the whole earth.'

> 5 Yahweh came down to see the city and the tower, which the children of men built. 6 Yahweh said, 'Behold, they are one people, and they all have one language, and this is what they begin to do. Now nothing will be withheld from them, which they intend to do. 7 Come, let's go down, and there confuse their language, that they may not understand one another's speech.' 8 So Yahweh scattered them abroad from there on the surface of all the earth. They stopped building the city." Genesis 11:1-8

After the world-wide flood, God commanded mankind to spread abroad and repopulate the earth. But rather than spreading out, men disregarded God's injunction, and decided to stick together and build a city. Nimrod, the world's first king and Antichrist type, in direct defiance of God, established a series of inter-connected cities creating the world's first empire with himself as its head. The chief city, Babel, (meaning 'Gate of God', also known as 'Babylon'), was the location of a tower reaching to heaven. Both the tower and the city were constructed of brick and mortar by the world's first masons.

Concentrating humanity in cities held decided advantages for would-be despots, as it allowed tyrants, like Nimrod, to exercise greater control over the masses. The tower, with its top in heaven, was designed to be the focal point of Nimrod's newly created religion; a religion which clearly existed in opposition to the God of heaven.

In addition to building a city and a tower, the community also sought to secure their reputation, to establish a 'name for themselves'. They wanted to be special. Rather than choosing to regard all of mankind as one extended family, they elevated themselves above the rest, insisting that they were a special group of people, who deserved to be feared and revered. The ethnic and religious rivalries and conflicts we see in the world today are the full-flower of this aspect of the spirit of Babel.

⁸ Cush became the father of Nimrod. He began to be a mighty one in the earth. ⁹ He was a mighty hunter before Yahweh. Therefore it is said, 'like Nimrod, a mighty hunter before Yahweh.' " Genesis 10:8,9,

Nimrod was a mighty one—a tyrant—on the earth, hunting the souls of men to further his desire for world domination and worship. He opposed God to His face and sought to establish himself as the sole ruler of the world. Under the satanic and calculated control of Nimrod, mankind's growing achievements were intended to move them further and further away from the worship of the one true God, and create a class of willing slaves for himself, and in the process, usurping God's place in the hearts of mankind.

When the Lord came down from heaven to see the activity at Babel, He stated that if things continued unabated in the direction they were going, that humanity would, in fact, be able to achieve *anything* they could imagine. At some point, man's rebellion would become irreversible and God's plan for the redemption of mankind would not be possible.

We know the rest of the story: God intervened by confusing their language. He interjected a communication barrier between the people, breaking their common language into many different languages. Frustrated by their inability to communicate, they were unable to complete the city. The people abandoned the project and dispersed themselves over the face of the earth.

Though the people left Babel, Babel never left the people, and the seeds of that infamous city were sown throughout the world. In every place that people settled, Babel lived on and became the unwritten spiritual foundation of civilization. Malignant satanic forces, in opposition to both God and man, would reanimate the spirit of Babel in the psyche of humanity. Generation after generation, powerful men, following Nimrod's example, would seek to conquer, subjugate, use and abuse the rank and file of humanity. Deifying themselves, they would insinuate themselves at the top of a system of hierarchical control which could, and would, be applied to every aspect of human society.

This is how the 'Matrix' got its REAL start!

The "Mystery" of Babylon

>"On her forehead a mysterious name was written:
>
>BABYLON THE GREAT,
>THE MOTHER OF PROSTITUTES
>AND OF THE ABOMINATIONS OF THE EARTH." Revelation 17:5

mustérion: 'to shut' as in to 'shut the mouth' or 'keep silence'; a mystery or secret doctrine; a mystery, secret, of which initiation is necessary; also used of "the initiatory rites of the pagan mysteries".

Though the city of Babel was never completed and the great tower fell into ruins, the religion of Babel was far from finished—indeed, religious Babylon was only getting started! Like a noxious weed, the religious pattern begun by Nimrod reproduced itself over the four corners of the world and became the template for every man-made system on earth, including religious systems. Without exception, all religious *systems* carry the DNA of Nimrod's efforts to supplant God.

The nefarious genius of his scheme was the creation of a *reproducible system of control,* flexible enough to be adapted to the spiritual climate of any culture, and with enough apparent legitimacy to allow it to continue to exist without opposition, resulting in *maximum control* over the people.

There are a number of traits that characterize the Babylonian religious system, and Babylonian-style systems in general. They include: a 'priesthood', a hierarchy, the perpetuation of the system, the use of symbols, and multiple support systems.

Power and control

The *power* of Babylonian religion has always resided in the priesthood. The priests of the various iterations of Harlot religion may be known by different names among the various religious groups: shaman, yogi, imam, pastor, minister, president, rabbi or pope; but they all refer to the clergy class. Special training, apprenticeships, higher education, internships, etc, allows the elite few access to the 'mysteries' of their religion. This specialized training imparts esoteric, secret knowledge to the 'priest', mysteries which are generally withheld or concealed from the rank and file, ordinary person.

Being the repository of special knowledge invests the priest class with power, influence and control—especially spiritual control—over the masses. The priests are relied upon to use their special knowledge to act as intermediaries between the god(s) and man. The rituals and rites that are performed by the priests are believed to enable ordinary people to safely interact with, or appease the god(s). Since the priests have the distinction of being initiated into the mysteries of the religion, and they are perceived as being closer to God/the gods than ordinary people, they invariably hold a position of prestige and status in the community.

This is a template which holds true in all worldly systems and institutions: in the medical system, doctors are the 'priests'. In the educational system, professors with PhD's make up the 'clergy' class. Every system has its priests—people who know the secrets and know how to use their secret knowledge to exercise influence, power and control over the 'laity'.

Hierarchical Structure

The *'structure'* of Babylonian religion is *hierarchical*. In a hierarchy, power is centralized and concentrated at the top, and then trickles down through various layers of initiates until it reaches the uninitiated at the very bottom. The pyramid is an apt symbol of how the Harlot system both retains and dispenses her power and control, from the top, down; from the capstone to the base.

No where is religious hierarchical structure more evident than in the Roman Catholic church. The Pope sits at the top of the hierarchy, and below him are the bishops, cardinals and priests and finally, the laity at the bottom. For centuries, the Roman church penalized the reading of the Bible except by the members of the clergy and scholars loyal to the Church. They forbade the translation of the Bible into the common language of the people, and went so far as to keep the masses illiterate so that they would not be able know the truth as revealed in God's word.

Deception and Legalism

The *method* used to control the masses employs a mixture of deception, legalism and sorcery. The Harlot system utilizes arbitrary rules, procedures, commandments, revelations, systems, rewards and the like, to brainwash the people and keep them in their places. The people at the top know that the masses can be manipulated through repeated doses of fear and guilt. People are threatened with various punishments should they get out of line, and the right 'encouragement' can motivate the flock to do, say or give almost anything in order to assuage a guilty conscience or ensure both temporal and eternal tranquility.

Nimrod's Babylonian system was based on the lie that people can live quite well apart from a relationship with the living God. Any religion, any doctrine or dogma will do...as long as the religion presents itself as 'legitimate' and 'feels spiritual'. The rightness of the religion is assumed by the people, and those who question the system are viewed as heretics and outsiders. The persecution of heretics functioned as a powerful lesson and deterrent to anyone who might consider questioning the established authorities.

The Goal

The *goal* of the Babylonian system is *self-perpetuation,* which is actually a kind of *immortality*...making a name for oneself. This desire for self-perpetuation is what lies behind all the magnificent cathedrals and temples in the world, many of which were constructed hundreds of years ago. These edifices were designed to promote and reinforce the grandeur and immutability of their religion. What Harlot religion may lack in actual spiritual substance, it more than makes up for in earthly assets—with the ordinary people footing the bill. A heavy burden, usually financial in nature, tends to be placed on the people at the bottom of the hierarchy. It's their *privilege* and duty to feed the system and keep it running. They are responsible for the construction and up-keep of elaborate cathedrals and temples, the salaries and support of the priest class, schools of initiation and higher learning, and so on. This is how Harlot religion has ensconced herself in the middle of society. The unspoken assumption is that this fat, overblown and ravenous entity must endure forever, whatever the cost to others.

Symbols

The need for language to communicate basic information between initiates was replaced through the use of *symbols*. Symbols, by their very nature are universal, requiring no translation in order to be understood by the initiated. In religion, symbols can also manifest as symbolic actions: rites, rituals, holy days, traditions, forms of worship and the like.

Support Systems

The false religious system, depicted by the Harlot in Revelation, always seeks a 'lover'...a *support system*. She has no qualms about joining forces with other powerful organizations and institutions in order to enrich herself and enhance her reputation. Her bedfellows include presidents and kings, governments, universities, wealthy patrons, financial institutions, and the like. She generously shares her over-whelming influence over the masses of humanity in exchange for perks that add to her coffers and fame, all the while denying any culpability for her lack of true concern and fidelity to her followers.

Up until now, I have not mentioned how evangelical Christianity has been influenced by this system, yet I am sure that many believers reading this are feeling uncomfortable and perhaps even a bit defensive at this point. It's plain to see that the evangelical church has been heavily influenced by Babel as well. We're all in the 'matrix', my friends, and much to our dismay, the Babylonian, 'Harlot' expression of Christianity has found its way into our churches and, for most of us, it's all we have ever known.

False Christianity In the Church

Through no fault of our own, we were cleverly channeled into a controlled version of Christianity. For millennia, Satan has used the Harlot system to keep believers from knowing the fulness of all that God has intended for us to experience in worship and Christian fellowship. Most of us are unaware that God even *has* a radically different plan for His people! His plan runs contrary to the world's system of how things are done. It feels unnatural and wrong. Just as the religious leaders of Jesus' day were offended by His teaching, we may find ourselves offended as well. What we think we know, and what we have been taught by our parents, well-meaning pastors and Bible teachers is, most likely, infused with Babylon.

Is there another way?

Systems can be dangerous. God knows that religious systems are benign at best and fiendishly diabolical at worst. Satan knows that wherever there is a system in place, whoever controls the system, also controls the people. That's why God's way of being the 'church' is *not systematized*; nor does it come in a tidy, pre-packaged format.

The gathering of believers foregoes a spiritual hierarchy, as Christ alone desires to be the Center and Source of the gathering. He eliminates the priest class by making all believers priests, with the Lord Jesus Himself as the High Priest. Rather than relying on rites, rituals and holy days, He insists that His people rely on the unseen moving of His Spirit. His secrets are freely available to all who desire to know them. His law is love and Christ Himself leads from the center through the Person of the Holy Spirit.

The church that God desires has no need to perpetuate itself except through reproducing the Life it possesses. Flexible and responsive, the church that He desires can change directions at the drop of a hat. It opposes the status quo and offends the prudent. It is outwardly weak, yet inwardly unassailable. It is humble yet powerful; other-worldly yet engaged in the lives of others. It is simultaneously confident in Christ and self-less in actions. It thrives in economic downturns and grows through persecution. It changes the world from the inside, out. It turns the world upside down.

In short, God's people were meant to be controlled, *not by a system, but by a Person—Christ Himself, who is its Head.* The church that God desires was meant to operate solely under the Headship of Christ, led by the Holy Spirit.

Coming Out of Babylon: Persecution

So, some of you may be asking, "Surely a little bit of Babylon won't harm anyone, will it?"

That's like asking, "What's wrong with a little bit of arsenic in my soup?".
In the case of the Christian gathering, even minute, frequent, undetectable doses of 'Babel' injected into a gathering over time, may be all that is necessary to quench the Spirit.

A very interesting thing happens when the church undergoes heavy persecution: she inevitably returns to her spiritual roots. The church—of necessity—must dive 'underground'. It quickly decentralizes and the hierarchy dissolves. False leaders disappear and the lukewarm scatter. Many new and unlikely shepherds rise to take their place, and leadership is shared under the supreme guidance of the Chief Shepherd. The Gospel spreads like fire, from one warm heart to another, as disciples are made and people are won to Christ.

Of necessity, new believers are motivated to press into the life of the Spirit, and spiritual growth takes place very quickly. This rapid growth sometimes means that relationships within the gathering can get a bit messy. Meetings may not be predictable and consistent; but love and forgiveness flow from person to person. The work of the kingdom of God takes precedence over personal preference, because when God's people are undergoing persecution, petty issues become irrelevant, and love and forgiveness become a matter of life and death.

Because God loves mankind and God loves the church, He will allow persecution to take place during the end times. He will allow the most terrible persecution the world has ever seen, or ever will see. The religious systems of the world, including false Christianity, will persecute God's people. The Harlot will work in conjunction with the 'earth dwellers'—worldly *religious* people—who oppose God, His Word and His people. As a result of this persecution, not only will untold millions of people be killed for their faith, but untold millions of people will come to a saving knowledge of Christ.

The saying, "The blood of the martyrs is the seed of the church", will prove true once more.

Chapter 15: Even More Principles of Interpretation...

There are certain Bible study principles that hold true, no matter what book of the Bible one is studying: whether examining a 'Greek-style' passage in the New Testament book of Romans or a 'Hebraic-style' passage in the Old Testament prophets or Revelation. Reading and interpreting a passage *in its context,* is a principle that can be universally applied.

Every passage needs to be interpreted in the light of the surrounding verses and chapters, as well as in the context of the book as a whole. We all know about unscrupulous teachers who often 'pull verses out of context', and twist the scriptures for their own gain.

Let's take a look at the martyrs again. If we read the passage in Revelation 7 that speaks about the martyrs who appear in heaven waving palm branches, we read that they are people who "keep coming out of the *great tribulation*". If we don't pay attention to what the passage is actually saying in *its context,* we could easily assume that every 'great tribulation' we read about in the Bible is talking about the same 'great tribulation'. We would then equate the 'great tribulation' found in Revelation 7 which concerns the *gentile* martyrs, with the 'great tribulation' Jesus spoke about which concerns the *Jews* in Matthew 24. And we would be wrong.

When attempting to crack the code of some passage in Revelation, we should *always comb through Revelation first* and see if we can find the answer somewhere in the book itself before we look elsewhere. We search Revelation first, because Revelation provides the context, and the book of Revelation often has *its own definition* of words, ideas and people, and sometimes will use terms quite differently than the way other books of the Bible use them. The 'great tribulation' is an example of this. Understanding how a word, phrase or idea is used in its context can prevent a lot of misinterpretation.

• *Interpret passages in the context in which they appear*

Most of the names of people and groups of people in Revelation are actually communicated in symbolic 'code'. The "Lamb" is the code name for Jesus. The "144,000 of Israel" is the code name for the first believers who come to Christ from Israel, a symbolic 12,000 from each of the 12 tribes of Israel. The "Harlot" is the code name for the false religious system. "Stars" are angels, "lampstands" are churches and so on. In fact, *Revelation* will tell us who and what *everything* is. If we search, we will find the key to the code lies somewhere within the book itself, or Revelation will carefully point us to a *specific passage or passages* in the Old or New Testament where the code will be 'cracked'.

Reading and understanding a passage in its context, is a basic principle for correctly interpreting all biblical passages. We need to ask, "What does this verse (or word, or idea, etc) mean in the *context* of the verses and chapters around it?" When we consider that Revelation is the *only* apocalyptic book in the New Testament, this becomes even more important, as we soon discover that the words used in Revelation often have a precise, specific and unique meaning not shared by other passages of scripture; and that only Revelation can really tell you what that meaning is.

Old Testament "Layers" in Revelation: The Two Witnesses

Revelation utilizes between four and five hundred Old Testament references and allusions in its brief 22 chapters! Some references and allusions are used multiple times. For example Jesus is referred to as the "Lamb" over and over again in the book. The 'Lamb' of course, harkens back to the slain Passover lamb that preserved the firstborn of the Israelites from the Death Angel prior to their exodus from Egypt. This is a fairly straightforward use of an Old Testament allusion in Revelation.

You'll recall that though Revelation was originally written in the Greek language, its perspective and style are not Greek at all, but actually Hebraic—meaning the prophecies will be given in a way that is indirect, symbolic and multi-layered. This multi-layered, symbolic approach is manifested in Revelation when we see multiple Old Testament allusions 'layered' over one another. An example of how more than one Old Testament reference provides multiple layers of information, is evidenced in the vision about the Two Witnesses.

In the case of the Two Witnesses, the Old Testament prophetic allusions which form the various 'layers' of information, at first glance, seem to be totally unrelated to each other, and unrelated to the story in general. However, when viewed as a whole, a very clear picture of the identity and ministry of the Two Witnesses emerges. Remember, the end time story is veiled beneath layer(s) of symbolism. Sometimes one or more layers of symbolic allusions will be added to the symbols already present in Revelation's end time narrative.

• *Old (and New) Testament passages often provide another layer of symbolic 'code', in addition to the symbolism already present in Revelation.*

Revelation 11 describes the story of the two end time 'witnesses', and provides a number of clues which point to their identity and ministry:

3 " I will give power to my two witnesses, and they will prophesy one thousand two hundred sixty days, clothed in sackcloth.4 " These are the two olive trees and the two lamp stands, standing before the Lord of the earth. 5 If anyone desires to harm them, fire proceeds out of their mouth and devours their enemies. If anyone desires to harm them, he must be killed in this way. 6 "These have the power to shut up the sky, that it may not rain during the days of their prophecy. They have power over the waters, to turn them into blood, and to strike the earth with every plague, as often as they desire." Revelation 11:3-6

Below is a list of clues gleaned from the verses in Revelation concerning the Two Witnesses. All these clues direct us to examine *specific, relevant passages* in the Old Testament which expand the story even further. The additional Old Testament passages will enable us to 'decode' the meaning of the clues found in Revelation:

1) The Two Witnesses are wearing sackcloth.
2) They are symbolized by two olive trees and two lampstands who 'stand before the Lord of all the earth'.
3) Fire flows from their mouths to devour their enemies.
4) They have power to shut up sky so it doesn't rain for 3.5 years.
5) They have power to turn the water to blood.
6) They are mortal men.

Clue #1: Sackcloth

After the Babylonian captivity, two men led the returning Jewish exiles back to Jerusalem: a priest named Ezra, and Nehemiah, a civil leader. Both of these men sought to instruct the Jews in the ways of God:

> "13 On the second day, the heads of fathers' households of all the people, the priests, and the Levites were gathered together to Ezra the scribe, to study the words of the law. 14 They found written in the law how Yahweh had commanded by Moses that the children of Israel should dwell in booths in the feast of the seventh month; 15 and that they should publish and proclaim in all their cities and in Jerusalem, saying, 'Go out to the mountain, and get olive branches, branches of wild olive, myrtle branches, palm branches, and branches of thick trees, to make temporary shelters, as it is written.' " Nehemiah 8:13-15

The Feast of Tabernacles, referenced in the passage above, (also called the 'feast of the 7th month') had not been celebrated by the Jews during the time of their exile in Babylon. Though this feast of the Lord had been instituted by God centuries before at Mount Sinai, the returning exiles knew nothing about the feast until Ezra read the words of the law to them. The people were immediately moved to obey the command and celebrate the feast. At the completion of the eight days of celebration, the 'sons of Israel' entered into a time of mourning for their sins, and the sins of their fathers; particularly those sins that had brought about the exile in the first place:

> [1] "Now in the twenty-fourth day of this month the children of Israel were assembled with fasting, with sackcloth, and dirt on them. [2] The offspring of Israel separated themselves from all foreigners and stood and confessed their sins and the iniquities of their fathers." Nehemiah 9:1.2

Sackcloth was worn by all the sons of Israel as an outward demonstration of their inner sorrow, shame, and national repentance. They also separated themselves from foreigners as they confessed, not only their own sins, but the sins of their fathers, including the sin of idolatry. This leads us to another passage in the book of Malachi concerning the law of Moses and the coming of Elijah:

> [4] "Remember the law of Moses my servant, which I commanded to him in Horeb for all Israel, even statutes and ordinances. [5] Behold, I will send you Elijah the prophet before the great and terrible day of Yahweh comes. [6] He will turn the hearts of the fathers to the children and the hearts of the children to their fathers, lest I come and strike the earth with a curse." Malachi 4:4-6

The phrase, "turning the hearts of father to the children, and children to the fathers", refers to the sharing and receiving of biblical truth between the generations. When the fathers believe that God's laws are worthy of being passed on, they share them with their children. The it becomes the duty of the children to receive this information from their parents and pass it on as well. If each generation dispenses and then receives God's truth, all will go well. Should any generation fail to do this, God's curse would then come upon the nation.

Decode: Sackcloth is connected with repentance, confession, and obedience to the commands of God. We can expect that the Two Witnesses will be men who will humbly lead the sons of Israel, fathers and children, in repentance before God.

Clue #2: "The Two Olive Trees and the Two Lampstands who stand beside the Lord of all the earth"

The symbols of the 'two olive trees' and the two 'lampstands' very clearly points to a passage in the book of Zechariah.

¹¹ "Then I asked him, 'What are these two olive trees on the right side of the lamp stand and on the left side of it?'¹² I asked him the second time, 'What are these two olive branches, which are beside the two golden spouts that pour the golden oil out of themselves?' ¹³ He answered me, 'Don't you know what these are?' I said, 'No, my lord.'¹⁴ Then he said, 'These are the two anointed ones who stand by the Lord* of the whole earth.' " Zechariah 4:11-14

In the previous passage in Revelation we saw the identical symbols—the olive trees, the lampstands and the 'anointed ones who stand beside the Lord of the earth'—describing the Two Witnesses. Revelation very clearly lifted these symbols from the Zechariah passage. If we can discover what these symbols represent in Zechariah, we will be able to uncover what they mean in Revelation.

Examining the passages in Zechariah in the larger context of the surrounding verses indicates that the two olive trees and two lampstands represent two individuals: Joshua, the high priest, and a man named Zerubbabel. Like Ezra, Joshua was a priest; and like Nehemiah, Zerubbabel was a governor. These two men—Joshua and Zerubbabel—were instrumental in the rebuilding of the second temple after the exiles returned from Babylon. (God used Ezra and Nehemiah to rebuild the city of Jerusalem.)

Zerubbabel laid the temple's foundation, and, we are told that he was also able to complete the temple, as symbolized by Zerubbabel placing the top stone on the newly rebuilt temple. Though this was a seemingly insurmountable task, the Spirit of the Lord empowered both Zerubbabel and Joshua the high priest in their efforts, and they were able to complete the construction of the rebuilt temple in a surprisingly short period of time:

⁶ "Then he answered and spoke to me, saying, 'This is Yahweh's word to Zerubbabel, saying, "Not by might, nor by power, but by my Spirit," says Yahweh of Armies. ⁷ "Who are you, great mountain? Before Zerubbabel you are a plain; and he will bring out the capstone with shouts of 'Grace, grace, to it!'" ⁸ Moreover Yahweh's word came to me, saying, ⁹ 'The hands of Zerubbabel have laid the foundation of this house. His hands shall also finish it; and you will know that Yahweh of Armies has sent me to you.' " Zechariah 4:6-9

Decode: The Two Witnesses will be empowered by the Spirit of God to begin and complete a third temple in Jerusalem.

Clue #3: Fire flows from their mouths to devour their enemies.

28 "The prophet who has a dream, let him tell a dream; and he who has my word, let him speak my word faithfully. What is the straw to the wheat?" says

119

Yahweh. 29 'Isn't my word like fire?' says Yahweh; 'and like a hammer that breaks the rock in pieces? 30 Therefore behold, I am against the prophets,' says Yahweh, 'who each steal my words from his neighbor. 31 Behold, I am against the prophets,' says Yahweh, 'who use their tongues, and say, "'He says.'" Jeremiah 23:28-31b

In Jeremiah's time there were many false prophets who based their prophecy on personal dreams and visions. Jeremiah was commanded by God to only speak God's word. God's words were compared to a fire and a hammer. The word of God has power that dreams do not have. Just as a fire will destroy the works of men, the Spirit of God will empower the words spoken by His prophets enabling their words to carry His divine power.

Decode: The Two Witnesses will speak God's word in a powerful way. Their words will have power to destroy their enemies.

Clues #4 and #5: They have power to cause the rain to cease and turn water to blood.

Revelation 11 tells us that these two individuals can turn water to blood and cause droughts. There are only two people in the Bible who ever performed these two miracles. Revelation uses these two miracles as a kind of 'code' to tell us the actual identity of the Two Witnesses.

15 "Go to Pharaoh in the morning. Behold, he is going out to the water. You shall stand by the river's bank to meet him. You shall take the rod which was turned to a serpent in your hand. 16 You shall tell him, 'Yahweh, the God of the Hebrews, has sent me to you, saying, "Let my people go, that they may serve me in the wilderness. Behold, until now you haven't listened." 17 Yahweh says, "In this you shall know that I am Yahweh. Behold: I will strike with the rod that is in my hand on the waters which are in the river, and they shall be turned to blood." Exodus 7:15-17

Though the magicians in Pharaoh's court were able to replicate this miracle through their secret arts, Moses was the only one of God's prophets who ever turned water to blood.

The Bible tells us that Elijah prayed that it would not rain, and it didn't rain for 3.5 years.

"1 Elijah the Tishbite, who was one of the settlers of Gilead, said to Ahab, 'As Yahweh, the God of Israel, lives, before whom I stand, there shall not be dew nor rain these years, but according to my word.'" 1 Kings 17:1

"[1] After many days, Yahweh's word came to Elijah, in the third year, saying, "Go, show yourself to Ahab; and I will send rain on the earth." 1 Kings 18:1

"[17] Elijah was a man with a nature like ours, and he prayed earnestly that it might not rain, and it didn't rain on the earth for three years and six months." James 5:17

Decode: These two miraculous signs point to Moses and Elijah as being the Two Witnesses of Revelation.

Clue # 6: They are mortal men.

Revelation 11:7 tells us that the Two Witnesses will be put to death by the Beast. In order to die, they need to have mortal bodies that are capable of being put to death. We know that Elijah never physically died. He was taken alive into heaven by a whirlwind.

"[11] As they continued on and talked, behold, a chariot of fire and horses of fire separated them; and Elijah went up by a whirlwind into heaven." 2 Kings 2:11

But what about Moses? We know he died and God buried him:

"[5] So Moses the servant of Yahweh died there in the land of Moab, according to Yahweh's word. [6] He buried him in the valley in the land of Moab opposite Beth Peor, but no man knows where his tomb is to this day. [7] Moses was one hundred twenty years old when he died. His eye was not dim, nor his strength gone. " Deuteronomy 34:5-7

After Moses died, a dispute arose about his body:

"[9] But Michael, the archangel, when contending with the devil and arguing about the body of Moses, dared not bring against him an abusive condemnation, but said, 'May the Lord rebuke you!'" Jude 9

Scriptural evidence indicates that the body of Moses did not remain in the grave where God buried him. We know that Moses appeared with Elijah on the mountain when Christ was transfigured:

"²⁸ About eight days after these sayings, he took with him Peter, John, and James, and went up onto the mountain to pray. ²⁹ As he was praying, the appearance of his face was altered, and his clothing became white and dazzling. ³⁰ Behold, two men were talking with him, who were Moses and Elijah." Luke 9:28-30

Moses was not a disembodied spirit when he appeared with Elijah: he appeared on the mountain in a body, along with Elijah, who we know never died. Both men were transported by a cloud from heaven to the mountain, and then back into heaven again. The only conclusion we can draw from this is that Moses was raised from the dead—not into a glorified body—but back into his mortal body, similar to the kind of resurrection experienced by Lazarus; a resurrection in which he would ultimately have to die again. Moses could not be raised into his permanent, glorified body because Jesus had not yet died, or been resurrected into *His* glorified body. Jesus was the first Person to receive a glorified body, and as a result of His glorification, all those who trust in Him will one day receive a glorified body as well—including Moses and Elijah.

So what happened to Moses after he died?

1) God buried him.
2) His mortal body was resurrected—similar to Lazarus' resurrection.
3) After a dispute with the devil, most likely about the 'legality' of Moses being resurrected and taken to heaven, Michael took Moses to heaven.
4) Moses appeared in his mortal body along with Elijah, who never died, on the Mount of Transfiguration.
5) Moses will return with Elijah during the last days as one of the Two Witnesses.
6) Moses, along with Elijah, will be killed by the Beast.
7) He will resurrect and ascend into heaven at the midpoint of the seven years.

Decode: We have another confirmation that Moses and Elijah are the Two Witnesses of Revelation. Both of them existed heaven in their mortal bodies, then appeared at the Transfiguration and both will return during the end times, minister in power and then be killed by the Beast.

Some people have surmised that because Enoch never died, he may be one of the Two Witnesses. However, the symbolic clues given to us in Revelation don't point to Enoch as being one of the Two Witnesses. If anything, Enoch is a type of the raptured saints who will *never* taste death:

"5 By faith Enoch was taken away, so that he wouldn't see death, and he was not found, because God translated him. For he has had testimony given to him that before his translation he had been well pleasing to God." Hebrews 11:5

Here's what we know about the identity of the Two Witnesses and their ministry:

1) The symbols seem to indicate that the Two Witnesses are Moses and Elijah.
2) They will oversee the rebuilding of the Third Temple, from start to finish.
3) They will be super-naturally anointed by the Spirit of God.
4) They will proclaim the Word of God powerfully.
5) They will come against False Prophets.
6) They will punish the world by means of any and every type of plague.
7) They will lead the nation of Israel in repentance.
8) They will teach the ways of God to the sons of Israel.
9) They will destroy any who come against them.

This is an example of how multiple passages from the Old Testament are used by Revelation to expand on the end time story. Each new passage added another 'layer'. Revelation points directly to a number of radically different, and somewhat obscure passages in the Bible. Each of these passages provided additional clues about the identity and ministry of the Two Witnesses and each passage added more key information to the story. The narrative of the Two Witnesses is 'fleshed out' in the Old Testament passages—thereby adding dimension and details not present in Revelation. We now know the identity of the Two Witnesses and some of the things they will be doing during the time of their prophesying.

When Jesus told the readers of Revelation that they were not to add, nor subtract from, the words of the book, I believe that this caution also applies to how we *interpret* Revelation. We need to exercise great care, even when comparing 'scripture with scripture', as every word, phrase, idea and action in Revelation is communicating something important, and will give us a specific piece of the puzzle to help us understand the story. When putting together the prophetic and apocalyptic puzzle known as "Revelation", it's important that we only use the 'puzzle pieces' provided for us in the book itself, and only introduce passages from other parts of the Bible as Revelation directs.

Chapter 16: A Third 'Great Tribulation'

There are actually three 'great tribulations' that will take place during the last days. We've already looked at two of them: the first one being the tribulation of believers who will be martyred by the Harlot, which will take place prior to the midpoint of the 7 years. The martyred believers are the 'called out ones' from every 'tribe, tongue, people and nation' who will be martyred by "Mystery" Babylon and the 'earth dwellers'.

The second 'great tribulation' is found in Matthew 24:23, where Jesus spoke of a 'great tribulation' taking place after the event known as the "abomination of desolation". The book of Daniel tells us that this event will begin at the midpoint of the 7 years, and last for 3.5 years, or 'time, times and half a time". The second 'great tribulation' involves Israel, and remaining believers,will be 'cut short' when the wrath of God brings it to an end.

> 21 "For then there will be a *great tribulation*, such as has not occurred since the beginning of the world until now, nor ever will. 22 Unless those days had been cut short, no life would have been saved; but for the sake of the elect *those days will be cut short*." Matthew 24:21,22

The third 'great tribulation' is for 'Jezebel' and those who commit adultery with her. We read about Jezebel in the letter to the church of Thyatira:

> "But I have this against you, that you tolerate your woman Jezebel, who calls herself a prophetess. She teaches and seduces my servants to commit sexual immorality and to eat things sacrificed to idols. 21 I gave her time to repent, but she refuses to repent of her sexual immorality. 22 Behold, I will throw her and those who commit adultery with her into a bed of *great tribulation*, unless they repent of her works. 23 I will kill her children with Death, and all the assemblies will know that I am he who searches the minds and hearts. I will give to each one of you according to your deeds." Revelation 2:20-23

In the Old Testament, Jezebel was the daughter of a pagan priest who married Ahab, the king of the northern ten tribes of Israel. Though Ahab may have been the king, Jezebel was the power behind the throne. She was skilled in manipulating both people and circumstances to get what she wanted:

> "25 But there was no one like Ahab, who sold himself to do that which was evil in Yahweh's sight, whom Jezebel his wife stirred up." 1 Kings 21:25

'Jezebel' is a symbolic representation of people—both men and women—who will be used as agents of the Harlot religious system, to infiltrate the church of Thyatira. These people will promote themselves as 'prophets', and claim they speak for God.

'Jezebel' will use seduction to persuade believers to violate their consciences and commit 'sexual immorality' and 'eat meat sacrificed to idols'. These actions are not referring to *literal* sexual immorality or *literal* meat sacrificed to idols; they are merely symbols representing how believers will be tempted to become entangled in the Harlot religious system. Revelation is talking about *spiritual* immorality, not physical immorality. (Though physical immorality should be avoided as well!)

Jezebel represents individuals who will attempt to persuade some end time believers that the Harlot system is 'legitimate', and that participation in the rites, rituals and holy days belonging to the Harlot system is acceptable and to be encouraged—that God says it's 'okay'. In Jesus' estimation however, being associated in any way with the Harlot—having any kind of fellowship with her or her ilk—is the same as eating meat offered to idols or committing sexual immorality.

Jezebel is not a literal person. She represents a group of people who will infiltrate the local assemblies, and, through whatever means, attempt to draw believers into the 'system'. Everyone who gets sucked into the system will be given an opportunity to repent of having one foot in the true assembly and one foot in the 'false' system. Those who fail to repent will be cast into 'great tribulation'. This is the 'great tribulation' of the Harlot, who along with her 'daughters' will be destroyed at the 6th Trumpet.

In Revelation 18:4, the Lord pleads with His people to 'come out of her':

> "Come out of her, my people lest you take part in her sins, lest you share in her plagues." Revelation 18:4

Christ warns the church of Thyatira—and ALL the churches—that He knows what is going on in all their hearts and minds. He knows those who are true to Him and those who have divided loyalties. Believers during the last days are strongly admonished to remain pure in their devotion to Christ alone. They are told, in no uncertain terms, to have no dealings with the compromised Harlot system.

Chapter 17: The Tribulation

The Tribulation and the Wrath of God

Though the Bible refers to several 'great' tribulations which will take place during the end times, there are no passage(s) in scripture which support the idea of a seven-year Tribulation. Not one verse. Nada. Zip. Let that sink in.

This is a REAL problem because almost every single end time doctrinal position, held by many intelligent and trained Bible scholars, is *defined* in terms of a seven year period of time commonly known as 'The Tribulation'! Even the 'rapture' of the church is viewed from the vantage point of a seven year 'tribulation' and—depending on your eschatology—the rapture of believers will either be pre-tribulation—taking place before the seven years begins; mid-tribulation—with the rapture in the middle of the 7 years; or post-tribulation—where believers are gathered at the end of the seven years of Tribulation. For such a firmly held doctrine as the 'pre-*tribulation* rapture' to be so widely accepted, one would think that a seven year 'tribulation' would be a proven doctrine, fully supported by the weight of scripture—but, unfortunately, it's not.

People confuse 'tribulation'—persecution—with 'wrath'. When we read through the book of Revelation, and we see the breath-taking scope and devastating effects of the various Seal, Bowl and Trumpet judgments we are *sure* that this time of trouble, this time of sorrow and tribulation, *must be* the wrath of God! During the course of seven years, millions of people will die from war, famine and cosmic disturbances. Even more will be killed by the Harlot and the Beast. We know that the church is not destined for wrath (1 Thessalonians 5:9), but do all the horrors described in the book of Revelation constitute the 'wrath of God'? Or is the wrath of God something different?

The logic goes like this: 1) Terrible things take place during the 7 years before the Lord returns. 2) The terrible things that take place during the 7 years are so catastrophic that they *must* be the wrath of God. 3) The church is not destined for God's wrath, therefore, 4) the church will be removed in the rapture before the seven years begins.

The Bible defines 'tribulation' as persecution. The wrath of God is not the same thing as persecution and *Revelation is clearly delineates the difference between persecution (tribulation) and wrath*. The time when the wrath of God will be poured out is described for us in Revelation: the wrath of God will commence with the 7 Bowl judgments in Revelation 15, which will take place sometime toward the end of the seven years, along with the 6th and 7th Seal judgments, and the 7th Trumpet, all of which will occur one after the other, in rapid succession towards the very end of 7 years. Before the wrath of God can be poured out, the Beast kingdom must be in existence and that will not happen until the midpoint, 3.5 years before the return of Christ to earth. The wrath of God is not generalized or random—it is *specifically directed toward the Beast kingdom.*

From the passages examined previously in this book, we noted that the wrath of God does not last seven years. The wrath is not every single Seal, Trumpet and Bowl judgment, stretched out over seven long years. The wrath encompasses the 6th-7th Seals, the 7 Bowls and will end at the 7th Trumpet. Thus, if we use an artificial and biblically unsupported concept such as a seven year 'wrath/tribulation' to determine the timing of the rapture of the church, we can only be led into error and misunderstanding—and not just misunderstanding about the timing of the rapture—but about many other doctrines concerning the end times as well.

The 'Tribulation' and the "70th Week" of Daniel?

Bible teachers who hold to a seven year 'tribulation' usually point to Daniel 9:27 as the passage which supports this doctrine. This final 7 year interval of time—referred to as a 'week' of years in Daniel—is the final 'week' in a group of 70 'weeks' of years that form a prophecy directed to the nation of Israel:

> "Seventy weeks are decreed on your people and on your holy city, to finish disobedience, to make an end of sins, to make reconciliation for iniquity, to bring in everlasting righteousness, to seal up vision and prophecy, and to anoint the most holy." Daniel 9:24

The prophecy concerns the Jews, Jerusalem and the anointing of a holy 'thing' or holy 'One'. By the end of 70 weeks of years (490 years), the rebellion of the Jews will have been brought to an end—the same rebellion for which they had been exiled into Babylon for 70 years. God has a plan to bring the Jews to Himself—to take care of their 'sin problem'—and His plan involves the Jews, the city of Jerusalem and a holy One.

Nebuchadnezzar, the king of Babylon, was God's instrument to chastise Israel and bring her to her senses during the time of the Babylonian captivity. The city of Jerusalem was sacked and the temple destroyed by Nebuchadnezzar's armies. The upper class of Jewry—people like Daniel and his three friends—were carted off to the region of the Euphrates and told to make a go of it there. After 70 years spent in Babylon, God would allow them to return to their beloved city.

When, during a time of personal devotion and prayer, Daniel realized that the seventy years were coming to a close, he began fasting and praying for his nation, confessing the sins of Israel and their penchant for rebellion against God and His commands. The answer to Daniel's prayer was an angelic visitation and an astonishingly accurate, albeit somewhat cryptic, prophecy that foretold the history of the Jews over the next few centuries until the time of the Messiah—encompassing both His first and second comings.

> 25 "Know therefore and discern that from the going out of the commandment to restore and build Jerusalem to the Anointed One, the prince, will be seven weeks and sixty-two weeks. It will be built again, with street and moat, even in troubled times. 26 After the sixty-two weeks the Anointed One will be cut off, and will have nothing. The people of the prince who come will destroy the city and the sanctuary. Its end will be with a flood, and war will be even to the end. Desolations are determined. 27 He will make a firm covenant with many for one week. In the middle of the week he will cause the sacrifice and the offering to cease. And on the wing of abominations will come one who makes desolate; and even to the decreed full end, wrath will be poured out on the desolate." Daniel 9:25-27

The angel Gabriel informed Daniel through this prophecy, that the Jews would indeed return to Israel and rebuild Jerusalem, and that the temple would be rebuilt as well. Many years later the Messiah, the Anointed One, would arrive on the scene in Jerusalem and would be rejected. He would be "cut off and have nothing". He would die abruptly and without posterity.

Shortly after that, another army under the leadership of another 'prince' would replay what Nebuchadnezzar and his army had done in Daniel's day: they would destroy the city and the temple and disperse the Jews. That was exactly what happened. Christ was crucified without posterity. The Jews rejected God's Anointed One—and then God rejected the Jews. He allowed the Roman army, under the leadership of Titus, to destroy the city, the temple and to disperse the Jews throughout the known world.

All of this is historical fact, prophesied 400 years before it was fulfilled in 70 AD.

The last 'week' of years—the 70th Week—is the week that needs to be rightly understood.

> 27 "He will make a firm covenant with many for one week. In the middle of the week he will cause the sacrifice and the offering to cease. And on the wing of abominations will come one who makes desolate; and even to the decreed full end, wrath will be poured out on the desolate." Daniel 9:27

'Someone' makes a covenant, or 'strengthens' an already existing covenant for 7 years. Then, 3.5 years into the 'strengthening of the covenant', the sacrifices in the temple are brought to an end.

Who is it who 'strengthens' the covenant? The common teaching on the subject suggests that it is the Antichrist who makes a 'peace covenant' with Israel. Many people have been taught that the 'he' who makes a firm covenant with the 'many' is actually the 'prince' of the army that we read about in the previous verse...and then leap to the conclusion that the one who 'confirms the covenant' is the Antichrist! In other words, that the 'prince' who, along with his army sacked Jerusalem in 70 AD, has something to do with the Antichrist!

A lesson in grammar should help clarify exactly who 'confirms the covenant':

> Some commentators have stated that the word "he" in verse 27 refers to "the prince" in verse 26. As a result, they teach that whoever confirms the covenant' is associated with the 'prince', who is a type of the future Antichrist. "He" is a pronoun which must refer to a *specific preceding noun* in order to avoid ambiguity in the verse. The preceding noun is called the antecedent. An antecedent noun should *not* be found in a prepositional phrase.

> It is an accepted rule of grammar, in both English and Hebrew grammar, that a pronoun should not refer to noun within a prepositional phrase. The word "of" is a preposition and the word "prince" is in the prepositional phrase, "the people *of* the prince who is to come". "Prince" simply informs us about the "peoples" relationship with him. The prince is not the subject of the sentence. The word "prince" is an improper antecedent for the pronoun "he" in verse 27.

> The pronoun "he" cannot find its antecedent in the noun "people", either, because "people" is a plural neuter noun, and "he" is a masculine singular pronoun.

> The "he" refers back to the last masculine singular noun in verse 26:

> "Then after the sixty-two weeks **the Messiah** will be cut off..." Daniel 9:26

The Messiah is the last masculine singular noun—the Messiah who was 'cut off'. 'Seventy weeks' comes after 69 'weeks', and in the 70th and final week of years, Jesus 'confirmed' God's covenant with Israel at His first advent. His ministry encompassed 3.5 years and then, in the 'midst of the week', He was 'cut off'—rejected by the chief priests, the scribes and the Pharisees and condemned to die on a cross. Jesus' death put an end to 'sacrifice and offering'. The veil in the temple was torn in two and God made good on His promise to make 'atonement' for the sins of His people through the death of His One and only Son on a cross. When the Jews rejected Christ and compelled the Romans to crucify Him, God 'stopped the clock', as it were, for the nation of Israel. He put the last 3.5 years of the 70th week on hold until the time of the end.

"...**and** on the wing of abominations will come one who makes desolate, even until a complete destruction, one that is decreed, is poured out on the one who makes desolate." Daniel 9:27

The little word '**and**' separates two distinct thoughts and separates the 'week' into two separate 3.5 year periods of time. Said another way, there is a gap of 2,000 years inside that little word, '**and**'. Christ would confirm the covenant, putting an end to the temple sacrifices in the midst of the 'week', **AND** 2000 years later 'someone' would come on the 'wing of abominations' and make 'desolate'. The 'one' who comes on the 'wing of abominations' refers to the person we know of as the Antichrist.

The same people who teach that Israel will have seven years of tribulation, also believe that when Christ died, He was crucified in a 'gap' between the 69th and the 70th week. This doctrine takes the most important aspect of the Jew's redemption—the crucifixion of Christ, whose blood strengthened and ratified God's covenant with His people—and removes it from the prophecy altogether! The prophecy clearly states that Messiah would come after 69 'weeks' of years. What number comes after 69? The number seventy comes after 69. In the midst of the 70th week the Messiah was cut off...crucified:

> 25 "Know therefore and discern that from the going out of the commandment to restore and build Jerusalem to the Anointed One, the prince, will be seven weeks and sixty-two weeks. It will be built again, with street and moat, even in troubled times. 26 After the sixty-two weeks the Anointed One will be cut off, and will have nothing. The people of the prince who come will destroy the city and the sanctuary. Its end will be with a flood, and war will be even to the end. Desolations are determined." Daniel 9:25,26

In the middle of the 70th week, after 69 weeks, Christ would put an end to sacrifice and offering through His death on the cross. His premature death caused Israel's redemptive clock to be put on hold. *This means is that the Jews only have 3.5 years left on their 'clock'.* Their 'clock' will resume where it left off,   at Passover, in the middle of the 70th 'week' at an event we know of as the 'abomination of desolation'. At that time, the 'one who makes desolate'—the individual also known as the Antichrist and the 'son of perdition'—will take his seat in the temple of God proclaiming that he is God. Jesus predicted this day in Matthew 24:15-18:

> 15 "When, therefore, you see the abomination of desolation, which was spoken of through Daniel the prophet, standing in the holy place (let the

reader understand), [16] then let those who are in Judea flee to the mountains. [17] Let him who is on the housetop not go down to take out the things that are in his house. [18] Let him who is in the field not return back to get his clothes. " Matthew 24:15-18

Paul referred to this day as well:

> [3] "Let no one deceive you in any way. For it will not be unless the rebellion comes first, and the man of sin is revealed, the son of destruction. [4] He opposes and exalts himself against all that is called God or that is worshiped, so that he sits as God in the temple of God, setting himself up as God." 2 Thessalonians 2:3,4

The time preceding the 'abomination of desolation' is described in the book of Matthew as 'birth pains'.

> [6] "You will hear of wars and rumors of wars. See that you aren't troubled, for all this must happen, but the end is not yet. [7] For nation will rise against nation, and kingdom against kingdom; and there will be famines, plagues, and earthquakes in various places. [8] But all these things are the beginning of birth pains." Matthew 24:6-8

The events of Revelation take place over a period of 7 years, and give us the last days timeline for *believers*. Daniel, Jesus and Paul tell us that the 'end times' for the *Jews* will begin with the 'abomination of desolation', an event which will take place midway through the 70th Week of Daniel; at which time their timeline will continue for the last 3.5 years of the 70th Week. The Jew's time of trouble will be preceded by 'birth pangs': the first five Seal judgments and the first six Trumpet judgments that we read about in Revelation.

The bottom line is this: the Jews only have 3.5 years left on their 7 year redemption timeline. The first coming of Christ encompassed the first 3.5 years of the 70th Week, leaving only 3.5 years remaining. The timeline for believers will encompass the full 7 years. Both timelines—the one for believers in Revelation and the one for Israel in Daniel—will 'meet up' at the abomination/midpoint, and run concurrently from that point on.

People are watching and waiting for the Antichrist to make a 'peace covenant' with Israel so that they can predict the beginning of the 70th 'week' and get a feel for when the Church will be raptured. They think that once the covenant is made, the rapture of believers will be right around the corner. They do not realize that the covenant was already confirmed by Christ 2000 years ago!

132

The '70th week' of Daniel is not about the appearance of the Antichrist, but about the appearance of the *Christ*, and Christ's redemptive work on Israel's behalf. There is nothing in the brief prophecy recorded in Daniel 9:25-27 that intimates that the Antichrist will confirm a 'peace' covenant, thus kicking off a seven year tribulation, neither is there even a hint of a seven year time of 'tribulation' or persecution to be found anywhere in the Daniel 9:27 passage.

What is "tribulation"?

Simply put, 'tribulation' is the persecution and trials which the people of God must face while here on earth. The persecution of believers will intensify during the last days. We have already seen how the extermination of Christians will be undertaken by the Harlot and the 'earth dwellers' just before the midpoint/abomination; and after that, the extermination of both Jews AND Christians will take place from the midpoint on, during the 42 month/3.5 year reign of the Beast.

In summary: The 7 years prior to the visible return of Christ (commonly called 'the tribulation') does not consist of 7 years of the wrath of God; neither are the 7 years all persecution and trials. The persecution of God's people will come in waves. There is nothing in the scriptures that indicates that believers cannot, or will not, be present during the 7 years; thus the rapture(s) of believers can take place *within* the 7 year timeframe without contradicting passages pertaining to the wrath of God/Day of the Lord.

What about Israel in the Last Days?

Many dispensational Bible teachers are of the opinion that once the seven years of 'tribulation' begins, God's attention turns from the 'church' to Israel. They teach that God's primary interest at that point in time, is in leading His chosen people to Himself, and that the restoration of Israel alone, is the focal point of His plans and purposes.

The fact is, that God has *multiple* plans at work—at all times—and *all* His plans will converge in the last days. He has a plan for bringing His priests and kings—believers—into His heavenly Holy of Holies. He has a plan for His Son, making Him the Sovereign of the Universe. He has a plan for the demons, the 'Watchers', the fallen angels—to bring them into judgment. He has a plan for Satan, for the Harlot 'system', for the Beast/Antichrist, the False Prophet and those who rebel against Him. He has a plan for the restoration of all things, the resurrection of the dead and the creation of a new heaven and a new earth. AND He has a plan for Israel. ALL of these plans converge during the last days! Everyone's 'storyline' is present in the book of Revelation, and in Revelation, we see how *all* the stories of *all* the characters connect, intertwine and converge—ultimately culminating in the triumphant return of the Lord to the earth.

Chapter 18: The 'Church' in Revelation

What's the first thing that comes to mind when you think of the word, 'church'? Is it the building on the corner where you attend worship services on Sunday morning? A worship team leading the congregation in songs of praise? The pastor preaching a sermon? Sunday school? We all have our idea of what 'church' is...but —is the 'church' in our heads, the same as the 'church' that's described in our Bibles?

The Greek word translated 'church' in our English Bibles, is the word '*ekklesia*'. "*Ekklesia*" is derived from two Greek words: '*ek*', meaning 'out from, and to' and '*kaleo*' meaning 'to call or invite'. The '*ekklesia*', therefore, are the *"the assembly of all people that God is calling out from the world and to Himself."* The '*ekklesia*' are God's 'called out-and-to' people. His 'invited' people. His 'not of this world' people. His heaven-bound people.

Most believers understand that the "church" is not about buildings, services, Sunday school or preaching. Rather, the church is about people, and their individual and corporate relationship with God. The church is the '*ekklesia*'—a group of assembled individuals, called 'out of world' and invited into fellowship with God and each other.

The apostle Paul wrote extensively about the church—this assembly of 'called out-and-to' invited people. Just as God chose Israel out of all the nations to be His 'called out and chosen' people here on earth, God has also chosen believers to be His called out and chosen people who will live with Him in heavenly glory.

That God would invite people to dwell with Him in heaven is a concept that boggles the mind. Men and women, Jews and Gentiles, rich and poor have been called from the sea of humanity to be His 'chosen' people. This was a secret kept hidden by God until revealed to the apostle Paul by Christ. This mystery was not revealed to the Old Testament prophets in times past: the mystery that the *ekklesia*—believers in Jesus, both Jew and Gentile—would be personally chosen by God, in Christ, to be His special, holy people:

> 3 "Blessed be the God and Father of our Lord Jesus Christ, who has blessed us with every spiritual blessing in the heavenly places in Christ, 4 even as he chose us in him before the foundation of the world, that we would be holy and without defect before him in love." Ephesians 1:3,4

> 2 "Since you have heard of the administration of that grace of God which was given me toward you, 3 how that by revelation the mystery was made

known to me, as I wrote before in few words, 4 by which, when you read, you can perceive my understanding in the mystery of Christ, 5 which in other generations was not made known to the children of men, as it has now been revealed to his holy apostles and prophets in the Spirit, 6 that the Gentiles are fellow heirs and fellow members of the body, and fellow partakers of his promise in Christ Jesus through the Good News." Ephesians 3:2-6

This 'called out' group of people is likened to a 'body':

27 "Now you are the body of Christ, and members individually. "
1 Corinthians 12:27

The 'body' of believers is also compared to a 'virgin':

2 "For I am jealous over you with a godly jealousy. For I promised you in marriage to one husband, that I might present you as a pure virgin to Christ." 2 Corinthians 11:2

Everyone who is 'called out and invited', who in 'in Christ', who belongs to the Body and is a part of the Bride, is destined to dwell in heaven with God, as His blessed and blameless people.

Many sincere Bible teachers and Christians do not believe that the people who come to Christ during the time of 'tribulation' (which, according to them begins after the rapture of the church), are actually *bona fide* Christians, and thus full members of the Body of Christ. The doctrine of the pre-tribulation rapture holds that the 'church' leaves at the rapture, that the Holy Spirit leaves with the church, and that those who come to Christ after the rapture are not a part of the Body or Bride of Christ. They are 'saved', but somehow their destiny is not the same as believers who lived prior to the rapture.

Using the Bible's definition of 'church'—the "called out and invited" people of God—let's ask a question: "Do the people who come to Christ during the end times, during the time of 'tribulation', meet the definition of people who are 'called out and invited' by God to dwell with Him in heaven?" Are the martyrs, the 144K, and the Overcoming saints we read about in Revelation, members of the Body of Christ? Do they make up the Bride of Christ along with the rest of the believing church?

The very fact that each of these groups of people appear in heaven before the throne of God should provide the answer to the question: yes...they are a part of the '*ekklesia*', the Church. They were called 'out' of the world and 'to' God. They have access through the blood of Christ. They are in His heavenly temple, in His presence, ministering before Him as priests. The '*ekklesia*', the church, is composed of all believers—from Abel, to the very last 'tribulation' saint—all those who take refuge in the promises of God. (Hebrews 11)

Over the years, sincere Bible expositors have taught that chapters 1-3 of Revelation, including the letters to the seven churches, were describing the history of the church up until the time of the rapture of believers. In Revelation 4:1, John was told to 'come up here'—to go up into heaven. They believe that the 'Church Age' will end with the rapture, with the call to 'come up here'. Moreover, they believe that because the word, 'church' is absent from the book of Revelation from chapter 4 onward, the 'church' must also be 'absent' from the earth during the last 7 years, during the time of 'tribulation'! By using the linear, chronological Greek method to interpret Revelation, they have, by default, excluded multitudes upon multitudes of saved people from the assembly of 'called out' believers—millions of believers who are a part the '*ekklesia*'!

When the book of Revelation is interpreted through the lens of Western thinking; as though the chapters were placed in the order in which events transpire during the time of the end; as though the book were one, long vision instead of a series of many short visions; as though it were not possible that *we ourselves* may be living 'inside' the seven years—this is where one ends up: not acknowledging that the 'tribulation saints' are our brothers and sisters in Christ and part of the same Body and Bride to which we, ourselves, belong .

The word 'church' can have multiple meanings, including the Pauline concept of the universal spiritual Body of Christ, comprising both Jew and Gentile—all believers throughout the ages. However, when *Revelation* employs the word, 'church', it's referring to small, local assemblies of believers on earth. There's a world of difference between 'The Church Universal' in all its fullness, and a group of ten or 15 people gathered in someone's living room!

In Revelation, the idea of the fullness of the gathering of believers is symbolized, not by 'The Church', but by the holy city, the New Jerusalem, the Bride:

> 2 "I saw the holy city, New Jerusalem, coming down out of heaven from God, prepared like a bride adorned for her husband." Revelation 21:2

Prior to the glorious unveiling of the New Jerusalem in chapter 21, the 'church' is *never* presented in Revelation as a monolithic entity. The 'churches'—small local assemblies of believers—are what the book of Revelation means by the word 'church', not the all-encompassing expression of the Body of Christ. In fact, the small assemblies of believers are held in stark contrast to the world-wide religious institutions which will be in place during the end: specifically the Harlot religious system that 'sits on many waters' and the world-wide religion of the Beast. Those monstrous systems, bastions of evil, are to avoided at all costs. Jesus compared those systems to an abnormally over-grown shrub, in which the birds of the air (demonic spirits) were happy to make their homes:

> [18] "He said, 'What is God's Kingdom like? To what shall I compare it? [19] It is like a grain of mustard seed which a man took and put in his own garden. It grew and became a large tree, and the birds of the sky live in its branches.' " Luke 13:18,19

Not until we get a glimpse of the New Jerusalem do we see all believers, including those who came out of the 'tribulation', as a part of one glorious entity—the foundation, walls and gates of the New Jerusalem.

> [10] "He carried me away in the Spirit to a great and high mountain, and showed me the holy city, Jerusalem, coming down out of heaven from God, [11] having the glory of God. Her light was like a most precious stone, like a jasper stone, clear as crystal; [12] having a *great and high wall* with *twelve gates,* and at the gates twelve angels, and names written on them, which are the names of the twelve tribes of the children of Israel. [13] On the east were three gates, and on the north three gates, and on the south three gates, and on the west three gates. [14] The wall of the city had *twelve foundations,* and on them twelve names of the twelve Apostles of the Lamb." Revelation 21:10-14

The 24 Elders, seated on thrones, will be the first to arrive in heaven and they represent the 'foundation' of the Holy City. The foundation is solid—it's 'seated', just like the Elders. The overcoming believers who are killed during the 10 days of persecution by the Harlot and, later, those who refuse to take the mark of the Beast or participate in the worship of the Beast or its image, are represented by the great, high walls which stand on the foundation of the city. In Revelation 7:9, we see the 5th Seal martyrs *standing* before God's throne:

> [9] "After these things I looked, and behold, a great multitude which no man could count, out of every nation and of all tribes, peoples, and languages, standing before the throne and before the Lamb, dressed in white robes, with palm branches in their hands." Revelation 7:9

The believers who do not take the mark of the Beast during the last half of the seven years, are also seen *standing* in heaven:

2 "I saw something like a sea of glass mixed with fire, and those who over-came the beast, his image, and the number of his name, standing on the sea of glass, having harps of God." Revelation 15:2

All the 'overcoming' believers will have 'fought the good fight', having engaged in spiritual warfare and having secured the victory until the end, as evidenced by the fact that they remain *standing:*

11 "Put on the whole armor of God, that you may be able to stand against the wiles of the devil. 12 For our wrestling is not against flesh and blood, but against the principalities, against the powers, against the world's rulers of the darkness of this age, and against the spiritual forces of wickedness in the heavenly places. 13 Therefore put on the whole armor of God, that you may be able to withstand in the evil day, and having done all, to stand. 14 Stand therefore, having the utility belt of truth buckled around your waist, and having put on the breastplate of righteousness, 15 and having fitted your feet with the preparation of the Good News of peace, 16 above all, taking up the shield of faith, with which you will be able to quench all the fiery darts of the evil one. 17 And take the helmet of salvation, and the sword of the Spirit, which is the word of God. " Ephesians 6:11-17

The 144K who 'follow the Lamb' wherever He goes, are represented in the New Jerusalem by the 12 gates in the four walls of the city. Above each gate is an in-scription of one of the names of the 12 tribes of Israel:

12 "...having a *great and high wall* with *twelve gates,* and at the gates twelve angels, and names written on them, which are the names of the twelve tribes of the children of Israel. 13 On the east were three gates, and on the north three gates, and on the south three gates, and on the west three gates." Revelation 21:12,13

As each company of believers arrives in heaven, they are incorporated into the New Jerusalem. The last group to be admitted to the city are those martyred by the Beast during the last 3.5 years of the seven years. They await their resurrec-tion upon the return of Christ to the earth:

"I saw the souls of those who had been beheaded for the testimony of Je-sus and for the word of God, and such as didn't worship the beast nor his image, and didn't receive the mark on their forehead and on their hand. They lived and reigned with Christ for a thousand years. 5 The rest of the dead didn't live until the thousand years were finished. This is the first resurrection. 6 Blessed and holy is he who has part in the first resurrection. Over these, the second death has no power, but they will be priests of God and of Christ, and will reign with him one thousand years." Revelation 20:4b-6

Once this last group of martyrs are raised as 'priests and kings', the Bride will have finally made herself ready:

> 7 "Let's rejoice and be exceedingly glad, and let's give the glory to him. For the wedding of the Lamb has come, and his wife has made herself ready." Revelation 19:7

Chapter 19: Christ in the midst...

Though the Pauline concept of 'the Church', which encapsulates the mystical body of Christ, is nowhere to be found in Revelation, the unity of Christ with His people is represented in the book in other ways. God goes to great lengths to depict the oneness Christ has with His people. Like all spiritual truths tucked away in Revelation, this union is depicted *symbolically and indirectly, using imagery and 'layering'.*

One of the ways Christ is portrayed in union with His people is described in the very first chapter of Revelation, where we see Him in the 'midst' of the seven golden lampstands:

> [12] "I turned to see the voice that spoke with me. Having turned, I saw seven golden lamp stands. [13] And among the lamp stands was one like a son of man, clothed with a robe reaching down to his feet, and with a golden sash around his chest." Revelation 1:12, 13

The seven lampstands represent the seven assemblies of 'called out and invited' believers. Christ is seen walking in their midst. He's present with them. He sees what goes on inside each assembly and what is going on inside the individual hearts and minds of each member of the fellowship. He knows how the enemy will come at them, where they can be 'seduced', where they may falter and stumble. **He is not far away**—He is *in the midst*—to guide, to comfort, encourage and exhort. He is close, at the very center of their assemblies.

In Revelation 5:6,7 we read this:

> [6] "I saw in the middle of the throne and of the four living creatures, and in the middle of the elders, a Lamb standing, as though it had been slain, having seven horns and seven eyes, which are the seven Spirits of God, sent out into all the earth. [7] Then he came, and he took it out of the right hand of him who sat on the throne." Revelation 5:6,7

The Lamb—Christ—is *in the midst* of the Elders. The Elders on their thrones are in close proximity to the throne of God, as close as is possible, and they are seated among the Four Living Creatures who surround and guard God's throne and His glory. Seated in the middle of the raptured saints, is the glorified and risen Lamb, who is Jesus. Rather than depicting Christ seated with His Father on His Father's throne, we see Him seated in the *midst of* the Elders. This is our clue that Christ and the 24 Elders are 'one' unified company—a band of heavenly priests, ministering to God in His presence.

The martyrs who come out of the 'great tribulation' are close to Christ as well:

> "So he said to me, 'These are the ones who come out of the great tribulation, and *washed their robes and made them white in the blood of the Lamb*. Therefore they are before the throne of God, and serve Him day and night in His temple. And He who sits on the throne will dwell among them. They shall neither hunger anymore nor thirst anymore; the sun shall not strike them, nor any heat; for the Lamb who is *in the midst of the throne will shepherd them* and lead them to living fountains of waters. And God will wipe away every tear from their eyes.' " Revelation 7:14-17

When these believers were persecuted and slain by the earth dwellers and the Harlot, Christ equated the shed blood of the martyrs with *His own* blood: "They washed their robes and made them white in the *blood of the Lamb*." The martyr's shed blood is described as being equivalent to the Lamb's shed blood.

This passage is not talking about the believer's salvation or being purchased by the blood of Christ. The 'robes' these saints 'wash' are the robes of their *bodies*. In Revelation, 'robes' is often a 'code' word signifying someone's body, whether a glorified body as when the 5th Seal martyrs are given a 'white robe', or a martyred body that has been covered in 'blood'. Christ, the slain Lamb, identifies with the deaths of the martyrs.

This martyred multitude will never leave God's temple—they will always have access to His presence as priests who minister to Him. The Lamb will shepherd them and tenderly care for them and God Himself will wipe away every tear, acknowledging all the suffering, sorrow and loss which they endured at the hands of the earth dwellers and the Harlot for the sake of Christ.

In Revelation 14, we see that the 144,000 of Israel are present on heavenly Mount Zion *with* the Lamb:

> "I saw, and behold, the Lamb standing on Mount Zion, and with him a number, one hundred forty-four thousand, having his name and the name of his Father written on their foreheads...4 These are those who were not defiled with women, for they are virgins. These are those who follow the Lamb wherever he goes. These were redeemed by Jesus from among men, the first fruits to God and to the Lamb. " Revelation 14:1,4

We'll be looking at this group of believers in greater detail later on, but for now we can see that the 144K and the Lamb are pictured *together* on heavenly Mount Zion. They are said to 'follow the Lamb wherever He goes'. They are His sheep and the Lamb is the Shepherd. Like the 12 disciples who followed Christ during

His earthly ministry, these 'first fruits' will also follow Christ. Their lives and His life will intertwine: they are seen as one 'flock', with one Shepherd.

When Christ returns to the earth, the Beast and the kings of the earth will come against Him and make 'war with the Lamb'. Christ will have His saints *with Him* as well, believers who are 'called and chosen and faithful':

> "These will war against the Lamb, and the Lamb will overcome them, for he is Lord of lords and King of kings; and those who are with him are called, chosen, and faithful." Revelation 17:14

Christ does not return to earth alone, He brings His faithful servants with Him. The 'called' go where He goes and His desire is to have them near Him, even when He goes into battle. His army of 'called, chosen and faithful' believers, who themselves 'conquered' the Beast through perseverance and faithfulness to Christ, will have already been battle-hardened:

> "I saw something like a sea of glass mixed with fire, and those who over-came the beast, his image, and the number of his name, standing on the sea of glass, having harps of God." Revelation 15:2

At the end of the Millennium, the unity of believers with Christ will be expressed in an even greater way, as God Himself, along with Christ and the glorified inhab-itants of New Jerusalem, come to dwell with resurrected and immortal people who will live on earth:

> "I heard a loud voice out of heaven saying, 'Behold, God's dwelling is with people; and he will dwell with them, and they will be his people, and God himself will be with them as their God.' " Revelation 21:3

The fellowship that believers enjoy with the Lamb, and with God in the New Jerusalem, will ultimately be enjoyed by all people on earth. The men and women who inhabit the recreated New Earth after the thousand year reign of Christ, will experience the bliss of entering into God's presence as well.

Chapter 20: The Mystery of the Male-child

One of the most interesting and profound symbolic representations of Christ in union with His called-out people, is depicted in a series of visions found in Revelation 12. The whole chapter is loaded with symbols and imagery, which, when decoded, form a framework for the *actual timing of events* leading to the return of Christ. We'll be diving into chapter 12 in greater detail in subsequent chapters of this book, but right now, we're going to examine the mysterious entity known as the 'male child' (or 'man-child').

> "¹ A great sign was seen in heaven: a woman clothed with the sun, and the moon under her feet, and on her head a crown of twelve stars. ² She was with child. She cried out in pain, laboring to give birth. " Revelation 12:1,2

The twelve stars which crown the woman's head alludes to Joseph's dream in Genesis:

> "He dreamed yet another dream, and told it to his brothers, and said, 'Behold, I have dreamed yet another dream: and behold, the sun and the moon and eleven stars bowed down to me.' " Genesis 37:9

The 'stars' in Joseph's dream represent Joseph's eleven brothers, who along with Joseph, were the patriarchs of the twelve tribes of Israel. In this vision, the stars represent the 12 tribes of Israel.

We are told the identity of the 'woman' in the next vision:

> "Another sign was seen in heaven. Behold, a great red dragon, having seven heads and ten horns, and on his heads seven crowns. ⁴ His tail drew one third of the stars of the sky, and threw them to the earth. The dragon stood before the woman who was about to give birth, so that when she gave birth he might devour her child. ⁵ She gave birth to a son, a male child, who is to rule all the nations with a rod of iron. Her child was caught up to God and to his throne. ⁶ The woman fled into the wilderness, where she has a place prepared by God, that there they may nourish her one thousand two hundred sixty days." Revelation 12:3-6

The 'woman' gave birth to the 'one who is to rule all the nations with a rod of iron'. The "One who is to rule all nations" is, of course, referring to Christ, who descended from the nation of Israel. The following passage from the letter to the church at Thyatira confirms that Christ has received the authority to rule over the nations, and that He will share His authority with believers who 'conquer':

> "He who overcomes, and he who keeps my works to the end, to him I will give authority over the nations. 27 He will rule them with a rod of iron, shattering them like clay pots, as I also have received of my Father." Revelation 2:26,27

The physical lineage of Jesus, the "One who rules with a rod of iron", descended from the tribe of Judah, one of the 12 tribes which make up the nation of Israel, is represented by the 'woman' in this vision. We also know that after the midpoint/abomination of desolation, the remnant of Israel will flee into the wilderness for 1260 days. Israel's flight into the wilderness is mentioned again in the following verses, and lasts for a 'time, times and half a time' or 3.5 years:

> "When the dragon saw that he was thrown down to the earth, he persecuted the woman who gave birth to the male child. 14 Two wings of the great eagle were given to the woman, that she might fly into the wilderness to her place, so that she might be nourished for a time, times, and half a time, from the face of the serpent. " Revelation 12:13,14

Together, these passages inform us that the woman who will flee into the wilderness represents the nation of Israel during the last days. She is the one who gave birth to the Male child—the Messiah; and we also learn that the Male-child (or 'Man-child') represents Jesus.

The Male Child and the Child

The two Greek words which are translated as the 'male child' are *'huios arsen'*, meaning 'a son, a male'. Every time the word *"huios"* (or 'son') is used in Revelation, it *always* refers to the Son, who is Christ. The *'huios'* is the Son who carries the nature of the Father: He is the Son who inherits.

> "And among the lamp stands was one like a son of man, clothed with a robe reaching down to his feet, and with a golden sash around his chest." Revelation 1:13

> " I looked, and saw a white cloud, and on the cloud one sitting like a son of man, having on his head a golden crown, and in his hand a sharp sickle." Revelation 14:14

But the 'child' who is born to the woman, the one who is 'caught up to God and to His throne' is referred to by a different Greek word: *'teknon'*. The 'child' is a *'teknon'*, which is a generic term for 'a child or descendent':

146

"And the dragon stood before the woman who was about to give birth, so that when she bore her child (*'teknon'*) he might devour it. She gave birth to a male child (*"huios arsen"*), one who is to rule all the nations with a rod of iron, but her child ("teknon") was caught up to God and to his throne."

We are told that the Dragon wants to devour the 'child'. The Dragon (Satan) does *not* seek to devour the male child, but rather seeks to destroy the 'child'/*'teknon'*. Then we read that the 'child'—the *'teknon'*—is 'caught up'. The *'huios arsen',* the Son, who is Christ, is *not* 'caught up.' The phrase 'caught up' is the English translation of the Greek word *'harpazo'* which refers to the rapture, the 'catching away' of believers.

The Son rules the nations, *but* the 'child' is 'caught up' and is taken into God's throne room in heaven. The little word, *'but'*, lets us know that the 'male child' and the 'child' are actually *two different entities*: one is Christ, who rules, and other—the 'child' who is 'caught up'—represents believers, who will be 'caught up' into the throne room of heaven in a rapture event. The *'huios arsen'* is layered over the *'tekon'* because we are meant to think of them as one 'baby'—one entity!

These verses combine two entities—the male child, who is Christ, and the child who represents believers—into the single symbol of the baby. This is the beauty of the Hebraic style: multiple ideas can be communicated simply and indirectly with an economy of words which is nothing short of amazing. To me, this is evidence of Revelation's divine origin. The Son who 'rules', the 'child' who will be raptured, the nation of Israel in 'labor'—and more—are all depicted in a very brief story about a woman giving birth.

There are many more layers found in Revelation 12 that will be discussed in another chapter, including evidence that the whole 7 year timeline for believers is outlined in the series of visions which are described in this chapter. In many ways, Revelation 12 is the hinge on which pivots the two halves of the seven years. The middle verse of Revelation—when Satan is cast out— falls in the middle of the 7 year timeline!

In summary: Using the indirect and layered Hebraic method of interpretation, rather than the conventional 'Greek-style' of interpretation, the spiritual reality of the union between Christ and believers is depicted in Revelation as:

1) Christ *in the midst* of His people
2) Christ *with* His people
3) The blood of the martyrs being equated with the blood of the Lamb

4) The 'male child' and the 'child' of Revelation 12, representing two different entities, whose union is symbolized by a singular 'baby'.

Chapter 21: Heavenly Signs

Three 'signs' are described in Revelation. The first sign—the great sign—is found in the first vision of Revelation 12:

> "A great sign was seen in heaven: a woman clothed with the sun, and the moon under her feet, and on her head a crown of twelve stars. ² She was with child. She cried out in pain, laboring to give birth." Revelation 12:1,2

The second sign is in the next vision of the same chapter:

> "Another sign was seen in heaven. Behold, a great red dragon, having seven heads and ten horns, and on his heads seven crowns. ⁴ His tail drew one third of the stars of the sky, and threw them to the earth. The dragon stood before the woman who was about to give birth, so that when she gave birth he might devour her child. ⁵ She gave birth to a son, a male child, who is to rule all the nations with a rod of iron. Her child was caught up to God and to his throne.
>
> ⁶ The woman fled into the wilderness, where she has a place prepared by God, that there they may nourish her one thousand two hundred sixty days." Revelation 12:3-6

The third sign—"great and marvelous"—is recorded in Revelation 15:1:

> "I saw another great and marvelous sign in the sky: seven angels having the seven last plagues, for in them God's wrath is finished." Revelation 15:1

There are also three different 'heavens' depicted in the book of Revelation. The first heaven is the abode of God and His angels. Other spirit beings are present in heaven as well, and we know that right now, Satan and his angels also dwell in heaven. Satan has a throne in heaven and he is actively worshiped by the fallen angels *in heaven!* After a brief war around the midpoint of the 7 years, the whole lot of them will be cast out of heaven by Michael and his angels. Contrary to Milton and some Christian teaching, the fallen angels (those who have not been consigned to the Pit), at the present time, call God's heaven their home.

The second 'heaven' refers to the starry heavens; the place where the sun, moon, stars and planets mark the passage of time. The luminaries are God's celestial 'clock'—keeping track of, and announcing God's 'appointed seasons'—His feast days. The moon waxes and wanes every month and the sun determines both the

24 hour day and the passage of years. Anomalies in the sun, moon and stars are 'attention grabbers' and are used by God to point to significant events (like the star of Bethlehem which heralded the birth of Christ) or to direct our attention to spiritual inflection points:

> "God said, 'Let there be lights in the expanse of the sky to divide the day from the night; and let them be for signs to mark seasons, days, and years; 15 and let them be for lights in the expanse of the sky to give light on the earth;' and it was so." Genesis 1:14,15

Finally, the sky above us, the expanse where the birds fly, is also referred to as 'heaven' or 'mid-heaven'. The specific meaning of the word 'heaven' in Revelation will be understood from the context of the passage.

A Great Sign...

> "A great sign was seen in heaven: a woman clothed with the sun, and the moon under her feet, and on her head a crown of twelve stars. 2 She was with child. She cried out in pain, laboring to give birth." Revelation 12:1,2

Like the star of Bethlehem, which was the sign in the heavens signaling the sages from the East that the Savior of the world had been born, the 'great sign' in Revelation 12:1, was meant to tell us that a monumental event of great spiritual significance was about to take place; and that God was about ready to move into a new phase of His redemptive plan. Because the sun, the moon and the stars are specifically named in this vision, we can assume that this sign actually took place in the starry heavens, among the sun, moon and stars—as did the star of Bethlehem.

God created the sun and the moon to separate the day from the night, and to delineate the months and years. The stars, particularly the twelve signs of the zodiac ("*mazzaroth*" in Hebrew), were understood by the ancients to act as signs in the night sky, each constellation representing a cosmic character, role-playing in the celestial drama of salvation.

In Bible times, people of faith understood that the story of salvation and the redemption of mankind was recounted through the various constellations which comprise the *mazzaroth*. They knew the 'story in the stars' foretold the coming of the Messiah, and His role in our redemption. Like all things spiritual, the constellations, and the information they both conceal and reveal, has been hijacked by the enemy for his own purposes. Rather than prophesying the story of Christ and telling HIS story, astrologers use the zodiac to foretell the future. Having one's horoscope read is fortune-telling, something which is forbidden in scripture. As a result, most sincere Christians believe that anything having to do with the signs of the zodiac is 'off-limits'; and most evangelical Christians are leery of ascribing any biblical or spiritual significance to the stars. Modern humanity in general is ignorant and unaware of the true message God has placed in the stars; a message the luminaries are silently communicating night after night.

We know that the starry host originated with God. The stars tell the story of salvation: from the virgin birth of Christ, represented by the constellation, Virgo the Virgin; to the reign of Christ who is the Lion of the Tribe of Judah, represented by the constellation, Leo, the Lion:

> "The heavens declare the glory of God.
> The expanse shows his handiwork.
> 2 Day after day they pour out speech,
> and night after night they display knowledge.
> 3 There is no speech nor language
> where their voice is not heard.
> 4 Their voice has gone out through all the earth,
> their words to the end of the world." Psalm 19:1-4

Every night, year after year, the stars bear silent witness to the gospel story. The individual constellations which comprise the zodiac are recognized throughout the world. There is a universal story in the stars, which has been read by humanity since ancient times, and it's basically the same story from culture to culture, told in varying ways, by nearly every people group on earth.

What's compelling about the 'great sign' described in Revelation 12:1,2, is that this vision seems to depict an actual astronomical alignment in the 'starry heavens', an alignment which took place in September of 2017.

Every September, the sun 'clothes' the constellation of Virgo—the only constellation on the ecliptic represented by a woman. The nine star constellation of Leo is always over Virgo's 'head', but in 2017 the 'wandering stars' of Mercury, Mars and Venus moved into the constellation of Leo adding 3 more stars to the 9 stars already present in Leo, thus creating a 'crown' of 12 stars for the 'woman'.

The planet Jupiter moves through each of the constellations on the ecliptic every 12 years. In 2017, Jupiter was in Virgo, and had been in retrograde motion inside of Virgo for nine months—the length of an average human gestation. Then, on the 23rd of September in 2017, the crescent moon appeared under Virgo's 'feet' and Jupiter began its exit from the constellation, having been in Virgo's 'womb' the length of a full-term pregnancy. Many who researched this rare alignment concluded that this indeed *was the fulfillment* of the 'great sign' which Revelation 12 described in such detail—a 'once in 7000 years' astronomical alignment, which took place during the closing hours of the two day Feast of Trumpets, which began on September 21, 2017.

The 'great sign' in the starry heavens was the climax of the Feast of Trumpets, and I believe this sign was the 'sounding of a trumpet' — a very loud wake up call to all those with ears to hear—that God was now beginning a new phase in the story of redemption: the end game.

The Second Sign: Sign of the Dragon and the Child

> "Another sign was seen in heaven. Behold, a great red dragon, having seven heads and ten horns, and on his heads seven crowns. 4 His tail drew one third of the stars of the sky, and threw them to the earth. The dragon stood before the woman who was about to give birth, so that when she gave birth he might devour her child. 5 She gave birth to a son, a male child, who is to rule all the nations with a rod of iron. Her child was caught up to God and to his throne.
>
> 6 The woman fled into the wilderness, where she has a place prepared by God, that there they may nourish her one thousand two hundred sixty days." Revelation 12:3-6

The first sign, the sign of the woman in travail, clothed with the sun, which appeared in the heavens in the fall of 2017, was, I believe, the starting point of the seven years which will culminate in the return of Christ to earth. Revelation 12 depicts a second sign following the first: the sign of the Dragon and the Child.

The same symbols that were used to tell the story in the starry heavens, will also be used to symbolically tell the rest of the story which will take place *on the earth*. We know that the woman represents the nation of Israel. In the second vision, the Dragon—who is Satan—is seen standing before the woman who is about to give birth. Israel is on earth, and this vision depicts—in symbolic fashion—the events that will take place on the earth, sometime after the Great Sign, but before the time when the woman will flee into the wilderness at the midpoint. (The significance of the Dragon's seven heads and 10 horns will be covered later in this book.) The important thing to note, is that Satan has positioned himself in such a way so as to devour the child—believers—*not the woman* who represents Israel. His goal is to prevent believers from entering the heavenly Holy of Holies. If the priesthood does not arrive into the throne room of God, Christ will not leave the heavenly altar to take the scroll and begin His reign, and thus Satan's judgment will have been preempted, or at least postponed.

152

The woman—Israel—is in travail, meaning she is enduring an intense time of suffering, most likely in the form of a war. In addition to the travail of the woman, the Dragon has used his tail to cast a third of his 'stars', his angels, to the earth. The fallen angels will most likely be disguised as aliens or 'angels of light'. They will be presented as benevolent and wise beings who only want to help humanity. It's also possible that they may show up as malevolent creatures bent on destroying humanity. Or they may be disguised as both good and evil beings. In any case, Satan will have his minions here on the earth, assisting him in his evil plan, which is to thwart the plans of God and set up his own kingdom on earth ruled by the Beast and himself.

We have already seen how the Male Child represents Christ. He is the One who will rule all nations with a rod of iron during the Millennium. The 'child' represents believers who will be born—changed into their glorified bodies—and after a brief period of persecution by the Dragon, they will be caught up into heaven. The child is then represented by the 24 Elders who serve as priests and kings in the presence of God.

The events described in the second sign will take place during the summer of 2020. These events could have taken place in 2018, 2019, and at the very latest, the fall of 2020. Since I am writing this book in the winter of 2019/20, we can expect the war in Israel and the 'alien' invasion/disclosure to take place over the next few months and the catching away of the child will be on the Day of Atonement, 9.28.20

Another highly significant series of events which will no doubt take place, will involve the collapse of the USA as a world power, and the rise of the kings of the east, especially China and her allies. How will this happen? Well, a virus that holds the potential of becoming a world-wide pandemic is in the news right now (2/2020). If the virus, which has shut down major cities in China, comes to the USA, it would cripple our infrastructure and economy; and not just the USA, but the whole world. Throw in some natural disasters like a devastating earthquake in California or along the Cascadia subduction zone, and the greatness of the USA would go up in smoke. Our enemies would take advantage of our weakness and possibly invade our borders, and/or further weaken our infrastructure and economy. When war comes to Israel, the United States will not be in a position to help her—we'll be fighting our own wars.

By late summer of 2020, the world will be on the brink of global warfare, (if it hasn't taken place already). We can also expect the arrival of fallen angels. Chaos, shortages, disease, lack of communication, and famines will spread until the Angel of the Lord arrives on the Feast of Trumpets to raise the dead and change the living who trust in Him. Ten days later, on the Day of Atonement, believers will be taken to heaven. Five days after that, on the Feast of Tabernacles, the first new believers in Christ will be sealed with the Holy Spirit.

The Third Sign

> "Then I saw another sign in heaven, great and marvelóus: seven angels having the seven last plagues, for in them the wrath of God is complete." Revelation 15:1

The third and last sign will take place on the 'day that no man knowns the day or hour'. This sign is in the *real* heaven—the abode of God. Seven beautiful angels will bring out the vials of God's wrath. Believers in heaven will see the sign and know that the judgment of the earth is about to begin. In Revelation, signs are meant for believers, so that they will know where they are in the cycle of redemption. The signs are the clock for God's people, even in heaven.

The first sign—the great sign of the woman in travail—appeared in the stars. The sign could be seen with one's eyes, even if only on a computer screen using an astronomy program like Stellarium. The second sign will be obvious and not secret in any way. Though Christians may have missed the significance of the first sign— the sign which initiated the 7 years telling us how close to the rapture believers actually were—they will not miss the second sign of the Dragon: a catastrophic war in Israel, a possible alien invasion and the rapture of believers.

Chapter 22: The Commandments of God & the Testimony of Jesus

Those who believe that 'the church' will not be present on earth during the last days, also believe that the in-dwelling and empowering ministry of the Holy Spirit will be taken from the earth at the same time that the 'church' is raptured. They believe that the 'age of grace' ends with the rapture, and that the new believers who come to Christ during the tribulation, after the rapture has taken place, are not under grace, but under the law. (The ministry of the Holy Spirit—which will be very active during the last days—is the subject of another chapter.)

However, we ourselves who confess Christ right now, are technically not living in the 'age of grace' either, but in the 'age of grace *through faith*', with 'faith' being the operative word. We know that faith is what pleases God:

> "*Without faith it is impossible to be well pleasing to him*, for he who comes to God must believe that he exists, and that he is a rewarder of those who seek him." Hebrews 11:6

> "For by grace you have been saved *through faith*, and that not of yourselves; it is the gift of God." Ephesians 2:8

> "Therefore we are always confident and know that while we are at home in the body, we are absent from the Lord; 7 for we walk by faith, not by sight. 8 We are courageous, I say, and are willing rather to be absent from the body and to be at home with the Lord. 9 Therefore also we make it our aim, whether at home or absent, to be well pleasing to him." 2 Corinthians 5:6-9

Faith is believing the promises of God—without seeing or possessing the fulfillment of the promises here on earth. Faith is believing that God can, and will, do everything He has said He will do. Faith *does* not—indeed *cannot*—come to an end until 'sight' begins, and people will continue to be saved by 'grace through *faith*' during the time before the visible return of Christ. Once 'every eye' sees Jesus at His Second Coming, *faith will no longer be possible*: for everyone *will see Him* and everyone will know the truth. Anyone who comes to Christ at *any time* prior to His visible return to the earth, comes to Him by *faith*—they are "saved by grace, through faith." That includes anyone who believes in Christ during the last of the 'last days'.

The Commandments of God

"The dragon grew angry with the woman, and went away to make war with the rest of her offspring, who keep God's commandments and hold Jesus' testimony." Revelation 12:17

The woman in this passage is Israel. She's the one who bore the Male child, the Messiah, who is to rule all nations. Layered beneath the symbol of the baby and the Male child, is the 'child', who represents believers who will be 'caught up'—raptured to God—and appear in His heavenly throne room. In addition to the Male child and the raptured 'child', verse 17 of Revelation 12 tells us that the woman has 'other children'! Who are these 'other children'?

The 'other children' are said to "keep the commandments of God and bear testimony to Jesus." We know that the 5th Seal martyrs also held the 'testimony' of Jesus:

> "When he opened the fifth seal, I saw underneath the altar the souls of those who had been killed for the Word of God, and for the testimony of the Lamb which they had." Revelation 6:9

The 5th Seal martyrs were killed for their testimony: their bodies were 'washed in the blood of the Lamb'. What 'testimony' did they bear? Were they also required to keep the 'commandments of God'?

I have already mentioned how Revelation uses words in a way that is unique to the book. I described the 'great tribulation' as being a case in point, where three distinct 'great tribulations' are depicted taking place during the last days. Two of them are mentioned in Revelation: the 'great tribulation' of the martyrs prior to the midpoint of the seven years, and the 'great tribulation' of believers who are seduced by 'Jezebel', and judged along with the Harlot at the 6th Trumpet, which will take place at the midpoint. In Matthew 24, Jesus describes a third 'great tribulation' which takes place after the midpoint/abomination of desolation and involves Israel and the escape of the remnant into the wilderness.

The 'testimony of Jesus' is a phrase which actually refers to a specific 'testimony' in the book of Revelation. At first glance, we might think that the martyrs who 'hold to the testimony of Jesus' are simply acknowledging that they are Christians—which they clearly are, even to the point of yielding their lives for Christ. The apostle John was exiled to the island of Patmos for 'bearing testimony to Jesus':

> "I John, your brother and partner with you in the oppression, Kingdom, and perseverance in Christ Jesus, was on the isle that is called Patmos because of God's Word and the *testimony* of Jesus Christ." Revelation 1:9

Those who 'hold to the testimony of Jesus' are believers who hold to the truth of the gospel. Like the apostle John, they are so convinced that Jesus is who He says He is, that they are willing to suffer and even lay down their lives for their faith.

In Revelation, there is another 'layer' to what it means to 'hold to the testimony of Jesus':

> "This is the Revelation of Jesus Christ, which God gave him to show to his servants the things which must happen soon, which he sent and made known by his angel to his servant, John, ² who testified to God's word and of the *testimony of Jesus Christ, about everything that he saw.*" Revelation 1:1,2

> "I fell down before his feet to worship him. He said to me, 'Look! Don't do it! I am a fellow bondservant with you and with your brothers who hold the testimony of Jesus. Worship God, for *the testimony of Jesus is the Spirit of Prophecy.*'" Revelation 19:10

What we can infer from these two passages is that the book of *Revelation itself*, including all the visions and all the prophecy contained within its pages, comprises the 'testimony of Jesus'. Believers who 'hold the testimony of Jesus', believe in the triumphal return of Christ to earth, the rapture of believers, the resurrection of the dead, the defeat of the Beast and the judgement of the Beast kingdom—everything foretold in the book. Those who believe this prophecy are said to 'hold the testimony of Jesus', which is the 'spirit of *prophecy*'. The last days *'ekklesia'* believe that God will do what He says He will do, as described in the Apocalypse. They believe that Christ will return and they demonstrate faith in God's revealed word by obeying His commandments.

Many people think that 'keeping the commandments of God' means that end time believers will need to obey the ten commandments and follow the Old Testament laws. The verse about 'keeping the commandments of God' seems to suggest that God 'reverts' to the 'old' way of doing things, moving from 'grace' back to the 'law'. True believers, people who come to Christ during the time of tribulation, would then need to demonstrate their faith in Christ by keeping God's commandments: observing the Sabbath, adhering to the kosher dietary laws and observing the feast days of Israel. But is this what 'keeping the commandments' means *in Revelation*?

Remember—Revelation is written in the Hebraic style which means that spiritual truth will be communicated *indirectly*, using imagery. This includes the use of symbols and 'layering' one scripture over another. Revelation will also point us to specific scriptures that enable us to decode the symbols. When we read about keeping 'the commandments of God', we are being directed to the Old Testament, to the book of Exodus and the giving of the law to the children of Israel:

> "Now therefore, if you will indeed obey my voice and keep my covenant, then you shall be my own possession from among all peoples; for all the earth is mine; 6 and you shall be to me a kingdom of priests and a holy nation.' These are the words which you shall speak to the children of Israel."

> "Moses came and called for the elders of the people, and set before them all these words which Yahweh commanded him. 8 All the people answered together, and said, 'All that Yahweh has spoken we will do.' " Exodus 19:5-8

God told the sons of Israel that if they would obey His voice and do as He commanded them, that they would be a kingdom of priests and a holy nation. God chose Israel, singling them out from among the nations of the world. He called them to be His special people. In this way, the nation of Israel is a type of the 'ekklesia', the 'called out' people of God, and Israel in Sinai is even referred to as the 'church in the wilderness':

> "This is he who was in the assembly in the wilderness with the angel that spoke to him on Mount Sinai, and with our fathers, who received living revelations to give to us." Acts 7:38

Moses went up the mountain to speak with God. He came down the mountain to deliver God's word to the people below. Moses then went back up the mountain to tell God what the people said. God's commands were always delivered via an *intermediary*. Reading through chapter 19 of Exodus, we know that the people did not hear from God directly. The commands of God were given via an intermediary (Moses) and the passage in Acts 7 tells us that God spoke first to 'the angel' who then passed the commands to the man, Moses. So the commandments given to the nation of Israel when they were at Mount Sinai were first given by God to an angel, who passed them on to Moses who then delivered the commands to the people.

The 'revelation' of end time events—including God's new commandments to His end time people, follows the same pattern of communicating His commands through the use of an *intermediary*. The 'revelation' originated with God, who delivered the message to His Son. However, Jesus is not the one who passed the message on to John.

Jesus' deity is confirmed in Revelation 1:1, because He, like His Father, used an angelic intermediary to communicate the end time revelation to John. Jesus gave the message to an angel, who then passed it on to the apostle John who wrote it in a book for us—a book which carries a curse for anyone who tampers with its contents, and bestows a blessing to all who 'keep' the message of the book.

> "Now I, John, am the one who heard and saw these things. When I heard and saw, I fell down to worship before the feet of the angel who had shown me these things. 9 He said to me, 'You must not do that! I am a fellow bondservant with you and with your brothers, the prophets, and with those who keep the words of this book. Worship God.' " Revelation 22:18,19

> "Blessed is he who reads and those who hear the words of the prophecy, and keep the things that are written in it, for the time is near." Revelation 1:3

Revelation is the very last word we have from God, recorded in the very last book of the Bible. Yet it is a message given to us 5th hand—through 4 intermediaries: from God to Jesus to an angel to John to the written book of Revelation! No wonder both Jesus and John emphasized that the testimony they were giving was true and they represented themselves as faithful witnesses to the visions entrusted to them by God! Even the angel who gave the message to John declared the truth of his words:

> "He said to me, "Write, 'Blessed are those who are invited to the wedding supper of the Lamb.' " He said to me, 'These are true words of God.'10 I fell down before his feet to worship him. He said to me, 'Look! Don't do it! I am a fellow bondservant with you and with your brothers who hold the testimony of Jesus. Worship God, for the testimony of Jesus is the Spirit of Prophecy.' " Revelation 19:9, 10

When Revelation refers to the 'commandments' of God, the first thing we need to understand is that whatever 'commandments' are given in Revelation were delivered with the same authority, and in the same manner, that the Law was delivered to the children of Israel in the wilderness.

This method of communication—using an intermediary—also applies to the messages delivered to the seven churches. Notice that seven angels deliver Christ's messages to the 7 churches in chapters 2 and 3, as seen in the following 2 examples:

"To the angel of the church in Ephesus write..." Revelation 2:1
"And to the angel of the church in Smyrna write..." Revelation 2:8

The seven 'stars' that the glorified Christ holds in His hands, represents the angels of these seven churches:

> "The mystery of the seven stars which you saw in my right hand, and the seven golden lamp stands is this: The seven stars are the angels of the seven assemblies. The seven lamp stands are seven assemblies." Revelation 1:20

The word for 'angel' can also be translated 'messenger'. For many years Bible scholars thought that the 'angel' of each of the seven churches was its pastor, the one who delivered the 'message' from God each Sunday. These scholars did not understand that the 'angel' of the church had nothing to do with a local pastor declaring the gospel; but was another proof of the deity of Christ. Like His Father, Jesus does not give messages to the church directly, but through the agency of an intermediary, in this case, the angel of each assembly.

Each of the seven letters to the seven churches contain God's commands to a special group of end time believers. Everything written in the letters to the seven churches is, in essence, a command of God which needs to be obeyed. The believers in these churches are not called to obey the 10 commandments or the dietary laws of ancient Israel, but to keep the specific commandments of God contained within the letters to the seven churches, and the commands found in Revelation as a whole!

> "Blessed is he who reads and those who hear the words of the prophecy, and *heed the things which are written in it*; for the time is near." Revelation 1:3

Believers are called to 'heed' or 'keep' the things which are *written in the book of Revelation*. The 'commandments of God and the 'testimony of Jesus', consist of everything written to the end time saints contained within the book of Revelation.

Just before the midpoint, believers who keep the commandments of God and the testimony of Jesus, will be martyred and appear in heaven, as represented by the 5th Seal martyrs and the great multitude that appears before God's throne in Revelation 7. The 'woman' has 'other children' who will need to endure *after* the midpoint, after Israel flees into the wilderness. These 'other children' will need to keep the commandments of God and hold onto their faith in Jesus. They appear victorious in Revelation 15, standing as Over-comers before the throne of God.

The 'Commandments' of God in the Letters to the Seven Churches

As we have already discovered, God's commands to the *'ekklesia'* during the last days will not be about keeping the Sabbath or adhering to any previous commandments issued by God. His commands in Revelation are *completely new*—a revised set of instructions for believers living in a very unusual period of time, in unprecedented circumstances.

God's commands to each of the seven churches are specific to a particular gathering, with different commands being given to different churches. Each group is given warnings and promises which are directed to that group of believers in particular, being personalized according to the issues and needs of each assembly. The church of Smyrna, for example, is told not to fear the persecution that is about to come upon them. If they are faithful unto death, they will receive the crown of life. The commandments contain blessings and the promise of rewards for those who persevere in obedience and faithfulness. In the case of the *'ekklesia'* at Smyrna, they are told that they will be given a 'crown of life' and they will not be subject to the second death:

> "Don't be afraid of the things which you are about to suffer. Behold, the devil is about to throw some of you into prison, that you may be tested; and you will have oppression for ten days. Be faithful to death, and I will give you the crown of life. [11] He who has an ear, let him hear what the Spirit says to the assemblies. He who overcomes won't be harmed by the second death." Revelation 2:10, 11

In addition, every church is commanded to heed the voice of the Spirit:

> "He who has an ear, let him hear what the Spirit says to the churches."

The Spirit Himself will testify to the truth of the messages in each of the letters. The Holy Spirit will personally confirm the words of God and the words of Christ to each individual, in each assembly, *if* they have 'spiritual' ears that are working. The Spirit adds His 'Amen!' to the commandments of the Father and the Son in the book of Revelation. The Spirit will be present to encourage and enable believers to persevere during the very difficult last days.

Chapter 23: The Seven Letters to the 144,000 of Israel

Revelation is an integrated book. Everything in the book, beginning with chapter 1, is a part of the same body of stories; and much of Revelation has to do with how the priests of God are brought into the heavenly Holy of Holies. This is not the story of how the Bride is raptured into heaven, but a story of how God's priests arrive in His presence.

Determining the Recipients of the Seven Letters

Believers, both now, and those who will come to Christ during the last seven years before the Second Coming of Christ, are *all priest/kings*. (The believers who will be beheaded during the reign of the Beast will be resurrected and they will rule with Christ on earth. We are also specifically told that they will be 'priests to God'.) The story is told via symbols and imagery. Every detail in the book is important, and tells us something about the characters, the plot and timing of events. This includes all the details found in Revelation chapters 1-3 which includes the letters to the seven churches.

When John encountered the vision of the glorified Christ in chapter one, he gave us a description of what he saw: one like a Son of Man, with eyes like flames of fire, dressed in a robe with a golden sash, and so on. But the description of Christ in chapter one does not give us the complete description: the description is actually continued in each of the 'greetings' to the letters to the seven churches.

Who exactly are the recipients of the letters? And what is Christ's relationship with these churches? We'll need to examine the details closely, and use the process of elimination to find the answer to that question. We'll compare what we find in these 3 chapters with other passages in Revelation in order to deduce the identity of the recipients of the letters.

Here's what we know:

1. The letters were not written to first century believers. Revelation was written to people who will be alive just prior to the return of Christ.
2. The letters do not describe successive eras of church history, beginning with the apostles through to the present age. For the most part, there is no history in Revelation.

Here's what we can deduce:

1. Because there is no warning against taking the mark of the Beast, nothing about the Antichrist or the False Prophet, we can assume that the people to

whom the letters are addressed, will *not* be present on the earth *after* the midpoint of the seven years when the Beast/Antichrist begins his reign.

2. This eliminates the Over-comers of Revelation 15, who 'overcome' because they don't take the mark; and it also eliminates those who are beheaded by the Beast. These people clearly ARE warned against taking the mark, worshipping the Beast etc, by the 'gospel angels' in Revelation 14, at the time the Beast starts to rule.

3. The rapture of present day believers (as depicted by the child being caught up), is one of the first things that will need to take place. The only 'warning' given to believers, is the one found in Revelation 12:5: that the dragon will attempt to devour the child. We know this will not work, and the child will enter into heaven without facing additional trials. The 'Mighty Angel' in Revelation 10, tells us that once the dead are raised and the living are changed, that there will be "no more delay". The rapture of present day believers into the throne room of God will be the trigger for the rest of the end time events. Therefore, the letters were not written to those of us who believe in Christ as of the time of this writing.

Remaining believers left to be considered:

- Gentile believers who will be martyred before the midpoint.
- The 144k of Israel.

We know that multitudes of people will be martyred just prior to the midpoint and we know that the Harlot/earth dwellers will be responsible for their deaths. Martyrdom is described in the letter to the church of Smyrna. We also see that only 'some' of the people to whom this letter is addressed will be killed or imprisoned, which means that some (or most) will *not* be killed. This would seem to eliminate the great multitude of martyred Gentile believers from "every tribe, tongue, people and nation" that we see before the throne of God in Revelation 7.

That leaves the 144K of Israel. Let's see if there are clues that indicate that the letters may be addressed to the 144K.

Sitting or Standing: Identifying 'Over-comers'

As we have already seen, most people who study Revelation tend to use the 'Greek' method of interpretation, rather than the Hebraic style. They begin interpreting the book starting with the seven letters to the seven churches. They assume that, chronologically speaking, the instructions given in the letters must apply to believers early in the 'story'. Many believe that each 'church' represents the successive 'ages' of church history, or, they may apply the letters to the first century believers. The problem with interpreting the book using the seven letters as the foundation of the story, is that we don't even know who all the characters are yet! It's not until we read much further into the book that we are told who all the players are. The 'foundation' of the book is not laid out chronologically, chapter by chapter, but symbolically; and it is imperative that we see the book as a *whole* before we attempt to identify the particulars.

The child and the woman are both rescued from Satan: the child, by being 'caught up, and the woman by being carried into the wilderness on "eagle's wings". Though both will be persecuted by Satan, neither the child nor the 'woman' are called to 'overcome'. Both the child and the woman will be delivered by God. The 'child' will be raptured and the 'woman' will be taken to a place of safety in the wilderness. The 24 Elders in the throne room of God are meant to be equated with the 'child' of the woman. They are seated on thrones in God's throne room, which is the destination of the raptured child.

The fact that the 24 Elders are *seated* means that they have already been rescued and that they were not required to be 'over-comers' the way the rest of the believers during the end times will need to be victorious. Those who must engage in spiritual warfare during a time of persecution and tribulation, will conquer through 'standing'. "Standing" in the scriptures, is how one gets the victory over the enemy:

> "Finally, be strong in the Lord and in the strength of his might. Put on the whole armor of God, that you may be able to stand against the wiles of the devil. For our wrestling is not against flesh and blood, but against the principalities, against the powers, against the world's rulers of the darkness of this age, and against the spiritual forces of wickedness in the heavenly places. Therefore put on the whole armor of God, that you may be able to withstand in the evil day, and having done all, to stand. 14 Stand therefore, having the utility belt of truth buckled around your waist, and having put on the breastplate of righteousness, and having fitted your feet with the preparation of the Good News of peace, above all, taking up the shield of faith, with which you will be able to quench all the fiery darts of the evil one." Ephesians 6:10-16

There are several divisions of 'priests' who described as 'standing' in heaven.

- The martyrs of the Harlot. The vast multitude of believers standing before the throne (Rev. 7);
- The 144K who 'follow the Lamb' (Rev. 14)
- The raptured 'over-comers' who stand before the sea of glass in heaven. (Rev. 15)

- The martyrs of the Beast who are resurrected at the return of Christ (Rev. 20). The Greek word 'resurrect' means 'to stand'! All of these groups must persevere in their own ways, gaining the victory through faithfully 'standing' with Christ.

The martyrs of the Harlot must 'overcome' through the 'blood of the Lamb'. They overcome by 'loving not their lives, willingly laying them down for Christ at the time of the ten days of persecution during the first half of the 'tribulation'.

The 144K must 'overcome' by enduring the persecution they will suffer at the hands of their fellow Jews. In addition, some will be imprisoned and some will be martyred during the ten day purge of the Harlot. This also takes place before the midpoint.

Those living during the reign of the Beast—both the martyrs of the Beast, and those that remain alive until the Lord comes to get them—must overcome by not taking the mark of the Beast, or worshiping the Beast or its image during the last half of the seven years.

The process of elimination...

The letters to the seven churches were written to those who must 'overcome', who must be victorious over their foes. This eliminates the present day church and the remnant of Israel as being the 'over-comers'. Both of these groups will be 'delivered', with no need to 'overcome'.

As we read through the seven letters, we see references to "Jews who are not Jews" and the "synagogue of Satan". These clues (among others) suggest that the 144K may be the intended recipients of the letters. The 144K will be the people who will be the very first to receive Christ once the 'child' is in heaven. These new Israeli believers will be persecuted almost immediately upon their 'sealing' and, as Jesus warned, their greatest enemies will be members of their own families!

The seven churches, represented by the seven candlesticks, are assemblies of Israelite believers. The 144K of Israel will be the "ekklesia", the 'called out ones', the apostles of the Lamb to whom the letters are addressed. The letters to the seven churches are placed early in the book of Revelation because the people to whom the instructions apply, will be the first to need the guidance they offer! So though Revelation is not deciphered chronologically, the chapters *are placed* in the right order, according to who will actually benefit from their contents during the last days!

Chapter 24: Firstborn, First Fruits

The One who knows the beginning from the end, chose to embed pieces of the end time story within the pages of both the Old and New Testaments. We have already seen how various Old Testament scriptures were 'layered' into the prophetic narrative of the Two Witnesses in Revelation. The origin of the Harlot—"Mystery Babylon"—was found in the Genesis account of the tower of Babel and Nimrod. We saw how Revelation provided clues in the form of 'coded' words telling us where to look in the scriptures to find the 'rest of the story'.

Two other very important templates are embedded scripture: the seven feasts of the Lord and in the harvest pattern of Israel. Both of these have to do with our redemption and *the order* in which God's people will arrive into heaven's throne room. Understanding the role of the 'first born' and their birthright adds another layer of illumination as well.

It's as though God had taken His choice spiritual 'jewels' and skillfully set them into the glorious end time narrative with beautiful precision. In many ways, Revelation is both the pinnacle and convergence of all scripture, drawing from the wealth of biblical prophecies, stories, rituals and symbols in order to create a sublime picture of the victory of Christ and the future bliss of His called out and chosen people, the '*ekklesia*' of God.

The "First Born-First Fruits" Pattern

In order to grasp the intricacies of God's end time plans and purposes, the student of Revelation needs to be familiar with Old Testament types and shadows. Of special importance are those types which relate to the harvest festivals in Israel, and in particular, that portion of the harvest known as the 'first fruits', and its related concept, the 'firstborn' son.

Jesus used agricultural metaphors and analogies when talking about the end time gathering of God's people, as well as the 'ingathering' of the wicked. The parable of "The Sower" (Matthew 13:3-9,18-23) and the parable of "The Wheat and the Tares" (Matthew 13:24-30) are two examples of Jesus using agricultural symbols when speaking about the end of the age:

> "He answered them, 'He who sows the good seed is the Son of Man, 38 the field is the world, the good seeds are the children of the Kingdom, and the darnel weeds are the children of the evil one. 39 The enemy who sowed them is the devil. The harvest is the end of the age, and the reapers are angels.' " Matthew 13:37-39

First Fruits, Firstborn...

In the Bible, we read that God commanded the children of Israel to give Him the first portion of everything: their crops, the first issue of their herds and even their firstborn males:

> "All that opens the womb is mine; and all your livestock that is male, the firstborn of cow and sheep. 20 You shall redeem the firstborn of a donkey with a lamb. If you will not redeem it, then you shall break its neck. You shall redeem all the firstborn of your sons. No one shall appear before me empty." Exodus 34:19, 20

> "You shall observe the feast of weeks with the first fruits of wheat harvest, and the feast of harvest at the year's end. 23 Three times in the year all your males shall appear before the Lord Yahweh, the God of Israel." Exodus 34:22,23

The males of Israel were to appear with their 'first fruits' offering three times a year: at the celebration of Passover/Unleavened Bread in the spring; at the Feast of Weeks,(also known as Pentecost or Shavuot) in the early summer; and at the Feast of Ingathering also known as the Feast of Tabernacles (or Sukkot) in the fall.

A sheaf of the first fruits of the barley harvest was presented at Unleavened Bread. Two loaves of leavened bread (among other things) were presented at the first fruits of the wheat harvest at Pentecost, and the first fruits of the olives, grapes and other fruits were presented at Tabernacles.

The firstborn son is a kind of 'first fruits'

The firstborn of the children of Israel and the firstborn of the animals belonged to God:

> "Yahweh spoke to Moses, saying, 2 'Sanctify to me all the firstborn, whatever opens the womb among the children of Israel, both of man and of animal. It is mine.' " Exodus 13:1,2

Firstborn sons were redeemed:

The firstborn of clean animals were sacrificed to the Lord. The firstborn son was not sacrificed, but 'redeemed':

> "When the days of their purification according to the law of Moses were fulfilled, they brought him up to Jerusalem to present him to the Lord

[23] (as it is written in the law of the Lord, 'Every male who opens the womb shall be called holy to the Lord'), [24] and to offer a sacrifice according to that which is said in the law of the Lord, 'A pair of turtledoves, or two young pigeons...' " Luke2:22-24

The Birthright of the Firstborn

The firstborn son was entitled to the double portion of the father's wealth and honor, and held a preeminent place in the family. This privilege was called the 'birthright'.

The birthright was the *promise of future blessing* reserved until the time the firstborn son reached majority age or upon the death of the father. The birthright was a unique opportunity not granted to every child. The birthright came to the firstborn son through no merit of his own, but simply because he was born first!

However, the birthright had certain conditions attached to it, and the birthright was only the *promise* of future blessing. It could be 'lost' or even sold. Esau sold his birthright to his brother, Jacob, for a bowl of soup. Jacob's oldest son, Reuben, forfeited his birthright through having sexual relations with his father's concubine. Neither Esau or Reuben were totally disinherited, and they continued on as sons, but they lost the preeminence that could have been theirs as the first-born.

The nation of Israel is also God's 'firstborn':

"You shall tell Pharaoh, 'Yahweh says, Israel is my son, my firstborn." Exodus 4:22

Israel was chosen from among the nations of the world to be doubly blessed by God. As God's 'firstborn' they were entitled to the 'birthright' not offered to the rest of the nations of the world. This birthright included the promised land, the covenants, the temple and the Messiah. They were to be a blessing to the rest of the world by sharing the blessing of the birthright with the nations.

The Levites/priests replaced the 'firstborn':

The sons of Levi belonged to God as well, with the tribe of Levi being chosen from among the 12 tribes to take the place of the firstborn sons of all the tribes. The special honor of serving God as priests in the tabernacle, and later in the Temple, was their 'birthright':

"Yahweh spoke to Moses, saying, [12] "Behold, I have taken the Levites from among the children of Israel instead of all the firstborn who open the womb among the children of Israel; and the Levites shall be mine." Numbers 3:11-12

Levites and priests who were not faithful were set aside. Nadab and Abihu who offered 'strange' fire to the Lord were killed. (Leviticus 10:1-3) Eli's priestly line was discontinued due to his failure to discipline his sons. (1 Samuel 2:12-36) In addition, any of the priestly line who had a physical defect were not permitted to serve in the temple.(Leviticus 21:16-24)

Christ is God's 'firstborn':

"When he again brings in the firstborn into the world he says, "Let all the angels of God worship him." Hebrews 1:6

When the writer of Hebrews referred to Jesus as the 'firstborn', he did not mean that the Eternal Son was a created being. Rather the term, 'firstborn', indicates Jesus' unique status among humanity; and that Jesus is entitled to receive the 'double-portion' inheritance, including the preeminence reserved for the first born son.

Firstborn, first-fruits, chosen, consecrated and sanctified are all words the Bible uses when referring to people and things that belong to God in a unique way. All of these are specifically chosen, set apart or 'called out' from a larger group or entity.

We know that God chose Israel out of the larger entity of the nations of the world. The tribe of Levi was then chosen out of all the 12 tribes to be the priestly tribe. The Messiah came as 'firstborn' out of the tribe set apart to produce the kings of Israel, the tribe of Judah.

When the firstborn of the flock or herd was given to God through sacrifice, it was offered in faith that there would be more offspring to take its place in the future. When people gave the first fruits of their crops, they were demonstrating faith in God's promise of a greater harvest to come. God takes 'His pick' of the first issue of herds, crops and sons before His people enjoy their portion.

The church is also God's 'firstborn'

"But you have come to Mount Zion and to the city of the living God, the heavenly Jerusalem, and to innumerable multitudes of angels, [23] to the festal gathering and assembly of the firstborn who are enrolled in heaven, to God the Judge of all, to the spirits of just men made perfect." Hebrews 12:22,23

God has a special group of 'called out' people whom He has separated from humanity and they have been designated to serve Him as priests and kings forever. Like the tribe of Levi who were separated out to be God's priests, and the tribe of Judah who received the royal blessing, we have been chosen to receive a 'double portion' in the age to come as both priests and kings.

"But you are a chosen race, a royal priesthood, a holy nation, a people for God's own possession, that you may proclaim the excellence of him who called you out of darkness into his marvelous light." 1 Peter 2:9

"Grace to you and peace from God, who is and who was and who is to come; and from the seven Spirits who are before his throne; 5 and from Jesus Christ, the faithful witness, the firstborn of the dead, and the ruler of the kings of the earth. To him who loves us, and washed us from our sins by his blood—6 and he made us to be a Kingdom, priests to his God and Father—to him be the glory and the dominion forever and ever. Amen." Revelation 1: 4b-6

Once the Millennial reign of Christ begins, God will have already obtained His portion of the first fruits of mankind in the form of the 'ekklesia'—the 'called out ones'—the priests and kings who make up His Church. And as a type of the firstborn, the church will have entered into the 'double portion' of her birthright, being made 'royal priests', the double portion inheritance reserved for the Father's faithful children.

Mortal people who enter the Millennium, and the children who are born to them during the Millennium, will *never be a part of this group of glorified, firstborn saints*. However, if these mortal people remain faithful and loyal to Christ their King during the thousand years, they will enter into eternity as 'immortal-mortal' people, on a world without the presence of death, sin or evil; and they will dwell on a new, re-created earth:

"I saw the holy city, New Jerusalem, coming down out of heaven from God, prepared like a bride adorned for her husband. 3 I heard a loud voice out of heaven saying, 'Behold, God's dwelling is with people; and he will dwell with them, and they will be his people, and God himself will be with them as their God. 4 He will wipe away every tear from their eyes. Death will be no more; neither will there be mourning, nor crying, nor pain any more. The first things have passed away.' " Revelation 21:2-4

171

God's special 'called out' ones, those believers who, from Abel to the last tribulation saint, walk and live by faith during the time leading up to the visible return of Christ at His second coming, will live eternally in the place Christ has prepared for them: the New Jerusalem. At the time of the re-creation, believers who dwell in the Holy City will descend from heaven. God, the Lamb, and the inhabitants of the New Jerusalem will at that time, dwell on earth with mankind, forever:

> "But you have come to Mount Zion and to the city of the living God, the heavenly Jerusalem, and to innumerable multitudes of angels, 23 to the festal gathering and assembly of the firstborn who are enrolled in heaven, to God the Judge of all, to the spirits of just men made perfect, 24 to Jesus, the mediator of a new covenant, and to the blood of sprinkling that speaks better than that of Abel." Hebrews 12:22-24

First fruit feasts

Three times a year the people of God were to bring the first fruits of their harvest into the temple. These gatherings celebrated the first fruits of the crops that were harvested; the barley crop at First Fruits/Passover; the wheat at Pentecost and at Tabernacles the fall crops of the olives, grapes, other fruit.

The first fruits of the crops—like the firstborn sons—belonged to God in a special way. The 'crops', and the people the crops represented, were considered 'holy to the Lord'.

Year after year, the children of Israel brought their first fruits into the temple in Jerusalem. Though people were instructed to set apart (sanctify) the first fruits of their crops into God's house, the fulfillment of all first fruits festivals actually take place when special *people* are separated unto God for His service. The Nation of Israel was God's first fruits:

> "Israel was holiness to Yahweh,
> the first fruits of his increase." Jeremiah 2:3

The nation of Israel belonged to God in a unique way, taken out from among all the nations of the earth. They were chosen—not because of inherent greatness on their part—but because of God's sovereign choice.

> "Not only so, but Rebekah also conceived by one, by our father Isaac. 11 For being not yet born, neither having done anything good or bad, that the purpose of God according to election might stand, not of works, but of him who calls.12 it was said to her, 'The elder will serve the younger.' 13 Even as it is written, 'Jacob I loved, but Esau I hated.' " Romans 9:10-12

172

Christ is called the 'first fruits' of the the resurrection

> "But now Christ has been raised from the dead. He became the first fruit of those who are asleep." 1 Corinthians 15;20

Christ's first fruits resurrection is the guarantee of a greater harvest of resurrected souls to come.

The church is called first fruits:

> "Of his own will he gave birth to us by the word of truth, that we should be a kind of first fruits of his creatures." James 1:18

Believers will be the very first of God's creation to be sanctified and redeemed. All of creation holds the promise of a future renewal and redemption once the first fruits (believers) are brought into God's heavenly temple.

The first Christian in an area is called the 'first fruits':

> "Greet the assembly that is in their house. Greet Epaenetus, my beloved, who is the first fruits of Achaia to Christ. " Romans 16:5

In summary, the first fruits are that portion of the harvest that belongs especially to God, chosen from among a larger crop, set apart for His plan and purposes. The firstborn son is also a type of 'first fruits', redeemed and set apart for God. The firstborn son is entitled to a special portion of the inheritance called the 'birthright'. The birthright is the promise of a double blessing upon receiving the inheritance, but the birthright can be forfeited through immoral behavior or through despising the birthright itself.

Chapter 25: The 12 Tribes, the 12 Apostles and the 144,000 of Israel

In the scriptures, divine government is often symbolized by the number 12, and the number 12 is also associated with those who have been 'chosen' by God to have a unique part of His plan and purposes. God chose the 12 sons of Jacob to be the heads of the 12 tribes of God's people, Israel. Jesus called 12 men to be His disciples. These 12 disciples, also called apostles, would later become the foundation of the church.

The 12 tribes of Israel were entrusted with proclaiming God's covenantal message and representing His nature and character in the world. They were given the promises, the temple, the Law and the prophetic writings. The Messiah was born from the nation of Israel, descending from the tribe of Judah.

Ultimately, Israel did not fulfill the purpose for which she had been called. When, in the fullness of time, her Messiah came, the priests, scribes and Pharisees rejected Him and had Him crucified. Within 40 years, the Romans destroyed the temple and the nation was dispersed. God set Israel aside and chose believers in Messiah to take His blessing to the world. Paul tells us in Romans 11:25-30, that because of unbelief—expressed as Israel's rejection of their Messiah—the nation of Israel lost their special spiritual status and were temporarily 'set aside'. God will give Israel another chance after 'the fulness of the Gentiles comes in'; that is, after the bulk of Gentiles come to Christ.

During the last days, God will restore Israel to Himself, not because of any righteousness on Israel's part, but for the sake of their forefathers, the patriarchs. God's promises to Abraham, Isaac and Jacob will be fulfilled when Israel accepts Jesus as their Messiah, and then the nation will enter into the fulness of the plan God has for them.

The 12 Tribes

Jacob (also known as 'Israel') had 12 sons by four different women. Those sons and their descendants make up what we know of as the nation of Israel. When we come across lists of the names of the 12 tribes/sons of Jacob in the Bible, an astute observer will note that the same 12 names are not always included on the various lists. On some lists, a name of one of the sons of Jacob may be omitted and another name added in its place. For example, Joseph's two sons, Ephraim and Manasseh, replace Joseph's name in some lists. In Revelation 7, the tribes of Dan and Ephraim are omitted and Joseph and Manasseh are included. In all, there are 14 different names vying for 12 spots in any list of the 12 tribes of Israel.

We have already seen how through poor choices, Isaac's son, Esau, and Jacob's son, Reuben, disqualified themselves from inheriting the birthright. Treating the birthright with contempt, and living in gross immorality kept them from possessing the rights of the 'firstborn'. They still belonged to the family and received an inheritance, but they forfeited the preeminence that could have been theirs.

The 12 Apostles

God Himself chose the men who would become Jesus' disciples and apostles:

> "In these days, he went out to the mountain to pray, and he continued all night in prayer to God. 13 When it was day, he called his disciples, and from them he chose twelve, whom he also named apostles: 14 Simon, whom he also named Peter; Andrew, his brother; James; John; Philip; Bartholomew; 15 Matthew; Thomas; James the son of Alphaeus; Simon who was called the Zealot; 16 Judas the son of James; and Judas Iscariot, who also became a traitor." Luke 6:12-16

Jesus received the 12 disciples from God's hand as His personal stewardship, and He shared God's truth with them during His 3.5 year ministry. The night before He was crucified, Jesus gave them back to God, entrusting them to His Father:

> "I revealed your name to the people whom you have given me out of the world. They were yours, and you have given them to me. They have kept your word. 7 Now they have known that all things whatever you have given me are from you, 8 for the words which you have given me I have given to them; and they received them, and knew for sure that I came from you. They have believed that you sent me. 9 I pray for them. I don't pray for the world, but for those whom you have given me, for they are yours. 10 All things that are mine are yours, and yours are mine, and I am glorified in them.
>
> 11 "I am no more in the world, but these are in the world, and I am coming to you. Holy Father, keep them through your name which you have given me, that they may be one, even as we are. 12 While I was with them in the world, I kept them in your name. I have kept those whom you have given me. None of them is lost except the son of destruction, that the Scripture might be fulfilled.
>
> 13 "But now I come to you, and I say these things in the world, that they may have my joy made full in themselves. 14 I have given them your word. The world hated them because they are not of the world, even as I am not

of the world. 15 I pray not that you would take them from the world, but that you would keep them from the evil one. 16 They are not of the world, even as I am not of the world. 17 Sanctify them in your truth. Your word is truth. 18 As you sent me into the world, even so I have sent them into the world. 19 For their sakes I sanctify myself, that they themselves also may be sanctified in truth." John 17:6-19

The disciples were chosen by God, called by Christ and, with the exception of Judas, they confirmed their call by continuing with Christ to the end. The disciples were not perfect: Peter denied Christ, Thomas doubted Christ and Judas betrayed Christ. Through repentance and forgiveness, both Peter and Thomas recovered and maintained their 'called-out' status as the 'first fruits' of a future, larger assembly of believers. Judas lost his inheritance, and his salvation as well, in fulfillment of the Old Testament prophecies.

"Yes, my own familiar friend, in whom I trusted, who ate bread with me, has lifted up his heel against me." Psalm 41:9

"While I was with them in the world, I kept them in your name. I have kept those whom you have given me. None of them is lost except the son of destruction, that the Scripture might be fulfilled. " John 17:12

Matthias was chosen by casting lots to replace Judas:

"For it is written in the book of Psalms,
'Let his habitation be made desolate.
Let no one dwell in it;' and, 'Let another take his office.'

21 "Of the men therefore who have accompanied us all the time that the Lord Jesus went in and out among us, 22 beginning from the baptism of John to the day that he was received up from us, of these one must become a witness with us of his resurrection."

23 "They put forward two: Joseph called Barsabbas, who was also called Justus, and Matthias. 24 They prayed and said, 'You, Lord, who know the hearts of all men, show which one of these two you have chosen 25 to take part in this ministry and apostleship from which Judas fell away, that he might go to his own place.' 26 They drew lots for them, and the lot fell on Matthias; and he was counted with the eleven apostles." Acts 1:20-26

Paul was also chosen by Christ to be an apostle, and was personally taught by Christ after His resurrection:

"…and last of all, as to the child born at the wrong time, he appeared to me also." 1 Corinthians 15:8

"But I make known to you, brothers, concerning the Good News which was preached by me, that it is not according to man. 12 For I didn't receive it from man, nor was I taught it, but it came to me through revelation of Jesus Christ." Galatians 1:11,12

14 Names —and only 12 Positions!

Just as there are 14 different names as possible choices for the 12 tribes of Israel; there are also 14 different names of apostles, vying for 12 available 'apostolic positions'.

Just because someone is chosen and called as a first fruit/firstborn, does not mean that they automatically receive the preeminence and double portion reserved for the firstborn/first fruits. Judas lost position his forever—as well as his eternal salvation, being referred to as the 'son of perdition'. Peter and Thomas were close to the edge of losing—not their salvation—but the promise of the 'double portion' that God had so graciously offered them as Jesus' disciples.

The 144K of Israel

Like the 12 disciples, the 144K of Israel, (a symbolic 12,000 from each of the 12 tribes), will be offered a place of preeminence in God's eternal kingdom. In Revelation 14:4 we learn that the 144K on Heavenly Mount Zion are called 'first fruits to God and to the Lamb'. They are called 'first fruits' because they will be the first believers to come to Christ after the rapture of believers:

"These are those who were not defiled with women, for they are virgins. These are those who follow the Lamb wherever he goes. These were redeemed by Jesus from among men, the first fruits to God and to the Lamb." Revelation 14:4

The 144K were also said to have been 'redeemed' from the earth. The concept of redemption harkens back to the redemption of the firstborn who was 'redeemed' and not sacrificed. The promise to this firstborn group is the potential of entering into the special blessing reserved for the firstborn. One of their special blessings—their 'birthright'—will be to be taken from the earth before the 'hour of trial':

"I know your works (behold, I have set before you an open door, which no one can shut), that you have a little power, and kept my word, and didn't deny my name. 9 Behold, I make some of the synagogue of Satan, of those who say they are Jews, and they are not, but lie—behold, I will make them to come and worship before your feet, and to know that I have loved you. 10 Because you kept my command to endure, I also will keep you from *the hour of testing which is to come on the whole world, to test those who dwell on the earth.*" Revelation 3:8-10

Remember, the offer of the birthright itself is not a guarantee of actually *possessing* the birthright. The birthright is an opportunity to enter into a special blessing, a blessing reserved for the firstborn. Those called from the 12 tribes of Israel during the last days must be faithful and persevere in the face of trials and persecution—including the 10 days of bloodshed at the hands of the earth dwellers and the Harlot—in order to inherit the birthright. If they are martyred for their faith during the 10 days, they will be raised up and given the crown of life (Smyrna):

"I know your works, oppression, and your poverty (but you are rich), and the blasphemy of those who say they are Jews, and they are not, but are a synagogue of Satan. 10 Don't be afraid of the things which you are about to suffer. Behold, the devil is about to throw some of you into prison, that you may be tested; and you will have oppression (*tribulation*) for ten days. Be faithful to death, and I will give you the crown of life. " Revelation 2:9, 10

If they are tempted to compromise their beliefs and be unfaithful to the Lord, they will need to repent while they are able, in order to enter into the promises reserved for those who are victorious. (Pergamum)

"But I have a few things against you, because you have there some who hold the teaching of Balaam, who taught Balak to throw a stumbling block before the children of Israel, to eat things sacrificed to idols, and to commit sexual immorality. 15 So also you likewise have some who hold to the teaching of the Nicolaitans. 16 Repent therefore, or else I am coming to you quickly and I will make war against them with the sword of my mouth." Revelation 2:14-16

If they are lured into defilement by 'Jezebel', and they do not repent, they may forfeit the prerogatives of their high calling as first born. (Thyatira)

"But I have this against you, that you tolerate your woman Jezebel, who calls herself a prophetess. She teaches and seduces my servants to commit sexual immorality and to eat things sacrificed to idols. 21 I gave her time to repent, but she refuses to repent of her sexual immorality. 22 Behold, I will throw her and those who commit adultery with her into a bed of great oppression, unless they repent of her works. " Revelation 2:20-22

If they grow cold in their love for the Lord, they may lose their special position—their "lamp stand will be removed from its place", but their salvation is still assured:

> "But I have this against you, that you left your first love. 5 Remember therefore from where you have fallen, and repent and do the first works; or else I am coming to you swiftly, and will move your lamp stand out of its place, unless you repent." Revelation 2:4,5

In summary, every one of the 144K who will be present on Heavenly Mount Zion, 'will have self-selected' through maintaining their call; heeding and obeying the commands given to them by God through Christ, in the letters to the 7 churches.

They, like the 12 apostles, will experience tremendous difficulties and some of them will stumble along the way. If they repent and move forward in the power of the Spirit, they will keep their first fruits/firstborn status like Peter and Thomas maintained their status as 'first fruit' apostles through repentance. If they don't repent, those of the called among the 144K will be 'left behind' when Jesus takes this group in a rapture event—the rapture which will take place just before the 6th Trumpet/'hour of trial'. Those left behind will no doubt weep as did Esau when he sold his birthright for a bowl of pottage and then wanted it back:

> "Follow after peace with all men, and the sanctification without which no man will see the Lord... 16 lest there be any sexually immoral person or profane person, like Esau, who sold his birthright for one meal. 17 For you know that even when he afterward desired to inherit the blessing, he was rejected, for he found no place for a change of mind though he sought it diligently with tears." Hebrews 12:14,16-17

When Christ comes for the 144K, each one of this group of first believers must be ready or they will be left behind to endure the reign of the Beast. Should they have disqualified themselves for this rapture, they will still be saved, but they will not receive the double blessing which belongs to the firstborn/first fruits of Israel.

Chapter 26: The Holy Spirit and First Fruits

The Holy Spirit is God's first fruits offering to us! The Holy Spirit is the down-payment given to believers, assuring us that our final, complete redemption, including the glorification of our bodies, will take place:

> "Not only so, but ourselves also, who have the first fruits of the Spirit, even we ourselves groan within ourselves, waiting for adoption, the redemption of our body." Romans 8:23

The 'first fruits' sanctify the rest of the crop

The presence of the Holy Spirit dwelling in our spirit, lets us know that the rest of of 'us', our bodies and souls, will be made holy as well.

> "If the first fruit is holy, so is the lump. If the root is holy, so are the branches " Romans 11:16

Jesus, the 12 apostles and the 144K are all a type of first fruits. They are the first in a company of holy people from the various harvests of souls. They are the first to be sanctified by the Spirit and sent into the world. The first fruits company are not immediately taken into heaven in a rapture event. The first fruit feasts of the Lord have more to do with the ministry of the Holy Spirit—a ministry which includes sealing and setting individuals, or groups of people apart for service—than they do with identifying potential rapture dates.

The 'first fruits' are not taken out of the world, but sent into the world:

> "As you sent me into the world, even so I have sent them into the world. 19 For their sakes I sanctify myself, that they themselves also may be sanctified in truth." John 17:18, 19

The Old Testament saints, including the 12 apostles, will be glorified with the living, when the dead in Christ are resurrected and living believers are changed on a future Feast of Trumpets:

> "These all, having been commended for their faith, didn't receive the promise, 40 God having provided some better thing concerning us, so that apart from us they should not be made perfect." Hebrews 11:39, 40

God sent Jesus—the Firstborn/First Fruits of God—into the world as His ambassador:

"And we have seen and testify that the Father has sent His Son to be the Savior of the world." 1 John 4:14

"You know of Jesus of Nazareth, how God anointed Him with the Holy Spirit and with power, and how He went about doing good and healing all who were oppressed by the devil, for God was with Him." Acts 10:38

Jesus and the Holy Spirit

When Jesus began His ministry, the Holy Spirit marked Jesus (first-born/first fruits) as being the Christ by descending upon Him in the form of a dove. Then, 'full of the Holy Spirit', Jesus was driven into the wilderness to be tempted by the devil. After 40 days of temptation, He returned in the *power* of the Spirit. This indicated two different actions of the Spirit: filling and empowering.

> "Jesus, *full of the Holy Spi*rit, returned from the Jordan and was led by the Spirit into the wilderness. " Luke 4:1

> "Jesus returned in the *power of the Spirit* into Galilee, and news about him spread through all the surrounding area." Luke 4:14

The Holy Spirit marks those whom God chooses. He sets them apart from the rest of mankind (sanctifies) them, and then He empowers them for service. Jesus was marked at His baptism, sanctified in the wilderness and then empowered as He resisted all the temptations of the devil.

The Day of Atonement may have been the day when Jesus was baptized, the day the Holy Spirit came on Him in the form of a dove. Baptism is a picture of death and when Jesus went into the baptismal waters of the Jordan, He was, in effect, demonstrating His willingness to 'die' to Himself, and be raised as one of us, becoming our Representative. Like the first of two goats which were brought to the high priest in the temple on the Day of Atonement, and was slain, Jesus was set apart to identify with sinful man and would die a criminal's death on the cross. Then, like the second goat—the scapegoat which was spared—Jesus was driven into the wilderness by the Holy Spirit to be tested and tried. Jesus prevailed over all the temptations of the enemy and returned from the wilderness in the power of the Spirit.

The Holy Spirit and the Day of First Fruits

The Bible refers to Jesus as the 'Lamb of God'. Like the Passover lamb which was slain, and whose blood—when applied to the doorposts and lintel of the house, caused the 'death angel' to 'pass over' that home, Jesus was crucified on Passover and His blood will cover the sins of all those who apply the blood to their 'home'. Jesus was the Lamb of God who takes away the sins of the world. When Jesus died on the cross, He was made to be sin for us:

> "For him who knew no sin he made to be sin on our behalf, so that in him we might become the righteousness of God." 2 Corinthians 5:21

The Holy Spirit gave life to Christ

Jesus died on Passover and was resurrected from the dead on the feast of First Fruits, 3 days later. Jesus' dead body was given life by the Holy Spirit:

> "But if the Spirit of Him who raised Jesus from the dead dwells in you, He who raised Christ Jesus from the dead will also give life to your mortal bodies through His Spirit who dwells in you." Romans 8:11

However, the first 'death' Jesus experienced, was not physical, but spiritual, as the fellowship He had always known with the Father was broken while He hung on the cross. Though He Himself was sinless, when He took our sins upon Himself, He experienced the same kind of 'spiritual' death that all sinners experience: separation from God:

> "About the ninth hour Jesus cried with a loud voice, saying, 'Eli, Eli, lima sabachthani?' That is, 'My God, my God, why have you forsaken me?'" Matthew 27:46

When Jesus died, He went to Sheol, the place of the dead. While His body was still lying dead in the tomb, His spirit was given life. He was spiritually reunited with His Father through the agency of the Holy Spirit *before He was physically resurrected.* Jesus' first resurrection was spiritual, not physical. Like us, He had to be spiritually 'born again'...brought back into relationship with God:

> "Because Christ also suffered for sins once, the righteous for the unrighteous, that he might bring you to God, being put to death in the flesh, but *made alive in the Spirit.* " 1 Peter 3:18

The Holy Spirit was active on First Fruits: first in healing the rift between the Father and Christ by causing Jesus to made 'alive in the Spirit'; and then resurrecting Jesus' lifeless body.

The 12 Apostles and the Holy Spirit

The 12 apostles were chosen by God to be specially trained by His Son. The Holy Spirit worked through Jesus to instruct the 12 disciples, and sanctify them as they lived, ministered and were taught by Christ. The Holy Spirit was 'with' the disciples in the Person of Christ:

> "I have said these things to you while still living with you. 26 But the Counselor, the Holy Spirit, whom the Father will send in my name, will teach you all things, and will remind you of all that I said to you." John 14:25, 26

> "The Spirit of truth, whom the world can't receive, for it doesn't see him and doesn't know him. You know him, for he lives with you and will be in you." John 14:17

On the day of His resurrection, when the first fruits of the barley harvest were brought into the temple, Jesus breathed on His disciples, and imparted the Spirit to them in a unique way:

> "When therefore it was evening on that day, the first day of the week, and when the doors were locked where the disciples were assembled, for fear of the Jews, Jesus came and stood in the middle and said to them, 'Peace be to you.' "

> 20 "When he had said this, he showed them his hands and his side. The disciples therefore were glad when they saw the Lord. 21 Jesus therefore said to them again, 'Peace be to you. As the Father has sent me, even so I send you.' 22 When he had said this, he breathed on them, and said to them, 'Receive the Holy Spirit!' " John 20:19-22

This was a real impartation of the Holy Spirit—given only to the disciples—taking place on the very day that Jesus was resurrected! This impartation of the Spirit is distinct from the out-pouring of the Spirit that would take place fifty days later, with a larger group of 120 believers, on Pentecost.

The impartation of the Spirit by Jesus to the disciples on the day of First Fruits, indicates that the disciples were *sealed as first fruits*. They were the first to believe in Christ as the Messiah, and the first believers to be sealed by the Spirit when Christ breathed on them. This was yet another action of the Holy Spirit on the day of First Fruits. Christ was made alive in the Spirit, then bodily resurrected by the Spirit, and then the breath of the Spirit sealed the disciples—all on the day of First Fruits!

The Spirit and Pentecost

Fifty days later, the 12 disciples (including Matthias) would receive another, different impartation of the Spirit—this time an impartation of power coming from heaven itself—along with about 100 or so other people:

> "But you will receive power when the Holy Spirit has come upon you. You will be witnesses to me in Jerusalem, in all Judea and Samaria, and to the uttermost parts of the earth." Acts 1:8

> "Now when the day of Pentecost had come, they were all with one accord in one place. 2 Suddenly there came from the sky a sound like the rushing of a mighty wind, and it filled all the house where they were sitting. 3 Tongues like fire appeared and were distributed to them, and one sat on each of them. 4 They were all filled with the Holy Spirit and began to speak with other languages, as the Spirit gave them the ability to speak." Acts 2:1-4

After being empowered by the Spirit on Pentecost, Peter preached a sermon in which 3000 people repented, and then they, too, received the promise of the Spirit. God's intention was that the Spirit be given to all whom the Lord calls to Himself:

> "Peter said to them, 'Repent and be baptized, every one of you, in the name of Jesus Christ for the forgiveness of sins, and you will receive the gift of the Holy Spirit. 39 *For the promise is to you and to your children, and to all who are far off, even as many as the Lord our God will call to himself.'*" Acts 2:38, 39

The 12 disciples, plus the rest of the 100 or so disciples present with them in Jerusalem that day (120 in all), received power from on high on the very day that the 2 loaves of bread, the first fruits offering of the wheat harvest, were offered in the temple on Pentecost.

There is much symbolism in the feast of Pentecost that applies to the completed, finished work of preparing the disciples as a first fruits offering from Christ to God. The scriptures tell us "no one was to appear before the Lord empty handed", and that included Christ! Jesus presented HIS offering to God, His disciples; the number of disciples having now been multiplied by a factor of 10—from 12 to about 120 souls. The fruit of Jesus' death and resurrection and the empowerment of the Spirit, brought an immediate increase of those trusting in Christ, as the "40, 60 and 100 fold" were already beginning to spring up as a result of the one Seed that had been sown in death.

On Pentecost, God accepted Christ's offering of the 120 disciples by sending a spiritual fire from heaven, as tongues of fire rested on each person in the room. Just like the Spirit filled Christ at His baptism and then empowered Him after the temptation, the 12 disciples, as firstborn/first fruits also had a 'double' experience of the Holy Spirit: once on First Fruits when Christ breathed on them; and then again on Pentecost when they, along with others, were empowered by the Spirit.

In summary, the actions and activity of the Holy Spirit came to the fore at the resurrection of Christ on First Fruits. The apostles were also 'sealed' by Christ on First Fruits when He breathed the Spirit on them. From the resurrection onward the active presence of the Holy Spirit would become the primary way God would live and move in the lives of believers.

Chapter 27: The First Fruits of the Harvest of Souls

The first fruits feasts of Israel are not so much about the first harvest of crops as they are about the first harvest of souls who are set apart and sanctified. The disciples of Christ, who were the first fruits of Christianity, were empowered by the Spirit of God for service. Sanctified and filled with the Spirit, they were anointed and sent to proclaim God's message to the world.

Many people believe that when God chooses to take possession of His 'first fruit harvest', that the first fruits will be taken in a rapture or 'transfer' event of some kind, and brought into His presence in heaven. Because the 12 apostles weren't raptured on First Fruits or Pentecost, some people do not believe at the 12 apostles represented the first fruits presentation of souls to God, and that another group of people—perhaps the present day church—may actually be the first fruits of the Pentecost presentation.

Let me emphasize again: all first fruits offerings were sanctified and set apart in a special way, unlike the rest of the 'harvest'. They were not to be used by any one other than God. Jesus prayed specifically that God would *not* take His disciples out of the world, but that He would 'sanctify' these men and set them apart—not for an immediate departure into heaven—but for service in the world:

> "I pray not that you would take them from the world, but that you would keep them from the evil one. 16 They are not of the world, even as I am not of the world. 17 Sanctify them in your truth. Your word is truth. 18 As you sent me into the world, even so I have sent them into the world. 19 For their sakes I sanctify myself, that they themselves also may be sanctified in truth." John 17:15-19

The names of the 12 apostles, written on the 12 foundations of the New Jerusalem, indicate their special status in the world to come:

> "The wall of the city had twelve foundations, and on them twelve names of the twelve Apostles of the Lamb." Revelation 21:14

The ministry of the Holy Spirit is intimately connected with the 'first fruits' of each of the 'harvest' festivals of First Fruits, Pentecost and Tabernacles. On these first fruit feasts, the Holy Spirit sets apart and sanctifies individuals for service. The 12 apostles were set apart from all other people in the world. They were the first to believe on Christ and the first Christians to be given the Holy Spirit. The day they were set apart was on First Fruits, when the first fruits of the Barley harvest were offered.

On First Fruits, Jesus officially commissioned His disciples to go into the world. He set them apart for service to God:

> "So Jesus said to them again, 'Peace be with you; as the Father has sent Me, I also send you.' And when He had said this, He breathed on them and said to them, 'Receive the Holy Spirit.' " John 20:21-22

Fifty days later, the 12 apostles plus the rest of the 120 disciples at Pentecost would be filled with the power of the Spirit, on the same day the first fruits of the wheat were offered in the temple.

We can expect this same pattern—of a special group of people being sealed by the Spirit and then being sent into the world—to be repeated with the 144K of Israel who are also depicted as first fruits.

There is one yet unfulfilled first fruits feast: the 7 day feast of Tabernacles. The first fruits of the olive tree are offered at Tabernacles and since spiritual Israel is represented by an olive tree (Romans 11:17-24), the 144K (spiritual Israel) will most likely be sealed with the Holy Spirit and set apart for service at the time of the olive harvest in the fall, at the feast of Tabernacles.

Just as a great number of people—both Jews and 'proselytes/Gentiles' were filled with the Spirit at Pentecost, which took place 50 days after Jesus breathed on the 12 disciples at First Fruits; the impartation of the Spirit to the 144K will immediately be followed by the Spirit in-filling and sealing believing Gentiles as well:

> "After these things I looked, and behold, a great multitude which no man could count, out of every nation and of all tribes, peoples, and languages, standing before the throne and before the Lamb, dressed in white robes, with palm branches in their hands." Revelation 7:9

The Holy Spirit and the Feast of Tabernacles

The 144K can expect to be 'sealed'—to receive the Holy Spirit—on the Feast of Tabernacles, the only first fruits feast that has yet to have the first fruits sanctified. In Bible times, the first fruits offering was offered in faith in the promises of God, as a guarantee of a greater harvest to come. The 144K will be the first of Israel who will come to faith and they guarantee that more will follow.

Gentiles will receive the Spirit during that time as well. In addition to being a feast of the Jews, the Feast of Tabernacles was a feast that encompassed all nations of the earth. The seventy bulls which were offered during the 7 days of the feast—one bull for each for the symbolic 70 nations on the earth—testified to the universality of this feast of the Lord.

Jesus may have been speaking prophetically about the future out-pouring of the Spirit on a future feast of Tabernacles, at which time the last day believers will be filled with the Spirit:

> " Now on the last and greatest day of the feast, Jesus stood and cried out, 'If anyone is thirsty, let him come to me and drink! 38 He who believes in me, as the Scripture has said, from within him will flow rivers of living water.' 39 But he said this about the Spirit, which those believing in him were to receive. For the Holy Spirit was not yet given, because Jesus wasn't yet glorified." John 7:37-39

The Old Testament prophet, Joel, refers to an out-pouring of the Spirit coming upon all mankind as well:

> "It will happen afterward, that I will pour out my Spirit on all flesh;
> and your sons and your daughters will prophesy.
> Your old men will dream dreams.
> Your young men will see visions.
> 29 And also on the servants and on the handmaids in those days,
> I will pour out my Spirit. " Joel 2:28, 29

The invitation to drink of the Spirit is open to anyone who thirsts, whether Jew or Gentile, man or woman. If you are thirsty, you may come and draw the water of the Spirit of Life from the Person of Jesus Christ, the Giver of Life, and receive the indwelling Holy Spirit.

This is the same invitation issued by the Spirit and the Bride at the marriage supper of the Lamb at the end of the Millennium:

> " Then he showed me a river of the water of life, clear as crystal, coming from the throne of God and of the Lamb... 17 The Spirit and the bride say, 'Come!' He who hears, let him say, 'Come!' He who is thirsty, let him come. He who desires, let him take the water of life freely." Revelation 22:1,17

In summary, on a future feast of Tabernacles, the Holy Spirit will seal the first fruits of Israel, the 144K. The Spirit will come upon that first group of people from all Israel who will put their trust in their Messiah, Jesus. This new group of Israelite believers are symbolically represented by the 144,000 'servants of God'.

On the last day of the feast, the 8th day, all those belonging to the nations who come to Christ will be filled with the Spirit as well.

Chapter 28: Believers and the Gift of the Holy Spirit

All true believers are marked by God, being sealed with the Holy Spirit. The presence of the Holy Spirit in our hearts is the down-payment that guarantees our heavenly inheritance. The indwelling Holy Spirit assures us that God will make good on His promises to us:

> "Now he who establishes us with you in Christ and anointed us is God, 22 who also sealed us and gave us the down payment of the Spirit in our hearts." 2 Corinthians 1:21,22

Once we are given the gift of the Holy Spirit, we belong to God. We can be secure in the knowledge that all our sins—past, present and future—are forgiven and that we have an entrance into God's kingdom. Forgiveness of sins is the free gift of God—we are saved by grace through faith:

> "But God, being rich in mercy, for his great love with which he loved us, 5 even when we were dead through our trespasses, made us alive together with Christ—by grace you have been saved—." Ephesians 2:4,5

We receive the Spirit by faith as well:

> "…that the blessing of Abraham might come on the Gentiles through Christ Jesus, that we might receive the promise of the Spirit through faith." Galatians 3:14

Only those who have the Spirit of God to belong to Him:

> "But if any man doesn't have the Spirit of Christ, he is not his." Romans 8:9b

The Spirit of God in our hearts gives us assurance that we are God's children:

> "For you didn't receive the spirit of bondage again to fear, but you received the Spirit of adoption, by whom we cry, 'Abba!⁺ Father!' 16 The Spirit himself testifies with our spirit that we are children of God; 17 and if children, then heirs—heirs of God and joint heirs with Christ, if indeed we suffer with him, that we may also be glorified with him. " Romans 8:15-17

> "By this we know that we remain in him and he in us, because he has given us of his Spirit. " 1 John 4:13

God intends for us to live securely in the knowledge that He loves us and that He will be faithful to save all who trust in Jesus for the forgiveness of sins. The blood of Jesus is able to deliver believers from the wrath to come—the punishment which will inevitably fall on a sinful world. When we trust in Christ to forgive our sins, we are filled with the Holy Spirit by faith. The Holy Spirit is our assurance that God will keep His promises to us.

In summary, anyone who has received Christ by faith is given the gift of the Holy Spirit by faith. The presence of the Spirit in our hearts is our guarantee that our sins have been forgiven and that we will have eternal life with God in heaven.

Chapter 29: The Gospel of John and the Book Revelation

The 12 Apostles were a 'type' of the 144K of Israel who will, in the future, be God's new apostles during the last days. The 144K (not the actual number, but a representative and symbolic number) will follow the pattern of discipleship already established in the gospels, particularly in the Gospel of John. The main difference between the first group of 12 disciples and the 144K, will be that Christ will not be physically present with the 144K as He was with the twelve; but He has promised that He *will* be present in the Person of the Holy Spirit. The Holy Spirit's active role with the 144k is emphasized in each of the seven letters to the seven assemblies: "He who has an ear, let him hear what the Spirit says to the churches." Again, John is not speaking about believers hearing the literal voice of the Spirit, but the 'voice' speaking to their hearts. The Spirit's voice *will be the voice of Christ,* and to hear the Spirit, is to hear Christ.

The gospel of John was written by the same John who penned the book of Revelation. Echos of Revelation appear in the gospel record bearing John's name, and many scholars believe that John wrote his gospel *after* he had received the Revelation from Christ, and long after the other three gospels were written.

The number "7", a number we see throughout the pages of Revelation, also finds its way into the message of John's gospel. Seven times Jesus refers to Himself using the phrase, "I AM", essentially equating Himself with God. Out of the many miracles which Jesus performed, John recorded only 7 of Jesus' miracles, which he called 'signs'. These seven signs were specifically chosen to draw the reader's attention to *Christ's divine nature* which is the central theme of John's gospel. At the close of his gospel, John attested that Jesus performed many other miracles as well. (John 21:25) John recorded the following seven signs, which emphasize Christ's creative and life-giving power, and His authority over the forces of nature, were specifically chosen to emphasize Christ's deity:

1. changing water to wine
2. healing a nobleman's son,
3. healing a paralytic
4. multiplying the loaves and fishes
5. walking on the Sea of Galilee
6. healing a blind man in Jerusalem
7. raising Lazarus from the dead

Rather than calling these acts 'miracles', using the Greek word "*dunamis*", meaning an 'act of power', John refers to them as 'signs'—using the Greek word, "*sémeion*". A sign points, not to itself, but to something else; it attests to a greater spiritual truth. The miracles of Jesus recorded in the book of John were all signs meant to point the reader to Christ's divinity; emphasizing that He is the "I AM" and that He existed as a member of the Godhead from eternity past. John's gospel is less about narrating facts about Christ's life and ministry, as it is about pointing to the fact of His divine origin and nature.

In the Old Testament, God revealed His Name to Moses as "I AM WHO I AM" (Exodus 3:14). The Jews of Jesus' day understood that when Jesus referred to Himself as "I AM", He was equating Himself with the God of the Old Testament. Seven times in the book of John, Jesus uses the Divine "I AM" when speaking about Himself and, just as Revelation uses symbolism and imagery to convey spiritual realities, the gospel of John also employs the use of many symbols and metaphors to do the same thing. The seven "I AM's" in John's gospel are an example of Jesus using metaphors to equate Himself with the God of the Old Testament:

> "I am the Bread of Life" (John 6:35, 41, 48, 51)
> "I am the Light of the World" (John 8:12; 9:5)
> "I am the Door" (John 10:7)
> "I am the Good Shepherd" (John 10:11, 14)
> "I am the Resurrection and the Life" (John 11:25)
> "I am the Way, the Truth and the Life" (John 14:6)
> "I am the True Vine" (John 15:1,5)

The Father is the Essence of all these "I AM's"; and Jesus, as God's Son and Representative, came to reveal the essential heart of the Father to the world. The words of God are spiritual food, He IS light, He is the One who throws open heaven's door to all who will come to Him through His Son.

• *Jesus will be all these same things to the 144K during the last days: spiritual food, spiritual revelation, Shepherd and the way to the Father.*

Following the Lamb

The title that is most often used for Christ in Revelation is "the Lamb". John is the only gospel writer who refers to Jesus as the "Lamb of God":

> "Again, the next day, John was standing with two of his disciples, 36 and he looked at Jesus as he walked, and said, *'Behold, the Lamb of God!' 37 The two disciples heard him speak, and they followed Jesus."* John 1:35-37

The following passage in Revelation echos John's gospel, this time concerning the 144K, and not the early disciples:

"These are the ones who follow the Lamb wherever He goes." Revelation 14:4b

Both groups of 'first fruits'—the original 12 apostles and the last day apostles—the 144K of Israel—*follow the Lamb*. Both groups of disciples are chosen and called to follow Christ as His disciples and apostles.

Both groups of disciples belong to the Lamb and to His Father in a special way:

> "I saw, and behold, the Lamb standing on Mount Zion, and with him a number, one hundred forty-four thousand, having his name and the name of his Father written on their foreheads." Revelation 14:1

> "I revealed your name to the people whom you have given me out of the world. They were yours, and you have given them to me. They have kept your word. 7 Now they have known that all things whatever you have given me are from you, 8 for the words which you have given me I have given to them; and they received them, and knew for sure that I came from you. They have believed that you sent me. 9 I pray for them. I don't pray for the world, but for those whom you have given me, *for they are yours. 10 All things that are mine are yours, and yours are mine, and I am glorified in them. "* John 17:6-10

Both groups of disciples—the 12 apostles and the 144K of Israel—are said to 'follow the Lamb' and they both are 'first fruits', belonging exclusively to God and the Lamb.

John the Baptist and the Two Witnesses

John tells us that several of Christ's disciples had previously been disciples of Christ's forerunner, John the Baptist, who came preaching a message of repentance. The gospel of John provides patterns for interpreting Revelation, and because of this, we can expect that some of Christ's end time disciples, the 144K of the twelve tribes of Israel, will also be disciples of Christ's end time 'forerunners', the 2 Witnesses—Moses and Elijah.

Jesus likened the ministry of His cousin, John, with that of "Elijah, who is to come":

> "As these went their way, Jesus began to say to the multitudes concerning John, 'What did you go out into the wilderness to see? A reed shaken by the wind? 8 But what did you go out to see? A man in soft clothing? Behold,

those who wear soft clothing are in kings' houses. 9 But why did you go out? To see a prophet? Yes, I tell you, and much more than a prophet. 10 For this is he, of whom it is written, "Behold, I send my messenger before your face, who will prepare your way before you."

11 'Most certainly I tell you, among those who are born of women there has not arisen anyone greater than John the Baptizer; yet he who is least in the Kingdom of Heaven is greater than he. 12 From the days of John the Baptizer until now, the Kingdom of Heaven suffers violence, and the violent take it by force. 13 For all the prophets and the law prophesied until John. 14 *If you are willing to receive it, this is Elijah, who is to come.'*" Matthew 11:7-14

The 2 Witnesses will also preach a message of repentance, as symbolized by the sackcloth they wear:

"I will give power to my two witnesses, and they will prophesy one thousand two hundred sixty days, clothed in sackcloth." Revelation 11:3

Similar to the humble beginnings of John the Baptist's ministry in the wilderness of the Jordan, the ministry of the 2 Witnesses will likely begin in obscurity in a lonely place, preaching a gospel of repentance to those whom God draws to hear them, and proclaiming the necessity of repentance before the arrival of the King. Following the pattern of John, some of 144K—God's 'first fruits'—may be among the disciples of the 2 Witnesses. The Witnesses will lay a foundation of repentance from dead works, so that, when the time comes, these disciples will readily accept the call to 'follow the Lamb'.

John the Baptist was compared to a lamp:

"He was the burning and shining lamp, and you were willing to rejoice for a while in his light." John 5:35

The 2 Witnesses are also 'lights':

"These are the two olive trees and the two lamp stands, standing before the Lord of the earth." Revelation 11:4

In the Bible, light and lamps are often used to describe the revelation of spiritual truth and heavenly realities to the human heart, and both John the Baptist and the 2 Witnesses will have an anointing from the Holy Spirit to bring spiritual illumination to those with ears to hear.

In Revelation, the Holy Spirit is symbolized by the seven torches of fire before the throne of God in heaven. We know that John was filled with the Holy Spirit from his mother's womb and the Two Witnesses will also be anointed by the Spirit as prophesied in Zechariah:

> "This is Yahweh's word to Zerubbabel, saying, 'Not by might, nor by power, but by my Spirit,' says Yahweh of Armies." Zechariah 4:6b

The 2 Witnesses will prophesy, which means that they will speak forth God's message. The message given to John the Baptist was, "Repent, for the kingdom of God is at hand!". The message of the Two Witnesses will also include the necessity for repentance and the nearness of Christ's return to establish His kingdom on earth.

Because the Messiah will come twice—first as our sacrifice and then as our King, there must also be two forerunners: a forerunner for each coming of Christ. Both John the Baptist and the 2 Witnesses are forerunners for Christ:

> "This is Yahweh's word to Zerubbabel, saying, 'Not by might, nor by power, but by my Spirit,' says Yahweh of Armies." John 1:23

> "Remember the law of Moses my servant, which I commanded to him in Horeb for all Israel, even statutes and ordinances.

> 5 "Behold, I will send you Elijah the prophet before the great and terrible day of Yahweh comes. 6 He will turn the hearts of the fathers to the children and the hearts of the children to their fathers, lest I come and strike the earth with a curse." Malachi 4:4,5

John the Baptist was a type of 'Elijah who is to come'. John was the forerunner who announced Jesus' first coming and his job was to prepare the hearts of the nation of Israel to receive their Messiah. Elijah and Moses—the two end time Witnesses—will also be the forerunners of the Messiah during the days preceding the second coming of Christ. In addition to rebuilding the temple and killing the Scarlet Beast, their calling will also include encouraging Israel to turn to the Lord in repentance, as did John the Baptist.

Each of these forerunners have disciples: people who's hearts will have been prepared to receive the Lord. At the first coming of Christ, some of the disciples of John the Baptist were included among the 12 apostles of the Lord, and before the second coming of Christ, we can expect that some of the 144K of Israel will have first spent time as the disciples of the 2 Witnesses.

We have already seen how Jesus is represented as the Lamb of God in both the gospel of John and Revelation, and how the use of 'signs' and the number '7' also ties the two books to each other. There is yet another strong correlation between these two books as well: Jesus, who is the Lamb of God, is also presented to us as God's 'Faithful Steward'. Jesus is the One to whom God entrusted the stewardship of training each group of disciples—both the first century apostles *and* the last days apostles, the 144K.

The night before Jesus was crucified, He shared some final instructions with His disciples in the upper room. After sharing the Passover meal with His disciples, John records what many refer to as Jesus' 'high priestly prayer' in John 17. While many see Jesus in His role as our faithful High Priest in this passage in John, there is yet another, more accurate analogy: Jesus as God's steward.

At the close of one's stewardship, all stewards were required to give an account of how they handled the responsibilities entrusted to them, and Jesus was no exception. On the night He was betrayed, as His earthly life was coming to a close, Jesus gave an account to His Father concerning the stewardship of the 12 disciples. In the prayer recorded in John 17, Jesus' intention was not to intercede for the disciples as would a priest, but rather He was giving an account of His ministry—an account of His stewardship—especially as it touched upon the training of the twelve men entrusted to Him by God.

In this prayer, Jesus told His Father that He had performed the duties of a faithful steward; that He had given God's words to the disciples, and that all the disciples had come to believe that He was sent from God. He didn't lose any of the twelve except Judas, that the word of God might be fulfilled. Jesus then asked that God would protect and care for the disciples whom He loved, and that they would be 'sent out', just as Jesus Himself had been sent out by God into the world. He asked that they would be one, and that ultimately, they would see Him in His heavenly glory in the place He would prepare for them.

In the passages recorded in John chapters 13-16, a section of scripture also known as the "upper room discourse", Jesus gave final instructions and commandments to His disciples before He was about to be crucified. The most important commandment He gave them was a 'new commandment': they were to love one another *as He had loved them*. They were to wash one another's feet—that is, forgive and serve one another. *The goal of Christ's commands was to replicate among His followers the unity of heart and mind that exists between the Father and His One and Only Son.* Once Jesus was no longer with them in person, He would send the Holy Spirit to guide them in the truth and be their Teacher. Just as Christ had declared the words of the Father to the disciples, the Spirit would disclose the words of Christ to the disciples after His departure.

In addition to giving his disciples their final instructions before His crucifixion, Jesus also warned His disciples that they, too, would be persecuted. The persecution that Jesus received at the hands of the Jews would be shared by the disciples who would follow in His footsteps. Because they were not 'of the world', the world would hate them and deliver them up:

> "If the world hates you, you know that it has hated me before it hated you. [19] If you were of the world, the world would love its own. But because you are not of the world, since I chose you out of the world, therefore the world hates you. [20] Remember the word that I said to you: 'A servant is not greater than his lord.' If they persecuted me, they will also persecute you. If they kept my word, they will also keep yours. [21] But they will do all these things to you for my name's sake, because they don't know him who sent me." John 15:18-21

Jesus is the 'same yesterday, today and forever'. His commandments for His chosen ones have not changed since He first gave them to the disciples in the upper room, and we can be assured that they will not change in the future. His commandments to the 144K will be the same as the commands He gave His 12 disciples 2,000 years ago. Likewise, the 144K can expect to be persecuted for their faith in Christ, at the hands of the same people who persecuted Jesus and the early disciples—the Jews.

The gospel of John left us a record of Christ's accounting to His Father of how He handled the stewardship entrusted to Him by God. What this accounting tells us is that one of the roles of Christ during His earthly ministry was that of the Steward of God's household.

The book of Revelation also makes reference to Christ as the Faithful Steward. In Revelation chapters 1-3, we see Jesus symbolically portrayed as Eliakim, a relatively obscure Old Testament character, who was the royal steward of King Hezekiah. In ancient times, the royal steward had the same authority as the king in matters pertaining to the king's household. Eliakim replaced an unfaithful steward named Shebna. In Isaiah 22, Eliakim is dressed in Shebna's robe and sash, and he was given the keys of the house of David:

> "It will happen in that day that I will call my servant Eliakim the son of Hilkiah, [21] and I will clothe him with your robe, and strengthen him with your belt. I will commit your government into his hand; and he will be a fa-

ther to the inhabitants of Jerusalem, and to the house of Judah. [22] I will lay the key of David's house on his shoulder. He will open, and no one will shut. He will shut, and no one will open. " Isaiah 22:20-22

In Revelation 1, Jesus is wearing a robe with a golden sash:

> "I turned to see the voice that spoke with me. Having turned, I saw seven golden lamp stands. [13] And among the lamp stands was one like a son of man, clothed with a robe reaching down to his feet, and with a golden sash around his chest." Revelation 1:12,13

We might be inclined to pass over this description of Christ walking in the midst of the lampstands, not fully understanding the implications of the description given in this passage. It's easy to think that what we read about Christ in chapter one, is only a description of Christ in His glory, and that this description contains all the symbolism necessary to know the identity of the Individual who is standing before John. What we don't know, however, is that the description of Christ in chapter one, is actually *continued* in chapters 2 and 3, in the letters to the seven churches, with more defining details added. Each of the seven letters adds yet another aspect of the person of Christ to what we already know about Christ from chapter 1. Some of the descriptions of Christ given in the letters to the seven churches share characteristics with the description of Christ in chapter one. The commonalities are:

- the presence of Christ in the midst of the golden lampstands
- feet like bronze
- voice like many waters
- the seven 'stars' in His hand
- the sword of His mouth

In the letters to the seven churches, there are additional symbolic characteristics describing Christ that are *not* listed in the first chapter, characteristics that are necessary to know before we draw any conclusion about exactly *who* John saw standing before him in the first chapter, and what would be the end time role of that glorious Person.

Christ is always represented symbolically in Revelation. The descriptions given in chapters 1-3 were meant to point us to the passage in Isaiah about Eliakim, the steward of the king. We were meant to see Christ's relationship with the 144K as one of stewarding and training God's future first fruit apostles. It's only in chapters 2 & 3, that the description of Christ—which began in chapter 1—is completed, and it's not until Revelation 3:7—where we are told that Christ has the Key of

David—that we actually have the 'give away' clue, that Christ is being symbolically represented by Eliakim, the faithful steward:

> "He who is holy, he who is true, he who has the key of David, he who opens and no one can shut, and who shuts and no one opens, says these things." Revelation 3:7

In chapters 2 and 3 we read the following additional characteristics of Christ as God's steward:

- He is the Son of God
- He holds the 7 Spirits of God
- He is Holy and true
- *He has the Key of David*
- *He shuts and no one can open; and opens and no one can shut*
- "Amen"
- He is the Faithful and true Witness
- He is the Originator (Firstborn) of God's creation

Like Eliakim, Christ possesses the key of David, the keys to the King's house. What He "opens, no one will shut, and what He shuts no one will open". In those days, the eldest adult son was often given the stewardship of his father's household. We are told that Christ is the 'Son of God'. He holds the 'seven Spirits of God' indicating His divine nature. He is holy, true and faithful—all characteristics of a faithful servant. He is the firstborn, the one who is entitled to administer God's kingdom. He is the 'Amen', the 'so be it', who does the will of His Father.

In this way, Christ is positively identified as the Steward of God's house, the fulfillment of the prophetic type of Eliakim—each having received a stewardship from their respective Kings. Christ's 'stewardship' includes the care and instruction of God's servants: the 12 apostles at His first coming and, in the last days, the 144K of Israel.

In Revelation chapters 1-3, Jesus is seen taking responsibility for new group of servants—new disciples—and He will issue the guidelines, commandments and warnings that will be necessary for them to faithfully serve the Lord and successfully persevere in the faith. In the gospel of John, Jesus gave the *final* accounting of His stewardship in His 'stewardship' prayer, at the end of His three-and-a-half year ministry. In Revelation, at the beginning of a new stewardship over the 144K of Israel, Jesus furnishes the basic requirements for those under His care. The Holy Spirit will reinforce Christ's instructions as the future disciples listen to and heed the Spirit's voice.

Jesus is the steward over God's household, those who make up the '*ekklesia*' of God. Jesus has been granted the authority to issue commands on behalf of His Father, and He also has the ability to provide for the needs of the members of God's household out of the treasuries of heaven. In the letters to the seven churches, Christ identifies Himself as the ruler of God's house, with the authority to act on God's behalf; the goal being that none of the 'first fruits' of Israel would be disinherited from the birthright, and thus lose their special standing and status before God.

In order for all of the 144K to attain to the promise of the birthright, they must maintain their 'first fruits/firstborn' status. The 'double portion' of the birthright is theirs as long as they do not violate the conditions of the birthright, as did Reuben and Esau. Differentiating between the blessings of the birthright— which are preserved though righteous living—and the gift of salvation, which cannot be earned, is critical. The 144K cannot lose their salvation, only the pre-eminence that the birthright promises them if they overcome. One of the benefits of the birthright is the promise of being removed from the earth before the 'hour of trial or testing' begins. We have already noted that the 'hour of testing' refers to the destruction of the Harlot at the 6th Trumpet (in one hour, on a single day) on the very same day as the abomination of desolation, at the midpoint:

> "Because you kept my command to endure, I also will keep you from the hour of testing which is to come on the whole world, to test those who dwell on the earth." Revelation 3:10

The promise of being kept from the hour of testing is given to the 'called out ones' of the assembly of Philadelphia, but the church of Philadelphia is not the only church who received the promise that Christ will come for them. With the exception of the letter to the church of Smyrna, Jesus states that He is coming to *all* of the churches. If these believers overcome, they will be taken in the First Fruits rapture God has promised especially for them, a rapture which will take place in the spring of 2021. Later in this book, we'll be examining each of the seven letters in greater detail and we'll discover how the 144K can obtain the victory and the birthright.

In the parable of the 10 virgins in Matthew 25, Jesus told the story of five wise and five foolish virgins who were eagerly awaiting the announcement of the bridegroom's arrival. All ten were invited to attend the wedding—at night—and all brought lamps with them to light the way, but only the wise brought extra oil. Since it was nighttime, all ten virgins fell asleep while they were waiting. Suddenly they were awakened with the announcement of the bridegroom's imminent arrival. All of their lamps had gone out, but the 5 wise virgins who brought additional oil, simply refilled their lamps and were ready to go. The 5 foolish virgins, with no extra oil, tried to beg some oil from their friends, but to no avail. The unprepared virgins would have to go to the shops to buy more oil. While they were going, the 5 wise virgins were taken into the marriage feast. Later, the foolish ones begged entrance to the marriage feast, but were denied.

Jesus told this parable so that people would be ready for His coming. For the 144K, the door will be open to those who, like the 5 wise virgins, are spiritually prepared, with their lamps trimmed and who are carrying enough oil of the Spirit to light their path. For those of the 144K who were called, but failed to live up to the birthright—who failed to spiritually prepare—the door to heaven will be closed to them as it was to the five foolish virgins. Those 'left behind' will need to wait until the third rapture—the 'Over-comer' rapture, which will take place just prior to the day of the Lord/wrath of God.

Jew vs Israelite

Another similarity between the gospel of John and the book of Revelation is more subtle and regards the use of the words, "Jew" and "Israelite" (or 'of Israel'). Strictly speaking, a Jew is someone who can trace their lineage back to the tribe of Judah, or they are someone who hails from the part of Israel known as Judea. An 'Israelite' is someone who can trace their lineage back to *any* of the 12 tribes of Israel.

In both the gospel of John and Revelation, a 'Jew' generally carries a negative connotation. In John, there are numerous references to the 'Jews', who seek to test, trap, accuse, arrest and ultimately hand Jesus over to the Romans for crucifixion. Jesus warned His disciples that they would be put out of synagogues and even thrown out of their own families because of their faith in Him. Most of the persecution they would receive would come from 'the Jews'. In Revelation, it is the Jews who are of the 'synagogue of Satan', who persecute the 144K of Israel:

> "I know your works, oppression, and your poverty (but you are rich), and the blasphemy of those who say they are Jews, and they are not, but are a synagogue of Satan." Revelation 2:9

> "Behold, I make some of the synagogue of Satan, of those who say they are Jews, and they are not, but lie—behold, I will make them to come and worship before your feet, and to know that I have loved you." Revelation 3:9

We read the following in John's gospel, at the time Jesus called Nathanael:

> "When Jesus saw Nathanael approaching, He said of him, 'Here is a true Israelite, in whom there is no deceit.' "

Jesus did not call Nathanael a Jew, but an 'Israelite', one who's heart was true to God, who did not cling to the traditions of men: Nathaniel's heart was true, with no deceit. The book of Revelation also draws a distinction between those who are chosen from the 12 tribes of Israel, "who do not lie"—and those Jews "who do lie":

> "In their mouth was found no lie, for they are blameless." Revelation 14:5

> "Behold, I make some of the synagogue of Satan, of those who say they are Jews, and they are not, but lie—" Revelation 3:9a

What truth do the "Israelites" possess that the "Jews" do not? It's the truth about the Messiah! Just as the Jews of Jesus' day preferred their own traditions to the authority of God's Word and His commandments, especially as revealed through the Person and work of Christ, Revelation tells us that the Jews will do the same during the last days. The Jews—both in John's day and in the future—will not be interested in pursuing spiritual truth, but in preserving their position and traditions.

> "The chief priests therefore and the Pharisees gathered a council, and said, 'What are we doing? For this man does many signs. 48 If we leave him alone like this, everyone will believe in him, and the *Romans will come and take away both our place and our nation.*'" John 11:47, 48

> "Then Pharisees and scribes came to Jesus from Jerusalem, saying, 2 'Why do your disciples disobey the tradition of the elders? For they don't wash their hands when they eat bread.' 3 He answered them, 'Why do you also disobey the commandment of God because of your tradition?' " Matthew 15:1-3

Jesus said that He would bring division, with brother pitted against brother, and family members opposing each other:

> "Don't think that I came to send peace on the earth. I didn't come to send peace, but a sword. 35 For I came to set a man at odds against his father, and a daughter against her mother, and a daughter-in-law against her mother-in-law. 36 A man's foes will be those of his own household. 37 He who loves father or mother more than me is not worthy of me; and he who loves son or daughter more than me isn't worthy of me." Matthew 10:34-37

The most zealous persecutors of "Israelites"—those who believe in Jesus as the Christ—will be the Jews, whom Jesus refers to as being of their father, the devil:

204

> "You are of your father the devil, and you want to do the desires of your father. He was a murderer from the beginning, and doesn't stand in the truth, because there is no truth in him. When he speaks a lie, he speaks on his own; for he is a liar, and the father of lies. " John 8:44

The letter of 1 John also tells us about liars:

> "Who is the liar but he who denies that Jesus is the Christ? This is the Antichrist, he who denies the Father and the Son. 23 Whoever denies the Son doesn't have the Father. He who confesses the Son has the Father also." 1 John 2:22,23

When the explosive end time events get underway at the rapture of the child, the 144K of Israel will be awakened to the knowledge that *Jesus* is their Messiah! They will be the first people who come to Christ, almost immediately after we've been taken. Fast on the heels of their conversion, the 144K will be sealed, and then persecution will begin in earnest. These newly born again Israelites will be persecuted by fellow Jews, and some of the 144K will die at their hands.

Within a brief time, *anyone* who is a Spirit-filled believer in Christ, whether of Israel, or a Gentile, will be persecuted by the Harlot and the earth dwellers during the 10 days of persecution, which will take place before the midpoint. Those who die will be resurrected into their incorruptible bodies in heaven, and the 144K who are not martyred, who 'overcome', will be taken in their own rapture before the midpoint. Finally, during the last half of the 7 years, believers *and* the nation of Israel will be persecuted by the Beast. The remnant of Israel will be taken to a safe place in the wilderness, while believers who are still present on earth, who survive until the 3rd rapture, will be taken on a day that 'no man knows the day or hour' just prior to the wrath of God/Day of the Lord. Not all believers will survive the reign of the Beast—some will be beheaded and then be resurrected at the 2nd Coming of Christ at the end of the wrath of God.

Because the 144K will be the first to come to Christ, with the most to lose should they not persevere as over-comers, and because they will be the first group to suffer persecution, the opening chapters of Revelation—including the letters to the seven churches—are addressed specifically to them, to help them be victorious in the face of trial.

Chapter 30: Angels in Revelation

The book of Revelation records more angelic activity than any other book of the Bible. Both the fallen angels and God's holy angels populate its pages, appearing in almost all of the visions of Revelation. We see angels in heaven offering praise and worship to God. We read about Michael and his angelic army; trumpet angels and bowl angels; angels of fire and angels of water. Some angels dispense plagues, some are assigned to announce events; but no matter what their task, all respond in obedience to the commands of the Lord. Even fallen angels must obey God. In Revelation 9, a fallen angel in heaven is given the key to the bottomless pit and is assigned the unpleasant task of unlocking the Abyss to release the "worst of the worst" of the fallen angels: the Watchers.

I believe that angels will interact with believers in the future in ways that are un-paralleled in human history. After the rapture of the church, end time believers can expect to have angelic encounters; encounters that are not a part of our experience as believers right now. As prophecy unfolds, supernatural entities—both good and evil—will interact with this world in ways which do not reflect our current experience. The interaction and involvement in human affairs by both the fallen angels and the holy angels, will be a source of fear for many, but a source of comfort and blessing for God's people.

Spiritual Inflection Points

When God shifts to a new phase or turning point in His plan of salvation, the inflection point is often accompanied by supernatural manifestations of angels. At the first coming of Christ for example, Mary, Joseph and others received angelic visitations. The angel, Gabriel, announced to Mary that she would be the mother of the Messiah. (Luke 1:26-38) Zechariah was also informed by an angel that he would be the father of the forerunner of the Messiah, John, who became known as 'the Baptist' (Luke 18-23). Joseph was told in a dream by an angel to take Mary as his wife, and then, after Jesus was born, Joseph was instructed by an angel to flee Bethlehem and go to Egypt (Matthew 1:20-25; 2:13-14). A herald angel, accompanied by an angelic host, announced to shepherds in the field, that the Savior had been born (Luke 2:8-14). Later, after the resurrection of Christ, Mary Magdalene spoke with an angel at the site of the empty tomb (Luke 24:22,23; Matthew 28:1-7). Christ, Himself, on two occasions, was ministered to by angels, first at His temptation (Matthew 4:11) and then in the garden of Gethsemane (Luke 22:43, 44).

A disproportionate amount of demonic activity also seemed to be present during the life and ministry of Christ. Demon-possessed people received deliverance from their afflictions; and events such as the violent storm that came upon the disciples on the Sea of Galilee, may have also had demonic origins.

The beginning of the church age was also accompanied by an influx of angelic activity: the apostles saw two angels at the ascension of Christ (Acts 1:10.11). An angel released the apostles from prison, after the Jewish leaders sought to make an example of them (Acts 5:17-21). Peter was led out of prison by an angel (Acts 12:6-11). An angel informed Paul that all would survive the shipwreck which would take place (Acts 27:21-25). No doubt there were other angelic visitations which were not recorded in scripture.

Angels announced coming events: (Zechariah, Mary, Joseph, Paul on ship)
Angels brought physical relief: Jesus after temptation, in Garden of Gethsemane
Angels brought release from prison: Peter, apostles in prison

In Revelation chapters 1-3, we read that Christ stands in the midst of 7 candlesticks or assemblies. He holds seven stars in His right hand—the right hand being the hand of power. These 7 stars symbolize angels. The number '7' represents the fulness of the angelic host available to Christ to aid His people. Each angel is responsible to deliver a message from Christ to the various assemblies. The message, in the form of letters, explains the experiences His end time apostles—the 144K of Israel (the first fruits/first born of God)—may encounter during the end times. Christ dictated the letters to 7 angels. The angels were not pastors or elders of the churches, but actual angels, messengers who will be assigned to serve God's people.

In the letter to the church of Sardis, Christ says that He has the seven stars (the angels of each assembly), implying that these angels are there to do Christ's bidding; to communicate and reinforce the message Christ has given them for each assembly.

Just as the apostles of the early church were visited by angels, many of the 144K may receive encouragement from angels who will bring messages from God to warn them of future events, reinforce the Word of God, and bring deliverance and provision—both physical and spiritual.

Christ will make His angels available to serve His elect in the end times. Hebrews 1 tells us about the role of angels with regard to believers:

> "Aren't they all serving spirits, sent out to do service for the sake of those who will inherit salvation?" Hebrews 1:14

The writer of Hebrews tells us that many have entertained angels unawares. (Note: I'm more and more persuaded that the book of Hebrews will have special application for the 144K.)

> "Don't forget to show hospitality to strangers, for in doing so, some have entertained angels without knowing it." Hebrews 13:2

It's possible that as events ramp up this year (2020) that God's people even now, will receive visits from angels, to warn, encourage and bring messages from God.

The seven assemblies of called out saints will have angels assigned to them, to serve and minister to them. All believers will have the indwelling presence of the Holy Spirit. Everything they need to maintain their faith and promote perseverance in their spiritual walk, will be made available to them, including angels as necessary.

Psalm 91

1 He who dwells in the secret place of the Most High
will rest in the shadow of the Almighty.
2 I will say of Yahweh, "He is my refuge and my fortress;
my God, in whom I trust."
3 For he will deliver you from the snare of the fowler,
and from the deadly pestilence.
4 He will cover you with his feathers.
Under his wings you will take refuge.
His faithfulness is your shield and rampart.
5 You shall not be afraid of the terror by night,
nor of the arrow that flies by day,
6 nor of the pestilence that walks in darkness,
nor of the destruction that wastes at noonday.
7 A thousand may fall at your side,
and ten thousand at your right hand;
but it will not come near you.
8 You will only look with your eyes,
and see the recompense of the wicked.
9 Because you have made Yahweh your refuge,
and the Most High your dwelling place,
10 no evil shall happen to you,
neither shall any plague come near your dwelling.
11 For he will put his angels in charge of you,
to guard you in all your ways.
12 They will bear you up in their hands,

so that you won't dash your foot against a stone.
¹³ You will tread on the lion and cobra.
You will trample the young lion and the serpent underfoot.
¹⁴ "Because he has set his love on me, therefore I will deliver him.
I will set him on high, because he has known my name.
¹⁵ He will call on me, and I will answer him.
I will be with him in trouble.
I will deliver him, and honor him.
¹⁶ I will satisfy him with long life,
and show him my salvation."

Chapter 31: The Letters to the Seven Churches and the Covenant with Death

The New Apostles

At the time of the Apostle Paul, the Jews were scattered far and wide over the face of the earth, having synagogues in every nation:

> "For Moses from generations of old has in every city those who preach him, being read in the synagogues every Sabbath." Acts 15:21

Currently, the descendants of the 12 tribes of Israel are dispersed throughout the world. When God chooses and calls out His end time first fruits of Israel, they will be called from every nation on earth, not just from the Jewish State of Israel. The fact that the seven churches in Revelation 2 & 3 do not bear the names of Israeli towns, but of cities outside of Israel, tells us that the 144K will reside primarily among the Gentiles. The meaning of the names of the cities are symbolic, and each city itself supplies a pattern which gives us clues about the challenges the 144K will face once they are sealed by the Spirit.

Several of the letters make reference to Satan, but from the context in which these references appear, we know that Satan is the entity who will incite and energize the Jews to oppose the gospel. Their 'father', the devil, who is the "father of lies", will be the inspiration behind the Jews that causes them to persecute Hebrew believers. The Jews will persecute the 144K just as they did the Lord Jesus and the early apostles.

We've already seen how the first century apostles who were 'firstborn/first fruits' to God, provided a pattern for the 144,000 Israelite believers. The apostles were a special class of believers, trained and equipped by Jesus and the Holy Spirit to spread the message of the gospel. They received supernatural abilities to perform miracles of healings, the ability to transport from place to place (Philip, in Acts 8:39), the power to strike their enemies with blindness (Paul, Acts 13:11); and even death (Peter, Acts 5:1-11). Their shadows healed the sick (Acts 5:12-16).

> "By the hands of the apostles many signs and wonders were done among the people. They were all with one accord in Solomon's porch. 13 None of the rest dared to join them; however, the people honored them. 14 More believers were added to the Lord, multitudes of both men and women. 15 They even carried out the sick into the streets and laid them on cots and mattresses, so that as Peter came by, at least his shadow might overshadow some of them. 16 The multitude also came together from the cities

around Jerusalem, bringing sick people and those who were tormented by unclean spirits; and they were all healed." Acts 5:12-16

God authenticated Paul's apostolic ministry through the miracles and signs which he performed among the people in church at Corinth.

"Truly the signs of an apostle were worked among you in all perseverance, in signs and wonders and mighty works. " 2 Corinthians 12:12

If the first century apostles received the ability to work supernatural signs, wonders and miracles, we can expect that the latter day apostles—the 144K— will be able to operate in the same manner, perhaps performing even greater miracles than did the early apostles. They will also be given supernatural ability to preach the Word effectively, prophesy, to impart words of knowledge and wisdom. They will walk in the power of the 'double anointing' of the Holy Spirit.

Many teach that the 144K will have an evangelistic ministry, that their calling will consist primarily of sharing the gospel with the nations. Though evangelization of the nations will be a part of their ministry, their gifting and anointing will not be limited to preaching. They will demonstrate the power of the Holy Ghost just as He operated through the Lord Jesus in the days of His humanity. As a result of their double anointing, many among the 144K will wield tremendous spiritual power and influence. They will turn the world up-side down for Christ, initiating a great end time revival; a revival which will continue through the opening of the first 5 Seals and the first 5 Trumpets.

Template for the Letters to the Seven Churches

Each of the letters that are dictated by Christ to the angels of the assemblies in Revelation chapters 2 and 3, follows the same basic pattern or template. According to the custom of the day, the author of the letter was given at the beginning of the correspondence, and not at the close of the letter as we do today.
The author of the letters is, of course, the Lord Jesus. The message contained in the letters represents the authoritative words of Christ, as the faithful Steward over the household of God. Since Christ is responsible for the instruction of these new disciples, and because He will not be present in person to instruct them, He communicates God's warnings, encouragement and promises in letter form. *His goal is that each one of the 144K apostles would enter into the full inheritance promised to those who overcome.*

Christ begins each letter by stating some aspect of His nature, essence or character that will apply to the specific issues which that particular group of believers will encounter. Some of His divine attributes have already been enumerated in

Revelation 1, and the rest will be contained in the greetings of the letters. Each assembly was meant to read all of the letters and the warnings, for the encouragements, and promises in each letter would be applicable to every church.

The main body of each letter contains commendations, warnings and areas where there is room for improvement. Promises for those who endure and overcome are given at the close of each letter. The promises reflect Christ's desire for intimacy with His people, eternal fellowship with God and the right to rule with Christ on earth.

The Covenant With Death

The 144K will face opposition on several fronts. False Jews will represent their biggest challenge. The new apostles can expect to be treated with contempt by their fellow Jews, and, as Jesus said, some of their most potent enemies will be members of their own families.

> "Don't think that I came to send peace on the earth. I didn't come to send peace, but a sword. 35 For I came to set a man at odds against his father, and a daughter against her mother, and a daughter-in-law against her mother-in-law. 36 A man's foes will be those of his own household." Matthew 10:34-36

In the future, false Jews will utilize anything—and everything—at their disposal, in their attempt to rein in the new believers. If threats of being cut off from their families and communities doesn't deter them, their adversaries will seek to entice them back into the fold through empty promises and worse. More and more pressure will be applied to these saints, especially those who live in Israel and other large Jewish communities.

As the days draw closer to the midpoint—and the time of their promised rapture on the Feast of First Fruits—they will be faced with a looming danger: the imminent 10 day persecution of believers by the Harlot religious system. Those who practice traditional Judaism will be exempt from this persecution, and false Jews will try and persuade the Israelite believers to take refuge in Judaism. The 144K will face opposition from fellow Jews, and they will be enticed to join Judaism to escape the coming conflagration. (Jesus will address this particular problem in the letter to the church of Pergamum.)

The nation of Israel and the Jews will make a 'covenant with death' to exempt themselves from the tribulation that is coming upon all unaffiliated, non-politically correct religions. In Isaiah, this persecution is called the 'overflowing scourge':

"Therefore hear Yahweh's word, you scoffers, that rule this people in Jerusalem: 15 'Because you have said, "We have made a covenant with death, and we are in agreement with Sheol. When the overflowing scourge passes through, it won't come to us; for we have made lies our refuge, and we have hidden ourselves under falsehood." ' " Isaiah 28:14,15

In essence, the covenant with death is an agreement that the religious leaders of the nation of Israel will make with the Harlot religious system, in conjunction with the Scarlet Beast. (The Roman church will most likely spear-head the Harlot religion.) The covenant will need to be in place prior to the midpoint of the seven years. When the Harlot begins her ten day eradication of the people of God in a world-wide bloodbath, (the 'overflowing scourge') the Jews will be exempt—but only temporarily. In a very few days, the Harlot herself will be destroyed by the Beast and the 10 Kings at the 6th Trumpet. The Harlot, who 'rides' the Beast, will not expect to be double-crossed by him; and when she finds herself the victim of *his* wrath at the 6th Trumpet, all bets are off; and any agreement the Jews had made with the Harlot, will be null and void.

The realization that they, too, have been double-crossed will take place at the time of the abomination of desolation, when the newly resurrected Beast takes his seat in the rebuilt temple of God claiming that he is God. The sound of bombs and missiles exploding will provide the backdrop for the abomination, as all the holy places connected with Harlot religion will be attacked and destroyed.

In addition to Hebrew believers being enticed to join false Judaism, they will also be tempted to join up with the 'mother' church—the Roman church and her daughters, and for the same reason: to escape persecution. The letter to the church of Thyatira was written to warn believers not to join up with her.

The Harlot seems to be unaware that the Beast hates her and everything she stands for. After the Harlot has done her best to wipe out true Christianity, the Beast and the 10 Kings will destroy the Harlot, and then the Jews will be on their own to face the wrath of the newly resurrected Beast from the Sea. On April 3, 2021, the day the Jews see the Antichrist take his seat in the temple of God, many will realize that they have been tricked. The 'covenant with death', which was the agreement Israel made with the Harlot, will be annulled.

Satan's goal will be to neutralize the ministry of the 144K, and he will use false Jews, false Christianity, and false apostles to try and accomplish his goal.

Ephesus and the Apostles of Satan"

"To the angel of the assembly in Ephesus write:

214

"He who holds the seven stars in his right hand, he who walks among the seven golden lamp stands says these things:

2 'I know your works, and your toil and perseverance, and that you can't tolerate evil men, and have tested those who call themselves apostles, and they are not, and found them false. 3 You have perseverance and have endured for my name's sake, and have not grown weary. 4 But I have this against you, that you left your first love. 5 Remember therefore from where you have fallen, and repent and do the first works; or else I am coming to you swiftly, and will move your lamp stand out of its place, unless you repent. 6 But this you have, that you hate the works of the Nicolaitans, which I also hate. 7 He who has an ear, let him hear what the Spirit says to the assemblies. To him who overcomes I will give to eat from the tree of life, which is in the Paradise of my God.' " Revelation 2:1-7

This assembly will find itself needing to discern between those who are apostles—those who are among the chosen 'first fruits'—and those who aren't:

"I know your works, and your toil and perseverance, and that you can't tolerate evil men, and have tested those who call themselves apostles, and they are not, and found them false." Revelation 3:2

We have already seen that any person who denies that Jesus is the Christ does not belong to God. This church will encounter Jews who will try and present themselves as being 'apostles', claiming special authority over them and even that they are among the 144K. This assembly will recognize that these so-called apostles are not one of them. They are false brethren, devoid of the Spirit, and liars. The theme of 'liars'—those Jews who are of the synagogue of Satan who 'lie'—is first mentioned here in this passage. Should any of Satan's minions seek to infiltrate the work of God at Ephesus, this assembly will be quick to notice. Blessed with discernment, they will expose the messengers of Satan. This church will endure much for Christ:

"You have perseverance and have endured for my name's sake, and have not grown weary." Revelation 3:3

They are deficient in one area, however—a very important area—which has the potential to cause them to lose their firstborn status, but not their salvation:

"But I have this against you, that you left your first love. 5 Remember therefore from where you have fallen, and repent and do the first works." Revelation 3:4, 5a

Some believers in this group will have abandoned their first love. Many assume that the love this church has abandoned is their love for Christ, and that it's their love for *Him* that has grown cold, but it's evident that they *do* have a devotion to Christ which extends even to a willingness to endure hardship for the sake of the Lord. Christ connects their abandoned 'first love' with the *deeds* they did at the first. The love they used to have had been evidenced by *works* done by them when they were first saved and sealed.

The works of new believers are recorded in the book of Acts:

> "They continued steadfastly in the apostles' teaching and fellowship, in the breaking of bread, and prayer. 43 Fear came on every soul, and many wonders and signs were done through the apostles. 44 All who believed were together, and had all things in common. 45 They sold their possessions and goods, and distributed them to all, according as anyone had need. 46 Day by day, continuing steadfastly with one accord in the temple, and breaking bread at home, they took their food with gladness and singleness of heart, 47 praising God and having favor with all the people. The Lord added to the assembly day by day those who were being saved." Acts 2:42-47

In addition to following the true teaching of authentic apostles, the early church fellowshipped with one another, shared meals together, and ensured that the physical needs of their brothers and sisters were met. Their unfeigned love for one another stemmed from pure hearts, which, in turn, drew others into the community of faith.

The most important commandment that believers will need to follow, is the 'new' commandment which Jesus delivered to His disciples the night of His betrayal. Jesus commanded his disciples to *love one another as He had loved them*. The works Christ desires to see in His church are deeds of love, as demonstrated in how believers care for *one another*. Correct doctrine and discernment are important, but *lack of love for the brethren has the potential to cause the loss of one's birthright and status in the coming age, especially among the 144K*:

> "...or else I am coming to you swiftly, and will move your lamp stand out of its place, unless you repent." Revelation 2:5b

Jesus tells the church of Ephesus that He will *come to them*. In six of the letters dictated to the seven churches, Jesus tells the 'ekklesia' that He will come to them. As I have pointed out before, this is not a reference to Christ's glorious visible return to earth at His second coming, but a personal coming: "I will come to *you...*" If, at His coming, they have not repented of abandoning their first love, their lampstand will be "removed from its place". This warning about being 're-moved from your place', does not imply that they will lose their salvation, rather they will lose their 'place' in the coming kingdom; they will forfeit their status as first born and the accompanying birthright. In other words, if they don't 'do the works they did at first', which consisted of loving one another through tangible expressions of care and concern, this *alone* would be enough to exempt them from the 'first fruits' rapture, and any other privilege which is a part of the birthright.

Dear friends...Christ is emphasizing the high priority He places on loving one an-other! Love for the brethren is *not an option* but a requirement of the highest or-der for all who would serve in God's kingdom. God is love, and love for the brethren should be the hallmark of all who belong to Christ:

> "We know and have believed the love which God has for us. God is love, and he who remains in love remains in God, and God remains in him. [17] In this, love has been made perfect among us, that we may have boldness in the day of judgment, because as he is, even so we are in this world. [18] There is no fear in love; but perfect love casts out fear, because fear has punish-ment. He who fears is not made perfect in love. [19] We love him, because he first loved us. [20] If a man says, 'I love God,' and hates his brother, he is a liar; for he who doesn't love his brother whom he has seen, how can he love God whom he has not seen? [21] *This commandment we have from him, that he who loves God should also love his brother.*" 1 John 4:16-21

When God's people are perfected in love, they abide in God and they have confi-dence on the day of judgment. God's love in and through the believer, casts out fear. Anyone who says they love God, but hates their brother is a liar. (There's that word, "liar" again!) When we love our brothers and sisters in the Lord, we are demonstrating that we belong to God and that we understand that God's kingdom is a kingdom of love.

> "So also you likewise have some who hold to the teaching of the Nicolai-tans. " Revelation 2:15

The word, Nicolaitans, comes from two Greek words, "*nike*" meaning 'to conquer or to have the victory' and "laos" meaning 'people'. The Nicolaitans symbolically represent those who desire to 'conquer the people', that is, they seek to place themselves over other believers in a hierarchical relationship. They desire to replicate the hierarchical structure of Babylonian Christianity and false Judaism by placing themselves over other believers. They do not recognize that all believers are 'brothers among brothers'. Instead, they will see themselves as superior and thus they will attempt to dominate and control the people of God, claiming they have God's authorization to rule over them. Establishing themselves as leaders in the household of God, they, whether knowingly or unknowingly, will attempt to replicate a work which Christ hates and will ultimately destroy.

Notice that Christ hates the works of the Nicolaitans, not the Nicolaitans themselves. This may indicate that many who are doing the works of Nicolaitanism may actually be believers whom Christ loves, believers who have fallen into the snare of Babylonian-style religion. Christ hates the works of the Nicolaitans because the individuals who follow this teaching usurp the place that rightly belongs only to Christ as the Head of the Church. He personally walks among the golden lampstands. Christ, as the Steward of God's household, is in the midst of His people through the agency of the Spirit, over-seeing their works and their progress. Any human control other than that which flows from Christ via the Holy Spirit, is a usurpation of Christ's place as Head of the 'ekklesia':

> "To the angel of the assembly in Ephesus write:
>
> "He who holds the seven stars in his right hand, he who walks among the seven golden lamp stands says these things." Revelation 2:1
>
> "He put all things in subjection under his feet, and gave him to be head over all things for the assembly." Ephesians 1:22

This assembly of believers are to look to Christ alone for guidance. Christ is the Faithful Steward over everyone in the household of God, and over everything which pertains to true spiritual life and holiness. He is the One who 'walks' among them.

> "To the angel of the assembly in Philadelphia write:
>
> "He who is holy, he who is true, he who has the key of David, he who opens and no one can shut, and who shuts and no one opens, says these things..." Revelation 3:7

The ultimate reward for those who are victorious, is access to the Tree of Life in the paradise of God—the New Jerusalem—the beautiful city which Christ is preparing, even now, for those who love Him.

The Tree of Life

The Tree of Life was one of two trees which stood in the midst of the garden of Eden, the other tree being the Tree of the Knowledge of Good and Evil. The Lord forbade our first parents to eat from the Tree of the Knowledge of Good and Evil. Satan tempted Eve with promises of wisdom and divinity, and she, being deceived by the serpent, ate from the forbidden tree. Adam, knowing that his wife had believed the lie, ate from the fruit his wife gave him, and that's how sin and death entered into the world.

The Tree of the Knowledge of Good and Evil—the tree whose fruit brought sin and death to the world through our first parents when they ate of it—is the origin of all Satanically-inspired religion. The fruit of the Tree of Knowledge was never meant to, nor was it ever able to, impart spiritual life. Those who apprehend true Christian spirituality know that spiritual life consists, not in knowledge of good and evil—trying to do the 'good' and avoid the 'evil'. Instead, true spiritual life is found in Christ, who is Life eternal. He, Himself is the Fruit of the Tree of Life. Those who 'eat' of Christ and participate in His life—as well as in His death here in this world—will have access to more of His Life in the next world, in the Paradise of God.

> "Jesus therefore said to them, 'Most certainly I tell you, unless you eat the flesh of the Son of Man and drink his blood, you don't have life in yourselves. 54 He who eats my flesh and drinks my blood has eternal life, and I will raise him up at the last day. 55 For my flesh is food indeed, and my blood is drink indeed. 56 He who eats my flesh and drinks my blood lives in me, and I in him. 57 As the living Father sent me, and I live because of the Father, so he who feeds on me will also live because of me.' " John 6:53-57

Those who listen to the voice of the Spirit will be reminded of Christ's words. They will receive additional words from the Lord as the Spirit guides them into all truth:

> "However, when he, the Spirit of truth, has come, he will guide you into all truth, for he will not speak from himself; but whatever he hears, he will speak. He will declare to you things that are coming. 14 He will glorify me, for he will take from what is mine and will declare it to you." John 16:13, 14

Being sensitive to the leading of the Holy Spirit will be imperative for the 144K, in order that they may receive the birthright which is promised to those who faithfully love and serve the Lord. Those who are faithful will be taken by Christ when He comes for them in their own rapture, just prior to the midpoint.
Smyrna and the Slander of Satan

> "To the angel of the assembly in Smyrna write:

"The first and the last, who was dead, and has come to life says these things:

"I know your works, oppression, and your poverty (but you are rich), and the blasphemy of those who say they are Jews, and they are not, but are a synagogue of Satan. 10 Don't be afraid of the things which you are about to suffer. Behold, the devil is about to throw some of you into prison, that you may be tested; and you will have oppression for ten days. Be faithful to death, and I will give you the crown of life. 11 He who has an ear, let him hear what the Spirit says to the assemblies. He who overcomes won't be harmed by the second death." Revelation 2:8-11

Myrrh was one of the ingredients that was a component of the holy incense used in the temple worship of ancient Israel. The incense was offered on the altar of incense which stood before the ark of God in the temple. Myrrh, along with other spices, was also used to embalm the dead; being one of the 'spices' brought by Nicodemus to embalm the Lord after His crucifixion. To the Hebrew mind, this aromatic gum was a symbol of sorrow, death, and of prayers ascending as perfumed smoke before God's throne.

With these connections in mind, Smyrna is an appropriate name for the city which foretells the tribulation of believers, as represented by the martyred 'souls under the altar' at the 5th Seal. In addition to believing Gentiles, some of the 144K of Israel will also be imprisoned during the 10 day persecution of the Harlot and the earth dwellers; and some of the 144K will be martyred at this time as well. The devil will allow some of these believing Israelites to be tested and die along with other members of the body of Christ who will be killed *en masse* during the ten day purge. Those of the 144K who will be imprisoned, but not killed, will be taken into heaven at the end of the 10 days, at their First Fruits rapture. If they can endure the 10 days of trial, they will be released to join Christ and their brethren in heaven, regardless of whether they were imprisoned or martyred.

The 'slander' of the 'synagogue of Satan' will lead to the death and imprisonment of some of the 144K. Slander is when a falsehood is manufactured and spread with the goal of causing injury to the person being defamed. To slander someone is to use lies to hurt them and their reputation. The Greek word translated as slander can also be translated as 'blaspheme'. Blasphemy is calling good, evil and evil, good. Right and wrong are turned upside down. The truth of the gospel is exchanged for the lie. False Jews of the synagogue of Satan will twist the truth of God, insisting that *they* are the true 'believers' and that the 144K are heretics.

The 'synagogue of Satan' will oppose the new Israeli believers. We know that Satan is the father of lies and that Satan will be the entity who will energize the

220

slander, lies and blasphemies of the Jews, all of which will be directed toward the servants of God. Just as in Jesus' day, the end time 'synagogue of Satan' will attempt to cut short the testimony of true Christians, whether by imprisoning believers, or by killing them. If these believers remain faithful, even unto death, they will be made alive again—they will receive the 'crown of life'.

Jesus doesn't specifically say that He is 'coming' for the church of Smyrna. What He *does* say, is that these believers will only need to endure for 10 days—whether imprisoned or martyred. In either case, they will be brought to heaven along with the rest of the 144K, and their Gentile brethren, the martyrs from every tribe, tongue, people, and nation. All of the resurrected and raptured believers will receive their glorified, resurrection bodies at that time.

The church of Smyrna is given no reprimand or correction. Christ only encourages them to persevere with the knowledge that their time of tribulation will be brief.

Pergamum and the Seat of Satan

> "To the angel of the assembly in Pergamum write:
>
> "He who has the sharp two-edged sword says these things:
>
> 13 "I know your works and where you dwell, where Satan's throne is. You hold firmly to my name, and didn't deny my faith in the days of Antipas my witness, my faithful one, who was killed among you, where Satan dwells. 14 But I have a few things against you, because you have there some who hold the teaching of Balaam, who taught Balak to throw a stumbling block before the children of Israel, to eat things sacrificed to idols, and to commit sexual immorality. 15 So also you likewise have some who hold to the teaching of the Nicolaitans. 16 Repent therefore, or else I am coming to you quickly and I will make war against them with the sword of my mouth. 17 He who has an ear, let him hear what the Spirit says to the assemblies. To him who overcomes, to him I will give of the hidden manna, † and I will give him a white stone, and on the stone a new name written which no one knows but he who receives it." Revelation 2:12-17

There is something different about the location of this assembly that is not like the rest of the seven churches. Christ says 'I know *where you live*, where the throne of Satan sits." Satan's 'throne' represents his locus of control and influence. In Revelation, Satan (the Dragon) is the particular adversary of Israel, God's covenant people. Satan will work *through* the Beast and the Harlot, but sometimes he is symbolized as working *directly* to neutralize God's chosen ones.

Satan will use the Jews to persecute the 144K servants of God. The place where the Jews will have the most power and influence will be in the land of Israel, and specifically in Jerusalem. It was in Jerusalem that Jesus was crucified, and it was in that same city that Stephen, the first martyr of the infant church, was stoned to death. The first martyr(s) of the 144K bear the symbolic name, Antipas. Like Christ and Stephen, 'Antipas' (who is not an actual person but the name given to a group of martyrs) will be martyred in Jerusalem, the place of Satan's throne.

The meaning of the name, Antipas, is 'like the father'. All those who follow in the spiritual lineage of Antipas will reflect the character and nature of their heavenly Father. Those of the synagogue of Satan, who live in the satanic stronghold of Jerusalem, will be like their 'father' as well. Satan is both a liar and a murderer:

> "You are of your father the devil, and you want to do the desires of your father. He was a murderer from the beginning, and doesn't stand in the truth, because there is no truth in him. When he speaks a lie, he speaks on his own; for he is a liar, and the father of lies." John 8:44

The 144K can expect death in the holy city, Jerusalem. The persecution which the 144K will endure from fellow Jews will be the most intense in the land of Israel, and in Jerusalem in particular.

If threats of murder and persecution do not prove effective in neutralizing the ministry of the 144K, Satan will resort to Plan B: "if you can't beat them, join them". Enter Balaam—the Old Testament prophet, who would not curse the Israelites outright, but caused them to sin through intermarriage with foreign women:

> "But I have a few things against you, because some of you hold to the teaching of Balaam, who taught Balak to place a stumbling block before the Israelites so they would eat food sacrificed to idols and commit sexual immorality."

> "Israel stayed in Shittim; and the people began to play the prostitute with the daughters of Moab; 2 for they called the people to the sacrifices of their gods. The people ate and bowed down to their gods." Numbers 25:1,2

Once the ancient Israelites became 'unequally yoked' with pagan women, they forsook the Lord and followed after other gods, a practice which God equated with spiritual fornication and harlotry.

The end time version of 'Balaam' will be so-called prophets who try to encourage their brethren to join Judaism. Modern day Judaism is compromised because it does not accept Jesus as the Messiah. Anyone turning to Judaism will become unequally yoked. Modern Judaism has nothing in common with the gospel of Christ, and those who choose to adhere to the traditions of men and not the commandments of God, place a 'curse' upon themselves, as did the Israelites in the wilderness who intermarried with pagan women. This curse may fall on some of the 144K, who forsake Christ *only,* and who in turn, encourage others to adhere to the traditions of men. The Lord will use His double-edged sword to differentiate between those who follow Him in purity, and those who do not. He will also wage war against those who hold the teaching of the Nicolaitans.

'Hidden manna' and a secret name on a white stone will be the rewards for those who persevere in the face of these trials and temptations. The hidden manna represents Christ, who tells us that He is the Bread of Life, the heavenly, spiritual Food reserved for those who are the Lord's faithful servants. They will see Christ in all His glory. They will receive a secret, new name which represents a new depth of intimacy these believers can expect to have with the Lord once they are taken to the throne room of God.

The Thyatira-Harlot Connection

The city of Thyatira originally bore the name, 'Semiramis', in honor of the wife of Nimrod. Semiramis was the only queen who ever ruled Babylon and she was also known as the 'Queen of Heaven'. Semiramis (a former prostitute) claimed that she had miraculously conceived her son as a result of being impregnated by a sunbeam. In essence, she was the original 'virgin mother', from which sprang all other 'mother-child' cults. The Roman church is steeped in ancient 'mother-child' worship, and the worship of Semiramis and her son is only thinly disguised in the veneration of the Virgin Mary and the infant Jesus.

The city of Semiramis was eventually conquered by a Seleucid general, and, on the day of his victory, a messenger came to him with the news that his wife had given birth to a daughter. One of the many meanings of the name, Thyatira, is 'daughter'. The name of the city was changed from Semiramis—a name which honored the so-called Queen of Heaven and prostitute—to Thyatira which means 'Daughter'.

In Revelation, we learn that the Harlot has 'daughters', who are harlots as well:

> "And on her forehead a name was written: MYSTERY, BABYLON THE GREAT, THE MOTHER OF HARLOTS AND OF THE ABOMINATIONS OF THE EARTH." Revelation 17:5

Spiritual harlotry originated in Babylon with Nimrod and Semiramis, and spread to all corners of the world via her 'daughter' religions. All false religions trace their roots to Babel. Just as we can all trace our physical lineage back to Noah who became the father of the human race, with his three sons repopulating the world after the flood; Babel/Babylon became the spiritual mother of all who follow after other gods. Her daughters have even infused the Christian church with Babylonian beliefs and practices, practices which started gaining traction at the time of Constantine in the 4th century. Wherever Roman Catholicism spread, the local pagan practices and holy days were adopted and absorbed—then reworked to fit into Catholicism, and finally made official by the Pope.

At the time of John and the apostles, Thyatira was known for manufacturing and selling purple cloth. The local craftsmen had a proprietary dye with which they produced luxurious purple goods, which were sold throughout the Roman world. When Paul journeyed to Philippi, he met a woman named Lydia, who was a seller of purple goods from Thyatira. (Lydia was also the first Christian convert in Europe. See Acts 16.)

> "These will war against the Lamb, and the Lamb will overcome them, for he is Lord of lords and King of kings; and those who are with him are called, chosen, and faithful." Revelation 17:14

In all of Revelation, only the Harlot is described as wearing purple. The church of Thyatira will be tempted to join up with the Harlot church and it's in this context that the letter to the church of Thyatira, was written.

Thyatira and the Depths of Satan

> "To the angel of the assembly in Thyatira write:
> "The Son of God, who has his eyes like a flame of fire, and his feet are like burnished brass, says these things:
>
> [19] "I know your works, your love, faith, service, patient endurance, and that your last works are more than the first. [20] But I have this against you, that you tolerate your§ woman Jezebel, who calls herself a prophetess. She teaches and seduces my servants to commit sexual immorality and to eat things sacrificed to idols. [21] I gave her time to repent, but she refuses to repent of her sexual immorality. [22] Behold, I will throw her and those who commit adultery with her into a bed of great oppression, unless they repent of her works. [23] I will kill her children with Death, and all the assemblies will know that I am he who searches the minds and hearts. I will give to each one of you according to your deeds. [24] But to you I say, to the rest

224

who are in Thyatira—as many as don't have this teaching, who don't know what some call 'the deep things of Satan'—to you I say, I am not putting any other burden on you. 25 Nevertheless, hold that which you have firmly until I come. 26 He who overcomes, and he who keeps my works to the end, to him I will give authority over the nations. 27 He will rule them with a rod of iron, shattering them like clay pots, as I also have received of my Father; 28 and I will give him the morning star. 29 He who has an ear, let him hear what the Spirit says to the assemblies." Revelation 2:18-19

We know that Satan will attempt to use the Jews and Judaism to slander, persecute and otherwise seek to deprive the 144K of Israel of their spiritual double portion as firstborn/first fruits. We have already seen how the accuser will send false apostles to try to corrupt the gospel (Ephesus). He will slander, blaspheme and persecute Israelite believers, martyring some of them (Smyrna). He will use the Jews in Jerusalem and Israel to martyr those who are 'like the Father' (Pergamum). In the church of Thyatira, Satan will seek to lead the 144K astray through false 'Christianity', polluting the truth of the gospel and causing some believers to engage in spiritual immorality.

Departing from a faithful relationship with God is referred to as 'harlotry' in the Word of God. Some compromised believers will infiltrate the fellowship of true believers, attempting to infuse elements of the Harlot religion into the fellowship. When God's people fellowship with unregenerate individuals or compromised brethren, they are symbolically represented as "eating meat offered to idols". To eat with someone is to have fellowship with them. False Christians and false doctrines will enter into the fellowship of God, attempting to corrupt these true believers; and the saints of Thyatira are warned by Christ not to tolerate the teaching of the prophetess, 'Jezebel'.

In the Old Testament, Jezebel was the wicked queen of an Israelite king named Ahab. She intensified Baal worship in Israel, bringing idolatry and the worship of Baal to a whole new level. The priests of Baal, which were many, were supported by the queen, and by extension, they were also supported by the people of Israel. The true prophets and priests of God, numbering over 7,000, had been driven underground by the religious zealotry of the pagan queen. A similar situation will play out once again with true believers in the end times, who will be driven underground by the religious fervor of the Harlot.

Jezebel is called a prophetess, and she personifies those who teach another gospel, who will disguise their satanic lies as 'deep truths' from God. False believers will use seductive and compelling arguments to reinforce the claim that they speak for God. The Roman church today claims to possess the words of God, being the sole authoritative voice of Christ and the only means of salvation for all mankind. She presents herself as the mother church, wooing her way-ward daughters to 'come home'.

To 'prophesy' means to 'speak forth'. Jezebel will 'speak forth', but she will not speak the true words of God: she will speak forth words from the 'depths' of Satan, which are the doctrines of demons that Paul writes about in 1 Timothy:

> "But the Spirit says expressly that in later times some will fall away from the faith, paying attention to seducing spirits and doctrines of demons, 2 through the hypocrisy of men who speak lies, branded in their own conscience as with a hot iron." 1 Timothy 4:1,2

This faction will be given time to repent, and if they choose not to repent of their false teaching, they, along with their disciples, will be cast into 'great tribulation'. They will not be taken in the rapture granted to the faithful 144K, but will instead become a victim of the 6th Trumpet judgment of the Harlot at the midpoint, when a third of mankind will be killed.

Christ knows the hearts and minds of each person within the '*ekklesia*' of God. The thoughts and motives of all believers are open before Him and no one will be able to fool Him when He comes to remove His faithful from the earth:

> "For the word of God is living and active, and sharper than any two-edged sword, piercing even to the dividing of soul and spirit, of both joints and marrow, and is able to discern the thoughts and intentions of the heart." Hebrews 4:12

Christ is the 'Word of God' who carries the sharp sword. His eyes are like flames of fire, seeing into the depths of each heart, rewarding the good and punishing the wicked.

When the 144K are faced with the overwhelming scourge—the 10 day persecution of the Harlot and the earth dwellers—some among the 144K may be tempted to join up with the Harlot religion and thus escape the coming 10 days of tribulation. That there are believers who will do just that, is indicated in the following passage in Revelation:

> "I heard another voice from heaven, saying, 'Come out of her, my people, that you have no participation in her sins, and that you don't receive of her plagues.'" Revelation 18:4

As an aside, we also learn from this passage that being a part of the Harlot religion, or her daughter religions, doesn't damn anyone to an eternity in the Lake of

Fire. Believers are exhorted to come 'out of her', because of her imminent destruction—a destruction they, too, will be swept up in once the 6th Trumpet sounds. Revelation distinguishes between the Harlot religion and the Beast religion. To take the mark of the Beast, worship the Beast or worship the Image of the Beast WILL forever damn a person to the Lake of Fire. Being entangled in the Harlot religion will mean physical death in the plagues of fire, smoke and sulphur, but not eternal damnation.

The end time apostles—the 144K of Israel—will appear on heavenly Mount Zion with the Lamb. These are the ones who were victorious over the spiritual enemies that came against them. They are spiritual virgins, undefiled by the Harlot or her daughters:

> "These are those who were not defiled with women, for they are virgins. These are those who follow the Lamb wherever he goes. These were redeemed by Jesus from among men, the first fruits to God and to the Lamb. 5 In their mouth was found no lie, for they are blameless." Revelation 14:4,5

The 144k on Mount Zion are virgins because they refused to have relations with 'women'. The women that are being referred to are the Harlot religious system and her daughter religions, with false Christianity and false Judaism being among her off-spring.

Those who are victorious, who are not drawn into the false Christianity of the Harlot, will receive authority to rule over the nations, just as Christ received authority from His Father to rule over the nations. The worldly and satanic power brokers of the end times—who are symbolically represented by Jezebel, the wicked queen who ruled over Israel during the days of Elijah—will find the tables turned on them when God's people become *their* rulers, ruling over *them* with a rod of iron, during the Millennium.

The victors are also given the 'morning star'. The 'morning star' is the brightest and last star visible in the east before the rising of the sun. To be given the morning star is to be given the assurance that, after the long night of sorrow and pain, the reign of Christ is near and is about to arise:

> "For his anger is but for a moment.
> His favor is for a lifetime.
> Weeping may stay for the night,
> but joy comes in the morning." Psalm 30:5

Sardis: The Spirit-less Church

"And to the angel of the assembly in Sardis write:

"He who has the seven Spirits of God and the seven stars says these things:

"I know your works, that you have a reputation of being alive, but you are dead. 2 Wake up and strengthen the things that remain, which you were about to throw away,* for I have found no works of yours perfected before my God. 3 Remember therefore how you have received and heard. Keep it and repent. If therefore you won't watch, I will come as a thief, and you won't know what hour I will come upon you. 4 Nevertheless you have a few names in Sardis that didn't defile their garments. They will walk with me in white, for they are worthy. 5 He who overcomes will be arrayed in white garments, and I will in no way blot his name out of the book of life, and I will confess his name before my Father, and before his angels. 6 He who has an ear, let him hear what the Spirit says to the assemblies." Revelation 3:1-6

Christ begins this letter by telling the believers at Sardis that He has the seven Spirits of God, and the seven stars (angels of the churches). In Revelation 5:6, we read that the 7 horns and the 7 eyes on the Lamb are the seven Spirits of God that are sent out into all the earth. The Lamb sends forth the Spirit of God. His Spirit will seal the 144K of Israel once present day believers are taken from the earth. As the firstborn/first fruits of Israel, the 144K will receive the 'double portion' of the Spirit, the portion which is reserved only for them among all the end time believers.

Just because these believers have the Holy Spirit living inside of them does not guarantee that the provisions of the *birthright* will actually be granted to them. The Spirit can be grieved and quenched. The fire of God, which had once ignited the hearts of these believers at their conversion, may be reduced to a smolder if they don't fan the flames.

Just as the 12 apostles held a special status in the early church, so too, any of Israel who are among the 144K, will have the reputation of being special, powerful and spiritual. For some though, their reputation may live on after the glory has departed. Having received the Holy Spirit in the beginning of the revival and having performed the apostolic works associated with people possessing the double portion of the Spirit, somewhere along the way, some may cease depending upon the Holy Spirit as their source of life. They may seek to prop up their spiritual life from other sources, counterfeit sources. They may cling to the 'good old days', basking in the adulation of those who recognized their unique call at the beginning, when they were first saved and sealed.

The 144K were told to remember what they received (the Holy Spirit); and to remember what they heard—the words of Christ, if they have ears to hear the voice of the Holy Spirit. The angels of the churches and the Holy Spirit will both communicate the words of Christ.

This church does not seem to be suffering the attacks of false Jews as do the churches of Smyrna and Pergamum. In fact, there is no indication of persecution of any kind taking place among the believers at Sardis at all. Persecution tends to cause believers to cling to the Lord closer, watching for and anticipating His deliverance. Persecuted believers have a desire for the coming of Christ. One of the most important words that Christ gave to all His end time churches, is the promise that *He would come for them*! The believers at the church of Sardis who have fallen asleep, will need to wake up, 'get back to basics', and reestablish their connection with the Holy Spirit so that they can walk in the power and life of the Spirit. If they ignore this warning, they will be unprepared for the coming of the Lord, caught unawares and unworthy to meet Him. If they repent before His coming, their 'soiled' garments will be cleansed and they will walk with Him in white. If they do not repent, they will not be admitted into heaven when Christ opens the door for the rapture of the 144K on the Feast of First Fruits.

Another clue that the letter to the church of Sardis is written to the 144K is the little phrase: "they will *walk with Me* in white". The 144K, who are seen on heavenly Mount Zion after their rapture in Revelation 14, follow the Lamb wherever he goes...they *walk* with Him.

What does it means for the church of Sardis to overcome? They will need to remember how to walk in the life and power of the Spirit. They will need to be watching and waiting for the Lord's coming. They cannot rely on their former reputation, or the fact that they had once received an apostolic calling. They will need to 'confirm' their call and election and continue to stir up one another to love and good deeds:

> "Let's hold fast the confession of our hope without wavering; for he who promised is faithful. 24 Let's consider how to provoke one another to love and good works, 25 not forsaking our own assembling together, as the custom of some is, but exhorting one another, and so much the more as you see the Day approaching." Hebrews 10:23-25

> "Therefore, brothers, be more diligent to make your calling and election sure. For if you do these things, you will never stumble." 2 Peter 1:10

If they will do these things, they will receive eternal life as evidenced by their names not being blotted out from the book of Life. They will be welcomed by Christ into the presence of His Father and the angels. Christ will confess that He knows them and He will recount the stories of how each one gained the victory through dependence upon the life of the Spirit.

Philadelphia: "Brotherly Love"

"7 "To the angel of the assembly in Philadelphia write:

"He who is holy, he who is true, he who has the key of David, he who opens and no one can shut, and who shuts and no one opens, says these things:

8 "I know your works (behold, I have set before you an open door, which no one can shut), that you have a little power, and kept my word, and didn't deny my name. 9 Behold, I make some of the synagogue of Satan, of those who say they are Jews, and they are not, but lie—behold, I will make them to come and worship before your feet, and to know that I have loved you. 10 Because you kept my command to endure, I also will keep you from the hour of testing which is to come on the whole world, to test those who dwell on the earth. 11 I am coming quickly! Hold firmly that which you have, so that no one takes your crown. 12 He who overcomes, I will make him a pillar in the temple of my God, and he will go out from there no more. I will write on him the name of my God and the name of the city of my God, the new Jerusalem, which comes down out of heaven from my God, and my own new name. 13 He who has an ear, let him hear what the Spirit says to the assemblies." Revelation 3:7-13

The name, Philadelphia, means 'city of brotherly love'. Love of the brethren is the hallmark of believers, and when believers love one another, they fulfill the most important commandment of Christ. We are to love one another as Jesus loved us, being willing to lay down our lives for one another. The beauty of brotherly love and unity is spoken of in the Psalms as well:

"1 See how good and how pleasant it is
for brothers to live together in unity!
2 It is like the precious oil on the head,
that ran down on the beard,
even Aaron's beard,
that came down on the edge of his robes,
3 like the dew of Hermon,

that comes down on the hills of Zion;
for there Yahweh gives the blessing,
even life forever more." Psalm 133:1-3

There is so much in this psalm that speaks prophetically of the 144K first fruits of Israel. First, they are brethren whose hearts are united in love. Their love is the ultimate expression of the Spirit of Christ in their midst, flowing from within each believer. These believers are compared to Aaron, the first high priest of Israel. The anointing of the Holy Spirit that rested on Aaron is represented by the precious oil that flows down from the top of Aaron's head onto his beard and to the bottom of his robe. The anointing is continuous and bountiful. The 144K who will be sealed by the Spirit will have this same anointing.

The love of the brethren, as expressed in the anointing of the Spirit, is compared to the 'dew of Hermon'. Mount Hermon is the highest mountain peak in Israel. Snow covers the summit of the mountain much of the year, and in the spring the melting snow causes rivers to gush down the mountain, bringing life to the valley below. The anointing of the Spirit produces rivers of life, unity, and love among the brethren. These are qualities the believers in the church of Philadelphia will possess, much to Christ's pleasure and satisfaction. He knows that they will undergo persecution and trials from their fellow Jews, those who are of the 'synagogue of Satan'. In the end, however, false Jews will be required to acknowledge that these believers are especially loved of the King of Israel, and they will bow before them in the Millennial kingdom.

Because of their perseverance, Jesus tells this gathering of loving believers that He will keep them from the 'hour of trial' or 'testing', which will come on the whole world. Jesus is referring to the hour of the Harlot's judgment, which will result in the death of a third of the earth's population. All those who make up compromised Christianity, and other religions as well—including the followers of Islam, Hinduism and any other religion that aligns with Rome—have an appointment for destruction.

Jesus, the faithful Steward of God, has the 'key of David' which opens the gates of heaven. No one can keep Christ from opening heaven's door to allow His people entrance into the throne room of God. Likewise, not even Satan and his angels will be able to access the heavenly temple once the door is closed and locked. Satan and his angels will be cast from heaven at the same time the rapture of the 144K takes place, on the feast of First Fruits in 2021, never to return again.

The 144K will be an integral part of the heavenly New Jerusalem. Christ will write God's name on them, the name of the New Jerusalem and Christ's own new name on their foreheads. This writing will replace the 'seal' which they received on their foreheads at the time they were sealed with the Holy Spirit, during the feast of Tabernacles, a few days after the first group of priest/believers were taken into heaven on the Day of Atonement. The 'seal' is the 'promissory note', the guarantee that they will, one day, receive everything God has promised them.

In Revelation 14, the 144K have the Father's name written on their foreheads:

> "I saw, and behold, the Lamb standing on Mount Zion, and with him a number, one hundred forty-four thousand, having his name and the name of his Father written on their foreheads." Revelation 14:1

Many—if not most—who teach on eschatology from a pre-tribulation perspective, believe that the church of Philadelphia represents faithful 'present-day' Christians who will be taken to heaven before the 'hour of trial' begins. They interpret the 'hour of trial' as the seven year 'tribulation'. They believe that before the seven years of 'tribulation' can begin, the church of Philadelphia—present day believers—must be taken into heaven in order to escape the trials of the end times which they understand to be the wrath of God. This is a foundational doctrine of almost all who hold to the pre-tribulation rapture position. However, if there is evidence that can show that the letters to the seven churches were written, not to present day believers, but to the 144K of Israel, believers who will be living *during* the seven years—then this doctrine crumbles. The promise to be taken that is given to believers in the letter to the church of Philadelphia, applies to the 144K of Israel *and no one else,* not even present day believers.

What's that on your forehead?

We know that a symbolic 12,000 from each of the 12 tribes of Israel are 'sealed'. We have also seen that to be 'sealed' is to be filled with the Holy Spirit. Paul tells us that all Christians are sealed with the Holy Spirit. The Spirit imparts the life of Christ to every believer. It is not possible to be a Christian apart from the indwelling life and ministry of the Holy Spirit.

The Greek word for "sealed", is "*sphragizo*", and means "to attest to ownership; the equivalent of a legal signature guaranteeing the promise of what is contained in the sealed (scroll or document)". In this case, the Holy Spirit is the seal or 'earnest' of the promises God has made. (See Ephesians 1:13,14.)

In Revelation 14:1, we see the Lamb standing on heavenly Mt Zion with the 144K. Rather than having a seal on their foreheads, they now have the Lamb's name *written,* on on their foreheads, as well as His Father's name *written* on them:

"I saw, and behold, the Lamb standing on Mount Zion, and with him a number, one hundred forty-four thousand, having his name and the name of his Father written on their foreheads. " Revelation 14:1

The 144K no longer have a *seal* on their foreheads. The seal has been replaced by writing. The Greek word translated as 'written', is *grapho,* which means 'to write'. The seal, which represented the promissory note, has been replaced by writing, indicating that the promise that the seal guaranteed, has been kept. His new apostles will be transported to heaven in their own rapture, and stand with the Lamb on heavenly Mt. Zion. What does Mt Zion represent? It represents the *real* Holy City, the place where God dwells, the place where His temple is located in heaven.

In Revelation 3:12, we read about the promises that Christ makes to the church of Philadelphia:

1. They will be made a pillar in the temple of my God.
2. He **write** on them the name of my God.
3. He will **write** on them the name of the city of my God (New Jerusalem).
4. He will **write** His own new Name on them.

Three passages in Revelation talk about believers being sealed and/or having God's name written on them: Revelation 3:12, 14:1 and 7:3. The seal is the earnest of the promise; the writing indicates the promise was kept.

- Revelation 3:12 is passage telling us about the promise Christ has made to this group: "I will write on him...."

- Revelation 7:3 is the passage that tells us about the sealing of the 144K on their foreheads, which is the 'signature' or earnest of the promise of God.

- Revelation 14:1 tells us that the promises made to the 144K were kept. God and Christ's new name are written on their foreheads, as they stand on Mt Zion/ New Jerusalem!

In the letter to the church of Philadelphia, we read that the faithful overcomer will be 'kept from the hour of trial': that is, they will not be present on earth when the Harlot is destroyed at the 6th Trumpet. Revelation 13:6 tells us that the earth dwellers know very well that the 144K are in heaven at the time the Beast is resurrected. They "blaspheme God, His Name and His dwelling, that is, *those who dwell in heaven!*" The 144K, along with raptured and resurrected people who are already in heaven, are represented as God's dwelling, His Temple. The letter to the church of Philadelphia informs us that the 144K will be as pillars in the temple of God. The earth dwellers will know exactly where these servants of God have been taken, and they will blaspheme them—tell lies about them—and turn the truth of their deliverance up-side down, making their rapture seem like a punishment.

There are 4 passages which, when viewed together, indicate that the 144K are in heaven before the midpoint:

1. In Revelation 3:12 we read the promise to the church of Philadelphia to be 'kept from hour of trial.
2. In Revelation 13:6 the earth dwellers blaspheme them, which alludes to the Old Testament story in 2 Kings 2:23,24, where a gang of boys—mockers—cry "go up, bald-head!"', mocking Elijah's rapture. After which 2 she-bears mauled 42 of them. Elijah's catching away was not a secret, even these young teens had heard the story, and then they mockingly demanded that Elisha depart in the same way. (Also of interest is the number '42'. Forty-two of the boys were mauled, and the Beast will reign for 42 months.)
3. The placement of the passage detailing the 144K on Mt. Zion is placed within the book of Revelation just after the chapter where the details of the reign of the Beast are enumerated. The writing on the foreheads of the 144K (in Revelation 14) is contrasted with the mark of the Beast on the foreheads/hands of the deceived earth dwellers (Revelation 13).
4. Revelation uses chastity as a symbol of spiritual purity; that is, the 144K are 'spiritually chaste'. (We're not talking about people who are physical virgins. In Revelation 14:4, there is no word for 'man' or 'male' in this passage, even though people assume that the 144K must be male virgins!) The point is that the 144K were never a part of the Harlot religious system or her 'daughter' systems, or, if they had been sucked in at one point in their lives, they repented of their involvement. The Harlot system will be done away with at the 6th Trumpet, at the midpoint. The only world-wide false religious system that the 144K will be required to resist *is the Harlot's system*. (False Judaism is a part of the Harlot system as well.) They will be kept from the 42 months of Beast worship if they overcome. The 144K will not defile themselves with 'women', that is, they will not engage in spiritual harlotry which has its origins in Babel/Babylon, and is symbolized by Mystery Babylon and her 'daughters'.

How does this apply to standard pre-tribulational eschatology?

If my understanding is correct, then the believers of the church of Philadelphia *do not present day believers who will be raptured before the beginning of a 7 year 'tribulation'*. This is perhaps the most important 'take away' for those of us awaiting the rapture.

If the church of Philadelphia represents the 144K, we know that there will be more than one rapture, and that the rapture of the 144K will be "mid-tribulation", right before the midpoint of the seven years. If this is so, then there must have been a prior rapture: the rapture of present day believers, as represented by the child of Revelation 12.

We also know that the 144K are a *part of the church*, the Body of Believers and the Bride of Christ, and thus full-fledged members of the community of faith. They do not come to Christ in a different dispensation; they, like us, will be living in the dispensation of *grace through faith* and they will be full participants in all that God's grace has to offer, including the in-dwelling ministry of the Holy Spirit. The Holy Spirit will be with them, and in them, just as He is with, and in, believers right now.

We also have the assurance that God will make good on the promises He has made both to us and to the 144K. Present day believers possess the seal of God now, and that seal—the indwelling life of the Holy Spirit—is the guarantee of our up-coming promised salvation, which will eventually be written on *our* foreheads too. The in-dwelling Spirit gives us assurance and hope that we will one day be brought into God's throne room, into His very Presence. The 144K will inherit the same promises and the same seal of God: the Holy Spirit. They will be taken in their own rapture before the midpoint.

Laodicea: "The 'Safe' Church"

The name, 'Laodicea', means 'the equitable people'. The symbolism implied in the name, Laodicea, gives us a clue that this group of believers may attempt to live in an unbelieving world in as unbiased and inoffensive manner as possible, with respect to the people around them—the goal being to evade and avoid persecution. In the letter to the church of Laodicea, as with the church of Sardis, there is no hint that these believers are directly engaged in battling the forces of evil which will manifest in the end times as tribulation and persecution. This is surprising, especially when we consider the amount of evil that will be running rampant in the world at that time, and the fact that Jesus told His disciples that they should expect persecution.

"To the angel of the assembly in Laodicea write:

'The Amen, the Faithful and True Witness, the Beginning of God's creation, says these things...' " Revelation 3:14

Christ says that He is the "Amen". He is the truth and the 'so be it'. He doesn't change, and what He says is what He means. He is also called the Faithful and

True Witness. When Christ returns at His Second Coming to reclaim the earth for God, He bears the name, Faithful and True, at that time as well:

> " I saw the heaven opened, and behold, a white horse, and he who sat on it is called Faithful and True. In righteousness he judges and makes war." Revelation 19:11

Jesus is also described as being the Origin, Beginning or Source of God's creation. This does not mean that Jesus is a created being or that there ever was a time when He did not exist in fellowship with the Father and the Spirit. What this passage is saying, is that Jesus is the One *through whom all creation exists*, and that He is the sustainer of everything that He has made.

> "In the beginning was the Word, and the Word was with God, and the Word was God. 2 The same was in the beginning with God. 3 All things were made through him. Without him, nothing was made that has been made." John 1:1-3

> "15 He is the image of the invisible God, the firstborn of all creation. 16 For by him all things were created in the heavens and on the earth, visible things and invisible things, whether thrones or dominions or principalities or powers. All things have been created through him and for him. 17 He is before all things, and in him all things are held together." Colossians 1:15-17

Jesus is the Source of all things, and all things hold together in Him. He is also the source of all things for the church, His body.

> "He put all things in subjection under his feet, and gave him to be head over all things for the assembly, 23 which is his body, the fullness of him who fills all in all." Ephesians 1:22,23

In this letter, Christ chastises the assembly for deriving their source of supply from other places and other people, instead of from Himself. Christ alone is the only true Source of spiritual life and spiritual riches.

> "I know your works, that you are neither cold nor hot. I wish you were cold or hot. 16 So, because you are lukewarm, and neither hot nor cold, I will vomit you out of my mouth. 17 Because you say, 'I am rich, and have gotten riches, and have need of nothing,' and don't know that you are the wretched one, miserable, poor, blind, and naked; 18 I counsel you to buy from me gold refined by fire, that you may become rich; and white gar-

ments, that you may clothe yourself, and that the shame of your naked-ness may not be revealed; and eye salve to anoint your eyes, that you may see. [19] As many as I love, I reprove and chasten. Be zealous therefore, and repent." Revelation 3:15-19

In terms of their Christian walk and testimony, the Laodicean assembly will choose to adopt a middle-of-the-road approach—an 'equitable' approach. Rather than risk offending others by proclaiming the exclusive and politically incorrect doctrine of Jesus as the Messiah, this group of Israelite believers will attempt to live in such a way so as to avoid conflict with other religious groups, especially fellow Jews and members of the Harlot religious system. They will live as though they, themselves, bore the responsibility of keeping themselves safe in the world and providing for all their own needs. They may actually pride themselves in their ability to keep themselves safe and physically secure in the religiously hostile world of the end times.

Endeavoring to 'go along to get along', this group of believers, by doing whatever necessary to remain neutral and unoffensive to the world around them, may at-tempt to side-step the persecution that the other churches will face. They will not be on fire and zealous in their love for Christ and His people, but neither will they be totally indifferent to Him. They will 'be' whatever they need to 'be' in order to be safe and still be Christian.

Living equitably carries its own dangers, dangers which may have serious conse-quences for this group of believers. People-pleasing—rather than pleasing Christ —has the potential to nullify the birthright of this assembly of first fruits servants of God. In an effort to 'play it safe', using their own insight and resources, they will side-step the need to run to Christ for provision and true spiritual riches. If they do not repent of their fear and pride, they will have nothing to show for themselves when Christ comes for them, except the pitiful fruit of their own ef-forts and expediency. Those who live 'equitably' will be left behind and thus be required to endure the reign of the Beast until the 3rd and final, secret rapture.

Christ loves this group of end time disciples and He believes better things about them. He pleads with them to be zealous in their faith and love, to be on *fire for Him*. He wants them to come to Him for every need and not rely on their own self-sufficiency and natural resources.

"Hey! Come, everyone who thirsts, to the waters!
Come, he who has no money, buy, and eat!
Yes, come, buy wine and milk without money and without price.
[2] Why do you spend money for that which is not bread,
and your labor for that which doesn't satisfy?

Listen diligently to me, and eat that which is good,
and let your soul delight itself in richness." Isaiah 55:1,2

In the Sermon on the Mount, Jesus declared that those who recognize their spiritual poverty will receive true spiritual riches:

"Blessed are the poor in spirit,
for theirs is the Kingdom of Heaven.
4 Blessed are those who mourn,
for they shall be comforted.
5 Blessed are the gentle,
for they shall inherit the earth.
6 Blessed are those who hunger and thirst for righteousness,
for they shall be filled.
7 Blessed are the merciful,
for they shall obtain mercy.
8 Blessed are the pure in heart,
for they shall see God.
9 Blessed are the peacemakers,
for they shall be called children of God.
10 Blessed are those who have been persecuted for righteousness' sake,
for theirs is the Kingdom of Heaven.
11 Blessed are you when people reproach you, persecute you, and say all kinds of evil against you falsely, for my sake. 12 Rejoice, and be exceedingly glad, for great is your reward in heaven. For that is how they persecuted the prophets who were before you." Matthew 5:3-12

Those who truly follow Christ can *expect* insults, persecution, and false accusations. There is a heavenly reward for those who patiently endure trials and tribulations for the sake of the Lord.

Christ desires intimate fellowship with His Laodicean people; fellowship which can begin the moment Christ is brought back to the center of their gathering. For those who place *all* their trust in Christ, whether they live or die, they will experience true fellowship with Christ here on earth. This quality of intimacy with the Lord will continue on in glory, where they will feast with Him in *His* home, when He comes for them.

"Behold, I stand at the door and knock. If anyone hears my voice and opens the door, then I will come in to him and will dine with him, and he with me. 21 He who overcomes, I will give to him to sit down with me on my throne, as I also overcame and sat down with my Father on his throne.

238

[22] He who has an ear, let him hear what the Spirit says to the assemblies."
Revelation 3:20-22

Chapter 32: Suffering Loss During the Last Days

Though all believers are saved by "grace through faith" as a gift of God through the merits of Christ alone, *rewards* can be forfeited by the action, or inaction, of a believer. Any person of faith may incur spiritual loss as a result of something that they do—or fail to do—which can prevent them from receiving all that God has promised His children. If we are carnal, spiritually lazy and not watchful, we may not inherit all we have been promised by God.

So what are the losses that believers may incur?

The most grievous loss imaginable would be the loss of one's salvation. However, there is only *one way* to lose one's salvation, and the window of time when that is possible is during the last 3.5 years before the visible return of Christ, during the reign of the Beast. Any person who takes the mark of the Beast, or worships the Beast, or its image, will be irredeemable and lose their salvation. This includes any believer who transfers their allegiance from Christ to the Beast. Once a person decides to follow the Beast, they can not return to Christ: their decision, once made, is irreversible.

The scriptures seem to indicate that only during the reign of the Beast can a believer can lose their eternal salvation and forfeit their entrance into God's kingdom. Revelation is very clear about this: to take the mark of the Beast or worship the Beast or its image, is a one way ticket to the Lake of Fire:

> "Another angel, a third, followed them, saying with a great voice, 'If anyone worships the beast and his image, and receives a mark on his forehead or on his hand, 10 he also will drink of the wine of the wrath of God, which is prepared unmixed in the cup of his anger. He will be tormented with fire and sulfur in the presence of the holy angels and in the presence of the Lamb. 11 The smoke of their torment goes up forever and ever. They have no rest day and night, those who worship the beast and his image, and whoever receives the mark of his name.'
>
> 12 Here is the perseverance of the saints, those who keep the commandments of God and the faith of Jesus.' " Revelation 14:9-12

Those who come to Christ after the first rapture of the child, who are also not among the 144K, and are not martyred by the earth dwellers and the Harlot, must endure the reign of the Beast. If they can persevere without taking his mark or worshipping the Beast or its image, they will be saved and removed from the earth in the third rapture event—the one which takes place in conjunction with the Day of the Lord/wrath of God—just prior to the seven Bowl judgments. Believers who persevere will be a part of the heavenly priesthood and rule and reign on earth:

> "I saw something like a sea of glass mixed with fire, and those who overcame the beast, his image, and the number of his name, standing on the sea of glass, having harps of God. 3 They sang the song of Moses, the servant of God, and the song of the Lamb, saying,
>
> 'Great and marvelous are your works, Lord God, the Almighty!
> Righteous and true are your ways, you King of the nations.' " Revelation 15:2,3

Right now, born again and Spirit-filled believers cannot lose their salvation, but they *can* lose their rewards. *Salvation* is a free gift that we receive through the merits of Christ alone. *Rewards* are what we receive for faithfulness to Christ and for investing ourselves in the kingdom of God. Living a life which expresses the life of Christ, and bears the fruit of the Spirit, assures us of future reward and a position in the age to come.

Paul tells us that we must all appear before the judgment seat of Christ to receive rewards based on how we lived here on earth, whether our deeds were good or bad:

> "For we must all be revealed before the judgment seat of Christ that each one may receive the things in the body according to what he has done, whether good or bad." 2 Corinthians 5:10

Some believers, those who built on the foundation of their faith with 'wood, hay and stubble'—things without intrinsic value—will have nothing to show for their life: their works will be burned. Others who build with valuable materials like gold, silver and precious stones, will find their works survive the 'fire' on that day, and they will receive the rewards and blessings promised to them:

> "For no one can lay any other foundation than that which has been laid, which is Jesus Christ. 12 But if anyone builds on the foundation with gold, silver, costly stones, wood, hay, or straw, 13 each man's work will be revealed. For the Day will declare it, because it is revealed in fire; and the fire itself will test what sort of work each man's work is. 14 If any man's work remains which he built on it, he will receive a reward. 15 If any man's work is burned, he will suffer loss, but he himself will be saved, but as through fire." 1 Corinthians 3:11-15

Any believer—both those who are believers right now, and those who will become believers at the time of the end—can lose rewards. The 144k future 'first fruits' believers who come to Christ after the rapture of the child, have the potential to lose their rewards as well. One of their rewards is being removed from the earth before the 'hour of trial begins. The 144K will be raptured to Heavenly Mount Zion before that day, their rapture most likely taking place on First Fruits during the Feast of Unleavened Bread:

> "Because you kept my command to endure, I also will keep you from the hour of testing which is to come on the whole world, to test those who dwell on the earth." Revelation 3:10

The rapture of the 144K will take place before the reign of the Beast begins, and, in order to participate in this rapture, a person must be a part of the 'first fruits/ firstborn' of spiritual Israel, the 144,000. As we have seen, the 144K are a special class of firstborn/first fruits, given special promises which will be granted to them—but only if they fulfill the requirements inherent in the birthright.

The requirements of the birthright are spelled out in the letters to the 7 churches: faithfulness and perseverance, not 'fornicating' with the Harlot church, and love of the brethren. Obedience to these commands will be necessary to confirm one's call as 'firstborn', and in order to stand as one of the 144K on heavenly Mount Zion with Christ as those who are "redeemed from the earth". If any of the 144K should fall into a snare, hopefully they will have time to recover their birthright through repentance and faithfulness, before the second rapture overtakes them.

Remember that people who are called the 'first fruits' are a special class of people. They represent the very first people to believe the gospel and be saved, receiving a double portion of the Holy Spirit. Right now, that distinction belongs to the 12 apostles, who were the very first to believe in Christ in this age, and in whose steps we follow. The 12 apostles are the 'first fruits' and we are the main harvest of believers. The main harvest will be reaped—all at once—in the first rapture event, which will take place on a future Day of Atonement. The Day of Atonement is the appointed day when the 'priesthood' will be raptured into heaven, to begin their priestly service in the heavenly Holy of Holies.

The 12 apostles were the first to believe in Christ and so they have the honor of being the 'first fruits'. Though they belong exclusively to God, they were not raptured, nor brought into God's 'barn' while they were still living. Christ's prayer for His disciples, recorded in John 17, was that the Father would NOT take them out of the world! They were to be sanctified and sent out into the world, just as Jesus had been set apart and sent into the world. We believe in Christ today because these men were 'left behind'!

Those who will be chosen by God to be among the 144K, but who fail to live up to the requirements of the birthright, will be taken in the third and final rapture, when the 'main olive harvest' of Israel—as well as the 'other fruit' of believing Gentiles—are gathered into God's storehouse, but only under the condition that they have not taken the mark of the Beast. Those of the 144K who failed to gain the 'birthright' rapture—the second rapture taking place before the reign of the Beast begins—who then manage to persevere during the reign of the Beast without taking the mark or worshipping the Beast—will be removed from the earth before the wrath of God begins. They cannot lose their salvation, only their 'birthright'.

In summary:

1. The terms 'firstborn' and 'first fruits' indicate a special, sanctified person (like Christ) or a set-apart and sanctified class of people (the 144K, the 12 disciples) who are specifically chosen by God, and called to be His own for His sole pleasure and purposes. Chosen people are set apart to be used by God, and sent out to evangelize the world.
2. God's choice is sovereign and not the result of the merits of sinful man. All believers were chosen 'in Christ' before the foundation of the world, not because they were perfect and holy, but by virtue of Christ's finished work on the cross, expressing the out-working of God's sovereign plan and purpose:

   "Blessed be the God and Father of our Lord Jesus Christ, who has blessed us with every spiritual blessing in the heavenly places in Christ, 4 even as he chose us in him before the foundation of the world, that we would be holy and without defect before him in love." Ephesians 1:3

3. Though God chose certain people to belong to Him, His choice can be overruled by the individual. People must still 'self-select' to be a part of the 'chosen' people of God; that is, though God chooses us, and the Spirit 'woos' us, we must still individually heed the call and trust in Jesus. If anyone refuses the offering of God, the birthright will go to another.
4. The inheritance/birthright is a future blessing that belongs to the 'firstborn' but can be forfeited. Being 'chosen in Christ' does not automatically guarantee possession of the double portion. The chosen one must properly value the privileges and rights that belong to the firstborn, as well as participate in the training process (sanctification) which qualifies him or her to inherit the blessings of the birthright.
5. Anyone who is sanctified—who is in Christ—is part of the firstborn/first fruits class—a new race of humanity—birthed out of the Adamic race. As we have already discovered, one must also self-select to remain a part of the firstborn called out ones in order to receive the birthright.

Gaining the Inheritance

Since we have the assurance that we have eternal life because of the indwelling Holy Spirit, all believers should strive to obtain their full inheritance—the double portion. This is the reward that God has promised us, through Christ. Salvation is not a reward, because it is received by grace alone, through faith alone; it is a gift and not a reward. The blood of Christ has set us free from our sins and there is no condemnation. On the other hand, the inheritance is the reward we are given by God for what we have done in this life for the sake of Christ.

Those desiring the inheritance willingly submit to the chastening and perfecting work of the Spirit. The Spirit enables us to put to death our old nature, so that the life of the Firstborn may be manifested in us, that we may receive the double portion birthright.

If you have not been born again into the family of God, it's not too late to be adopted into His family:

> "For he says,
> 'At an acceptable time I listened to you.
> In a day of salvation I helped you.'
> Behold, now is the acceptable time. Behold, now is the day of salvation.' "
> 2 Corinthians 6:2

Christ will hear and answer the cry of anyone who calls out to Him in true repentance. Repentance is a change of heart and mind. It's a decision to turn away from one's own way of living, and follow the Lord...every day and every hour of every day:

"Dear Jesus: I want to be a part of God's family and I'm sorry for my sinful life. Please forgive my sins and give me your Holy Spirit so that I can be God's child."

If you prayed this prayer sincerely, you can have the assurance that God will forgive your sins, no matter what you have done, if you come to Him with a humble heart.

> "If we confess our sins, He is faithful and just to forgive us our sins and to cleanse us from all unrighteousness." 1 John 1:9

If you have been born again of the Spirit of God, but you are not living for Christ, it's not too late to repent and receive the assurance that you may obtain all the promises God has in store for you. Ask the Holy Spirit to guide you, to fill your heart and mind and sanctify you—to separate your affections from the things of the world—and transfer them to the eternal things of God. This is done through prayer as well, as an act of the will:

"Lord Jesus—I'm sorry that I have been living for myself and the things of this world. I ask that you change my thoughts and desires. I want to value the things you value. Please change me from the inside out. I cannot do this on my own, so I ask that you fill me with your Holy Spirit. I choose to submit my life to the Life of Christ flowing in and through me, and I choose to live for You." Amen

Chapter 33: The Ministry of the Holy Spirit in the Last Days

There is a common teaching concerning the last days ministry of the Holy Spirit which is tied in with the belief that 'tribulation saints' are not *bona fide* members of the Body of Christ. This doctrine states that once present day believers are removed from the earth, the Holy Spirit will leave the earth with them, never to return in the same way. Rather than dwelling inside of the believer as He does now, the Holy Spirit's interaction with believers during the 'tribulation' would more closely resemble the way He ministered during the Old Testament times. In those days, the Spirit would come 'on' people for a specific task or calling, and once the task or calling was accomplished, the Spirit could, and often would, leave them.

The Old Testament people of faith had a very different experience of the Holy Spirit than do believers right now. Since the time of the out-pouring of the Spirit on the 120 disciples at Pentecost 2,000 years ago, every true believer who receives Christ as their Savior, has been 'sealed' with the Spirit. Unlike the saints of old where the Spirit could only come *upon* them, believers now can experience the continual abiding presence of the Holy Spirit who *dwells inside* each 'born again' believer. Since the time of Pentecost, the Holy Spirit's presence in our hearts is a guarantee that we will receive everything God has promised us in Christ:

> "In him you also, having heard the word of the truth, the Good News of your salvation—in whom, having also believed, you were sealed with the promised Holy Spirit, 14 who is a pledge of our inheritance, to the redemption of God's own possession, to the praise of his glory." Ephesians 1:13,14

If anyone does not have the in-dwelling Holy Spirit, he does not belong to Christ:

> "But you are not in the flesh but in the Spirit, if it is so that the Spirit of God dwells in you. But if any man doesn't have the Spirit of Christ, he is not his." Romans 8:9

The Holy Spirit is a life-giving Spirit and He will resurrect the bodies of those who die in the Lord:

> "If Christ is in you, the body is dead because of sin, but the spirit is alive because of righteousness. 11 But if the Spirit of him who raised up Jesus from the dead dwells in you, he who raised up Christ Jesus from the dead will also give life to your mortal bodies through his Spirit who dwells in you." Romans 8 10, 11

The Holy Spirit empowers people to carry the message of the gospel and be witnesses for Christ:

> "He said to them, 'It isn't for you to know times or seasons which the Father has set within his own authority. 8 But you will receive power when the Holy Spirit has come upon you. You will be witnesses to me in Jerusalem, in all Judea and Samaria, and to the uttermost parts of the earth.' " Acts 1:7,8

The Holy Spirit guides us into all truth:

> "However, when he, the Spirit of truth, has come, he will guide you into all truth, for he will not speak from himself; but whatever he hears, he will speak. He will declare to you things that are coming." John 16:13

The Holy Spirit glorifies Christ and imparts the life and riches of Christ to the believer:

> "He will glorify Me, for He will take of Mine and will disclose it to you. All things that the Father has are Mine; therefore I said that He takes of Mine and will disclose it to you." John 16:14,15

The Holy Spirit baptizes us into the body of Christ:

> "For in one Spirit we were all baptized into one body, whether Jews or Greeks, whether bond or free; and were all given to drink into one Spirit." 1 Corinthians 12:13

The Holy Spirit reproduces the character of Christ in our lives:

> "But the fruit of the Spirit is love, joy, peace, patience, kindness, goodness, faith, 23 gentleness, and self-control. Against such things there is no law. " Galatians 5:22,23

These are just a few of the ways the Holy Spirit ministers to believers in this present age. The question is, how will He minister to believers during the last days?

Seven times in the letters to the seven churches believers are admonished to 'hear what the Spirit is saying to the churches'. This is a command from God, and this command implies that some sort of spiritual 'interaction' between believers and the Holy Spirit actually exists. What does this tell us about the Holy Spirit's relationship with the 144K and other end time saints? Does this mean that saints who are alive during the time of the end will be filled with the indwelling Holy Spirit? What else does the book of Revelation tell us about how the Holy Spirit moves and ministers in the last days?

The Seven Spirits

The first mention of the Holy Spirit in Revelation is found in the very first chapter of the book:

> "Grace to you and peace from God, who is and who was and who is to come; and from the seven Spirits who are before his throne." Revelation 1:4

In the opening greeting of the book of Revelation, the Holy Spirit is referred to as the 'seven Spirits before the throne' of God in heaven. A literal interpretation of this passage would lead one to believe that there are seven individual Holy Spirits! We know that there is only one Spirit, so we must assume that the number 'seven' is code, part of the symbolic representation of the Spirit in Revelation. As we have already noted, the number 'seven' represents 'fulness or completion' as well as divinity. The Holy Spirit is therefore the full and complete representation of God and is, Himself, a member of the Divine Community consisting of Father, Son and Holy Spirit. His presence in the heavenly throne room is in conjunction with the presence of both the Father and the Son.

The Holy Spirit before God's throne in Revelation 4, is symbolized by seven torches of fire:

> "Out of the throne proceed lightnings, sounds, and thunders. There were seven lamps of fire burning before his throne, which are the seven Spirits of God. " Revelation 4:5

The seven torches of fire remind us of the 7 branched menorah which stood in the tabernacle. The menorah was the only source of light in the Holy Place and the priests could only minister by the light of that source. One of the roles of the Spirit is to provide spiritual illumination to God's people. The 7 branched menorah represents the 7 Spirits of God before the throne of God. The Holy Spirit, as a Member of the Godhead, is the only source of true spiritual enlightenment and revelation.

The seven churches, represented by seven lampstands, are also meant to shine the light of truth in the midst of a dark and fallen world. They do this through the supernatural enabling of the Spirit. The fact that the seven churches are represented by seven lampstands is further confirmation that the Spirit of revelation and illumination will dwell in, and with, the end time believers who are represented by these seven assemblies.

In Revelation 5, the angel cries out for someone who is worthy to open the scroll so that the judgment of the wicked on the earth can get underway. A Lamb, appearing as though it had been slain, stands in the midst of the living creatures and the Elders. The Lamb has seven horns and seven eyes:

> "I saw in the middle of the throne and of the four living creatures, and in the middle of the elders, a Lamb standing, as though it had been slain, having *seven horns and seven eyes, which are the seven Spirits of God,* sent out into all the earth. 7 Then he came, and he took it out of the right hand of him who sat on the throne." Revelation 5:6,7

The slain Lamb is Christ. His seven horns symbolize the strength and power of the Spirit which is present in Christ. The eyes represent the omniscience of God which Christ also shares. The number 'seven' denotes both divinity and fulness. Therefore, Christ possesses all the power associated with divinity as represented by the seven horns; and He embodies all knowledge and wisdom as represented by the seven eyes. The horns and eyes we are told, also represent the *'seven Spirits of God which are sent out into all the earth.'*

In conjunction with the Father, Christ will once again send the Spirit out into all the earth. Christ does not send the Spirit to the world at large, but to His 'called out and chosen' people:

> "I will pray to the Father, and he will give you another Counselor, that he may be with you forever: 17 the Spirit of truth, whom the world can't receive, for it doesn't see him and doesn't know him. You know him, for he lives with you and will be in you. 18 I will not leave you orphans. I will come to you. " John 14:16-18

Though the apostles and the early church were the first to experience the abiding presence of the Spirit, they will not be the last. The ministry of the Spirit, which began with the early church, established the pattern for how the Holy Spirit would operate in and through all believers, at all times.

Christ referred to the Holy Spirit as the 'Spirit of truth'. As the end of the age draws near, the world at large will have less and less interest in the truth, particularly spiritual truth, choosing instead to embrace Satan's lies. Those who have been 'born from above' welcome the truth, the truth which shines like a light in their hearts and minds. As they walk in the light of the Spirit, they will also illuminate the world around them. Unlike the earth dwellers and false Jews, believers will gladly receive and welcome the Spirit of Truth.

Jesus told His disciples that the Spirit would one day dwell inside believers and that He would not just dwell 'with' them. While we walk through this world, Christ is with us via the Person of the Holy Spirit, so that we are never left without His companionship and care. Believers *are never abandoned* by God. The saints living during the last days will not be abandoned, either. Christ will be with them through the abiding presence of the Holy Spirit.

Chapter 34: The Resurrection of the Dead in Revelation

The Doctrine of the Resurrection

The resurrection of the dead has been a tenant of faith since before the days of Job. Numerous Old Testament passages speak of the truth of the resurrection of the dead. Even so, not all Jews in Jesus' day believed in the resurrection: the Pharisees held to this doctrine but the Sadducees did not. When challenged by the Sadducees with regard to the resurrection of the dead, Jesus confirmed to them that the dead would one day, indeed, be resurrected:

> "On that day Sadducees (those who say that there is no resurrection) came to him. They asked him, 24 saying, 'Teacher, Moses said, "If a man dies, having no children, his brother shall marry his wife and raise up offspring for his brother." 25 Now there were with us seven brothers. The first married and died, and having no offspring left his wife to his brother. 26 In the same way, the second also, and the third, to the seventh. 27 After them all, the woman died. 28 In the resurrection therefore, whose wife will she be of the seven? For they all had her.'
>
> 29 But Jesus answered them, 'You are mistaken, not knowing the Scriptures, nor the power of God. 30 For in the resurrection they neither marry nor are given in marriage, but are like God's angels in heaven. 31 But concerning the resurrection of the dead, haven't you read that which was spoken to you by God, saying, 32 "I am the God of Abraham, and the God of Isaac, and the God of Jacob?' God is not the God of the dead, but of the living." '
>
> 33 When the multitudes heard it, they were astonished at his teaching."
> Matthew 22:23-33

Old Testament saints before the time of Christ also believed in the resurrection of the dead. Even Job confessed that after his sufferings were over, he would see God, not through the eyes of a disembodied spirit, but in his (resurrected) flesh:

> "But as for me, I know that my Redeemer lives.
> In the end, he will stand upon the earth.
> 26 After my skin is destroyed,
> then I will see God in my flesh," Job 19:25, 26

The Transformation of the Living

The resurrection of the dead has been a doctrine of the faith since ancient times and was not a new doctrine at the time of Christ and the apostles. However, the idea that living saints would be 'changed'—transformed from mortal people to immortal, glorified people—*apart from dying*, was something totally new. The Apostle Paul was given a revelation from the Lord concerning a generation of believers whose bodies would be transformed from mortal, human bodies into immortal, glorified bodies, in the 'twinkling of the eye'. In addition, this change of the living would take place *at the same time that the dead in Christ were raised.* The dead will be raised, their bodies transformed from 'corruptible' to 'incorruptible' and living believers will be changed from mortal men to glorified, immortal men and women. The 'mystery' of glorification apart from death was a revelation given to the apostle Paul by Christ:

> "Behold, I tell you a mystery. We will not all sleep, but we will all be changed, 52 in a moment, in the twinkling of an eye, at the last trumpet. For the trumpet will sound and the dead will be raised incorruptible, and we will be changed." 1 Corinthians 15:51, 52

The 'last trumpet' to which Paul refers in this passage in 1 Corinthians, is a reference to the Roman 'victory trumpet'— the trumpet which announced that a military battle had just been won. The last trumpet for believers, is also a victory trumpet, announcing the victory Christ has obtained for believers over death and mortality:

> "But when this perishable body will have become imperishable, and this mortal will have put on immortality, then what is written will happen: 'Death is swallowed up in victory. 55 Death, where is your sting?' " 1 Corinthians 15:54, 55

Many people assume that the 'last trumpet' mentioned in 1 Corinthians 15:51, is the trumpet which announces *the rapture* of believers, and they do not understand that what Paul is referring to in this passage, is the *victory* trumpet, the signal that Christ's victory *over death* will be complete at the glorification of both the living and the dead in Christ. Paul is comparing the trumpet sounded by the Roman armies when victorious in a battle, with the victory blast that will accompany the resurrecting dead and the transformed living. The sounding of this trumpet has nothing to do with the rapture, or with the 7th Trumpet of Revelation, but with the glorification of both the dead in Christ at their resurrection, and the living believers who will be simultaneously changed when the dead are raised.

Many well-meaning Bible teachers have superimposed the rapture onto the mystery of 'glorification apart from death'. However, the concept that Paul is actually referring to in this passage, is the idea that there will be a generation of believers

254

who will enter eternity in glorified bodies *apart from dying*. Paul makes no mention of a rapture in these verses; and by reading the passage in its context, we are informed that this 'mystery' is not about the rapture at all, but about the fact of the resurrection, and that *living believers will be glorified without having to die first,* and that *the 'change' of the living will take place in conjunction with the resurrection of the dead.*

Surely, somewhere within its pages, the book of Revelation must describe this monumental event; the time when the dead in Christ are resurrected and the living are changed—and so it does! The vision of the "mighty angel" with the little scroll in his hand in Revelation 10, records for us—in symbolic form—the prophecy of the resurrection of the dead and the change of the living. This event is depicted for us in the typical spare, Hebraic style: indirect, symbolic and layered:

> "I saw a mighty angel coming down out of the sky, clothed with a cloud. A rainbow was on his head. His face was like the sun, and his feet like pillars of fire. 2 He had in his hand a little open book. He set his right foot on the sea, and his left on the land. 3 He cried with a loud voice, as a lion roars. When he cried, the seven thunders uttered their voices. 4 When the seven thunders sounded, I was about to write; but I heard a voice from the sky saying, 'Seal up the things which the seven thunders said, and don't write them.'

> 5 "The angel whom I saw standing on the sea and on the land lifted up his right hand to the sky 6 and swore by him who lives forever and ever, who created heaven and the things that are in it, the earth and the things that are in it, and the sea and the things that are in it, that there will no longer be delay, 7 but in the days of the voice of the seventh angel, when he is about to sound, then the mystery of God is finished, as he declared to his servants the prophets." Revelation 10:1-7

If we were to interpret this passage using the logical, rational, linear Greek interpretive method, it is doubtful that we would be able to see the resurrection of the dead or the glorification of the living in this passage at all! But by implementing the Hebraic method, whereby Revelation is interpreted via its symbols and imagery, we'll find that God has given us all the resources necessary to decode this vision. Like many passages in Revelation, this passage relies heavily on a number of Old Testament allusions, and these allusions are what will enable us to 'decode' the meaning of the symbols in Revelation 10.

The Mighty Angel

Revelation talks more about angels than does any other book in the Bible. Angels act as God's ministers during the last days, delivering His messages and carrying out His will. The seven Trumpet angels announce the various plagues and woes, and the seven Bowl angels are responsible for the out-pouring of the wrath of God on the world. We have already seen how the book of Revelation was communicated from Christ to John via an angel. Angels are mediators and message carriers, delivering both wrath and hope during the last days.

In the Bible's original languages of Hebrew and Greek, the word translated as 'angel' in our English Bibles, usually describes a class of ministering spirit beings. God has His angelic servants and Satan has his as well. The angels in heaven praise, worship and adore God, and God sends His angels on assignment to the earth to deliver messages, encourage His people, and to carry out His judgments. In imitation of God's angels, Satan's angels do many of these same things as well.

In the scriptures, the word 'angel' can also be translated as 'messenger'. Some scripture passages actually translate the Greek or Hebrew word for 'angel' as 'messenger', when it's clear that the passage is referring to mortal people who are message carriers.

Sometimes the word 'angel' is not referring to either a human messenger or a class of spirit beings. In these cases, the word 'angel' refers to appearances of Christ before He was born as a baby in Bethlehem. In Genesis, the 'Angel of the Lord' appeared to Abraham and Hagar; in Exodus, He appeared to Moses. The Angel of the Lord was no ordinary angel: He was the second Person of the Trinity, the One who led the children of Israel throughout their wilderness wanderings, manifesting His glory in the pillar of fire and cloud. The Angel of the Lord was a theophany of Christ—a pre-incarnate appearance of the Eternal Son of God.

The Almighty God rules from His throne in heaven and only infrequently does He interact with humans directly. It is not possible for mortal man to see the ineffable glory and majesty of the Almighty and live. Moses saw the 'backside' of God's glory when God placed him in the cleft of a rock; and Isaiah 'saw the Lord, high and lifted up' and declared "Woe is me!" Because of man's sinful nature, God sends an intermediary to carry out His will and deliver His messages. Sometimes God uses an angel as an intermediary, and sometimes, as He did in the Old Testament days, *He sends His Son*, who, in this case, appears as the Angel of the Lord.

In the last book of the Old Testament, the book of Malachi, the Angel of the Lord —Christ—is also referred to as 'the Messenger of the covenant':
" 'Behold, I send my messenger, and he will prepare the way before me!
The Lord, whom you seek, will suddenly come to his temple. Behold, the

messenger of the covenant, whom you desire, is coming!' says Yahweh of Armies." Malachi 3:1

This prophecy refers to Christ, who is the Messenger of God's covenant. Jesus was the Angel who came to God's people, Israel, 2000 years ago, appearing suddenly in His temple. The Hebrew word for 'messenger' in this passage is the same word that is usually translated as 'angel' in other passages.

There are three possible meanings for the word 'angel' in the scriptures: 1) a class of spirit beings; 2) a human messenger; or 3) a reference to Christ, as the Angel of the Lord—God's Messenger.

Unlike most of the angels in the book of Revelation, the Mighty Angel of Revelation 10 is described in great detail. He seems different from the other angels who populate the pages of Revelation. He's described as coming down from heaven, clothed with a cloud, a rainbow over his head; his face is like the sun, and his feet like pillars of fire. The cloud and the rainbow, "face like the sun", etc, are symbols which are intended to be 'decoded'. Once we break the code of the symbols, we can ascertain the identity of this particular angel.

First, the angel is described as being 'mighty' and coming down from heaven. This particular 'angel' has extraordinary power and we know that he originates from heaven:

> "I saw a mighty angel coming down out of the sky, clothed with a cloud. A rainbow was on his head. His face was like the sun, and his feet like pillars of fire." Revelation 10:1

The mighty angel doesn't 'fall from heaven' like Satan who is 'cast out' or like the angel who is tasked with the opening of the bottomless pit:

> "The fifth angel sounded, and I saw a star from the sky which had fallen to the earth. The key to the pit of the abyss was given to him." Revelation 9:1

The word, 'star', as we know from Revelation 1: 20, is the 'code' word for 'angel'. In Revelation 12:4, the word, 'star', applies to the fallen angels as well:

> "His tail drew one third of the stars of the sky, and threw them to the earth. The dragon stood before the woman who was about to give birth, so that when she gave birth he might devour her child." Revelation 12:4

Next, we see that this mighty angel is clothed with a cloud. In Revelation, clouds are often associated with Christ. Christ 'comes with the clouds' in Revelation 1:7, and He is the "One like a Son of Man" who is seated on a cloud, in Revelation 14:14:

> "Behold, he is coming with the clouds, and every eye will see him, including those who pierced him. All the tribes of the earth will mourn over him. Even so, Amen." Revelation 1:7

> "I looked, and saw a white cloud, and on the cloud one sitting like a son of man, having on his head a golden crown, and in his hand a sharp sickle." Revelation 14:14

There is also an Old Testament passage in Daniel which refers to 'One like a Son of Man coming with the clouds'. Christ is clearly the One who comes with the clouds in this passage:

> "I saw in the night visions, and behold, there came with the clouds of the sky one like a son of man, and he came even to the Ancient of Days, and they brought him near before him. 14 Dominion was given him, and glory, and a kingdom, that all the peoples, nations, and languages should serve him. His dominion is an everlasting dominion, which will not pass away, and his kingdom one that which will not be destroyed." Daniel 7:13,14

Clouds are associated with the glory and presence of God:

> "Yahweh said to Moses, 'Behold, I come to you in a thick cloud, that the people may hear when I speak with you, and may also believe you forever.' Moses told the words of the people to Yahweh. " Exodus 19:9

> "While he was still speaking, behold, a bright cloud overshadowed them. Behold, a voice came out of the cloud, saying, 'This is my beloved Son, in whom I am well pleased. Listen to him.' " Matthew 17:5

When God spoke to Moses on the mountain, He came in a thick cloud; and when God hovered over the mount of transfiguration in the New Testament, He was also enveloped in a cloud. The mighty angel of Revelation 10 is also said to be 'clothed' or 'wrapped' in a cloud:

> "I saw a mighty angel coming down out of the sky, clothed with a cloud. A rainbow was on his head. His face was like the sun, and his feet like pillars of fire." Revelation 10;1

This angel also has a rainbow over his head. The rainbow was first mentioned in Revelation in conjunction with the throne of God:

> "Behold, there was a throne set in heaven, and one sitting on the throne
> 3 that looked like a jasper stone and a sardius. There was a *rainbow
> around the throne,* like an emerald to look at. " Revelation 4:2b,3

When the prophet Ezekiel was given a vision of the Lord, both the cloud and the rainbow were used to depict His glory:

> "As the appearance of the rainbow that is in the cloud in the day of rain,
> so was the appearance of the brightness all around." Ezekiel 1:28

This angel also has a 'face like the sun'. When Jesus first appeared to John in Revelation 1, He was described as having a glorious countenance:

> "He had seven stars in his right hand. Out of his mouth proceeded a sharp
> two-edged sword. His face was like the sun shining at its brightest." Revela-
> tion 1:16

Jesus is described as having a face like the sun at His transfiguration:

> "He was changed before them. His face shone like the sun, and his
> garments became as white as the light." Matthew 17:2

This angelic being is also said to have legs like pillars of fire, similar to the depiction of Christ in Revelation 1:

> "His feet were like burnished brass, as if it had been refined in a furnace.
> His voice was like the voice of many waters. " Revelation 1:15

The prophet Daniel also saw a 'man' who bears a striking resemblance to the glorified Christ of Revelation 1:

> "In the twenty-fourth day of the first month, as I was by the side of the
> great river, which is Hiddekel, 5 I lifted up my eyes and looked, and be-
> hold, there was a man clothed in linen, whose waist was adorned with
> pure gold of Uphaz. 6 His body also was like beryl, and his face as the ap-
> pearance of lightning, and his eyes as flaming torches. His arms and his
> feet were like burnished bronze. The voice of his words was like the voice
> of a multitude." Daniel 10:4-6

Through the use of symbols which point us to *specific passages* in the Bible, we are provided with enough clues to enable us to identify this particular angel. The conclusion that we are intended to arrive at, is that the 'mighty angel' of Revelation 10, is none other than the Lord Jesus Himself, coming as the Angel of the Lord.

> " I saw a mighty angel coming down out of the sky, clothed with a cloud. A rainbow was on his head. His face was like the sun, and his feet like pillars of fire. 2 He had in his hand a little open book. He set his right foot on the sea, and his left on the land. 3 He cried with a loud voice, as a lion roars." Revelation 10:1-3a

Christ *is* the Mighty Angel sent by God to carry a message to the earth. Jesus is acting as God's agent, God's intermediary and as His 'messenger'. We read that this Angel is carrying a little scroll in His hand, further emphasizing the messenger aspect of Christ's role in this passage. For the record, I do not believe that Christ is one of a class of created spirit-beings known as 'angels'; rather He is an angel in the sense that He is God's Messenger and Intermediary—the Angel of the Lord—and it is in this capacity that Jesus is symbolized by the 'Mighty Angel' of Revelation 10.

Christ, the Mighty Angel, places His right foot on the sea and His left foot on the land. This action conveys His jurisdiction over both the sea and the land. He is assuming a posture of strength, authority and dominion.

The Sea and the Nephilim

To the Hebrew mind, the 'sea' and the 'land'—besides being geographical features—carry specific connotations which shed light on the passage concerning the Mighty Angel. Before we continue our study of Revelation 10, a little background will be necessary to understand the meaning of the symbols, the 'sea' and the 'land'.

In the Old Testament, the 'sea' was synonymous with the place of the dead; and the 'land' was the home of the living. That the sea would be equated with death is not surprising as the great flood of Noah's day brought about the death of all life on earth—save for eight people—and caused the earth to become one vast, watery graveyard of animals, men and *nephilim*. The sea became synonymous with the abode of demons, death and destruction.

The *nephilim* were hybrids: part human and part angel. Genesis tells us that the 'sons of God' saw the 'daughters of men', took them to wife and bore children by them:

> "When men began to multiply on the surface of the ground, and daughters were born to them, 2 God's sons saw that men's daughters were

beautiful, and they took any that they wanted for themselves as wives. 3 Yahweh said, 'My Spirit will not strive with man forever, because he also is flesh; so his days will be one hundred twenty years.' 4 The Nephilim were in the earth in those days, and also after that, when God's sons came in to men's daughters and had children with them. Those were the mighty men who were of old, men of renown." Genesis 6:1-4

The *nephilim* were the giants of the Bible stories, terrifying beings whose existence has been confirmed through archeology, and through the many legends found in cultures throughout the world. The angelic corruption of humankind, which produced the *nephilim* hybrids—the giants—was no doubt an intensional act on the part of the dark, spiritual, satanic forces to destroy God's crowning work of creation: mankind. In the processes of corrupting, defiling and defacing mankind, they hoped they could also *prevent the birth of the Messiah*, the promised 'seed of the woman', the One who would crush the serpent's head:

> "Yahweh God said to the serpent,
> 'Because you have done this,
> you are cursed above all livestock,
> and above every animal of the field.
> You shall go on your belly
> and you shall eat dust all the days of your life.
> 15 I will put hostility between you and the woman,
> and between your offspring and her offspring.
> He will bruise your head,
> and you will bruise his heel.' " Genesis 3:14,15

The 'sons of God', recorded in Genesis 6, are identified with the 'Watchers'—angels whom God had originally intended to watch over and care for mankind. However, instead of caring for them, they corrupted them. Through interbreeding with human women, the sons of God caused the human race to become less and less human. God knew that—were this kind of defiling procreation to continue unabated—mankind as originally created in God's image, would cease to exist. The bulk of humanity would reflect the nature of the fallen angels. The image of God would be completely erased, being replaced instead with the image of the Watchers. This genetic corruption would lead to the end of the human race. Mankind would become something other than man: he would be irredeemable and forever lost.

Noah, however, was perfect in his generation, that is in his genetics. (Genesis 6:14) Noah was not sinless, rather he was completely *human*, with no genetic 'defect'. He had no *'nephilim'* or Watcher genes which could be passed on, thereby

261

further corrupting the human race. The genetic code of the mass of humanity living at the time of Noah was defiled through the actions of the Watchers: only Noah and his family seemed to be free from this defilement.

> "The earth was corrupt before God, and the earth was filled with violence. [12] God saw the earth, and saw that it was corrupt, for all flesh had corrupted their way on the earth." Genesis 6:11,12

God sent the flood to wipe out the giants—the *nephilim*—in order to prevent the continued corruption of the human race. The bodies of the giants turned to dust, and their spirits were left to wander the earth looking for a 'home', for a body to possess. We call these wandering spirits, demons.

The judgement of 'sons of God' was severe. Their offspring, the giants, were drowned in the flood, and the angels who assumed human bodies and mated with human women, were placed in chains and assigned to the Pit:

> "Angels who didn't keep their first domain, but deserted their own dwelling place, he has kept in everlasting bonds under darkness for the judgment of the great day. [7] Even as Sodom and Gomorrah and the cities around them, having in the same way as these given themselves over to sexual immorality and gone after strange flesh, are shown as an example, suffering the punishment of eternal fire." Jude 6,7

Jude tells us that the fallen angels 'abandoned their proper abode'; that is, they intentionally put off their spiritual, angelic bodies and exchanged them for temporary 'human' bodies. They left their heavenly domain to indulge in sexual relations with human woman on earth, an act which was off-limits to them, and defiled both them and the people on earth.

These angels currently reside in the Pit, being held in chains until the time of the end, when they will be judged:

> "For if God didn't spare angels when they sinned, but cast them down to Tartarus, and committed them to pits of darkness to be reserved for judgment..." 2 Peter 2:4

In Revelation, the 'Pit' is synonymous with the 'Abyss', and the word, 'abyss', carries the connotation of the depths of the sea. The angelic beings who simultaneously corrupted not only themselves, but also contributed to the corruption of the human race, are currently being held in chains in the abyss, and they will be released at the 5th Trumpet:

"The fifth angel sounded, and I saw a star from the sky which had fallen to the earth. The key to the pit of the abyss was given to him. 2 He opened the pit of the abyss, and smoke went up out of the pit, like the smoke from a burning furnace. The sun and the air were darkened because of the smoke from the pit." Revelation 9:1,2

"They have over them as king the angel of the abyss. His name in Hebrew is "Abaddon", but in Greek, he has the name 'Apollyon.' " Revelation 9:11

The fact that the Pit will be opened during the last days is another indicator that the conditions corresponding to the 'days of Noah' will once again infect the earth. The phrase, 'the days of Noah' does not simply refer to an increase in violence and wickedness, but refers to the unlawful interaction of the 'sons of God' with mankind. Those 'who kept not their first estate', will be released on the earth one last time before they are forever consigned to the Lake of Fire. We'll be looking at the occupants of the Abyss/Pit in greater detail later, including their king, Apollyon, who is also known as Abaddon—the Destroyer.

The flood destroyed the children of the Watchers, and at the same time the Watchers themselves were imprisoned in the Pit, also known as the Abyss. To the Hebrew mind, the flood, the sea and the Abyss were all places of death, evil and darkness. In the Old Testament book of Jonah, the runaway prophet also likened the sea to Sheol, the place of the dead:

"Out of the belly of Sheol I cried.
You heard my voice.
3 For you threw me into the depths,
in the heart of the seas.
The flood was all around me.
All your waves and your billows passed over me." Jonah 2:2b,3

In Exodus, the sea, which is a symbol of death, is held in contrast to the dry land, the place of the living:

"In the morning watch, Yahweh looked out on the Egyptian army through the pillar of fire and of cloud, and confused the Egyptian army. 25 He took off their chariot wheels, and they drove them heavily; so that the Egyptians said, 'Let's flee from the face of Israel, for Yahweh fights for them against the Egyptians!'

26 "Yahweh said to Moses, 'Stretch out your hand over the sea, that the waters may come again on the Egyptians, on their chariots, and on their horsemen.' 27 Moses stretched out his hand over the sea, and the sea re-

turned to its strength when the morning appeared; and the Egyptians fled against it. Yahweh overthrew the Egyptians in the middle of the sea. [28] The waters returned, and covered the chariots and the horsemen, even all Pharaoh's army that went in after them into the sea. There remained not so much as one of them. [29] But the children of Israel walked on dry land in the middle of the sea, and the waters were a wall to them on their right hand and on their left." Exodus 14:24-29

The Egyptians perished in the waters, and the Red Sea became their grave. The children of Israel passed over on dry land *through* the Red Sea. They were preserved from Pharaoh's army, and also preserved from death in the sea. To those who believe in Christ, 'crossing over on dry land' is symbolic of crossing over from death into life:

> "Most certainly I tell you, he who hears my word and believes him who sent me has eternal life, and doesn't come into judgment, but has passed out of death into life. " John 5:24

Later in Revelation, we'll read that the Beast who was mortally wounded, will be resurrected. He is depicted as rising out of the sea or place of the dead:

> "Then I stood on the sand of the sea. I saw a beast coming up out of the sea, having ten horns and seven heads. On his horns were ten crowns, and on his heads, blasphemous names...[3] One of his heads looked like it had been wounded fatally. His fatal wound was healed, and the whole earth marveled at the beast. " Revelation 13:1,3

This Beast is also described as ascending or coming up from the Abyss or bottomless pit, after which he will kill the Two Witnesses:

> "When they have finished their testimony, the beast that comes up out of the abyss will make war with them, and overcome them, and kill them." Revelation 11:7

At the final resurrection of the dead, at the Great White Throne judgment, the sea will give up the dead inside it. The 'sea' is a reference to Sheol, the place of the dead, which will deliver up the souls of the dead contained therein:

> "The sea gave up the dead who were in it. Death and Hades gave up the dead who were in them." Revelation 20:13

There will be 'no sea' when God recreates the new heavens and the new earth. The absence of the sea described in the scriptures, is not referring to the absence of a literal body of water called 'the sea', but the absence of death, and the place of the dead. The 'sea', Death and Sheol will be no more because the 'former things' will have passed away:

> "I saw a new heaven and a new earth, for the first heaven and the first earth have passed away, and the sea is no more...4 He will wipe away every tear from their eyes. Death will be no more; neither will there be mourning, nor crying, nor pain any more. The first things have passed away."
> Revelation 21:1,4

The Land of the Living

The Mighty Angel places one foot on the sea and one foot on the land. If the sea represents death and the place of the dead, what does the 'land' represent? The 'land' represents the abode of the living:

> "I am still confident of this:
> I will see the goodness of Yahweh in the *land of the living*." Psalm 27:13

> "I said, 'I won't see Yah,
> Yah in the land of the living.
> I will see man no more with the inhabitants of the world.' "
> Isaiah 38:11

We have already seen that the children of Israel were preserved through the sea, crossing over on 'dry land'. The land is the place where the living dwell, as opposed to the sea, which represents the place of the dead.

If the Mighty Angel in Revelation 10, is identified as Christ, who places one foot on the 'sea'/Sheol, indicating that He has authority over those who dwell in the sea—place of the dead, then by placing His other foot on the land, we know that He also has authority over those who dwell in the 'land of the living'.

The Mighty Angel—Christ—is seen taking authority over people who belong to Him, both the dead, as represented by the sea, and the living who are on the land.

The Lion's Roar and the Seven Thunders

Next, we read that the Mighty Angel—Christ—'roars like a lion':

"And he set his right foot on the sea and his left foot on the land, and cried with a loud voice, as when a lion roars."

In Revelation 5, the Lamb—Christ—has already been referred to as the 'Lion of the tribe of Judah':

"One of the elders said to me, 'Don't weep. Behold, the Lion who is of the tribe of Judah, the Root of David, has overcome: he who opens the book and its seven seals.'" Revelation 5:5

Jesus is the Lion of Judah, and the King who will rule and reign on earth. The reason *why* the 'lion roars' is given to us in the book of Amos:

"Do two walk together,
unless they have agreed?
4 Will a lion roar in the thicket,
when he has no prey?
Does a young lion cry out of his den,
if he has caught nothing?
5 Can a bird fall in a trap on the earth,
where no snare is set for him?
Does a snare spring up from the ground,
when there is nothing to catch?
6 Does the trumpet alarm sound in a city,
without the people being afraid?
Does evil happen to a city,
and Yahweh hasn't done it?
7 Surely the Lord Yahweh will do nothing,
unless he reveals his secret to his servants the prophets.
8 The lion has roared.
Who will not fear?
The Lord Yahweh has spoken.
Who can but prophesy?" Amos 3:3-8

This passage assumes a 'cause and effect' between two actions: a snare will only spring when something falls into it. Two people must make travel plans *first*, before they can go on their journey together. The Lord reveals His plans to His people and THEN He performs what He said He would do. *A lion roars only when he has 'taken prey'.*

Christ is portrayed as a roaring lion in Revelation 10, and Amos 3 tells us that a lion doesn't roar unless he has taken 'prey'. If Christ is the 'lion who roars', what is the 'prey' that He has taken?

Since the Mighty Angel is taking authority over the place of the dead (the 'sea') and everyone in it; and the land of the living (the 'land') and all who dwell in it, I believe that the 'prey' He has taken are *His people* in the 'sea' and *His people* on the 'land; both the dead in Christ and the living believers who will be changed. This passage depicts the resurrection of the dead in Christ and the transformation of living believers into their immortal, glorified bodies.

Immediately after the Lion roars, the 'seven Thunders' respond to His roar. Who or what are the 'seven Thunders'?

> "He cried with a loud voice, as a lion roars. When he cried, the seven thunders uttered their voices. 4 When the seven thunders sounded, I was about to write; but I heard a voice from the sky saying, 'Seal up the things which the seven thunders said, and don't write them.' " Revelation 10:3,4

After the Lion 'roars', we are introduced to the seven 'Thunders'. We've already noted how the number, '7', represents divinity and completion. We have also noted that there are seven Spirits before the throne of God, which represent the fulness of the divine attributes present in the Holy Spirit. In the case of the seven Thunders, the number, '7', tells us that the Thunders are divine, representing the Spirit. There are also 'thunderings' which emanate from the throne of God, in conjunction with the seven Spirits:

> "Out of the throne proceed lightnings, sounds, and thunders. There were seven lamps of fire burning before his throne, which are the seven Spirits of God." Revelation 4:5

In Revelation 22:1, the Spirit before the throne is no longer represented by the thunderings, lightnings, and voices which proceed from the throne, but by the River of Life which flows from the throne of God. The Spiritual River of Life flows from God's throne *after* all things have been made new, *after* the earth has been judged and the Millennium and the Great White Throne judgment are things of the past. Until that time, the Spirit is represented by the seven torches *and* the "lightnings, thunderings and voices" which proceed from the throne of God.

Christ will take authority over the living in the world, and over the dead in the place of the dead. He will resurrect the dead and change the living. He will roar like a lion roars when He has taken His 'prey' and the Spirit of God, as represented by the 7 Thunders, will respond to the Lion's roar with a message of His own. The words John heard uttered by the 7 Thunders, have been sealed up. This is the only aspect of the revelation which John received from Christ that he was not permitted to share.

We know that both Christ and the Holy Spirit are instrumental in the resurrection of the dead:

> "Most certainly I tell you, the hour comes, and now is, when the dead will hear the Son of God's voice; and those who hear will live. 26 For as the Father has life in himself, even so he gave to the Son also to have life in himself. 27 He also gave him authority to execute judgment, because he is a son of man. 28 Don't marvel at this, for the hour comes in which all who are in the tombs will hear his voice 29 and will come out; those who have done good, to the resurrection of life; and those who have done evil, to the resurrection of judgment." John 5:25-29

> "But if the Spirit of him who raised up Jesus from the dead dwells in you, he who raised up Christ Jesus from the dead will also give life to your mortal bodies *through his Spirit who dwells in you.*" Romans 8:11

The seven Thunders represent the voice of the seven-fold Spirit of God. The Spirit will add His 'Voice'—His power and authority to that of Christ's—and together the Sevenfold Spirit and the Lion of the Tribe of Judah, will bring immortality and glory to those who are in Christ: both the dead and the living.

The Voice of the Archangel

> "For the Lord himself will descend from heaven with a shout, with the voice of the archangel and with God's trumpet. The dead in Christ will rise first." 1 Thessalonians 4:16

When Paul described the resurrection of the dead, he said that the Lord will descend from heaven with a shout, and that's exactly what we see the Mighty Angel doing in Revelation 10, descending from heaven to the earth—but in the case of Revelation, His shout is symbolized by a 'roar', so that we know that He has taken 'prey'.

Paul tells us that Christ's voice is the 'voice of the archangel'. This description of the archangel's voice has been a source of confusion for many people, and because Christ is described as having the voice of an archangel, some people believe that Jesus must BE an archangel! (This is the position of the Jehovah's Witnesses who believe that Jesus is the archangel, Michael.)
As we have already discussed, whenever God wants to show His Son acting as His intermediary, whether by delivering a message or otherwise acting in His stead, the Eternal Son is often symbolized by an 'angel' or 'messenger'. The Mighty An-

gel of Revelation 10, is an example of this use of the word, 'angel', and there are two more examples of this embedded within the pages of the Revelation. The 'roar' of the Mighty Angel in Revelation 10, IS the voice of the archangel which Paul described in 1 Thessalonians 4:16, and the resurrection of the dead in Christ will be preceded by the voice of the archangel, who is Christ. In 1 Corinthians 15, we learn that the 'change' of the living, and the resurrection of the dead will happen at the same time!

> "Behold, I tell you a mystery. We will not all sleep, but we will all be changed, 52 in a moment, in the twinkling of an eye, at the last trumpet. For the trumpet will sound and the dead will be raised incorruptible, and we will be changed. 53 For this perishable body must become imperishable, and this mortal must put on immortality. " 1 Corinthians 15:51-53

The 'trumpet of God' in the Thessalonians passage may be connected with the 'victory trumpet' of 1 Corinthians 15:51, as well as with the voice of the 7 Thunders emanating from the throne of God. The Feast of Trumpets, also known as the Day of Shouting, is the most likely day for the appearance of the Angel of the Lord, who will resurrect the dead and glorify living believers.

The Delay

Revelation 10 goes on to say:

> "The angel whom I saw standing on the sea and on the land lifted up his right hand to the sky 6 and swore by him who lives forever and ever, who created heaven and the things that are in it, the earth and the things that are in it, and the sea and the things that are in it, that there will no longer be delay, 7 but in the days of the voice of the seventh angel, when he is about to sound, then the mystery of God is finished, as he declared to his servants the prophets." Revelation 10:5-7

The Angel—Christ—raises His hand to heaven and swears by God, the Creator of all things, that the 'delay' is over. This passage in Revelation alludes to Daniel 12, and yet another 'angel' who makes the same gesture and swears by God. The angel (called a 'man' in Daniel 12) is also a theophany of Christ:

> "Then I, Daniel, looked, and behold, two others stood, one on the river bank on this side, and the other on the river bank on that side. 6 One said to the man clothed in linen, who was above the waters of the river, 'How long will it be to the end of these wonders?'

7 " I heard the man clothed in linen, who was above the waters of the river, when he held up his right hand and his left hand to heaven, and swore by him who lives forever that it will be for a time, times, and a half; and when they have finished breaking in pieces the power of the holy people, all these things will be finished." Daniel 12:5-7

The Angel—referred to as "the man"—told Daniel how long the 'shattering of the power of the holy people' would last. The Angel was referring the time of the 'great tribulation' for the Jews, which, he said, would last for 'time, times and half a time' or 3.5 years/1260 days.

The 'delay' to which the Angel in Revelation was referring to, was the delay of the beginning of the judgment of God, which, up until this point in time, has been postponed. Before the judgments can begin, Christ must take the scroll and before He can take the scroll, the next 'rotation' of priests must be in place in the heavenly throne room. The resurrected 'dead in Christ' will be the first group to appear in heaven in their glorified bodies as represented by the 24 Elders in Revelation 4. Shortly thereafter, the newly glorified living saints will be 'caught up' and join their resurrected brethren in heaven as well, as represented by the 24 Elders in Revelation 5. The judgments of God cannot take place until the resurrection and rapture of this division of the priesthood of believers—symbolized by the 24 Elders—takes place.

The Mighty Angel of Revelation 10, declares that, upon the resurrection of the dead and change of the living into their immortal bodies, the 'delay' is now over and that the prophecies that were revealed to God's servants—in particular the prophetic details and events revealed to His end time servants recorded in the book of Revelation—would soon take place. By the time the 7th angel sounds his trumpet, the judgments prophesied in the book of Revelation will be over.

Once the Mighty Angel resurrects the dead believers, and changes and raptures the living saints, the events associated with the Seals, Trumpets and Bowls—as well as the rest of the events which take place in the book of Revelation—can begin. The 'delay' will be over.

When did the 'delay' begin?

Remember the Great Sign of Revelation 12:1,2? That sign was a 'once in 7,000 year' astronomical alignment which took place during the Feast of Trumpets in 2017. This astronomical alignment was the first 'sign' or indicator that the seven year timeframe depicted in Revelation, was getting underway. The next 'sign' in Revelation 12, will be the sign of the Dragon, which will involve a war in Israel (the 'travail' of the woman), Satan casting a third of his angels to the earth ("alien" invasion?), the 'birth/glorification' of the 'child'/believers, the Dragon seeking to devour the newly glorified believers and finally, the 'child' being caught up to God and to His throne. We learn that the woman—Israel—will flee from the Dragon into the wilderness for 1260 days. This is the framework for the events which take place during the 7 years, with the midpoint being when the woman flees into the wilderness.

If the seven years preceding the return of Christ began on September 21, 2017, the midpoint would then be on April 3, 2021. What that means for us, is that believers must be taken into heaven no later than the fall of 2020. What this also means is that believers *could* have been taken into heaven in 2018 or 2019—*after* the Revelation 12 Sign and but *before* the midpoint. Obviously, we weren't taken in any of those years. The resurrection and the rapture—the events which will initiate the Seals, Trumpets, Bowls, etc,—have been delayed. The last possible year for the rapture of the 'wheat' harvest, also symbolized by the 'child' being caught up to God in Revelation 12, is during the fall Feasts of the Lord in 2020. The rapture of the child to the throne of God, corresponds to the appearance of the 24 Elders, the first 'rotation' of priest/kings in the throne room of heaven in Revelation 4 & 5.

I believe that the 'Great Sign' was the signal that we are now in the seven years preceding the visible return of Christ to the earth! (What that also means is that this book will have a short 'shelf-life'!)

Chapter 35: Revelation 12—The Seven Year Framework

The Sequence of Events Prior to the 1st Rapture

Revelation 12 gives us the framework for the entire seven year period of time before the return of Christ. The Revelation 12 sign, which took place over the Feast of Trumpets, September 21-23, 2017, initiated the start of the seven years commonly known as the 'Tribulation'. The Jews consider this two day feast to be one long day, and in the case of 2017, the 'trumpet' which sounded on of the Feast of Trumpets, was the 'Great Sign', announcing that one 'era' was ending, and that God was beginning the end game of His glorious plan of salvation and redemption

Daniel 12 gives an interesting corroborating 'day count' that I believe relates to the last seven years before the return of Christ:

> "From the time that the continual *burnt offering* is taken away and the abomination that makes desolate set up, there will be one thousand two hundred ninety days. ¹² Blessed is he who waits, and comes to the one thousand three hundred thirty-five days." Daniel 12:11,12

The words '*burnt offering*' are not in the original Hebrew text in Daniel 12:11, but were added by the translators to help the passage make sense. The translators assumed that the 'continual' referred to the burnt offerings and sacrifices, which took place without fail, day and night in the temple, while the temple was still standing. But I believe that if God wanted us to know that there were 1290 days between the time the sacrifices were taken away and the time when 'the abomination that makes desolate' would take place, the word for *offering* or sacrifice would have been in the text. According to what is *actually* in the text, all we know is 'something' which had been continuing like clockwork for millennia, was now over; and that if one were to count 1290 days from the day 'it' was over, we'd land on a day known as the 'abomination of desolation'.

I believe that what may have ended was 'business as usual' and *time*...we've run out of time, and God, through the Revelation 12 Sign, was indicating a 'sea change', the beginning of something new; that the end was in sight; and that from the 'one long continual day' when the Revelation 12 Sign appeared, until the day of the abomination of desolation, there would be 1290 days. Adding an additional 1335 days to the midpoint date of the abomination, would then take us to the arrival of a 'blessed day'.

If we assume that the Revelation 12 Sign on the Feast of Trumpets was the starting date for the last seven years, we can then calculate where the 1290, 1260 and 1335 day counts contained in the book of Daniel (and Revelation) take us. What we discover is that if we begin our timeline on September 21, 2017, *many of the 'day counts' land on specific feast days of the Lord,* days which have significance in God's word with reference to the final days and the in-gathering of His harvest of souls. (I use Torah Calendar to determine the dates for the Feasts of the Lord, and 'timeanddate.com' to calculate the 'day counts'. There is an error of plus or minus 24 hours.)

If we begin our timeline on the Feast of Trumpets in 2017, and add the 'day counts' provided for us in the books of Revelation and Daniel, all the feast days of the Lord line up perfectly with regard to the events Revelation describes, including the 1260 day ministry of the Two Witnesses, the 10 day persecution of believers, the 42 month reign of the Beast and so on. *All the day counts align in such a way as to not be mere coincidence; but instead confirm the accuracy of the whole timeline.* We'll be examining all of this in greater detail later in the book.

This claim may seem implausible, and many who are reading this will no doubt conclude that I'm making an assertion for which there is no possible scriptural support; but I hope that you will take the time to consider the astounding claims I will be presenting in the rest of this book. Your life and the lives of those you love may be at stake.

There are 1290 days between the Feast of Trumpets in 2017 and the presumed date of the abomination of desolation (to which both Jesus and Daniel referred, and as has been discussed previously in this book) on April 3, 2017. We know there will be 1260 days or 42 months or 'time, times and half a time', from the date of the abomination until the return of Christ (on the Day of Atonement, 9/14/24). The woman/Israel will be in the wilderness for 1260 days during which time the Beast will reign for 42 months. In Daniel 9:27, the midpoint begins with the abomination event at the 3.5 year mark of the last 'week' or 7 years, of Daniel's 70 weeks of years, leaving but 3.5 years on Israel's clock, at the close of which the 'desolator'—the Antichrist—will be destroyed:

> "*and* on the wing of abominations will come one who makes desolate; and even to the decreed full end, wrath will be poured out on the desolate." Daniel 9:27b

The starting point of the 1335 days to which Daniel 12:12 refers, begins at the abomination of desolation (4/3/21) and ends on the 24th day of the 9th Hebrew month—Hanukkah eve (11/27/24). The prophet, Haggai, referred to the 24th day of the 9th month as a day of blessing:

> "Yahweh's word came the second time to Haggai in the *twenty-fourth day of the month, saying,* [21] 'Speak to Zerubbabel, governor of Judah, saying,

"I will shake the heavens and the earth. 22 I will overthrow the throne of kingdoms. I will destroy the strength of the kingdoms of the nations. I will overthrow the chariots and those who ride in them. The horses and their riders will come down, everyone by the sword of his brother.

23 In that day," says Yahweh of Armies, "I will take you, Zerubbabel my servant, the son of Shealtiel," says Yahweh, "and will make you like a signet ring, for I have chosen you," says Yahweh of Armies.' " Haggai 2:20-23

In this passage, Zerubbabel is a type of Christ, whom the Lord God has chosen as His Servant and Heir, to rule over all the earth after God disposes of the kingdoms of this world along with their rebellious kings, at the end of the seven years. The '24th day of the 9th month' is Hanukkah eve. Hanukkah commemorates the renewal of the sacrifices in the cleansed temple after Antiochus Epiphanes—a precursor of the Antichrist—defiled the second temple as prophesied in the book of Daniel, hundreds of years earlier.

The Great Sign and the Birth of the Child

Let's assume that the whole of Revelation chapter 12 provides the framework on which we can hang key events in Revelation, events which will unfold during the seven year period of time that most people refer to as the Tribulation. The first event would be the 'Great Sign'—a specific astronomical alignment—a sign in the starry heavens depicting a woman in travail about to give birth:

"A great sign was seen in heaven: a woman clothed with the sun, and the moon under her feet, and on her head a crown of twelve stars. 2 She was with child. She cried out in pain, laboring to give birth." Revelation 12:1,2

A second sign follows:

"Another sign was seen in heaven. Behold, a great red dragon, having seven heads and ten horns, and on his heads seven crowns. 4 His tail drew one third of the stars of the sky, and threw them to the earth. The dragon stood before the woman who was about to give birth, so that when she gave birth he might devour her child.

5 She gave birth to a son, a male child, who is to rule all the nations with a rod of iron. Her child was caught up to God and to his throne. 6 The woman fled into the wilderness, where she has a place prepared by God,

that there they may nourish her one thousand two hundred sixty days. "
Revelation 12:3-6

Whereas the first sign took place in the starry heavens, the second sign—using the same symbols of the woman, the dragon and the child—continues the story which will actually take place on earth. The Dragon—Satan—is on the earth and he uses his 'tail' to cast a third of his fallen angels from heaven to the earth. He essentially divides his angelic forces into two groups: two-thirds of them remain in heaven (the heaven where God dwells) and one-third are tossed to the earth. Satan does not choose to bring his whole contingent to earth to assist him; some must be left in heaven to 'hold the fort' in the realm he has carved out for himself in God's heaven.

Will the 'stars' that Satan casts to the earth manifest visibly on the earth? Or will these fallen angels merely be unseen spiritual beings? Will they possess a body of some sort? I'm of the opinion that these fallen entities will present themselves as 'aliens'. The introduction of the whole 'alien' agenda into modern culture is not by coincidence or as the result of runaway imaginations; rather Satan has implanted into our collective psyche the concept of a technologically advanced civilization of 'space brothers' dwelling somewhere 'out there' in the cosmos. 'Contact' or disclosure will come prior to the child being born, and it will also most likely take place around the time there is a war in Israel. Maybe the satanic cover story designed for mass consumption, will be that these visitors are here to help the world ascend to the next level of evolution. Once aliens are a part of the story, the disappearance of millions of believers will have an explanation: these people were removed from the earth by visitors from space, benevolent beings who only have humanity's best interests at heart.

The Travail of the Woman

The Old Testament prophets predicted that in the last days Israel would experience a crushing blow from her enemies who would invade her borders from the north. The fall of Damascus in Syria will precede the invasion of Israel which will come from the northern mountains bordering Syria. The fall of Damascus is predicted in Isaiah 17:

> "The burden of Damascus.
> 'Behold, Damascus is taken away from being a city,
> and it will be a ruinous heap.' " Isaiah 17:1

Not only will Damascus be destroyed, but Israel herself will be decimated:

" 'It will happen in that day that the *glory of Jacob will be made thin,* and the fatness of his flesh will become lean. 5 It will be like when the harvester gathers the wheat, and his arm reaps the grain. Yes, it will be like when one gleans grain in the valley of Rephaim. 6 Yet gleanings will be left there, like the shaking of an olive tree, *two or three olives in the top of the uppermost bough,* four or five in the outermost branches of a fruitful tree,' says Yahweh, the God of Israel.' " Isaiah 17:4-6

In the end, Israel will stand alone. Where are her military allies? Where is the United States in all of this?

The answer: the USA will either not have the ability, or the inclination to help—or both. The United States will be contending with over-whelming troubles of her own. Chaos, civil disorder, natural disasters, an invasion of enemy forces into her 'homeland', economic collapse, pandemics—one or all of these—may contribute to her demise as a world power...and all will take place during a volatile presidential election year--2020.

In conjunction with the implosion of the United States, the forces arrayed against Israel will take advantage of their window of opportunity to invade Israel to gain her natural resources. The prophet Ezekiel describes a last days invasion of Israel by a coalition of nations; nations which only recently have begun to meld together on the world stage: Russia, Turkey, Iran, Sudan, Libya and Ethiopia:

"Yahweh's word came to me, saying, 2 'Son of man, set your face toward Gog, of the land of Magog, the prince of Rosh, Meshech, and Tubal, and prophesy against him, 3 and say, 'The Lord Yahweh says: "Behold, I am against you, Gog, prince of Rosh, Meshech, and Tubal. 4 I will turn you around, and put hooks into your jaws, and I will bring you out, with all your army, horses and horsemen, all of them clothed in full armor, a great company with buckler and shield, all of them handling swords; 5 Persia, Cush, and Put with them, all of them with shield and helmet; 6 Gomer, and all his hordes; the house of Togarmah in the uttermost parts of the north, and all his hordes—even many peoples with you.

7 'Be prepared, yes, prepare yourself, you, and all your companies who are assembled to you, and be a guard to them. 8 After many days you will be visited. In the latter years you will come into the land that is brought back from the sword, that is gathered out of many peoples, on the mountains of Israel, which have been a continual waste; but it is brought out of the peoples and they will dwell securely, all of them. 9 You will ascend. You

will come like a storm. You will be like a cloud to cover the land, you and all your hordes, and many peoples with you.' " Ezekiel 38:1-9

The Lord will use this invasion as an opportunity to make Himself known to Israel and the nations, and He, Himself, will deliver Israel:

" 'I will call for a sword against him to all my mountains,' says the Lord Yahweh. 'Every man's sword will be against his brother. 22 I will enter into judgment with him with pestilence and with blood. I will rain on him, on his hordes, and on the many peoples who are with him, torrential rains with great hailstones, fire, and sulfur. 23 I will magnify myself and sanctify myself, and I will make myself known in the eyes of many nations. Then they will know that I am Yahweh.' " Ezekiel 38:21-23

We have already identified the woman as being Israel, from whom the Messiah descended physically. The woman is also identified with the remnant of Israel who will flee at the time of the abomination of desolation. In the passage in Revelation 12, we read that 'travail' has come upon the woman: 'travail' being the code word for a war or conflict. Jeremiah predicted such a time for Israel:

"Ask now, and see whether a man travails with child.
Why do I see every man with his hands on his waist,
as a woman in travail,
and all faces are turned pale?
7 Alas, for that day is great, so that none is like it!
It is even the time of Jacob's trouble;
but he will be saved out of it." Jeremiah 30:6,7

Many Christians believe that "the time of Jacob's trouble", is synonymous with seven years of 'tribulation'. As we have already noted, there IS a seven year timeframe that Revelation describes, but not all of that time consists of 'tribulation'. War, wrath and persecution in Israel, will not last seven years, nor does Israel even have seven years *left* on her timeline. Since the three and a half year ministry of Christ fulfilled the first half of the 70th and final 'week' of the prophecy in Daniel 9:27, only three and a half years remain for Israel on her prophetic timeline. The last half of the 'week' won't begin until the abomination of desolation takes place at the midpoint.

Thus we can infer from the passage in Revelation 12, that the United States must collapse as a viable world power, and will be unable to come to the aid of Israel, who will then find herself being invaded by her enemies from the north, as depicted in Ezekiel 38. Add a possible 'alien' invasion into the mix; and it's into this chaotic and otherworldly milieu, that the 'child' will be born.

The 'child' represents believers on the earth who will be physically regenerated and receive their glorified bodies. Believers who possess the Spirit of God have already been *spiritually* 'born again' and given new life in their spirit at the time they received Christ. The presence of the Holy Spirit in our hearts guarantees that we will one day receive a glorified, immortal body as well. In 1 Corinthians 15:51, Paul states that there are some who would receive their glorified bodies apart from dying, people who will be glorified at the same time the dead are given incorruptible bodies. We have already noted that Revelation draws a distinction between the 'birth' of the child and the 'rapture' of the child—that the birth and the 'catching away' are not the same event, but are separated by a brief period of time, during which the Dragon will attempt to 'devour the child'.

The birth of the child will take place on the earth and believers will have a brief period of time before they are caught up to God. The newly glorified saints may walk the earth much as Jesus did after His resurrection. Though He possessed a resurrected and glorified body, He appeared to others as a 'normal' human being. Mary supposed Him to be the 'gardener'. The disciples on the road to Emmaus thought He was a fellow traveler. There was nothing unusual about His physical countenance when He appeared to the disciples after His resurrection, and there will most likely be nothing unusual about the appearance of newly glorified saints on earth after their birth into glorified bodies. I'm of the opinion that the ten days between the glorification/birth of believers and the rapture of the child, will be spent in sharing Christ with the lost. No wonder Satan will want to devour the child!

The spirits of the dead in Christ who are in heaven will most likely be reunited with their glorified bodies *in heaven* and not on the earth. We have already seen how the 5th Seal martyrs received their 'white robes'—their glorified bodies—in heaven, not on the earth. There will not be millions of people bursting forth from their graves and flying into heaven at the time of the resurrection/change.

The newly embodied, previously 'dead in Christ' are represented by the 24 Elders around the throne of God in Revelation 4; and the 24 Elders in Revelation 5 depicts the newly glorified *living* saints seated as priests—with Christ in the midst of them as the High Priest.

If my interpretation is correct, the 'resurrection/change' will take place on the Feast of Trumpets, September 18, 2020, with the voice of the Archangel (Christ) and the trumpet of God.

The glorification of living believers will be followed by intense spiritual warfare. Satan and his angels will seek to prevent the next 'rotation' of priests from entering the Holy of Holies in heaven. Both the resurrected dead and the changed living believers who make up the main harvest of souls of the 'wheat' harvest, must be present in heaven before Christ will take the scroll from the hand of His Father and begin to judge the earth.

The rapture or catching away of glorified living believers will take place on the Day of Atonement, September 28, 2020. The 144,000 of Israel will be sealed with the Spirit five days later on the Feast of Tabernacles, and on the 8th Day of the Feast, both Jews and Gentiles will be baptized in the Holy Spirit as prophesied by Joel:

> "It will happen afterward, that I will pour out my Spirit on all flesh;
> and your sons and your daughters will prophesy.
> Your old men will dream dreams.
> Your young men will see visions.
> [29] And also on the servants and on the handmaids in those days,
> I will pour out my Spirit." Joel 2:28,29

Chapter 36: Revelation 12 (continued)—The War in Heaven

> "There was war in the sky. Michael and his angels made war on the dragon. The dragon and his angels made war. 8 They didn't prevail. No place was found for them any more in heaven. 9 The great dragon was thrown down, the old serpent, he who is called the devil and Satan, the deceiver of the whole world. He was thrown down to the earth, and his angels were thrown down with him.
>
> 10 "I heard a loud voice in heaven, saying, 'Now the salvation, the power, and the Kingdom of our God, and the authority of his Christ has come; for the accuser of our brothers has been thrown down, who accuses them before our God day and night. 11 They overcame him because of the Lamb's blood, and because of the word of their testimony. They didn't love their life, even to death. 12 Therefore rejoice, heavens, and you who dwell in them. Woe to the earth and to the sea, because the devil has gone down to you, having great wrath, knowing that he has but a short time.' " Revelation 12:7-12

Just prior to the midpoint—the day when the woman must flee into the wilderness—Satan will be cast out of heaven, forever. Michael and his angels will wage war with the devil and his angels, and Michael's army will prevail and cast Satan and his minions to the earth.

Once Satan has been evicted from heaven, the glorified saints in heaven will begin to worship and praise God, declaring that salvation at last has come! The devil, who continually sought to find fault with believers on earth so as to accuse them before God, was, at long last cast down! The martyred saints—now residing in heaven, wearing their glorious new bodies—along with their brethren, the Elders, burst out in praise to God.

The defeat of Satan and his angels by Michael and his armies, will be met with shouts of joy: the 5th Seal martyrs, the 24 Elders and the 144K, along with the angels—everyone who calls 'heaven' their home—will rejoice! But 'woe' to the earth! Satan knows that his days are numbered, and that he will be compelled to have the cooperation of the earth dwellers if he is to succeed in maintaining his position on earth as the 'prince of this world' and the 'prince of the power of the air'. He will deceive the earth dwellers concerning his true identity and the identity of his false 'son', the Beast. These two—the Dragon and the Beast—along with the False Prophet, will comprise a false 'trinity' that will seduce mankind into assisting them in a last ditch attempt at the usurpation of what rightly belongs to Christ—the earth.

With the expulsion of Satan from heaven, the continual priestly intercession at the altar of incense in heaven, once being an essential ministry of Christ and His brethren—the priest/kings—is now over. Because Satan no longer has access to heaven in order to bring accusations against the saints on earth, the intercessory role of Christ and the Elders will have come to a close for the time being.

I believe that the war in heaven between Michael and Satan, will take place in conjunction with the 10 days of persecution of believers on earth. The persecution will be initiated by the Harlot on earth, and be carried out by the earth dwellers. The two-thirds of Satan's angels who remained in heaven—those not having been cast to the earth by the 'dragon's tail'—will battle Michael and his heavenly angels. The remaining third of fallen angels who were cast to the earth—in addition to the 'locust army' from the Pit (more on this later)—will do their utmost to neutralize God's influence through the few believers that are left on the earth. The final day of the 10 day persecution will coincide with Michael finally casting Satan out of heaven, and it will also coincide with the rapture of the 144K of Israel, who will take their place on heavenly Mount Zion. I believe that the convergence of these events will be on First Fruits, March 30, 2021—three and a half days before the midpoint on April 3, 2021. (Later in this book I will demonstrate how I arrived at First Fruits being the date for the culmination of these events in Revelation.)

The prophet Daniel made an oblique reference to the heavenly war between the angelic armies of Michael and Satan, when he described Michael as 'rising up':

> "At that time Michael will stand up, the great prince who stands for the children of your people; and there will be a time of trouble, such as never was since there was a nation even to that same time. At that time your people will be delivered, everyone who is found written in the book."
> Daniel 12:1

Michael is referred to as the great angelic prince whom God has placed in charge of the nation of Israel. Michael is a powerful spiritual being and the way Michael will 'rise up' in the last days, is by initiating the war in heaven to rid heaven of Satan and his minions. The effects of the war in heaven will spill over on to the earth. Daniel indicates that when Michael 'rises up', the nation of Israel will experience the worst time of distress in her history. This is the effect that the war in heaven will have on God's chosen people. Michael will 'arise' and, once Satan is cast out, things will get worse before they get better, for the nation of Israel. Daniel also speaks of the deliverance that some of God's people will experience at that time. Everyone whose name is in the Book will be delivered. This no doubt refers to the 144,000 of Israel, who will be taken into heaven at the same time that Satan is cast out.

Satan's defeat and expulsion from heaven will not come about because of God's direct involvement. Neither the Almighty or the Lamb will participate in the war in heaven. Rather, Satan will be defeated by what he may consider a *peer*—another angel—Michael. The fact that God does not stoop so low as to get involved in this war is an indication that Satan never posed an actual threat to God's rule in heaven.

During the eons that Satan and his angels have been plotting the takeover of heaven and earth, Satan, believing that he could eventually 'conquer' God and his hosts, will ultimately become a victim of his own hubris. In comparison to God, the Dragon's power and majesty is nothing. The Dragon's presence in heaven has only been tolerated by God because Satan was deemed a useful instrument in God's larger plan and purposes. Once Satan's presence in heaven is no longer useful to God, Michael and his angels will make short work of Satan and his angels, ridding heaven of the devil and his angels forever. *What a blow to Satan's pride that will be!*

Once Satan finds himself on the earth—an outcast of heaven as a result of his defeat by Michael, Israel's angelic guardian—Satan's full fury will be unleashed on Israel. Israel will become the focal point of the Dragon's wrath. This will initiate the time of the end for the Jews: the beginning of the last half of Daniel's "70th Week" and the "time of Jacob's trouble". Once the Dragon's 'son', the Beast, resurrects from the dead—arises from the 'sea'—and is installed as the messiah in the temple of God, all hell will, literally, break loose onto the nation of Israel.

Judgement always begins with the house of God, and because of this, God's judgment will fall in His own 'house' in heaven *first*, before He judges the earth and her inhabitants. The war in heaven between the angelic forces loyal to God led by Michael, and the opposing forces loyal to Satan, will be how the final end time cleansing will begin, and it will take place in God's house first.

At the end of the Millennial reign of Christ, after the Great White Throne judgment, God will create a new heaven. Who knows what spiritual filth Satan will have left behind. Satan is a destroyer and he no doubt will have left destruction in his wake, even in heaven. This may be one of the reasons why God will create not only a new earth, but a new heaven as well.

Converging Timelines

The Bible gives us not one, but two 'end time' timelines. The timeline for *believers* is recorded in the book of Revelation and depicts a seven year duration of time. The end time sequence of events for *Israel*, is in the book of Daniel, specifically in the prophecy of the '70 Weeks' in Daniel 9:25-27, as well as in Daniel 12.

Israel's 70th week is divided into two halves of three and a half years each. The first half of the week has already taken place during Christ's three and a half year ministry, leaving only three and a half years left on Israel's 'timeline'. The two timelines—the one for believers and the one for Israel—will 'meet up' at the midpoint. In Revelation, the midpoint is found (among other places) in Revelation 12 when the woman flees; and the midpoint for Israel is found in Daniel 12—after 'Michael rises up' when Israel's time of trouble begins. Both Revelation 12 and Daniel 12 refer to the archangel Michael and a 'time of trouble' lasting for a 'time, times and half a time' for Israel.

The midpoint of the seven year *timeline for believers,* as well as the *beginning* of the last three and a half years *for Israel*, is found in the fourth (and last) vision contained in the twelfth chapter of Revelation:

> "When the dragon saw that he was thrown down to the earth, he persecuted the woman who gave birth to the male child. 14 Two wings of the great eagle were given to the woman, that she might fly into the wilderness to her place, so that she might be nourished for a time, times, and half a time, from the face of the serpent.
>
> 15 "The serpent spewed water out of his mouth after the woman like a river, that he might cause her to be carried away by the stream. 16 The earth helped the woman, and the earth opened its mouth and swallowed up the river which the dragon spewed out of his mouth. 17 The dragon grew angry with the woman, and went away to make war with the rest of her offspring, who keep God's commandments and hold Jesus' testimony." Revelation 12:13-17

One of the first things the Dragon will do upon finding himself on the earth, is take his wrath out on the woman: that is, he will attempt to wipe out the nation who 'gave birth' to the Messiah, the nation whom Michael protects. We know from Revelation 12:6, that God will have already made for provision for the woman to be kept safe in the wilderness. We are told that she will be in the wilderness for 1260 days:

> "The woman fled into the wilderness, where she has a place prepared by God, that there they may nourish her one thousand two hundred sixty days." Revelation 12:6

The Flight of the Woman

Revelation 12:13-17 fills in the details of the woman's 'flight' that were left out in the vision of the sign of the Dragon and the child. We learn that the woman "is given two wings of a great eagle that she might fly into the wilderness." The 'Greek/Western' interpretation of this passage would have us understand that the Jewish remnant may, somehow, be 'air-lifted' (in actual airplanes!) to safety by some friendly or sympathetic nation. However, when using the Hebraic method to interpret this passage, the 'great wings' which carry the woman are viewed as *symbols* that need to be decoded.

The book of Exodus tells us that when the children of Israel fled Egypt, they were carried *by God* into the wilderness:

> "You have seen what I did to the Egyptians, and how *I bore you on ea-gles' wings,* and brought you to myself." Exodus 19:4

The Old Testament allusion found in Exodus 19, tells us that God Himself is the One who will lead His people to safety in the wilderness. That's exactly how He cared for His people at the time of the first exodus from Egypt, and that's what He will do again in the last 'exodus'. At the time of the first exodus, the 'Angel of the Lord' guided the fledgling nation, manifesting in the pillar of cloud and fire, and He was their continual protection all the days of their wilderness wanderings. Later on we'll see how the Lord Jesus will appear again as the Angel of the Lord, the one who will guide His people into the wilderness once more.

During the last days, when remnant of Israel witnesses the abomination of deso-lation, the event which Jesus described in His Olivet discourse as a fulfillment of the prophecy in Daniel 9, this will be their signal that they must escape into the wilderness, and to flee as quickly as they can. The remnant is represented by the woman in Revelation 12, and when the woman begins to flee, the Dragon will at-tempt to destroy her with a 'flood':

> "The serpent spewed water out of his mouth after the woman like a river, that he might cause her to be carried away by the stream. 16 The earth helped the woman, and the earth opened its mouth and swallowed up the river which the dragon spewed out of his mouth."

Again, we're not talking about a literal flood of water, but a flood of *troops*—an army who will pursue the woman, just as pharaoh and his army went after the children of Israel at the time of the first exodus from Egypt; and, just as God's people escaped through the Red Sea on dry land and the Egyptian army was drowned when the waters closed in on them, the same fate will come upon the army of the Dragon: only this time the army will be swallowed by the *earth*, and not by the sea.

Zechariah 14 tells us that when the remnant of Israel takes flight from Jerusalem, an enormous earthquake will open the way for them through the Mount of Olives to the east of the temple in Jerusalem. The Lord Jesus Himself will be the cause of the earthquake:

> "His feet will stand in that day on the Mount of Olives, which is before Jerusalem on the east; and the Mount of Olives will be split in two from east to west, making a very great valley. Half of the mountain will move toward the north, and half of it toward the south.

> 5 "You shall flee by the valley of my mountains, for the valley of the mountains shall reach to Azel. Yes, you shall flee, just like you fled from before the earthquake in the days of Uzziah king of Judah. Yahweh my God will come, and all the holy ones with you." Zechariah 14:4,5

Because most Bible teachers don't understand the symbolism of Revelation, or the sequence of end time events described in the prophetic word, they do not realize that Christ will be intimately involved in the rescue of His people during the last days, including serving as the Guide for the remnant of Israel, taking her to her place of safety in the wilderness—on 'wings of eagles'.

Many Bible teachers believe that the last seven years before Christ's return to earth will consist of seven years of 'tribulation'/wrath, during which time Christ and His Bride will be in heaven, feasting at a wedding supper, oblivious to the destruction taking place on the world below. Furthermore, many teach that not until the 'wedding feast' is over, will Christ make an appearance on earth, with His feet touching down on the Mount of Olives, *at the end* of seven years of 'tribulation' and wrath. Revelation contradicts this rather shallow and callous understanding of Christ's role as Savior and Deliverer. *Christ will appear to personally deliver the nation of Israel*, just as He will appear 'wrapped in a cloud, with a face like the sun' to raise the dead and change the living.

As a result of having an incomplete understanding of Christ's personal and intimate involvement with His people during the last days as described in Revelation (and other places in scripture), many believe that this passage in Zechariah must refer to the visible, triumphant 2nd Coming of Christ. They believe that Jesus will step down on the Mount of Olives at the *end* of the seven years, instead of in the middle of the seven years to rescue the woman—the remnant of Israel. Which interpretation is correct? The context in Zechariah 4 tells us exactly what is happening, and *when* it takes place: Christ steps down on the Mount of Olives, setting in motion an enormous earthquake. The mountain splits in half, north to south, and the remnant of Israel will flee through the valley that is formed as a result of the earthquake.

Revelation tells us the rest of the story and in chapter 12, verse16:

> "But the earth helped the woman and opened its mouth to swallow up the river that had poured from the dragon's mouth."

The Dragon's army, as it attempts to pursue the remnant, will be 'swallowed up' as the split in the Mount of Olives closes back up again. This interpretation is in harmony with what we have already read in Revelation about the 'earth coming to the rescue of the woman' and swallowing the flood, imagery which suggests that the ground has opened up. In Matthew, Jesus emphasized the need for haste on the part of the fleeing remnant; for once the enemy begins to pursue the remnant, their way of escape through the newly created valley in the Mount of Olives will soon disappear as the mountain returns to its place.

The split in the Mount of Olives will remain open for a very brief interval of time —long enough for the people to pass through, but *not* long enough for people to go home and retrieve their belongings before they flee:

> "When, therefore, you see the abomination of desolation, which was spoken of through Daniel the prophet, standing in the holy place (let the reader understand), 16 then let those who are in Judea flee to the mountains. 17 Let him who is on the housetop not go down to take out the things that are in his house. 18 Let him who is in the field not return back to get his clothes." Matthew 24:15-18

We know that the Two Witnesses will resurrect at the midpoint, and Revelation tells us that at the same hour they resurrect and ascend, that there will be a great earthquake in Jerusalem. This is the same earthquake we have already read about in Zechariah:

> " After the three and a half days, the breath of life from God entered into them, and they stood on their feet. Great fear fell on those who saw them. 12 I heard a loud voice from heaven saying to them, "Come up here!" They went up into heaven in a cloud, and their enemies saw them.
>
> 13 "In that day there was a great earthquake, and a tenth of the city fell. Seven thousand people were killed in the earthquake, and the rest were terrified and gave glory to the God of heaven." Revelation 11:11-13

The prophecies contained in Revelation 12, Zechariah 4 and Matthew 24, when 'layered' over one another, provide the details for the story of the flight of the woman—the remnant of Israel—into the wilderness. Christ will be the Angel of the Lord who leads them to the place prepared by God, bearing them on 'eagles' wings'.

The length of time that the woman will be in the wilderness is 1260 days or 'time, times and half a time', which is the equivalent of three and a half years. Daniel 12 refers to this same duration—"time, times and half a time"—as the length of time that Israel would undergo tremendous persecution, which he refers to as the 'shattering of the holy people':

> "I heard the man clothed in linen, who was above the waters of the river, when he held up his right hand and his left hand to heaven, and swore by him who lives forever that it will be *for a time, times, and a half;* and when they have finished breaking in pieces the power of the holy people, all these things will be finished." Daniel 12:7

The Jews who do not move quickly enough to escape with the remnant, who remain in Jerusalem, will be terribly persecuted by the Beast from the Sea. Many Jews would rather die rather than be absorbed into the empire of the Antichrist. Zechariah tells us that two-thirds of those left in the land will die and the remaining third will come to faith in Christ:

> " 'It shall happen that in all the land,' says Yahweh, 'two parts in it will be cut off and die; but the third will be left in it 9 I will bring the third part into the fire, and will refine them as silver is refined, and will test them like gold is tested. They will call on my name, and I will hear them. I will say, 'It is my people;' and they will say, 'Yahweh is my God.' " Zechariah 13:8,9

At the end of 1260 days, Christ will return to the earth and He will gather His remnant from the place where they have been kept safe from the machinations of the Dragon. The prophet Micah, describes the remnant of Israel as a flock of sheep being kept safe in a sheepfold. The 'One who breaks open the way', who is their King and Shepherd, is none other than Christ. Christ is the 'Breaker'—the One who split the mountain in two, creating the path of escape for the remnant:

> 'I will surely assemble all of you, Jacob.
> I will surely gather the remnant of Israel.
> I will put them together as the sheep of Bozrah,
> as a flock in the middle of their pasture.
> They will swarm with people.

13 *He who breaks open the way* goes up before them.
They break through the gate, and go out.
Their king passes on before them,
with Yahweh at their head." Micah 2:12,13

In summary: the full seven years of the end time timeline for believers is encoded in the twelfth chapter of Revelation, commencing with the Great Sign which coincided with the Feast of Trumpets in 2017. This sign established the beginning of the seven years. Sometime between the Great Sign and the midpoint 1290 days later, Israel will be devastated in a war. The resurrection of the dead and the rapture of the child will also take place after a time of spiritual and earthly warfare. Around the midpoint, the war between Michael and Satan will arise in heaven, taking place in conjunction with the 10 day persecution of believers on earth. The war in heaven will abruptly end when Satan and his angels are cast to the earth. All this will take place just days before the midpoint. After the Dragon is cast from heaven he will begin to pursue the woman (at the time of the abomination of desolation—which is at the midpoint). Three and a half years later, Christ will return to the earth at His second coming.

Chapter 37: The Mighty Angel, the Little Scroll and the Rebuilt Temple

In addition to resurrecting the dead and transforming the bodies of living believers, the Mighty Angel—Christ, represented by the Angel of the Lord—has another mission: delivering the little scroll He holds in His hand:

> "I saw a mighty angel coming down out of the sky, clothed with a cloud. A rainbow was on his head. His face was like the sun, and his feet like pillars of fire. 2 He had in his hand a little open book. He set his right foot on the sea, and his left on the land." Revelation 10: 10:1,2

> "The voice which I heard from heaven, again speaking with me, said, 'Go, take the book which is open in the hand of the angel who stands on the sea and on the land.'

> 9 "I went to the angel, telling him to give me the little book.
> He said to me, 'Take it and eat it. It will make your stomach bitter, but in your mouth it will be as sweet as honey.' 10 I took the little book out of the angel's hand, and ate it. It was as sweet as honey in my mouth. When I had eaten it, my stomach was made bitter.

> 11 "They told me, 'You must prophesy again over many peoples, nations, languages, and kings.' " Revelation 10:8-11

The Little Scroll

John now becomes an active participant in the story he has been recording. A voice from heaven tells him to take the scroll from the Angel—who is Christ making an incognito appearance on earth. John asks the Angel to give him the scroll, and once John has taken the scroll, he is told to eat it; it would taste sweet in his mouth but would turn bitter in his stomach.

The little scroll is not to be confused with the seven-sealed scroll that the Lamb takes from His Father's hand in Revelation 5. The little scroll is open, not sealed. The little scroll contains an open message for anyone to read. In the beginning the contents of the scroll and its message would be 'sweet', but will turn 'bitter' in the end. The prophet Ezekiel was also told to eat a scroll:

> "Yahweh's word came to me, saying, 2 'Son of man, prophesy against the prophets of Israel who prophesy, and say to those who prophesy out of their own heart, "Hear Yahweh's word: 3 The Lord Yahweh says, 'Woe to

the foolish prophets, who follow their own spirit, and have seen nothing!'"
Ezekiel 3:1-3

The words of the scroll that Ezekiel ate contained the message he was told to preach to the house of Israel. Jeremiah also speaks of the joy and sweetness of God's word:

"Your words were found,
and I ate them.
Your words were to me a joy and the rejoicing of my heart,
for I am called by your name, Yahweh, God of Armies." Jeremiah 15:16

What would make the joy and sweetness of God's word turn to bitterness? What message does the scroll contain? I believe that the answer to that question lies in the verses that follow:

"A reed like a rod was given to me. Someone said, 'Rise and measure God's temple, and the altar, and those who worship in it. 2 Leave out the court which is outside of the temple, and don't measure it, for it has been given to the nations. They will tread the holy city under foot for forty-two months.' " Revelation 11:1,2

What starts sweet and then turns bitter? To a Jew, the temple of God is the sweetest place on earth, and the desecration and destruction of the temple represents the epitome of bitterness:

"One thing I have asked of Yahweh, that I will seek after:
that I may dwell in Yahweh's house all the days of my life,
to see Yahweh's beauty,
and to inquire in his temple." Psalm 27:4

The decree to rebuild the temple of God will prove to be both sweet and bitter.

Rebuilding the Temple of God

The temple of God will be measured and rebuilt. The altar will be erected in its proper place and worshipers will come to offer prayers and praise to God. The temple will be on a smaller scale than previous temples and we are told that the outer court will not be a part of the newly rebuilt temple; the outer court described as being 'given to the Gentiles':

> "Leave out the court which is outside of the temple, and don't measure it, for it has been given to the nations. They will tread the holy city under foot for forty-two months." Revelation 11:2

Jerusalem is called the 'holy city' because the temple of God is there and the Presence of God resides in the temple. Authorization *from God* will be granted to rebuild the temple during the last days. The authorization to rebuild the temple will be conveyed *at the same time* the dead in Christ are resurrected and the living saints are glorified, on the Feast of Trumpets in 2020. The altar will be rebuilt and the people who worship there will be 'counted'. The only people who are ever 'counted' in Revelation are the 144,000 of Israel: 12,000 from each of the 12 tribes; and thus we are indirectly being informed that some of the 144K will worship in the rebuilt temple. (Remember, the number '144,000' is a symbolic number.)

The beginning of the seventh month on the Hebrew calendar marks the Feast of Trumpets. In the book of Ezra, the Feast of Trumpets was the day the returning exiles rebuilt the altar and offered sacrifices to God. After the Babylonian exile, temple worship began with the construction of the altar of burnt offering:

> "When *the seventh month had come*, and the children of Israel were in the cities, the people gathered themselves together as one man to Jerusalem. ² Then Jeshua the son of Jozadak stood up with his brothers the priests and Zerubbabel the son of Shealtiel and his relatives, and *built the altar of the God of Israel*, to offer burnt offerings on it, as it is written in the law of Moses the man of God." Ezra 3:1,2

After the Babylonian captivity, the altar was rebuilt on the Feast of Trumpets. Nearly 2000 years since the destruction of the temple in 70 AD, the altar will again be rebuilt on the Feast of Trumpets and God's people will worship before Him in truth and sincerity. God's time-keeping method, the one He uses for delineating spiritually significant events, does not travel in a straight line, but in a circle or spiral. The things that have taken place in the past, will take place again.

There are some who believe that rebuilding the temple in Jerusalem is a bad thing, and that those who desire to rebuild the temple are only preparing a temple for the Antichrist to defile. The book of Revelation, however, is very clear that the 3rd temple will be the 'temple of God' in the 'holy city'. Not until the temple is desecrated will the temple lose its sweetness, and be transformed into the bitter, defiled temple of the Beast.

Why would God reinstate the sacrificial system, the very system He put an end to when the veil was torn in two when Christ died on the cross? There are a couple of reasons why He may do this. First, the sacrificial system was never intended to remove the sins of the people, but only temporarily cover sin until such a time as the Lamb of God would provide perfect atonement for the sins of the world. All things having to do with the temple—the sacrifices, the rituals, the feast days, sabbaths and so on—*all point to Christ and God's plan of redemption*. If ever there was an object lesson that graphically demonstrated the high price of sin and the lengths to which God was willing go to pay for sin in sending His One and Only Son, there is no better object lesson than the sacrifices, offerings and feast days of Israel. The book of Hebrews sheds light on the meanings behind the various aspects of temple worship, and I believe that this particular New Testament book—the book of Hebrews—will be a source of encouragement and instruction for new believers in Israel.

"Those Who Worship There..."

In a previous chapter, I showed how Jesus made a distinction between 'Jews' and 'Israelites'. A 'Jew' was someone who emphasized tradition and appearances rather than the word of God and truth in the innermost being. Upon meeting His future disciple, Nathaniel, for the first time, Jesus called him an 'Israelite':

> "Jesus saw Nathanael coming to him, and said about him, 'Behold, an Israelite indeed, in whom is no deceit!' " John 1:47

Jesus could sense that Nathaniel desired 'truth in the inward parts'. Nathaniel was not impressed by the outward expressions of Jewish tradition and religious 'show'; and because of this, he stood in stark contrast the scribes, Pharisees and religious leaders of his day; people who emphasized slavish obedience to the traditions of men. This soon-to-be disciple of the Lord discerned the difference between the commandments of God and the commandments of men.

The 144,000—who are sealed are from the 12 tribes 'of Israel'—are *never referred to as 'Jews'*:

> "And I heard the number of those who were sealed, 144,000 from all the tribes of Israel." Revelation 7:4

Though we tend to use the terms 'Jew' and 'Israelite' interchangeably, each word carries a different connotation in both the book of Revelation and the Gospel of John. A 'Jew', *technically* refers only to the descendants of Israel who belong to the tribe of Judah. The term, Israelite, refers to those who descend from any of the 12 tribes of Israel. The 144K hail from *all 12 tribes* of Israel, not just Judah.

After the northern kingdom of Israel was cast to the four winds by Assyria, the southern kingdom of Judah was all that remained of God's people. Decades later the kingdom of Judah was transported to Babylon by Nebuchadnezzer, where, for 70 years, they would be humbled by God. Babylon also became the place from whence came many Jewish traditions, and it was there in Babylon that the synagogue system originated. Because the Babylonian captivity was recognized by the Jews as a punishment for their father's rebellion against the commandments of God, the Jewish religious leaders, out of a desire to keep themselves from departing from God's ways in the future, developed a system of rules that, if kept, would prevent them from straying from God once the exile was over. They believed that if they obeyed these additional commandments, they could prevent a future national captivity from ever occurring again.

After the Babylonian exile, obeying these man-made rules took precedence over obeying the laws of God. By the time of Christ, the Word of God had been largely supplanted by the traditions of men:

> "Then Pharisees and scribes came to Jesus from Jerusalem, saying, 2 'Why do your disciples disobey the tradition of the elders? For they don't wash their hands when they eat bread.'

> 3 He answered them, 'Why do you also disobey the commandment of God because of your tradition? 4 For God commanded, "Honor your father and your mother," and, "He who speaks evil of father or mother, let him be put to death." 5 But you say, "Whoever may tell his father or his mother, 'Whatever help you might otherwise have gotten from me is a gift devoted to God.'" Matthew 15:1-6

In the gospels, Jesus drew a distinction between those who desired to follow the commandments of God from a sincere heart, and the hypocrisy of those who kept the commandments of men in order to appear pure in the eyes of men. In Revelation, we see this same distinction:

> "I know your works, oppression, and your poverty (but you are rich), and the blasphemy of those who say they are Jews, and they are not, but are a synagogue of Satan. " Revelation 2:9

> "Behold, I make some of the synagogue of Satan, of those who say they are Jews, and they are not, but lie—behold, I will make them to come and worship before your feet, and to know that I have loved you. " Revelation 3:9

> "In their mouth was found no lie, for they are blameless." Revelation 14:5

The 144K of Israel will be sincere worshipers of God, and they will desire to keep the commandments of God as revealed in the book of Revelation: specifically the commands communicated by Christ in the letters to the seven churches.

The 'synagogue of Satan' refers to Jews who are blind to spiritual truth; especially the truths about Christ, truths which the 144K will embrace. The Person of Christ, the plan of salvation and the very future of God's people, are all embedded in the temple system, represented in every aspect of temple worship. In future days, the Jews will once again harass and oppress the true worshipers of God—the 144,000 of Israel—just as they came against those who trusted in Jesus at His first advent.

The rebuilt temple will be a sore spot for the Jews during the last days. In Revelation 11, the 144K are counted as 'worshipers'. Their detractors are not 'counted' at all because they are not true worshipers. The possibility exists that the newly rebuilt temple may not be viewed as a legitimate temple by mainstream Judaism. The authorization to rebuild the temple will come from God through Christ to the Two Witnesses. The Two Witnesses will receive the commission to rebuild the temple—from start to finish—once the decree to rebuild is given; but that doesn't mean that the rank and file of Judaism will accept this temple—especially at the beginning. The Beast/Antichrist WILL however, recognize the newly constructed temple as the authorized dwelling place of God on earth. This very temple—the place where the 144k will worship, which will be constructed by the Two Witnesses—will be the location of the abomination of desolation.

Some Jews will eventually come to their senses and turn to the Lord, but most will not believe in Christ until the Second Coming. When they 'see Him', they will repent of their error, and acknowledge Christ's Lordship; *and they will bow* before those who, through faithfulness to Christ, will stand before them as those who will rule and reign over them on the earth.

The sweetness of fellowship with God which the 144K will enjoy in the rebuilt temple will be short-lived. Before many months have passed, the 'holy city' will be transformed into 'Sodom and Egypt'—two places of corruption and bondage that, in the past, God's people fled *from*. The Two Witnesses will be slain in Jerusalem, by the Beast:

> " When they have finished their testimony, the beast that comes up out of the abyss will make war with them, and overcome them, and kill them. [8] Their dead bodies will be in the street of the great city, which spiritually is called Sodom and Egypt, where also their Lord was crucified." Revelation 11:7,8

By the time the Two Witnesses are slain and their dead bodies lie exposed in the streets of Jerusalem, the 'holy city' will be 'holy' no more, for the man of sin—the Beast—will sit himself in the temple of God:

> " Let no one deceive you in any way. For it will not be unless the rebellion comes first, and the man of sin is revealed, the son of destruction. 4 He opposes and exalts himself against all that is called God or that is worshiped, so that he sits as God in the temple of God, setting himself up as God." 2 Thessalonians 2:3,4

The 'little scroll' is telling us that the temple of God *will be rebuilt* in the city of Jerusalem. The altar will be constructed and the 144K of Israel will worship there. We already know that the ministry of the Two Witnesses will include their active participation in the rebuilding of the temple—from foundation to capstone—as symbolized by the 'two lampstands and the two olive trees', which harken back to Joshua, the High Priest and Zerubbabel, the two builders of the second temple—who are Old Testament shadows of the Two Witnesses.

The 'Beast who ascends from the bottomless pit' will be responsible for the death of the Two Witnesses at the close of their 1260 day ministry. Three and a half days after they are killed, they will resurrect and ascend into heaven—on the same day and hour that the remnant flees:

> " From among the peoples, tribes, languages, and nations, people will look at their dead bodies for three and a half days, and will not allow their dead bodies to be laid in a tomb. 10 Those who dwell on the earth will rejoice over them, and they will be glad. They will give gifts to one another, because these two prophets tormented those who dwell on the earth.
>
> 11 After the three and a half days, the breath of life from God entered into them, and they stood on their feet. Great fear fell on those who saw them. 12 I heard a loud voice from heaven saying to them, "Come up here!" They went up into heaven in a cloud, and their enemies saw them. 13 In that day there was a great earthquake, and a tenth of the city fell. Seven thousand people were killed in the earthquake, and the rest were terrified and gave glory to the God of heaven." Revelation 11:9-13

We can calculate the arrival date of the Two Witnesses by using the date associated with the beginning of the seven years, a date which was marked out for us in the starry heavens by God Himself in the Great Sign of Revelation 12. If we use the beginning of the Feast of Trumpets in 2017 as our starting date, and count forward 1290 days, we arrive at the midpoint— *April 3, 2021.*

Revelation describes a number of events that will take place on the day of the abomination of desolation. The midpoint is the day the remnant will flee into the wilderness through the split in the Mount of Olives, and the day the Two Witnesses will resurrect and ascend into heaven. These events loom large among other notable events which will take place on that day as well.

If we subtract 3.5 days from April 3, 2021, we arrive at the date the Two Witnesses will be slain, which will be on the feast of First Fruits, March 30, 2021. They will be killed on the tenth and final day of the ten days of persecution instigated by the Harlot. This is the same day the 144K will be taken into heaven. To calculate the starting date when the Two Witnesses actually began their 1260 day ministry, we subtract 1260 days from March 30, 2021, (the day they will be slain), which takes us back to October 17, 2017.

"Prophesy Again..."

Before John measures the temple, he is told that he must prophesy again:

> "I took the little book out of the angel's hand, and ate it. It was as sweet as honey in my mouth. When I had eaten it, my stomach was made bitter. 11 They told me, 'You must prophesy again over many peoples, nations, languages, and kings.' " Revelation 10:10, 11

What's happening here? Why the command to 'prophesy again'? Remember—the decree to rebuild the temple will be delivered on the day that the dead in Christ are raised and the living saints are glorified. On the Feast of Trumpets, *all the deceased dead in Christ from the beginning of time* up until that day will finally receive their glorified bodies. All believers—from Old Testament days through the present—believers who have been patiently waiting to receive their permanent dwelling places, will finally receive their 'white robes'—their resurrection bodies. Men and women of faith from ancient times, whose names are recorded in the Hebrews 'Hall of Faith' (Hebrews 11), as well as multitudes of unnamed saints who, during their lives anticipated inheriting the eternal promises of God, will at that time finally receive their inheritance. These brothers and sisters—who themselves are future inhabitants of the New Jerusalem—currently exist only in spirit form before the Father, and they are awaiting their completion: the resurrection and glorification of their bodies.

Though many think that these saints are already enjoying the wonders of heaven in glorified bodies, the scriptures tell us that these brethren are waiting for us, so that as 'one' we may possess the perfection and wholeness that God has promised us:

"These all, having been commended for their faith, didn't receive the promise, [40] God having provided some better thing concerning us, so that *apart from us they should not be made perfect*." Hebrews 11:39, 40

No wonder Paul tells us that the 'dead in Christ' rise first! Though we all receive our glorified bodies at 'the last trumpet', the 'dead in Christ' will be the first to appear before the Lord in their glorified state, appearing as 24 Elders seated on thrones wearing crowns of gold. Their first act upon receiving their new bodies will be to worship God, casting their crowns at His feet:

"When the living creatures give glory, honor, and thanks to him who sits on the throne, to him who lives forever and ever, [10] the twenty-four elders fall down before him who sits on the throne and worship him who lives forever and ever, and throw their crowns before the throne, saying,

[11] 'Worthy are you, our Lord and God, the Holy One, to receive the glory, the honor, and the power, for you created all things, and because of your desire they existed and were created!' " Revelation 4:9-11

The 'dead in Christ' will be the first to appear in resurrected bodies in heaven, and living saints who, having received their glorified bodies on earth, will need to wait 10 more days before they join them in heaven, on the Day of Atonement when they will be raptured. The raptured Elders in Revelation 5, are those who sing a new song with harps in their hands:

"They sang a new song, saying,
'You are worthy to take the book
and to open its seals,
for you were killed,
and bought us for God with your blood
out of every tribe, language, people, and nation,
[10] and made us kings and priests to our God;
and we will reign on the earth.' " Revelation 5:9,10

The fact that we see the 24 Elders worshiping twice, hints at two different but related appearances, of the same division of priests before God's throne. The spirits of the dead (in chapter 4) will have been present in the throne room for a period of time and the worship they bring is not a 'new song', but a response to the praise and worship of the Living Creatures. The 'child' of Revelation 12, who is 'born' and then 'caught up' to God, represents living saints on the earth who will be 'changed' on the earth and then taken to heaven. The 'birth' or glorification of living believers will take place on earth, but the dead in Christ will receive their immortal bodies in heaven. The dead are not 'caught up'—only the living child is swept up to heaven.

If we follow the rapture pattern already established in scripture—the 'Elijah/Elisha' rapture pattern—we know that shortly after the first group of priest/kings (the 24 Elders) is taken into heaven, the new believers (the 144K) will receive the 'double portion' of the Spirit, which is the spiritual inheritance reserved for the 'first born'. The 'baton' will pass from the child to this next group of people, the 144K of Israel, who will come to Christ after the child's departure to God's throne room.

At the rapture, the first 'division' of the priesthood, the 24 Elders, will be in heaven, but we know that the 24 Elders are not the only group of priests who will be serving God in His throne room. There will be more divisions of priests to follow. The 144K of Israel will arrive on First Fruits, preceded by the martyrs who will be killed by the Harlot—believers who put their faith in Christ. John must 'prophesy' about these people as well; they are part of the 'many people, nations, tongues and kings'—end time believers whose story is only just beginning! These people, along with many others, have roles to play during the last days. Though the first group of believers will no longer be present on the earth, the story is far from over, and John must prophecy again about the people who will take part in the next chapter of salvation.

Once the predominately Gentile believers have been taken in the first rapture, the commission of spreading the gospel will fall to the 144K of Israel. The new Gentile believers will join them as well. The descendants of Israel will once more be at the forefront of sharing the gospel of salvation through Christ. These new saints will welcome the presence of the indwelling Holy Spirit, who's presence will enable them to preach the Word with power, and give them strength to endure the difficult days which lie ahead.

The 144K, representing the 'first fruits' of the 'olive' harvest of Israel, will be the first to receive the Spirit. As 'first fruits' they will be sealed with the Spirit and then a few days later they will receive a second out-pouring of the Holy Spirit along with all the rest of the new believers. Just as Jesus' first disciples received the double portion of the Spirit being sealed on First Fruits by Christ, and then along with 100+ others, who were baptized in the Spirit on Pentecost. After Peter's sermon, 3000 more converted souls received the gift of the Holy Spirit . The 144K will be sealed on the first day of the feast of Tabernacles, when the first fruits of the olive are offered. At the end of the feast, on the 8th day, the 144K, along with believing Gentiles, will receive the out-pouring of the Holy Spirit a second time:

"Now on the last and greatest day of the feast, Jesus stood and cried out, 'If anyone is thirsty, let him come to me and drink! 38 He who believes in me, as the Scripture has said, from within him will flow rivers of living water.' 39 But he said this about the Spirit, which those believing in him were to receive. For the Holy Spirit was not yet given, because Jesus wasn't yet glorified." John 7:37-39

"It will happen afterward, that I will pour out my Spirit on all flesh;
and your sons and your daughters will prophesy.
Your old men will dream dreams.
Your young men will see visions.
29 And also on the servants and on the handmaids in those days,
I will pour out my Spirit." Joel 2:28,29

Chapter 38: The False Prophet (Part 1)

There are three 'beasts' mentioned in Revelation: the Scarlet Beast (also known as the 'first Beast'), the Beast from the Earth (also known as the 'second Beast') and the Beast from the Sea. Details concerning the first and second Beasts are described in Revelation 13. The beasts are not actually animals, they are men; but when God wants to depict men who refuse to acknowledge or worship God, He often uses the metaphor of a beast. This is especially true when describing kings or rulers who have turned from God.

The story of Nebuchadnezzar and his dream, (recorded in Daniel 4), is a good example of how people can turn into beasts. The king of Babylon, Nebuchadnezzar, was given a dream from God which troubled him. The dream contained a prophecy concerning the world empires that would succeed him and his empire, Babylon. God showed him a statue with a head of gold, arms and chest of silver, belly and thighs of bronze, legs and feet of iron and finally, toes mixed with iron and clay. Daniel was called upon to interpret the dream, and he gave the following interpretation: Nebuchadnezzar and his kingdom were the head of gold, and after Babylon, four other kingdoms would arise, symbolized by the parts of the statue made of the inferior metals. Eventually all the kingdoms would be destroyed by a Rock which would hit the statue's toes and cause it to crumble to dust.

Because God wasn't finished with what He wanted to communicate about the kingdoms represented by the statue, He also gave a disturbing dream to Daniel, which contained more prophetic details about the same kingdoms that were in Nebuchadnezzar's dream. In Daniel's dream, God chose to represent these same kingdoms, not by a statue made of precious metals, but by four terrifying beasts: a lion with wings, a bear with ribs in his mouth, a leopard with four wings and a fourth beast even more terrifying and dreadful than the first three.

From a human perspective, kingdoms and their kings can be viewed as the magnificent legacies of powerful men, as reflected in the precious metals of the statue in the kings' dream. Kingdoms and their kings can also be strong as represented by harder metals like bronze and iron. But from God's perspective, these kings were nothing more than brute beasts. In Daniel's dream, rather than being the head of gold, King Nebuchadnezzar and the Babylonian kingdom were represented by the lion with wings like an eagle. The lion is the king of the beasts and the wings represent swiftness and freedom of movement. Nebuchadnezzar was powerful and exceedingly proud of his magnificent kingdom, and he took great pride in his personal achievements:

"The king spoke and said, 'Is not this great Babylon, which I have built for the royal dwelling place by the might of my power and for the glory of my majesty?' " Daniel 4:30

Immediately after the king uttered those words, God caused him to lose his mind —to turn into a beast for seven long years. Nebuchadnezzar was driven out of his beautiful city and he lived as a beast of the field, eating grass—unkempt and uncared for. At the end of the seventh year, sanity returned to Nebuchadnezzar and he recognized that God was the One who presided over the rise and fall of kings and kingdoms:

"At the end of the days I, Nebuchadnezzar, lifted up my eyes to heaven, and my understanding returned to me; and I blessed the Most High, and I praised and honored him who lives forever, for his dominion is an everlasting dominion, and his kingdom from generation to generation. 35 All the inhabitants of the earth are reputed as nothing; and he does according to his will in the army of heaven, and among the inhabitants of the earth; and no one can stop his hand,or ask him, 'What are you doing?'

" At the same time my understanding returned to me; and for the glory of my kingdom, my majesty and brightness returned to me. My counselors and my lords sought me; and I was established in my kingdom, and excellent greatness was added to me. 37 Now I, Nebuchadnezzar, praise and extol and honor the King of heaven; for all his works are truth, and his ways justice; and those who walk in pride he is able to abase." Daniel 4:34, 37

After seven years of insanity, Nebuchadnezzar was changed from a beast back into a man again—his 'wings were plucked off and he was made to stand on his feet.' When he acknowledged that God was the true Ruler of the world, his sanity was restored—he became human—and was given the heart and mind of a man:

"The first was like a lion, and had eagle's wings. I watched until its wings were plucked, and it was lifted up from the earth and made to stand on two feet as a man. A man's heart was given to it." Daniel 7:4

In the scriptures, 'beasts' are men who have lost their minds *spiritually*, and thus their true humanity. Pride, arrogance, self-satisfaction, cruelty and an utter disregard for God and His ways causes men to think and behave irrationally, as beasts:

"Thus my heart was grieved,
And I was vexed in my mind.
I was so foolish and ignorant;

I was like a beast before You." Psalm 73:21,22

The Beasts of Revelation are no different. They are men who will exchange the truth of God for a lie and in the process lose their humanity. They will reap the judgment that is due them when Christ returns to earth at the 2nd Coming when He establishes *His* glorious kingdom. Christ is the Rock that will grind the statue to dust.

We'll be examining all the Beasts of Revelation, but because the Scarlet Beast and the Beast from the Sea have a complex relationship, we'll begin with the Beast from the Earth, as his identity is easier to unravel.

The Beast from the Earth

The Beast from the Earth is introduced in Revelation 13. He is also known as the False Prophet or the second Beast:

> "I saw another beast coming up out of the earth. He had two horns like a lamb and it spoke like a dragon. 12 He exercises all the authority of the first beast in his presence. He makes the earth and those who dwell in it to worship the first beast, whose fatal wound was healed. 13 He performs great signs, even making fire come down out of the sky to the earth in the sight of people. 14 He deceives my own people who dwell on the earth because of the signs he was granted to do in front of the beast, saying to those who dwell on the earth that they should make an image to the beast who had the sword wound and lived. 15 It was given to him to give breath to the image of the beast, that the image of the beast should both speak, and cause as many as wouldn't worship the image of the beast to be killed. 16 He causes all, the small and the great, the rich and the poor, and the free and the slave, to be given marks on their right hands or on their foreheads; 17 and that no one would be able to buy or to sell unless he has that mark, which is the name of the beast or the number of his name. 18 Here is wisdom. He who has understanding, let him calculate the number of the beast, for it is the number of a man. His number is six hundred sixty-six." Revelation 13:11-18

The Beast from the Earth—the False Prophet—is the 'forerunner' of the Beast we know of as the Antichrist. The False Prophet's job is to announce the coming of the false messiah. The False Prophet is to the Antichrist, what John the Baptist was to Jesus at His first coming. Both John the Baptist and the False Prophet are heralds, announcing the arrival of their respective kings.

The False Prophet is also the 'Aaron' to the first Beast's 'Moses'. The False Prophet speaks for the first Beast, and he instructs the earth dwellers to make an Image of the Beast that everyone must worship. In order for people to buy or sell, the False Prophet will also compel everyone to take the infamous mark of the Beast. Because the mark of the beast is also evidence that a person is willing to worship the Beast, taking the mark will be voluntary—no one will be forced to take it, but those that *refuse* to do so, will, if discovered, be beheaded.

> "I saw thrones, and they sat on them, and judgment was given to them. I saw the souls of those who had been beheaded for the testimony of Jesus and for the word of God, and such as didn't worship the beast nor his image, and didn't receive the mark on their forehead and on their hand. They lived and reigned with Christ for a thousand years." Revelation 20:4

Before the final battle of Armageddon, three foul spirits will issue from the mouths of the Dragon, the Beast and the False Prophet. These are 'demonic' spirits which will perform signs in order to persuade the kings of the earth to come to Armageddon. The signs which the False Prophet (and the demonic spirits) will perform must be powerful enough to convince the kings that if they participate in the battle against the Lord, they may actually be victorious. We know how the battle ends—with the blood of Christ's enemies flowing 'bridle deep' in the valley of Meggido.

The last time we see the False Prophet in Revelation, he and the Beast from the Sea are thrown into the Lake of Fire by the King of kings and Lord of lords—the Lord Jesus:

> "The beast was taken, and with him the false prophet who worked the signs in his sight, with which he deceived those who had received the mark of the beast and those who worshiped his image. These two were thrown alive into the lake of fire that burns with sulfur." Revelation 19:20

Later on in the book we'll be looking at the Beast from the Earth in more detail.

Chapter 39: The First Beast—The "Antichrist 1.0"

The Scarlet Beast and the Beast from the Sea

We've already seen how one person or entity can have more than one name in Revelation. The Beast from the Earth is also known as the False Prophet and the second Beast. The Lord Jesus is the Lamb, the King of kings, the Faithful Witness and so on. Satan is also called the Dragon, the Devil and the Deceiver of the whole world.

In addition to the Beast from the Earth, there are two more 'Beasts' in Revelation: the Scarlet Beast and the Beast from the Sea. Revelation 17 tells us about the rather complex relationship and identity of these two beasts:

> "The angel said to me, 'Why do you wonder? I will tell you the mystery of the woman and of the beast that carries her, which has the seven heads and the ten horns. 8 The beast that you saw was, and is not; and is about to come up out of the abyss and to go into destruction. Those who dwell on the earth and whose names have not been written in the book of life from the foundation of the world will marvel when they see that the beast was, and is not, and shall be present.' " Revelation 17:7,8

The Beast with seven heads and ten horns that is ridden by the Harlot, is the Scarlet Beast. The Scarlet Beast was the Beast that John saw who 'was' and 'is not' then 'rises from the bottomless pit' and 'goes to destruction'. John saw a man, personified by a beast, who will come on the scene. This man will die, rise from the dead and eventually be thrown into the Lake of Fire.

We are also told that this man 'rises from the bottomless pit.' We know that at the 5th Trumpet the locust army and their king, Apollyon, will also rise from the pit. We also know that the 'beast from the bottomless pit' (or abyss) is the one who makes war on the Two Witnesses in Revelation 11:

> "When they have finished their testimony, the beast that comes up out of the abyss will make war with them, and overcome them, and kill them." Revelation 11:7

Revelation 17 gives us more information about this beast:

> "They are seven kings. Five have fallen, the one is, and the other has not yet come. When he comes, he must continue a little while. 11 The beast that was,

and is not, is himself also an eighth, and is of the seven; and he goes to destruction. " Revelation 17:10, 11

Though all of this may seem rather confusing, it's not really that difficult to understand. The beast that 'was' and 'is not' and 'is about to rise from the bottomless pit' is "also an eighth king....but he is also one of the seven kings". This passage is telling us that the 7th King—the Scarlet Beast, the beast which the Harlot rides, will only be on the scene a 'little while' and then he will die. He will return to 'life' as the 8th King—also known as the Beast from the Sea. He is also referred to as the 'Beast who ascends from the Bottomless Pit/Abyss'. Apollyon, the angel of the Abyss, is an entity who will also ascend from the pit, and he will indwell the 7th King at his resurrection. The Scarlet Beast will be transformed from the 7th King into the 8th King/Beast from the Sea/Beast who ascends from the Bottomless Pit.

Even though we read about the Beast from the Sea (in Revelation 13), before we read about the Scarlet Beast/7th King (in Revelation 18), the passage in Revelation 17 is where we actually find out which beast comes first chronologically: whether the Beast from the Sea or the Scarlet Beast. The first beast is the Scarlet Beast, the Beast whom the Harlot rides. This Beast is the 7th King who will only remain a little while. We know that the 8th King (Antichrist) will reign for 42 months. We can deduce then, that sometime just prior to the midpoint of the seven years, the 7th King will die and then be transformed/resurrected as the 8th King. This 8th King, will, along with Apollyon (who will ascend *within* him) reign for 42 months:

> "A mouth speaking great things and blasphemy was given to him. Authority to make war for forty-two months was given to him." Revelation 13:5

> "The ten horns that you saw are ten kings who have received no kingdom as yet, but they receive authority as kings with the beast for one hour. 13 These have one mind, and they give their power and authority to the beast." Revelation 17:12,13

The Beast from the Sea will go to 'destruction' (or 'perdition'). He will join the False Prophet in the Lake of Fire when Christ returns.

The 'lawless one' that Paul wrote about in 2 Thessalonians is the 7th King who will die, then resurrect, and become the 8th King—the Antichrist. The 'lawless one' as Paul calls him, will not be positively identified until the time that he 'is not' and 'ascends from the bottomless pit' and presents himself as God in the rebuilt temple.

Apollyon

The Beast from the Sea and the Dragon have a relationship that imitates the relationship between God the Father and the Son. The Dragon will give his power, his throne and his great authority to the beast. Why would Satan share his power and his throne with a man? To answer that, we need to go back to Genesis, the first book in the Bible.

After God created man, He placed him in a garden and told the man that he was permitted to eat anything in the garden with one exception: he was not to eat from the Tree of the Knowledge of Good and Evil. The day he, or his wife, ate from that tree, they would die. Satan, in the form of a serpent, tempted the woman to eat and she took the fruit and then gave some of the fruit to her husband to eat. They quickly realized the terrible thing they had done, and the on-going effects of that one act has been written in the sad, sordid history of the world.

After Adam and his wife ate of the forbidden fruit in the Garden of Eden, the Lord spelled out for them in detail, the actual consequences of their actions. Satan, in the disguise of a serpent, would also be given consequences for his part in the fall of man. In the very first prophecy in the Bible, God gave the plan of salvation in 'seed' form:

> "I will put enmity between you and the woman,
> and between your offspring and her offspring;
> he shall bruise your head,
> and you shall bruise his heel." Genesis 3:15

God told Satan that his offspring (or 'seed') and the woman's offspring (or 'seed') would one day go 'toe to toe'; and that the woman's offspring would 'bruise the head of the serpent'. We know that Jesus is the 'seed' of the woman, born of the virgin Mary, and that Christ was the one who "bruised the serpent's head". Even though Jesus' 'heel' was bruised by Satan while He hung on the cross, the resurrection of Christ put an end to Satan's plan for world domination, and the serpent's head will, one day in the future, be crushed, permanently.

We know that Jesus is the 'seed of the woman' but who or what is the serpent's 'seed' or offspring? There are a lot of strange 'serpent seed' doctrines out there, and anytime someone starts talking about 'serpent seed', it's easy for people to tune out and shut down; but…Satan DOES have an 'offspring', as Genesis 3:15 tells us, and his 'offspring' is none other than the angel from the Abyss, Apollyon. Apollyon will indwell the Beast—the 7th-now-become-8th King—and rule as a god-man, for 42 months. Satan will give the Beast everything that he has at his disposal: his power, his might and his authority. Satan will withhold none of his resources from his 'son', the Beast. Neither Satan or Apollyon, however, can be the ruler of an earthly kingdom—which is what the Beast kingdom will be. A 'man' must reign on earth—those are the rules which God put in place eons ago. Satan knows the rules and he has *his* 'man', the resurrected Beast who will also be empowered by the 'seed of the serpent', who provides the 'host' body for Apollyon.

"666"

The number '666' has been the subject of much speculation for many years. We all know that '666' is the number that identifies the Beast; and that '666' is the number of a man, and also the "number of his name". What does that mean? Is it possible to know who the Beast might be? Can we calculate the "number of his name" through deciphering the gematria of his name?

Remember that Revelation uses numbers in a symbolic way, so we need to know what the base number, 6, means. Since man was created on the 6th day, the number, 6, is most often associated with man. Because '6' is used three times in the number, '666', we know that the *meaning of the number six will be magnified*. Therefore '666' means 'man magnified' or 'super-man'. Satan's man will appear to be a 'superman' or a man-god. When calculating the number of the Antichrist's literal, human name in gematria, the letters of his name may also have a sum of '666'; but in Revelation, the primary meaning of the number, "666", is "superman".

Chapter 40: The Life-cycle of the Beast

Most of us are aware that there will be a person appearing on the world's stage during the last days: a man known as the Antichrist. Paul calls the Antichrist, 'the man of sin' and the 'lawless one'. He is the false son of Satan and will be the host body to Apollyon, the 'seed of the serpent'. In Revelation, the Antichrist is also known by another name: the Beast from the Sea.

Revelation gives us many clues about the life, death and resurrection of the Beast, all veiled in symbolism and imagery. First, and foremost, the Beast—the Antichrist—is an imitator of Christ. He will be killed and then 'resurrect', imitating the death and resurrection of Christ. Before the Beast dies, he is known as the 'Scarlet Beast', and after his death he becomes the 'Beast from the Sea' and the 'Beast who ascends from the bottomless pit/Abyss'. He is the '7th king' who dies and comes back to life as the '8th king'. He is a 'hybrid'; first, a man and then a 'superman' embodying Apollyon, the king of the Watchers. The man Revelation refers to as the Scarlet Beast and the 7th King, is the "Antichrist 1.0"; and after his death and resurrection, he will be transformed into a man-god—a hybrid. Apollyon, the king of the angels of the bottomless pit, will enter into the dead body of the Scarlet Beast, turning him into the 8th King/Beast from the Sea/bottomless pit/Abyss—the "Antichrist 2.0".

"Like father...like son"

Revelation describes three different entities who each have seven heads and ten horns. These entities are the Dragon, the Scarlet Beast and the Beast from the Sea. The placement of the crowns on their horns and heads describe for us the 'evolution' of the Beast, and how he is transformed from the Scarlet Beast into the Beast from the Sea.

The Dragon is the 'father' and symbolic prototype of the 7th and 8th kings: the Scarlet Beast and the Beast from the Sea. Revelation describes the Dragon in chapter 12:

> "Another sign was seen in heaven. Behold, a great red dragon, having *seven heads and ten horns, and on his heads seven crowns.*" Revelation 12:3

The Scarlet Beast is described in Revelation 17:

> "He carried me away in the Spirit into a wilderness. I saw a woman sitting on a scarlet-colored beast, full of blasphemous names, h*aving seven heads and ten horns.*" Revelation 17:3

The Beast from the Sea is described in Revelation 13:

> "Then I stood on the sand of the sea. I saw a beast coming up out of the sea, having ten horns and seven heads. On his horns were ten crowns, and on his heads, blasphemous names. 2 The beast which I saw was like a leopard, and his feet were like those of a bear, and his mouth like the mouth of a lion. The dragon gave him his power, his throne, and great authority." Revelation 13:1,2

The Dragon and the two Beasts each have 7 heads and 10 horns. We are told the meaning of the 7 heads in Revelation 17:

> "Here is the mind that has wisdom. The seven heads are seven mountains on which the woman sits. 10 They are seven kings. Five have fallen, the one is, and the other has not yet come. When he comes, he must continue a little while." Revelation 17:9,10

The seven heads represent seven 'mountains' or empires, which the Harlot either has controlled in the past, or will control in the future. Since the time John penned the Revelation, six of the empires and their kings, have fallen, leaving *one last king* and kingdom yet to come. When the 7th king arrives on the scene, the Bible tells us that his rule will be short-lived—because he will be killed. The seven heads represent seven kings, and the seventh king only rules for a short while.

> "They are seven kings. Five have fallen, the one is, and the other has not yet come. When he comes, he must *continue a little while.*" Revelation 17:10

In addition to having seven heads, these three—the Dragon, the Scarlet Beast and the Beast from the Sea/Abyss—also have ten horns. A horn is a symbol of power and strength. Revelation 17 tells us who the 10 horns represent:

> "The ten horns that you saw are ten kings who have received no kingdom as yet, but they receive authority as kings with the beast for one hour. 13 These have one mind, and they give their power and authority to the beast. " Revelation 17:12,13

The Scarlet Beast has ten horns with no crowns. The horns are kings who will not receive their power until rather late in the game, which is why the horns have no crowns. The ten horns are ten kings who will quickly rise to power for the sole purpose of giving their authority to the Beast for 'one hour.' The one hour refers to the destruction of the Harlot at the 6th Trumpet, which will take place in one hour, on a single day. The ten kings will support the Beast in his desire to destroy 'Mystery Babylon':

> " The ten horns which you saw, they and the beast will hate the prostitute, will make her desolate, will strip her naked, will eat her flesh, and will burn her utterly with fire. 17 For God has put in their hearts to do what he has in mind, to be of one mind, and to give their kingdom to the beast, until the words of God should be accomplished." Revelation 17:16,17

The placement of the crowns on the 7 heads and horns indicate *who* is holding the power, *when* they hold it and when they *give their power away*. The Dragon has crowns on each of his seven heads, but no crowns on his horns. He controls the seven world empires and their kings. He does not have crowns on his horns because the kings represented by the horns will not have authority until just before the midpoint, and they will give their power to the Beast, not to the Dragon. The Scarlet Beast has no crowns on either his horns or his heads, indicating that he has no real power at all, since the Scarlet Beast is the Beast who is controlled by the Harlot, and *she* is the one who holds the reigns of power. The Beast from the Sea has crowns on his 10 horns, but none on his seven heads. The crowns on his 10 horns represents the 10 kings who will give their authority to the Beast at the time of the abomination of desolation.

Scriptures tell us that the Scarlet Beast will die and be raised from the dead. The following verses give us this information in the typical indirect Hebraic style:

> " The beast that you saw was, and is not; and is about to come up out of the abyss and to go into destruction. Those who dwell on the earth and whose names have not been written in the book of life from the foundation of the world will marvel when they see that the beast was, and is not, and shall be present." Revelation 17:8

The Beast that John saw was the Scarlet Beast, and John was told that the Scarlet Beast would die ("is no more"). The [Scarlet] Beast 'was' and 'is no more', but is about to 'come up from the Abyss'. The Beast will die and come up or resurrect from the Abyss or bottomless Pit. Apollyon, the king over the angels of the bottomless pit/Abyss, will 'come up' with the Beast when he resurrects. The Beast who dies is the 7th King, and when he resurrects he becomes the 8th King, AND we are informed that he is also *one of the seven*:

> "The beast that was, and is not, is himself also an eighth, and is of the seven; and he goes to destruction." Revelation 17:11

The 8th King is the same person as the 7th King...only different! This 'resurrected' 7th-now-8th King comes up from the Abyss incarnating the spirit of Apollyon. Apollyon was one of the 'Watchers'—one of the fallen angels who mated with human women before the time of the flood. What this means is that not only was Apollyon an extremely wicked angel in his day, but that he is still a very powerful and malevolent angel. After all, he's the king over *all* the angels who 'kept not their first estate'—angels described as 'locusts' in Revelation 9—who are being held prisoners, chained in the bottomless pit since the time of the flood:

> "The shapes of the locusts were like horses prepared for war. On their heads were something like golden crowns, and their faces were like people's faces. 8 They had hair like women's hair, and their teeth were like those of lions. 9 They had breastplates like breastplates of iron. The sound of their wings was like the sound of many chariots and horses rushing to war. 10 They have tails like those of scorpions, with stingers. In their tails they have power to harm men for five months. 11 *They have over them as king the angel of the abyss. His name in Hebrew is 'Abaddon', but in Greek, he has the name 'Apollyon'.*" Revelation 9:7-11

These spirit beings are represented by 'locusts', a symbol which gives us a very important clue as to their characteristics. For now, the important thing to understand is that during the days which preceded the flood of Noah's day, Apollyon posed such a huge threat to the human race and mankind's very survival, that he was placed in chains, and has been imprisoned for the last six thousand years. This malignant entity will be released during the time of the end to fulfill God's greater purpose in saving many souls—but more on this later!

> "The beast which I saw was like a leopard, and his feet were like those of a bear, and his mouth like the mouth of a lion. The dragon gave him his power, his throne, and great authority. 3 One of his heads looked like it had been wounded fatally. His fatal wound was healed, and the whole earth marveled at the beast. 4 They worshiped the dragon because he gave his authority to the beast; and they worshiped the beast, saying, 'Who is like the beast? Who is able to make war with him?' " Revelation 13:2-4

In the aforementioned passage, one of the Beast's 'heads' was mortally wounded. Remember that 'heads' represent kings—so one of the kings, the 7th king, will be killed and then his 'mortal wound' will be 'healed', which is another way of saying that the Beast will be brought back to life again. A 'mortal wound' is a wound which results in death. To be 'healed' from 'death' is to be resurrected. The resurrection of the Beast will cause the whole world to marvel and follow after him, and even to worship him.

The Beast is killed by being 'wounded', not because of an accident or illness. He will be 'wounded' by another person or persons. Who would be motivated to 'wound' or kill the Beast?

> "He deceives my own people who dwell on the earth because of the signs he was granted to do in front of the beast, saying to those who dwell on the earth that they should make an image to the beast who had *the sword wound and lived.*" Revelation 13:14

The False Prophet will direct the earth dwellers to "make an image to the beast that had been *wounded by the sword*...and yet lived." This text provides yet another clue about how the Beast is killed—he is 'wounded by a sword'; in other words, the Beast dies in battle.

In John's day, soldiers who fought in hand-to-hand combat often did so using swords. Most likely the Beast will not be killed by an actual sword; rather the sword is merely symbolic, telling us about the circumstances surrounding his death: that the Beast will face an enemy, perhaps a personal enemy, and during the course of a battle, the Beast will be killed by his adversary. The Scarlet Beast—the 7th King—will receive a mortal wound from someone who is more powerful than he—and he will die.

Who kills the Beast?

In my research on this topic, I've never come across anyone who even ventured to speculate on the identity of the person, or persons, who might want to kill the Beast. In fact, many Bible teachers resist the whole idea that the Beast is an actual individual who will die and resurrect. They claim that Satan doesn't have the power to raise the dead, etc. and that what is 'resurrected', therefore, must be an empire and not a person. During the last days, however, the Lord will allow the 'Pit'—the Abyss—to be opened, and once the door to the Pit is opened, it will not be closed until Satan is cast into the Pit at the return of Christ!

During the end times, fallen spirits—human and otherwise—will have unprecedented access between realms, both spiritual and earthly. They will move between heaven, earth, and the Pit. Once the Beast is killed and descends into the Pit, both Apollyon and the Beast will be free to return to earth to reanimate the dead body of the Beast. The door to the Pit will remain open, and the soul of the Beast will return to the land of the living and Apollyon will accompany him. Together, their spirits will reanimate the lifeless body of the 7th King. The dead Scarlet Beast will resurrect as the 8th King, also known as the "Beast who ascends from the Abyss', and he/they will rule the 7th empire during the reign of the Beast.

Contrary to popular thinking, an *empire* is not what is being resurrected in this passage in Revelation: rather, it's a *person* who comes back to life. The whole world will follow after the Beast who 'was and is not, and comes up from the Abyss'; the world follows an *individual*, not an empire. The earth dwellers will worship a resurrected person, not a governmental system!

The Beast will be killed by an adversary who has both the motivation—and the power—to actually be able to kill the Beast. Again, Revelation hints at the identity of the killer, without specifically naming names. At the time of the Scarlet Beast (and the Harlot who 'rides' or controls him) there will be two very powerful individuals on the earth: the Two Witnesses. These two men, who I believe are Moses and Elijah, have the power to inflict any type of plague they desire upon the earth. If anyone comes against them, *they have the power to destroy that individual*:

> "If anyone desires to harm them, fire proceeds out of their mouth and devours their enemies. If anyone desires to harm them, he must be killed in this way. " Revelation 11:5

The Two Witnesses are prophets who represent God in the world, and they will be given unlimited power to do whatever must be done in order to fulfill their commission, and to remain alive for the full 1260 days of their ministry. The Scarlet Beast is Satan's 'man', but he will not have Satan's power until after he resurrects from the dead: after he rises from 'the sea', which represents death:

> "Then I stood on the sand of the sea. I saw a beast coming up out of the sea, having ten horns and seven heads. On his horns were ten crowns, and on his heads, blasphemous names. 2 The beast which I saw was like a leopard, and his feet were like those of a bear, and his mouth like the mouth of a lion. The dragon gave him his power, his throne, and great authority." Revelation 13:1,2

Anyone who comes against the Two Witnesses will be killed. If the Scarlet Beast comes against the Two Witnesses, he will be killed. Not until he resurrects will he have the power to withstand the Two Witnesses, and only because their 1260 days of ministry will have expired. On the final day of their ministry, with their power gone, the Beast who 'ascends from the bottomless pit'—the resurrected 7th-now-8th King—will 'make war on them' and kill them.

When the Beast rises from the dead he will be given the Dragon's power:

"Then I stood on the sand of the sea. I saw a beast coming up out of the sea, having ten horns and seven heads...The dragon gave him his power, his throne, and great authority." Revelation 13:1a, 2b

When the Beast rises from the Pit and assumes the power and throne of his 'father', the earth dwellers will view the Beast's resurrection as proof that the Beast and the Dragon are more powerful than the true God and His servants! He alone can defeat the Two Witnesses. That's why the earth dwellers will follow after the Beast and worship him...they will believe that he is a god/man...the resurrected messiah! **THIS is the great deception.** And to make matters worse, the Beast will be killed on Passover, emulating the Lord's death; and he will be 'raised' on First Fruits, the same day that Christ was raised from the dead. Once the Beast has been empowered by his father, the devil, the Beast will kill the Two Witnesses, who will have just completed their ministry.

The false resurrection of the Beast will be the event that causes those on earth to worship the Beast. Once the Witnesses are dead and can no longer torment the people on earth with plagues and death, the people on earth, believing the lie about the Beast—that he is God—a lie that his 'resurrection' will seem to prove, will celebrate the death of the Two Witnesses by gift giving and merry making. They will not allow the bodies of the Two Witnesses to be buried; and for 3.5 days, the bodies of God's two prophets will lie exposed in Jerusalem...now become 'Sodom and Egypt':

> "When they have finished their testimony, the beast that comes up out of the abyss will make war with them, and overcome them, and kill them. [8] Their dead bodies will be in the street of the great city, which spiritually is called Sodom and Egypt, where also their Lord was crucified. [9] From among the peoples, tribes, languages, and nations, people will look at their dead bodies for three and a half days, and will not allow their dead bodies to be laid in a tomb. [10] Those who dwell on the earth will rejoice over them, and they will be glad. They will give gifts to one another, because these two prophets tormented those who dwell on the earth.
>
> [11] After the three and a half days, the breath of life from God entered into them, and they stood on their feet. Great fear fell on those who saw them. [12] I heard a loud voice from heaven saying to them, 'Come up here!' They went up into heaven in a cloud, and their enemies saw them. " Revelation 11:7-12

The Two Witnesses will kill the Beast on Passover, and the Beast, together with Apollyon, will enter into, and reanimate, the dead body of the Scarlet Beast. The Beast will resurrect on First Fruits in a blasphemous imitation of the Lord's death

317

and resurrection. The Two Witnesses will then be killed by the Beast on the last day of their 1260 day ministry—the day the Beast rises from the dead and receives the power and authority of the Dragon. Three and a half days later—at the midpoint—on April 3, 2021, the same day as the abomination of desolation and the great earthquake that splits the Mount of Olives in two, the Two Witnesses will rise from the dead and ascend into heaven.

Chapter 41: The False Prophet—The Most Dangerous Man on Earth (Part 2)

John 1:19-23

> *" This is John's testimony, when the Jews sent priests and Levites from Jerusalem to ask him, "Who are you?"*
> *²⁰ He declared, and didn't deny, but he declared, "I am not the Christ."*
> *²¹ They asked him, "What then? Are you Elijah?"*
> *He said, "I am not."*
> *"Are you the prophet?"*
> *He answered, "No."*
> *²² They said therefore to him, "Who are you? Give us an answer to take back to those who sent us. What do you say about yourself?"*
> *²³ He said, "I am the voice of one crying in the wilderness, 'Make straight the way of the Lord,' as Isaiah the prophet said."*

When John the Baptist came preaching a message of repentance, he preached with such passion and authority that the chief priests were compelled to send messengers into the wilderness to ascertain if, indeed, their redemption was drawing near. Had the Messiah had actually come? Was John the Messiah? Or was he the person who would act as the forerunner to the Messiah? The Old Testament prophets had predicted that before the coming of the Messiah, they were to expect Elijah to reappear, as well as another man simply known as The Prophet. The priests in Jerusalem wanted to know who John was, and if he was the Christ or maybe Elijah, the forerunner of the Messiah.

John told the religious officials who had been sent to question him that he was not the Messiah, Elijah or the mysterious coming prophet...he was simply a voice crying in the wilderness, "Prepare the way of the Lord!"

Since before the first coming of Christ, the Jews have been waiting for their Messiah's arrival. They rejected their true Messiah, the Lord Jesus, at His first coming, and two thousand years later, they are still watching and waiting for the appearance of their deliverer, as well as the appearance of Elijah and the Prophet. The messianic expectation among religious Jews has not diminished over the centuries, but, on the contrary, has only increased the last few years as Jews eagerly watch and wait for their Messiah to manifest on the world stage.

The Jews are also waiting for Elijah. Every Passover, Jews fill a cup of wine for Elijah and place it on the Passover table. Here's what "My Jewish Learning" has to say about this custom:

At this time when we recount the redemption of the Jews from Egypt in the Hagadah we also express our hope for the future redemption with the coming of the Messiah. The tradition is that Elijah the Prophet will be the one to announce the coming of Messiah. In fact, there's a tradition that Messiah will come in the month in which Passover occurs, 'Nissan' on the Jewish calendar. The cup is called 'Elijah's Cup' to express our hope that our guest will be Elijah himself coming to inform us of Messiah's coming and the rebuilding of the Holy Temple in Jerusalem. This theme of the future redemption rings throughout the Hagadah, and is stated explicitly at the beginning and the end in the words "Next Year in Jerusalem!"

Any Jew who has celebrated Passover is very familiar with the connection between the prophecy of Elijah's coming, and the expectation that he will arrive during the Passover.

The Jews are also waiting for someone they call the Prophet. This is a lesser known title for the Messiah. The Prophet is mentioned in a prophecy found in the book of Deuteronomy, chapter 18:

> "Yahweh your God will raise up to you a prophet from among you, of your brothers, like me. You shall listen to him."

> 18 "I will raise them up a prophet from among their brothers, like you. I will put my words in his mouth, and he shall speak to them all that I shall command him. 19 It shall happen, that whoever will not listen to my words which he shall speak in my name, I will require it of him. 20 But the prophet who speaks a word presumptuously in my name, which I have not commanded him to speak, or who speaks in the name of other gods, that same prophet shall die."

> 21 "You may say in your heart, 'How shall we know the word which Yahweh has not spoken?' 22 When a prophet speaks in Yahweh's name, if the thing doesn't follow, nor happen, that is the thing which Yahweh has not spoken. The prophet has spoken it presumptuously. You shall not be afraid of him." Deuteronomy 18:15,18-22

The False Aaron, the False Prophet and the False Elijah

We have already seen how the people, places and events recorded in the Old Testament will reappear again during the last times. Almost 70% of the verses in Revelation can be traced back to some passage or story in the Old Testament. As we delve more deeply into the identity of the individual known as the False

Prophet spoken of in Revelation 13:11-18, we also need to identify which Old Testament prophecies, stories and allusions apply to him.

In popular Christian culture, the Beast from the Sea is more commonly referred to as the Antichrist. The Antichrist is the counterfeit messiah who will appear during the last days. Like the true Messiah who had a forerunner—John the Baptist—who drew people's attention to the identity of their Messiah, the false messiah will also have a forerunner—known as the False Prophet or the Beast from the Earth. Let's review Revelation 13:11-18, the passage which addresses the False Prophet.

> "I saw another beast coming up out of the earth. He had two horns like a lamb and it spoke like a dragon. 12 He exercises all the authority of the first beast in his presence. He makes the earth and those who dwell in it to worship the first beast, whose fatal wound was healed. 13 He performs great signs, even making fire come down out of the sky to the earth in the sight of people. 14 He deceives my own people who dwell on the earth because of the signs he was granted to do in front of the beast, saying to those who dwell on the earth that they should make an image to the beast who had the sword wound and lived." Revelation 13:11-14

The second Beast arises out of the land, not the sea as did the first Beast. The first Beast was killed with the sword of war. He 'was not' and then returned from the place of the dead—metaphorically referred to as 'the sea'. This new Beast—the second Beast—does not arise from the sea of death: he will be from the land of the living.

The 'land' represents the place of the living. The 'land' can also represent something else which may provide another layer of interpretation. When the definite article, 'the' appears before the words, 'earth' or 'land', most Jews would understand that what is being referred to is the Land of Israel—the Land of Promise which God gave their forefathers. Therefore, it's also highly likely that the Beast who arises from the land, may actually be from *the land of Israel*—and he will be Jewish/Israeli.

The Beast from the Land is described as having two horns like a lamb. Horns signify power and strength; and because his horns are small and lamb-like, we can infer that this individual will possess little personal power. Like Jesus at His first coming, this individual gives the impression of being harmless, innocent and pure. Jesus is called the Lamb in Revelation, but, as we shall see, this second Beast is far from 'lamb-like'. He is more like a wolf in sheep's clothing. Revelation tells us that he will "speak like a dragon". The Dragon is Satan, the 'deceiver of the whole world'. (Revelation 12:9) The Beast from the Earth will speak 'Dragon words'. In other words, he will be a consummate liar and deceiver.

The Beast from the Land is represented as being as gentle and harmless as a lamb because he has *no power in and of himself.* He can only exercise power and authority *in the presence of the first Beast*, the Antichrist. Revelation 13:12 tells us that this Land Beast 'exercises all the authority of the first beast *in its presence'.*

We've seen this type of relationship before in the Bible, in the book of Exodus, where Aaron was the spokesman and miracle-worker for Moses.

> "Yahweh said to Moses, 'Behold, I have made you as God to Pharaoh; and Aaron your brother shall be your prophet. 2 You shall speak all that I command you; and Aaron your brother shall speak to Pharaoh, that he let the children of Israel go out of his land.' " Exodus 7:1,2

> "Yahweh spoke to Moses and to Aaron, saying, 9 'When Pharaoh speaks to you, saying, "Perform a miracle!" then you shall tell Aaron, "Take your rod, and cast it down before Pharaoh, and it will become a serpent."' " Exodus 7:8,9

Just like Aaron was able to work signs when in the presence of Moses, the False Prophet will work great signs *in the presence of the Beast* from the Sea/Antichrist. The signs that the False Prophet will perform when in the presence of the Beast will persuade the earth dwellers to worship and follow after the Beast. The Beast from the Earth (False Prophet) and the Beast from the Sea (Antichrist) will follow the pattern of Moses and Aaron. Moses had the God-given authority to lead the Israelites out of Egypt, but *Aaron* was the voice of God to the people, as well as the miracle-worker who performed miracles before Pharaoh.

The False Prophet will also seem to fulfill the prophecy of 'the Prophet' spoken of in the passage in Deuteronomy 18. The Prophet will be a man who is raised up from among Israel, a man like Moses, who supposedly has God's words in his mouth and who can confirm those words by working great signs. Jesus was the fulfillment of the Prophet, but the Jews today do not recognize that Jesus already fulfilled the prophecy of Deuteronomy 18, and so they are still waiting for the Prophet to appear.

Because the Jews of Jesus' day rejected the True Messiah, they demonstrated that they did not love the truth, nor were they able to receive the truth as it is found in Christ. This same lack of discernment will cause the end time Jews to be especially vulnerable to deception, and they will accept both the false messiah and the False Prophet, believing them to be the messengers from God. The Jews and the

322

rest of the earth dwellers will be duped by the deceptive 'dragon words' coming from the mouth of the False Prophet. The message the False Prophet will proclaim is that the Beast from the Sea—the Antichrist—is indeed the long awaited Messiah! The False Prophet will also cause "fire to come down from heaven in the sight of men." (v13) This sign will be the *coup de grace*—THE sign—that will clinch it for the Jews. This deceptive sign will cause them to believe that the resurrected Beast is the Messiah. The False Prophet will seem to meet all the criteria for the long-expected Prophet as prophesied by, and typified by, Moses. He will deceive the Jews into believing that the Beast from the Sea is their true savior, king and messiah, whose arrival signals the beginning of Israel's millennial reign.

The miracle of fire coming down from heaven reminds us of the prophet Elijah, who, in a contest between himself and the prophets of Baal, caused fire to come down and consume the sacrifice on the altar, proving that Elijah's God was the true God. (See 1 Kings 18:38.) The Jews, who will be expecting Elijah to return, will see the miracle that the 'anti-prophet' will perform—that of causing fire to come down from heaven—and they will be convinced that Elijah has returned! This miracle will serve several purposes:

1) Persuade the masses that the Beast from the Earth is 'the prophet' who is to come. (Deuteronomy 18:15)
2) Convince the people that the False Prophet is also the long-expected Elijah, the forerunner of the messiah. (Malachi 4:5)
3) Convince the people that the newly resurrected Beast is the long-awaited Messiah.

This spectacular sign will most likely take place on the day of the abomination of desolation, the day when the Beast/Antichrist takes his seat in the temple of God, at the time of the evening sacrifice (1 Kings 18:36). The time of the evening sacrifice may also be when the remnant of Israel suddenly will have their eyes opened and will recognize their mistake. At sun-down on that day, the Sabbath will be over and the awake remnant will hasten through the newly formed valley created by the earthquake that will split the earth when the Lord steps down on the Mount of Olives, east of the temple site.

Who the False Prophet is Not

There is a lot of confusion about the identity of the False Prophet. Most students of eschatology understand that the False Prophet will operate in conjunction with the Beast—the Antichrist—to usher in the one world religion. Then, when people look at current events and see how the Pope is taking steps right now to gather all religions under the umbrella of the Roman church, they conclude that the Pope must be the False Prophet. Since the Pope is bringing all world religions together, doesn't that make him a likely candidate for the False Prophet, the individual who will usher in the one world religion along with the Beast?

Earlier in this book I pointed out that the religion of the Harlot is not the same as the religion of the Beast. The Harlot has her own agenda. She 'rides' the Beast— meaning *she* controls *him*! She takes the reins of leadership and she uses the Beast to control the whole world, seeking to conform the world to her agenda and plans. This is one of the reasons—perhaps the main reason—why the Beast hates the Harlot and plots her destruction along with the 10 Kings, who also hate her. She has her own agenda and she is far too controlling.

Compromised Christianity will be a part of the Harlot religion and Catholicism has contributed to the compromise of Christianity over the centuries. The Pope, as head of the Roman church, will head up the *Harlot* religion, and he and his church will be destroyed by the Beast and the 10 Kings at the 6th Trumpet. On the same day and hour that the Harlot is destroyed, the fire will fall from heaven and the False Prophet will proclaim that the Beast is God. Everyone must worship the Beast who 'was not' and came to life again. At that moment, all other religions will be outlawed—including any vestiges of Catholicism and the Pope.

Some people confuse the False Prophet with the Antichrist and see them as being one and the same person. The Bible tells us that they are different people: the Antichrist comes from the sea—he rises from the dead; and the False Prophet arises from the land of the living, and most likely arrives from the land of Israel.

The Dragon, the Beast and the False Prophet form a false trinity. The False Prophet imitates the role of the Holy Spirit. The job of the Holy Spirit is to direct our attention to the Son. The False Prophet, as the false spirit, will direct attention to the Beast, and demand that people worship him as the true messiah. The Dragon imitates God the Father. The Father has given all authority to Christ; and the Dragon will give his throne and authority to the false messiah. The Beast, who is the 'seed of the serpent' imitates the Son, laying down his life and then rising from the dead. In another chapter we'll be looking other attributes of the Spirit, and other ways that the False Prophet will imitate the ministry of the Spirit during the last days.

Chapter 42: Back to Timelines...

Though many of the numbers in Revelation are symbolic (7, 12, 24, etc), measurements of time and the 'day counts' are meant to be taken *literally*. The time period of 3 1/2 years in Revelation is mentioned using 3 different metrics: days (1,260), months (42) and 'time, times and half a time' (which is a symbolic way of expressing 'one year, two years and half a year'). These interchangeable metrics reinforce the idea that we are talking about specific, literal periods of time.

There are three chapters in Revelation which provide specific day counts—precise units of time which make it possible to calculate when certain events will take place. The specific time and day counts which appear in chapters 11, 12 and 13 are as follows: 1,260 days, 42 months, 'time, times and half a time', and three and a half days.

In Daniel 9:27, we read about the '70th week'—a 7 year period of time, which is divided into two halves of three and a half years each. In the middle of the '70th week', at the three and a half year mark, the Antichrist will perform the abomination of desolation; and from what we read in other passages in the scriptures, we know that when the abomination of desolation takes place, the remnant of Israel will flee into the wilderness to the place prepared for her by God. She will be in the wilderness for 1,260 days or 3 1/2 years. (See Revelation 12:13, Matthew 24:15-20, 2 Thessalonians 2:3-7.)

The prophetic story presented in Revelation 12, gave us our starting date for the 7 years, beginning with the Great Sign in the heavens on the Feast of Trumpets in 2017; and brought us all the way to the end of the woman's exile, 1,260 days after the Dragon began his persecution of Israel at the midpoint.

First, let's consider the time/day-counts found in Revelation 11:1-12

> ¹ "A reed like a rod was given to me. Someone said, 'Rise and measure God's temple, and the altar, and those who worship in it. ² Leave out the court which is outside of the temple, and don't measure it, for it has been given to the nations. They will tread the holy city under foot for forty-two months. ³ I will give power to my two witnesses, and they will prophesy one thousand two hundred sixty days, clothed in sackcloth.' "

> ⁴ "These are the two olive trees and the two lamp stands, standing before the Lord of the earth. ⁵ If anyone desires to harm them, fire proceeds out of their mouth and devours their enemies. If anyone desires to harm them, he must be killed in this way. ⁶ These have the power to shut up the sky, that it

may not rain during the days of their prophecy. They have power over the waters, to turn them into blood, and to strike the earth with every plague, as often as they desire.

⁷ When they have finished their testimony, the beast that comes up out of the abyss will make war with them, and overcome them, and kill them. ⁸ Their dead bodies will be in the street of the great city, which spiritually is called Sodom and Egypt, where also their Lord was crucified. ⁹ From among the peoples, tribes, languages, and nations, people will look at their dead bodies for three and a half days, and will not allow their dead bodies to be laid in a tomb. ¹⁰ Those who dwell on the earth will rejoice over them, and they will be glad. They will give gifts to one another, because these two prophets tormented those who dwell on the earth.

¹¹ After the three and a half days, the breath of life from God entered into them, and they stood on their feet. Great fear fell on those who saw them. ¹² I heard a loud voice from heaven saying to them, 'Come up here!' They went up into heaven in a cloud, and their enemies saw them."

This vision describes the career and ministry of the Two Witnesses, and provides us with another 1260 day or 3.5 year scenario. The 1,260 days during which the woman is in the wilderness will take place during the *last* 3.5 years. The 1,260 days of the Two Witnesses' ministry will take place during the *first* 3.5 years.

The story begins with the Two Witnesses' arrival, and we learn that their ministry will continue for 1,260 days. At the end of their ministry, the 'Beast who ascends from the bottomless pit' will make war on them and kill them. The 'Beast who ascends from the bottomless pit is another name for the Beast from the Sea—the 8th King. Three and a half days later, after they are killed, the Two Witnesses will resurrect and ascend into heaven. The *actual* time period that concerns the Two Witnesses is 1,263.5 days, which includes the 1,260 days of ministry plus the 3.5 days they lie in the streets of Jerusalem before they are resurrected.

The 1263.5 days of the Two Witnesses' ministry, death and ascension occurs during the first half of the 7 years, and ends with their ascension at the midpoint/2nd Woe/6th Trumpet/destruction of the Harlot. The second half of the 7 years is briefly mentioned in Revelation 11:2, which states that the "holy city will be trampled" for 42 months—the last 3.5 years. We know the Beast reigns for 42 months during the last 3.5 years.

In Revelation chapter 11, there is a gap in the timeline between when the Two Witnesses ascend into heaven at the midpoint, and the blowing of the 7th Trumpet which takes place at the return of Christ. We read that, concurrent with the ascension of the Two Witnesses, there will be a great earthquake partially destroying the city of Jerusalem. Seven thousand people will be killed and one-tenth of the city will fall. Chapter 11 then skips over the whole rest of the second half of the seven years, proceeding directly to the 7th Trumpet at the return of Christ at the end of the seven years.

> "The seventh angel sounded, and great voices in heaven followed, saying, 'The kingdom of the world has become the Kingdom of our Lord and of his Christ. He will reign forever and ever!' " Revelation 11:15

In chapter 13, the timeline picks up on the Feast of First Fruits, *the same day that the 2 Witnesses are killed.* In Revelation 13, we are formally introduced to the 'Beast from the Sea/bottomless pit'—the individual most people refer to as the Antichrist. This is the same Beast who made 'war' on the Two Witnesses and killed them in chapter 11. In chapter 13, we learn that the Beast will rule for 42 months—the second half of the 7 years—the same 42 months that saw the Holy City will be trampled in Revelation 11.

> "Then I stood on the sand of the sea. I saw a beast coming up out of the sea, having ten horns and seven heads. On his horns were ten crowns, and on his heads, blasphemous names. 2 The beast which I saw was like a leopard, and his feet were like those of a bear, and his mouth like the mouth of a lion. The dragon gave him his power, his throne, and great authority.
>
> 3 One of his heads looked like it had been wounded fatally. His fatal wound was healed, and the whole earth marveled at the beast. 4 They worshiped the dragon because he gave his authority to the beast; and they worshiped the beast, saying, 'Who is like the beast? Who is able to make war with him?' 5 A mouth speaking great things and blasphemy was given to him. Authority to make war for forty-two months was given to him. 6 He opened his mouth for blasphemy against God, to blaspheme his name, his dwelling, and those who dwell in heaven. 7 It was given to him to make war with the saints and to overcome them. Authority over every tribe, people, language, and nation was given to him." Revelation 13:1-7

In addition to Revelation 12, Revelation chapters 10 through 13 furnish another framework for the entire seven years of the 'tribulation'. The ministry of the Two Witnesses will take place during the first 3.5 years (1260 +3.5 days), and the reign of the Beast will take place during the last 3.5 years (42 months) of the seven years. The narrative pivots from the first half of the seven years in chapter 11, to the second half in chapter 13, with special emphasis on the events which will take place around the midpoint.

Most of the narrative contained in Revelation is dedicated to the first 3.5 years of 'tribulation'. Only a few passages deal solely with the last 3.5 years. The stories of the martyrs, the Harlot, and the various raptures and resurrections that precede the reign of the Beast make up the bulk of the book. The last 3.5 years which describe the reign of the Beast, the mark of the Beast, the False Prophet, etc, represent only a small portion of the story that is being told in Revelation and, of *all* the chapters in Revelation, only chapter 13 is dedicated to the 42 month reign of the Beast. Most of the Revelation story concerns the persecution of believers *by the Harlot* and the earth dwellers, which will take place during the first half of the seven year time frame (persecution from which Israel will be exempt), along with the societal and earth changes which will take place as a result of various Seal and Trumpet judgments.

These four chapters—10 through 13—also introduce us to some of the main characters who appear in Revelation: the 'child', who represents present day believers on earth who will be caught up in the first rapture, who will then be represented by the Elders throughout the rest of the book; the woman—who represents the remnant of Israel; the Dragon who is Satan; the heavenly brethren represented by the Elders, 144K and the martyrs; the 'other offspring' of the woman who must endure the reign of the Beast, the Two Witnesses and finally, the Beast from the Sea/Abyss. The exact middle verses of the book of Revelation happen to coincide with the exact middle of the seven years (the war in heaven in chapter 12), illustrating how the story transitions from the persecution of just *believers* during the first half of the seven years, to also include the persecution *of Israel* during the last half.

We have already discovered that most Bible teachers utilize the non-symbolic, literal, linear Greek method of Bible interpretation when they interpret the book of Revelation; and, in so doing, they often place characters and events in the wrong places on the end time timeline, and they often confuse the events of the first 3.5 years with those events which take place during the last 3.5 years. Thus, the persecution of believers (which is instigated by the Harlot), is thought to coincide with the persecution that is instigated by the Beast and the False Prophet. The Pope (or some other religious figurehead who is a part of the Harlot religion) is confused with the False Prophet, and both Harlot religion and Beast religion are viewed as same 'one world' religion. In some scenarios, the Two Witnesses don't begin their ministry until the midpoint, when the temple is desecrated by the Antichrist; and they are not martyred until the end of the 42 months, at Christ's return. But Revelation 11 tells us—albeit indirectly—that the Two Witnesses are the individuals who will rebuild the temple; the temple that must be in place by the *midpoint* in order for the Beast to desecrate it. Only through interpreting Revelation in the Hebraic style can we arrive at a more accurate understanding of the events preceding the return of Christ to the earth.

Convergence

Using the multi-layered, Hebraic method of interpretation—where 'time' is tracked in cycles—we discover that the events which are described in the various visions, often converge on the exact same days, but from different perspectives, depending on which characters are involved. The *midpoint* is one such convergence date:

- the day when the Two Witnesses resurrect and ascend;
- the day when Satan begins his persecution of Israel;
- the day the remnant of Israel must flee into the wilderness;
- the day that the 10 Kings and the Beast destroy the Harlot at the 6th Trumpet/ 2nd Woe;
- the time of the great earthquake that will split the Mount of Olives;
- the official start of the worship of the Beast by the earth dwellers at the abomination of desolation;
- the beginning of the reign of the Beast along with the Dragon and the False Prophet.

The midpoint is when the restraining hand of God is finally removed from the earth, granting the Beast free rein to do as he pleases, until God brings the Beast kingdom to an end at the Second Coming of Christ to the earth.

In addition to the convergence of events which will take place at the midpoint/ abomination of desolation; the Feast of First Fruits in the spring of 2021 is another such convergence date. On that day Satan will be cast out of heaven and 'stand by the sand of the sea', waiting for his false 'son', the Beast from the Sea, to rise from the dead. The Beast will imitate Christ and rise on the same feast that Christ rose from the dead:

> " Then I stood on the sand of the sea. I saw a beast coming up out of the sea, having ten horns and seven heads. On his horns were ten crowns, and on his heads, blasphemous names." Revelation 13:1

Once the Beast rises from the sea of death, the Dragon will bestow on the Beast his power, his throne and his great authority. The authority of the Dragon, is represented by the 'crowns' on the seven heads of the Dragon, and will be transferred to the Beast from the Sea, who is depicted as having 10 crowns on his *horns*, representing the power that the 10 Kings confer upon the Beast. Once Satan gives the Beast *his* authority as represented by the 7 crowns on his heads, the Beast will possess ALL earthly and satanic power: all 7 crowns which were on the Dragon's heads, plus all the crowns of the 10 Kings will be his.

Just as Christ has been given all authority from His Father, the Dragon will bestow all his authority on his 'son', who is the 'seed of the serpent'. Contrary to popular opinion, there can be no Antichrist until the Beast rises from the dead—he must wait until then, for it's *only at that time* that the Dragon will transfer his power to the Beast so that the Beast will be able to reign during the false Millennium. The Beast's authority will be made 'official' three and a half days after he resurrects, when he will go into the temple of God, declaring that he IS God, to the acclaim and adulation of the earth dwellers.

With his newly acquired power, the Beast will, as one of his first acts of domination over the earth, kill the Two Witnesses, in direct defiance of the God of heaven. The death of God's prophets will be yet another event which will take place on First Fruits. The ten days of persecution by the Harlot and the earth dwellers, will have begun on the spring equinox, will also come to an end on that day, and a great multitude of people from every tribe and nation will stand before God in their resurrection bodies:

> "After these things I looked, and behold, a great multitude which no man could count, out of every nation and of all tribes, peoples, and languages, standing before the throne and before the Lamb, dressed in white robes, with palm branches in their hands." Revelation 7:9

The 144K of Israel—those who will be 'kept from the hour of trial'—will be taken into heaven on First Fruits as well. They are the "first fruits to God and to the Lamb". On that day, they may also receive yet another anointing of the Spirit, acknowledging that they were victorious over the temptations and trials which came their way.

The five months after the opening of the Pit, the 'locust army' will cease torturing people without the seal of God. The 150 days will end on the Feast of First Fruits, having begun on Halloween in 2020.

First Fruits is the day Christians celebrate Christ's resurrection from the grave. First Fruits will also be the 'resurrection day' of the Beast; and the earth dwellers will celebrate *his* 'victory' over the grave, worshiping him as God:

> " One of his heads looked like it had been wounded fatally. His fatal wound was healed, and the whole earth marveled at the beast. 4 They worshiped the dragon because he gave his authority to the beast; and they worshiped the beast, saying, 'Who is like the beast? Who is able to make war with him?' " Revelation 13:3,4

330

Spring of 2021 will mark the first time that the Jews will be able to celebrate the Passover in a temple since the destruction of Jerusalem by the Romans in 70AD. Naturally, the streets of Jerusalem will be packed with pilgrims streaming in from all over the world to attend the feasts. The events of that day may even be live-streamed for all the world to see:

> "From among the peoples, tribes, languages, and nations, people will look at their dead bodies for three and a half days, and will not allow their dead bodies to be laid in a tomb. 10 Those who dwell on the earth will rejoice over them, and they will be glad. They will give gifts to one another, because these two prophets tormented those who dwell on the earth." Revelation 11:9,10

When Two Witnesses resurrect from the dead, their enemies will watch them rise and go into heaven:

> "I heard a loud voice from heaven saying to them, 'Come up here!' They went up into heaven in a cloud, and their enemies saw them." Revelation 11:12

In order to communicate the myriad of details which will take place over a very compressed period of time in the spring of 2021, the stories were told in more than one vision in Revelation. In addition to the visions described in Revelation chapters 10-13, we must also incorporate the accompanying Old Testament allusions into the narrative as well, because they help us understand the symbolic details.

With such a plethora of information needing to be communicated, one vision alone would not suffice. Through many smaller visions, Revelation follows the story line of multiple characters, having many interactions, and each with their own timelines. The personal timelines of the various characters often intersect the timelines of other characters at crucial junctures: the Two Witnesses, the martyrs, the Beast(s) and the Dragon to name a few—and more than one vision is required to chronicle all the particulars. The only way to comprehend the complexity of the narrative, is to understand the book of Revelation from the Hebraic perspective: multiple visions and repeating cycles, which, when layered over one another, together create a multi-dimensional drama that reads less like a Bible story and more like science fiction.

Chapter 43: 'Unholy' Week Timeline

Equinox, 3/20/21:
- Begin 10 Day persecution of believers by the Harlot. Israel is exempt.
- Michael arises, war in heaven begins.

Passover, 3/28/21:
- The Scarlet Beast is killed by the Two Witnesses.

First Fruits, 3/30/21:
- The Beast rises from the 'sea'/death.
- Apollyon ascends from the bottomless pit/Abyss.
- End war in heaven.
- Satan/Dragon and his angels are cast out of heaven.
- The Beast receives power from the Dragon.
- The 1260 day ministry of the Two Witnesses ends.
- The Beast kills the Two Witnesses.
- End 10 day persecution of believers.
- All martyrs of the Harlot are in heaven in resurrection bodies.
- The 144K of Israel are taken to heaven.
- The earth dwellers exchange gifts.
- Earth dwellers begin to worship the Dragon and the Beast.

Midpoint/Abomination of Desolation, 4/3/21:
- The Man of Sin defiles the temple of God.
- The Two Witnesses rise from the dead and ascend into heaven.
- The Lord appears on the Mount of Olives and splits the mountain.
- Great earthquake in Jerusalem, 1/10 of the city is destroyed.
- 7,000 people are killed.
- The Dragon begins to persecute the remnant of Israel/the 'woman' of Rev. 12.
- At sundown on the Sabbath (7PM) the woman/remnant of Israel follows Christ through the valley created by the earthquake.
- The Dragon's army pursues the remnant until his army is crushed when the split in the Mount of Olives comes back together.
- 6th Trumpet: The Harlot is destroyed by the Beast and the 10 Kings, the 200 million man army and 4 angels who are released from the Euphrates.
- One third of the earth is killed in the destruction of the Harlot (6th Trumpet/ 2nd Woe).

Chapter 44: The Image of the Beast (Part 1)

God has graciously revealed the events which will take place during the time of the end by giving us the visions of Revelation. God told us through the prophet Amos, that He would do nothing without first revealing His plans to His servants, the prophets (Amos 3:7). God's end time prophetic revelation—which was entrusted to John—is contained in the book of Revelation, as well as in very specific Old and New Testament passages. The prophetic message of Revelation was given to us by God the Father, so that those of us who are alive at the time of the end, would not be caught off-guard when the events described in Revelation begin to unfold. The events of Revelation will take place rapidly, and 'to be forewarned is to be forearmed'.

During the 42 month reign of the Beast three things will be required of humanity:

1. In order to buy or sell, or engage in commerce, a person must take the 'mark of the Beast'. (Also called the 'name of the Beast' or the 'number of his name'.) The mark allows one to be a fully functioning member of the Beast empire and Beast society. Without the mark, one will be an out-cast of society and will be on their own in terms of survival. The mark is something a person must choose to receive as it is connected with the worship of the Beast. The mark will be received by people *with the understanding that they belong to the Beast* and his kingdom. Taking the mark by accident cannot happen as it is connected to willing and voluntary worship of the Beast. (The 144K, on the other hand, are marked or sealed by God. To be sealed means that God has placed *His* mark of ownership upon you. All who belong to Christ either have been, or will be, 'sealed' with the Holy Spirit.)
2. Those who choose to worship the Beast will receive the mark of the Beast on either their right hand or their forehead as a display of their allegiance to the Beast.
3. To be a functioning member of society, one must also worship the Beast: that is, pay homage to the Beast, honor him, revere him and obey him.
4. People will also be required to pay homage—give worship—to the Image of the Beast.

Those individuals who refuse the mark will be criminals and liable to the death penalty. Beheading will be the consequence for those who refuse to worship either the Beast or the Image of the Beast. Life will be very difficult for the remaining believers under these circumstances.

Old Testament type: Three Men in a Fiery Furnace

The story of Nebuchadnezzar's golden statue in Daniel 3, provides an Old Testament pattern of believers who will refuse to worship the Image of the Beast. Nebuchadnezzar, the king of Babylon, (the 'head of gold' in his dream of the image), constructed a statue entirely of gold—representing himself—with the intent that everyone in the land of Babylon should worship the image, under pain of death. Those who refused to worship the image would be cast into a furnace of fire. The image was 60 cubits by 6 cubits, and 6 different instruments signaled when the worship was about to begin. ("666" anyone?)

Shadrach, Meshach and Abednego, Daniel's three Hebrew friends, refused to worship the golden image. When Nebuchadnezzar found out about this, he gave the men a second chance—an opportunity to change their minds. However, they refused the second chance, and chose not to worship the image and were cast, bound, into a furnace of fire, heated seven times hotter than normal. When the king peered into the fiery furnace to watch how these three men would die, he saw one like a 'son of the gods' walking with the three men—who were still very much alive. Daniel's friends were commanded to step out of the furnace, and, to everyone's amazement, they showed no effects of the fire: they were not burned nor did they even smell of smoke! God had delivered them, and the Lord was with them in the fire.

The story of the deliverance of Daniel's three friends, is a pattern that will be repeated during the last days. There will be some believers who, when pressed to give homage to the image or take the mark, will refuse to do so. In this way they 'overcome the Beast and his image and the number of his name'. By refusing to worship the image, some—but not all of them—will be martyred by beheading.

Not all believers will be killed during the reign of the Beast. Some believer's lives will be preserved until the coming of the Lord, who will take them into heaven at the Overcomer rapture—the rapture immediately preceding the Day of the Lord. The surviving believers will be victorious over the Beast, remaining faithful to Christ even in very difficult circumstances.

In Revelation 1:9, the Apostle John uses himself as an example of patient endurance in the midst of tribulation:

> "I, John, your brother and partner with you in the oppression (*tribulation*), Kingdom, and perseverance in Christ Jesus, was on the isle that is called Patmos because of God's Word and the testimony of Jesus Christ."

When the Dragon leaves off his pursuit of the remnant of Israel at the midpoint, he will then persecute believers who refuse to take the mark. These will be the saints who must endure and be faithful to Christ in the midst of terrible trials, just as John was faithful in the face of intense persecution. Whether through offering their lives as martyrs or through steadfast perseverance until Christ comes to take them at the Overcomer rapture, they will remain faithful to Him. (Revelation 15:2; 1 Thessalonians 5:5-10)

> "(*These are those who*) keep the commandments of God and bear testimony to Jesus." Revelation 12:17

Image and Idol? The same thing...or different?

The False Prophet will instruct earth dwellers to make an image of (or 'to') the Beast: "the one who was wounded by the sword and yet lived". The False Prophet will then give 'breath' or 'spirit' to the image.

> "He deceives my own people who dwell on the earth because of the signs he was granted to do in front of the beast, saying to those who dwell on the earth that they should make an image to the beast who had the sword wound and lived. 15 It was given to him to give breath to the image of the beast, that the image of the beast should both speak, and cause as many as wouldn't worship the image of the beast to be killed." Revelation 13:14,15

Many people have the idea that the 'image' will be a physical idol that is set up—possibly in the Temple—at the time of the abomination of desolation. The book of Revelation, however, seems to make a distinction between an 'image' and an 'idol'. In Revelation 9:20, we read about idolaters who have evaded death at the time of the 6th Trumpet destruction of Mystery Babylon. They are people who persist in their idolatry: "did not give up worshiping demons, and idols of gold and silver and bronze and stone and wood..." The Greek word for *idol* in Revelation 9, is "*eidolon*", which means '*an image or a statute of a god*'.

The word for *image*, used in Revelation 13:15 and other places, is the Greek word, '*eikon*', which actually means a '*mirror-like representation', something which exactly reflects its source and is the exact 'replication of a prototype*'. (Strong's #1504)

To get an idea how the word 'image' is used in the New Testament, let's look at other passages where the Greek word, '*eikon*', is found:

> "Just as we have born the *image* of the man of dust, we shall also bear the *image* (*eikon*) of the man of heaven." 1 Corinthians 15:49

> "...and have put on the new nature, which is being renewed in knowledge after the *image* of its creator." Colossians 3:10

"For those whom he foreknew he also predestined to be conformed to the *image* of his Son, in order that he might be the first-born among many brethren." Romans 8:29

"And we all with unveiled face are being changed into his *image* from one degree of glory to another; for this comes from the Lord who is the Spirit." 2 Corinthians 3:18

"He (Christ)is the *image* of the invisible God, the first-born of all creation..." Colossians 1:15

In summary, these verses tell us that:

1) Christ is the exact reflection and *image of God.*
2) All of mankind bears the exact *image of Adam*, the man of dust.
3) Believers are being transformed into the i*mage of Christ.*
4) The 'earth dwellers' will manufacture something which is the exact *Image of the Beast.*
5) The False Prophet will give the *Image of the Beast 'breath or spirit'*, enabling it to 'speak'—to reflect and express the exact nature of the Beast.

This, of course, takes us back to Genesis and the creation of man.

> *"Then the Lord God formed man of dust from the ground, and breathed into his nostrils the breath of life; and man became a living being." Genesis 2:7*

The False Prophet, imitating the Holy Spirit, will animate the Image of the Beast which the earth dwellers will make. He will then impart breath and 'spirit' to the image. Just as man was created in the image of God and given life by the Spirit of God, there will be a *false creation of a new humanity made in the 'Image of the Beast'*, which will then be given a 'spirit'. *This image is more than an idol.* The reference to the Genesis story hints that the Image of the Beast will be a new 'Adam'; a new kind of god-man, created in the likeness of the Beast, an entity who must be worshipped under penalty of death.

Cooperation of the Earth Dwellers is Necessary

Adam and Eve were given dominion over the earth. They were to rule over the earth as God's stewards and God's representatives. One of the consequences of the fall was that Satan became the 'de facto' god of this world, and fallen mankind was placed in bondage to Satan. After the war in heaven, and once Satan is cast to earth, he will set up his kingdom here on earth, in conjunction with his false 'son' the Antichrist, and *replace humans who bear the image of God* with 'hybrids'/ replicants, non-humans who will be re-created in the *Image of the Beast*. Satan must have the 'buy in' of the earth dwellers in this final move to erase the fingerprints of God as revealed in mankind—just as he needed the 'buy in' of our first parents in Eden in order to seize dominion of the earth from man.

The earth dwellers will make the image; the False Prophet—the False Holy Spirit— will place 'spirit' inside of it. The False Prophet will not make the image, but instead he will instruct those made in the image of God—humans—to make it. This is part of the deception. Unlike God who may do as He wills, *the false trinity must have the cooperation, permission and/or agreement of mankind in order to create this new life form*. Satan exercises his power when people are in agreement with him. He is blocked when people resist him. So Satan uses subtlety, lies, half-truths, and 'helpful' suggestions to gain permission from people in order for him to act. Whether the earth dwellers will be cognizant of what they are doing is immaterial; the important thing is that, at some level, they will come into agreement with the prince of the world. The earth dwellers will make the image, which will then become "Adam 2.0", the first of a new 'race' of mankind, the god-men of the False Millennium.

Christ is both 100% God and 100% man: He carries a dual nature. The Beast will counterfeit Christ's dual nature: The Beast will be a man and he will be the 'host body' for the spirit of Apollyon, the king of the angels of the bottomless pit.

Our Culture Has Been Primed

As believers, it's hard to wrap our minds around this idea of a new Adam, a new race of fallen mankind. On the other hand, our culture has been primed for the arrival of this very thing. Entertainment is full of super heroes and mutants. Using advanced technology, mankind has the ability—through nanotechnology, neural lace and the like—to 'download' information into people's brains, to connect them with the internet, to turn people into cyborgs and more. Artificial intelligence— A.I.—is all the rage. The religion of the day is humanism, which is really just the worship of man. Trans-humanism, goes a step further, with the goal of controlling mankind's 'evolution' and deliberately creating god-like men. Hidden underneath all this are the shadowy vestiges of Hitler, and his desire to recreate the master race, to bring about the return of the Aryan gods.

The Days of Noah...

As I write this in the winter of 2019-20, the 'Watchers' are safely locked away, held in chains in the bottomless Pit/Abyss. Apollyon is the king of these beings, the one who will indwell the resurrected Beast. Will the other angels in the Pit, the Watchers, require host human bodies as well? What about the fallen angels who currently dwell in heaven, the angels who will be cast to earth just before the first rapture and again just before the midpoint. Will they also desire host human bodies in which to dwell?

During the days prior to the flood, the Nephilim were on the earth, the genetic products of fallen angels who mated with human women. The illicit union of angelic creatures with human women created the giants, who were hybrid beings, NOT created in the image of God. By the time of Noah, the race of mankind had been so corrupted by the fallen angels and the Nephilim, that eventually only Noah and his family were genetically uncorrupted. Noah was 'perfect' in his 'generation', ie, in his genetic code. He and his family were preserved in the ark when God sent a flood to wipe out the hybrids.

The giants were killed in the flood and the spirits of these monsters still roam the earth as demons, disembodied spirits seeking a host body in which to dwell. Will demon possession be common during the end days...and will a kind of demon possession even perhaps be considered *desirable*?

Satan's Goal

Satan's goal is the defilement, elimination, transmutation and corruption of everything that reflects or reveals God, or His Son, the Lord Jesus. Satan's deceptive promises to Eve in the garden will be repeated during the last days. Just as Satan deceived Eve into believing empty promises of immortality and wisdom, Satan will deceive mankind with promises of life-extension, unlimited knowledge and even divinity, through the use of technology and the illicit knowledge provided by the soon-to-be released occupants of the Abyss. Satan has always sought the destruction of the human race as we know it, for each person carries the image of God within them. That image must be stamped out, destroyed and replaced by the Image of the Beast. Humanity must evolve, and become 'trans-human'. We are about to enter the era where true humans will be rare indeed, just as they were in the days of Noah!

Satan will also seek to maintain his dominion, his foothold, on the earth. Once he is cast from heaven, he must, at all costs, retain his title to the earth as the prince of the power of the air and the prince of this world. If he can't maintain his hold of the earth, he knows that he will be cast into the Pit, and from there into the Lake of Fire. In order to be able to hold his ground here on earth, he will need to create a formidable army of super soldiers who will be available to fight against Christ and His hosts when Christ returns to earth at Armageddon.

Satan and the Watchers also want to finish what was started at Babel: to complete the tower which reaches to heaven, and make a name for themselves. In Genesis 11:6, God said of those building the tower, that this was "only the beginning of what they will do; and nothing that they propose to do will be impossible for them." Given enough time, and with no intervention from God, they, along with Satan and his minions, would rule the world—forever.

Chapter 45: Three Races of Humanity

Two kinds of people will be present during the thousand year reign of Christ on earth: mortal people and glorified people. The mortal people are those who will still be alive when Christ returns to the earth. Matthew 25 tells us that Christ will judge between the nations as a shepherd separates the sheep from the goats. what that means that not all people who live on the earth will be killed in the wrath of God: some among the nations will escape.

Glorified people are believers who will have received their immortal, glorified bodies at the time of the resurrection, or just prior to their rapture into heaven. Believers are people who will be transformed into the image of Christ, who Paul calls the Last Adam.

There will also exist 2 kinds of people during the Beast's false millennium: mortal people and 'replicants'—god-men who will be 'created' in the Image of the Beast. The 'replicants' will require mere mortals to worship them by order of the Beast and the False Prophet. The 'replicants' will possess a dual nature just like the Beast. They will have the appearance of human bodies, but they will be people chosen from among mankind to become 'immortal' hosts to fallen spirits. In essence, the replicants will embody the return of the ancient gods. Those who refuse to worship them will be beheaded by the False Prophet. Those who do homage to them will be cast into the Lake of Fire by Christ.

Satan has a false immortality and a false divinity for men who opt to be re-created in the Image of the Beast. Some, but not all, of those made in the image of God, will seek to abandon God's image in them and choose instead to reflect the Image of the Beast, who is himself, in the image of *his* father, Satan.

People who choose to be more-than-human (trans-human), who desire to transcend their current mortal state and become god-like, will no longer be considered human. Anyone who takes the mark or worships the Beast or becomes like the Beast, will be irredeemable. Christ's sacrifice on the cross will not be able to save or deliver them, even if they should have a change of heart. Christ died for people created in the image of Adam, who was created in the image of God. Christ did not die for 'non-image carriers'—those who carry the Image of the Beast. This is the danger of taking the mark or following the Beast in any way. An eternity in the Lake of Fire is all that remains for those who choose the path of deception and darkness.

Chapter 46: Salvation

The moment a man, woman or child is 'born again', he is adopted into God's family. He becomes a child of God and has the potential to inherit the Father's wealth. When a child of God is first saved, he does not *at that moment* receive everything that God has promised him. At the new birth our spirits are made alive to the things of God, and the Holy Spirit takes up residence inside of us. But a new Christian is still a babe, and must mature into his inheritance. The maturation process is called sanctification: the process whereby our souls—our mind, will and emotions—are made holy and whole.

Salvation comes in stages. The first stage of salvation happens more or less instantaneously: our spirits are made alive and responsive to God. An alive and awakened spirit is necessary for a loving and 'working' relationship with God's Holy Spirit. The Spirit makes His home inside of us and lets us know that we are loved and accepted and forgiven.

The second stage of salvation is the process of 'sanctification'. Paul calls it the process of 'being saved' (present tense, 1 Corinthians 1:18). At this stage of the process, believers are encouraged to live in communion with the Holy Spirit, moment by moment. As we yield our thoughts, will, emotions and actions to the gracious control of the Holy Spirit, little by little, the Spirit recreates the life of Christ inside of us, so that our thoughts, will, emotions and actions reflect the nature and image of Christ.

Paul tells us that all people bear the image of the man of dust, which is Adam. (1 Corinthians 15:49) Believers will also bear the image of the Man of heaven, who is Christ. With reference to our bodies, the physical comes first, and then the spiritual. With reference to the 'total package' of redemption, the new birth begins at salvation—being made alive in the Spirit. As the Spirit works in our lives, our souls and personality become transformed into the image of Christ as well.

> "...that you put away, as concerning your former way of life, the old man that grows corrupt after the lusts of deceit, 23 and that you be renewed in the spirit of your mind, 24 and put on the new man, who in the likeness of God has been created in righteousness and holiness of truth." Ephesians 4:22-24

When a person is 'born again' or 'born from above', the Spirit regenerates the fallen human spirit and the Holy Spirit comes to dwell inside the believer. The Spirit brings life to the believer's mind, will and emotions and, one day, He will transform their body into the likeness of Christ's body. Those of us who have been born again of the Spirit of God possess a dual nature: we are creatures of dust reflecting Adam's image, but we also bear the spiritual image of Christ, and will one day, also have a body like His. The resurrection and the 'change'...from mortal to immortal...will happen on the same day, in the 'twinkling of an eye'.

> "Behold, I tell you a mystery. We will not all sleep, but we will all be changed, 52 in a moment, in the twinkling of an eye, at the last trumpet. For the trumpet will sound and the dead will be raised incorruptible, and we will be changed." 1 Corinthians 15:51, 52

> "I saw a mighty angel coming down out of the sky, clothed with a cloud. A rainbow was on his head. His face was like the sun, and his feet like pillars of fire. 2 He had in his hand a little open book. He set his right foot on the sea, and his left on the land. 3 He cried with a loud voice, as a lion roars. When he cried, the seven thunders uttered their voices. 4 When the seven thunders sounded, I was about to write; but I heard a voice from the sky saying, "Seal up the things which the seven thunders said, and don't write them." Revelation 10:1-4

The third and final stage of salvation is the redemption of our bodies, also known as 'glorification'. (Romans 8:23) Our salvation will become complete once our lowly bodies are transformed into a glorious body like Christ's glorified body. The tendency toward sin, which dwells in our mortal body, will be removed forever. We will possess a body which is equally at home in heaven as it is on the earth, capable of interacting with and participating in both realms. Like being born again in our spirits, the final aspect of salvation—glorification—will also take place instantaneously: in the twinkling of an eye. We need to remember, though, that the change/transformation is not the same thing as the rapture, which is the 'catching away' of believers into heaven. The 'change' will precede the rapture. We must have a body like His in order to enter into the heavenly temple. The scriptures tell us that our bodies will become like Christ's glorified body.

John, the author of the Gospel of John and the recorder of Revelation, also wrote the epistles of 1-3 John. Hear what he has to say on this topic:

> "Beloved, now we are children of God. It is not yet revealed what we will be; but we know that when he is revealed, we will be like him, for we will see him just as he is. 3 Everyone who has this hope set on him purifies himself, even as he is pure." 1 John 3:2,3

Both 1 John 3:2, and the passage in Revelation 10, tell us that Christ is going to appear on earth in order to raise the dead and change the living. In Revelation,

He appears *incognito*, wrapped in a cloud. Somehow, believers will 'see Him' and at that moment, they will become like Him, being transformed into His Image.

What will our Glorified body be like?

There are quite a few passages that tell us something about the attributes of Christ's glorified body, which is the prototype of the new bodies all believers will one day possess.

Christ's appearance to Mary in the garden was the first appearance of Christ after His resurrection. She thought He was the gardener! (John 20:11-16)

> "But Mary was standing outside at the tomb weeping. So as she wept, she stooped and looked into the tomb, 12 and she saw two angels in white sitting, one at the head and one at the feet, where the body of Jesus had lain. 13 They asked her, 'Woman, why are you weeping?'
> She said to them, 'Because they have taken away my Lord, and I don't know where they have laid him.' 14 When she had said this, she turned around and saw Jesus standing, and didn't know that it was Jesus.
> 15 Jesus said to her, 'Woman, why are you weeping? Who are you looking for?'
> She, supposing him to be the gardener, said to him, 'Sir, if you have carried him away, tell me where you have laid him, and I will take him away.'
> 16 Jesus said to her, 'Mary.'
> She turned and said to him, 'Rabboni!' which is to say, 'Teacher!' "

On the same day the risen Christ appeared to Mary, on First Fruits, He also appeared to the disciples:

> "When therefore it was evening on that day, the first day of the week, and when the doors were locked where the disciples were assembled, for fear of the Jews, Jesus came and stood in the middle and said to them, 'Peace be to you.'
> 20 When he had said this, he showed them his hands and his side. The disciples therefore were glad when they saw the Lord." John 20:19,20

The disciples had locked themselves into a room for fear of being arrested and killed themselves. The locks on the door, however, posed no problem for Jesus, as He materialized in the room with them. He would appear before them on two different occasions, both times without walking through the door. Time and space did not seem to pose a problem for Him, and it won't pose a problem for us, either. Jesus had the ability to transport from one location to another.

Jesus bore the marks of crucifixion on His glorified body. That's how we know that His soul/spirit went back into His former human, crucified Body. The same thing will happen to us...the same body we now reside in now will one day be changed.

In John 21:12, Jesus appeared beside the Sea of Galilee, and no one dared ask if it was the Lord, because they knew it was Him.

> "Jesus said to them, 'Come and eat breakfast!'
> None of the disciples dared inquire of him, 'Who are you?' knowing that it was the Lord." John 21:12

We get the impression that there was something about the glorified Lord that resembled the 'old' Jesus that they remembered; but there was something different, too. Like Christ, we may appear different, yet somehow still be recognizable as being the same person we always have been. There will be some things about our bodies that will remain the same, and other things which will be different.

In the future, we will still possess a kind of physical body that will be able to interact with the physical earth. We will also have a spiritual body that can interact with the spiritual world. We will be 'ourselves', only different. When Jesus entered into the world, He became a physical, mortal Person just like us, being born of the virgin Mary. He became a glorified Man when He was raised from the dead. After His resurrection, He became the first of a new kind of man, and the progenitor of a glorified race of humanity. All those who believe in Him will one day reflect His image, just as all men currently reflect the image of our first father, Adam. This new race of glorified people will actually have their own home—the New Jerusalem—the heavenly city which will come down to earth at the end of the Millennium.

Because glorified people are neither 'fish nor fowl'—neither just spiritual or just physical, we will need our own domain, which is the place Christ is preparing for us even now. Heaven was created for spiritual beings, like the angels. The earth was for mortal people. The earthly, human aspect of our new glorified bodies will be able to interface with the physical world, and we will rule with Christ on the earth. The heavenly, spiritual aspect of our new bodies will enable us to access the throne room of Heaven, where we will be priests to God, spending time in His presence. Though glorified saints will have the ability to interact with both realms —the heavenly and the earthly—Christ is making a place for us which is perfectly suited for this New Race of glorified humanity, the New Jerusalem, which is now in heaven, but which will one day come to the New Earth.

How will the 'change' happen?

Voice of Christ will raise the dead, and the Spirit who lives inside of us will transform our mortal bodies. (Romans 8:9-11)

> "But you are not in the flesh but in the Spirit, if it is so that the Spirit of God dwells in you. But if any man doesn't have the Spirit of Christ, he is not his. 10 If Christ is in you, the body is dead because of sin, but the spirit is alive because of righteousness. 11 *But if the Spirit of him who raised up Jesus from the dead dwells in you, he who raised up Christ Jesus from the dead will also give life to your mortal bodies through his Spirit who dwells in you.*" Romans 8:9-11

The Spirit who lives inside of us is the member of the community of God who will transform our bodies at the time of the change. If the Spirit is living inside of you right now, and you are used to interacting with Him, this will seem like a perfectly natural event...similar to when you were born again. On one level, nothing will have changed, on another level, everything will be different!

The voice of Christ is the voice that the dead will hear when they are raised:

> "For the Lord himself will descend from heaven with a shout, with the voice of the archangel and with God's trumpet. The dead in Christ will rise first." 1 Thessalonians 4:16

This is exactly what we see in Revelation 10, when Christ descends from heaven to earth as the Angel of the Lord, and together with the Spirit of God (who is described as the 7 Thunders before the throne of God in heaven), they will raise the dead and change the living.

The dead in Christ will most likely receive their glorified bodies in heaven, as do the 5th Seal martyrs. (Revelation 6:11) The 5th Seal Martyrs are given a white robe—representing their new bodies—in heaven. There is no indication that their souls will need to travel from God's presence back to earth to receive their new bodies and then go back into heaven again. There is no need for this to happen, as a glorified body is trans-dimensional.

In the book of 2 Corinthians, Paul explains that our earthly bodies are temporary dwellings, like 'tents' and our glorified bodies are like permanent building.

> "For we know that if the earthly house of our tent is dissolved, we have a building from God, a house not made with hands, eternal, in the heavens." 2 Corinthians 5:1

Our earthly bodies are also compared to clothing. Right now our spirits and souls are being 'clothed' in our mortal bodies.

> "For most certainly in this we groan, longing to be clothed with our habitation which is from heaven, 3 if indeed being clothed, we will not be found naked. 4 For indeed we who are in this tent do groan, being burdened, not that we desire to be unclothed, but that we desire to be clothed, that what is mortal may be swallowed up by life. 5 Now he who made us for this very thing is God, who also gave to us the down payment of the Spirit." 2 Corinthians 5:2-5

Believers who have died are no longer 'clothed'—they no longer have a body. The goal is not to be souls with no bodies, but souls with better bodies! We don't want to die and have our bodies decay: we want to have our mortal life 'swallowed up' by the life of God! In this passage, Paul is referring to the 'change' at which time our mortal bodies will be transformed by the life of God. When that happens, we will be given our permanent glorified bodies. The Spirit in our hearts is the guarantee that this will happen. If the Spirit is present inside of us as a result of the new birth, we have the assurance that we will also receive our glorified bodies *through the power of the Spirit who dwells inside of us.*

Where will we receive our new bodies?

Jesus received His glorified body in the tomb in which He was buried. We will receive our new bodies on the earth and the dead will receive their glorified bodies in heaven. Just as the resurrected Christ spent some time on the earth before He was received up into heaven, it appears that we will have about 10 days here on earth in our glorified bodies as well. However, both the dead and the living will acquire their new bodies *at the same time*, on the Feast of Trumpets, but the dead in Christ will actually appear in heaven first, having received their new bodies *in* heaven. The 24 Elders before the throne in Revelation 4 seem to be this first group of resurrected (not 'changed') saints. The 24 Elders in chapter 5—the people we see acting as priests with golden bowls of incense in their hands—represent the recently raptured believers who were changed on earth, and raptured on the Day of Atonement.

The 144K will watch us go...and then they will be filled with the Holy Spirit as first fruits to God, on the Feast of Tabernacles 5 days later.

Chapter 47: The Image of the Beast (Part 2)

One of the roles of the Holy Spirit is to recreate the image of Christ in us. When we are born of the Spirit, we become one spirit with Christ, and we live by the power of the Spirit who dwells inside of us. Anything the False Prophet does regarding the Image of the Beast is guaranteed to be a poor counterfeit of God's plan of salvation and redemption.

The 'image' that the earth dwellers make, once it has been given the spirit/"breath" from the False Prophet, will become another kind of man, reflecting the Image of the Beast. He will become a hybrid being, part man and part demon. Just as we become one with the Spirit upon being regenerated, so too will the 'image' become like the Beast. People will be told that Satan wants to make good on the promises he gave to Adam and Eve in the garden, when he exclaimed to Eve: "Thou salt not surely die!" and "You shall be as God". Those created in the Image of the Beast, Adam 2.0—beast/men—will be worshipped as gods. They will be granted a kind of immortality, with a fallen spirit breathed or 'downloaded' into them.

In the Beast's kingdom, there will be up-graded 'god-men'—people who allow themselves to reflect the Image of the Beast—and there will be regular mortals; just as in Christ's coming kingdom there will exist both mortal people and glorified saints.

As much as is possible, Satan will attempt to erase the image of God from man and replace God's image with his own image. Whereas God created distinctions between male and female, between spirit beings and men, and between mankind and beasts, Satan will seek to erase those distinctions and meld men, women, spirit beings and animals into a new 'race' that resembles himself, most aptly represented in the Baphomet: part man, part beast, with both genders in one entity. We can already see the cultural conditioning at work which will make this acceptable to the masses.

This 'new man', created in the Image of the Beast, will also be worshiped. To become a 'god', you must receive the 'spirit' of the Antichrist. Just as the Holy Spirit seals believers with a mark of ownership, these children of the Beast will be permanently altered in their spirits, souls and bodies, signifying their choice to be sons of Satan. **This is irrevocable.** This is, I believe, the blasphemy against the Holy Spirit which Jesus spoke of in the gospels; it is the unpardonable sin. The deception (and self-deception!) will be so great, that many people will not be able to recognize or accept the truth. The promise of immortality and 'super powers' will be so tempting that even believers have the potential to be drawn into the deception.

During the last years of human history, during the 42 month reign of the Beast and before the 2nd Advent of Christ, abdication of one's salvation through taking the mark of the Beast, or 'worshiping' the Image of the Beast is something that *can happen to believers*. Though saved in spirit, the bodies of those believers who will be alive during the 42 month reign of the Beast, will not yet have been glorified, and free from sin. It's possible—and highly probable—that the mark of the Beast, as well as taking on the 'image' of the Beast, has the potential to affect the very DNA of the person who receives the mark or chooses to replicate the Image of the Beast inside of themselves. **Anyone who receives the 'mark' on hand or forehead or chooses to be 'altered' in one's body to reflect the Image of the Beast, will be forever damned.** The end game for Satan is the eradication of the 'image of God' in mankind. People are merely the hosts, the 'interface' with the three dimensional world. This is what the return of the days of Noah looks like: the return of the Nephilim and the 'gods' of old, living here on earth with men.

If the Image of the Beast were merely an idol or statue to be worshiped, as bad as that is, idolatry is a forgivable sin when it's repented of. But to choose to give worth, homage and value to a new kind of 'Adam', an entity created in the Image of the Beast, well, that's another thing altogether. Replacing the image of God in man will be the ultimate 'slap in the face' as far as God is concerned, and worship of the Image will be enough to send all who worship the Beast or its Image, into the Lake of Fire forever. (Revelation 14:9-11)

Mankind will have to choose: do they continue as they are, created in the 'image and likeness of God' or do they choose to give honor and glory to the 'Image of the Beast'? Will they choose to reflect the image of Christ, or replicate the image of the Antichrist? Everyone must choose, and however they choose, that choice will determine their ultimate, eternal destination.

The False Prophet is the 'Anti-Spirit', the 3rd member of the False Trinity of the Dragon, Beast, and False Prophet. Just as the Spirit lifts up and exalts Christ, so too will the false Spirit/False Prophet lift up and exalt the Antichrist...deceiving, if possible, the very elect of God. The Holy Spirit reproduces the image of Christ in believers and the False Prophet will reproduce the Image of the Beast in earth dwellers who choose to participate. In the last days, self-deception will be the very worst kind of deception. Anyone who allows himself to be deceived into believing the promises of Satan, the consummate liar and thief, will be swept away in the deception. God Himself, will send a strong delusion upon those who reject the truth and take pleasure in unrighteousness. (2 Thessalonians 2:11)

Chapter 48: The Three 'Woes' and the Opening of the Pit

Because Revelation is not chronological, there's no need to start at chapter one when interpreting the story. What may seem to be a 'hit and miss' approach to the book of Revelation, is really the only way that anyone can actually explain the events of the end times as described in Revelation. Working 'backwards' through the story, going from events which are more obvious—like the events associated with the wrath of God and the return of Christ—to those events which are less obvious, like the nature of the Beast, is a totally legitimate way to study the book.

In the opening chapters of this book, I began with 'The End'—the events connected with the Second Coming of Christ and the wrath of God. We examined the passages which describe the victory of Christ over His enemies, and how the end of the story has been incorporated into many of the visions. Early on in the book, I demonstrated how the 6th and 7th Seal, the 7 Bowls and the 7th Trumpet all have something to do with the wrath of God/Day of the Lord and the return of Christ.

Working backwards, we discovered that the 6th Trumpet—which coincided with the 2nd Woe—will take place at the midpoint initiating the destruction of the Harlot, also known as Mystery, Babylon. One-third of mankind—those who are implicated in Babylonian religion and idolatry—will be killed with fire, smoke and sulphur by the Beast and the 10 Kings and a 200 million man army, empowered and guided by 4 fallen angels.

We also know that the 5th Seal involves the martyrs who will be killed *by the Harlot* during the Great Tribulation *for Christians*, during the 10 days of persecution just before the midpoint. We also know that Seals 1-4 and Trumpets 1-4 will take place after the 24 Elders are in heaven, but not before the 144K are sealed. (These 'judgments' will be examined in detail later on in the book.)

The Three "Woes"

The three 'woes' are equated with Trumpets 5, 6 and 7, and are mentioned in Revelation 8:13:

> "I saw, and I heard an eagle, flying in mid heaven, saying with a loud voice, 'Woe! Woe! Woe to those who dwell on the earth, because of the other blasts of the trumpets of the three angels, who are yet to sound!' " Revelation 8:13

Working backward, from the 3rd Woe/7th Trumpet, here's what we know so far:

- *7th Trumpet (3rd Woe)*: This is the victory trumpet which announces Christ's rule on earth and takes place at the end of the 42 month reign of the Beast.
- *6th Trumpet(2nd Woe)*: This is when the judgment of the Harlot and her associates takes place, at the midpoint.
- *5th Trumpet (1st Woe)*: This is when the bottomless Pit is opened and the Watchers/fallen angels (also known as the 'locust army') are released.

The 5th Trumpet is the trumpet which announces the opening of the bottomless pit and the release of the 'Watchers'—fallen angels who are symbolically represented by locusts; and their king, Apollyon, the Destroyer. Apollyon is the entity who will indwell the Beast after the Beast is resurrected:

> "The fifth angel sounded, and I saw a star from the sky which had fallen to the earth. The key to the pit of the abyss was given to him. 2 He opened the pit of the abyss, and smoke went up out of the pit, like the smoke from a burning furnace. The sun and the air were darkened because of the smoke from the pit. 3 Then out of the smoke came locusts on the earth, and power was given to them, as the scorpions of the earth have power. 4 They were told that they should not hurt the grass of the earth, neither any green thing, neither any tree, but only those people who don't have God's seal on their foreheads. 5 They were given power, not to kill them, but to torment them for five months. Their torment was like the torment of a scorpion when it strikes a person. 6 In those days people will seek death, and will in no way find it. They will desire to die, and death will flee from them.
>
> 7 The shapes of the locusts were like horses prepared for war. On their heads were something like golden crowns, and their faces were like people's faces. 8 They had hair like women's hair, and their teeth were like those of lions. 9 They had breastplates like breastplates of iron. The sound of their wings was like the sound of many chariots and horses rushing to war. 10 They have tails like those of scorpions, with stingers. In their tails they have power to harm men for five months. 11 They have over them as king the angel of the abyss. His name in Hebrew is 'Abaddon', but in Greek, he has the name 'Apollyon'.
>
> 12 The first woe is past. Behold, there are still two woes coming after this."
> Revelation 9:1-12

A quick skim of chapter 9 can leave one reeling! How does one make sense of locusts and scorpion stings and women's hair and lion's teeth? The symbols used in this chapter point us to *very specific Old Testament allusions*, which will then provide additional details about the story, and help us to interpret the meaning of the symbols used in Revelation 9. Later in this book we'll be going through this chapter, verse by verse, in order to have a better understanding of the "who, what, when, where and how's" of this most extraordinary passage of scripture.

The 5th Trumpet/Revival Connection

God desires that everyone would repent and become a part of His forever family. He does not desire the death of the wicked, but that the wicked would repent and be saved. Some end time teachers believe that the door to salvation closes at the (first) rapture, and that all who are 'left behind' are left to endure the wrath of God as unrepentant unbelievers. Nothing could be further from the truth! The sounding of the 5th Trumpet—which will bring about immense suffering for all who are not sealed—will actually, I believe, result in the **greatest revival in the history of the world**. When the 5th angel sounds his trumpet, and an 'army' of fallen entities are released in a billowing cloud of smoke, *multitudes* will turn to Christ in faith. God can—and will—use EVERYTHING—even the fallen angels—to bring people to Himself. If God did not spare His one and only Son, but gave Him up for us, will God not use even the fallen angels in His plan of redemption?

The Hebraic roots of the Revelation story is manifested through the use of symbols and imagery, and the story of the locust army is told *indirectly through symbols*. Unlike other interpretations of Revelation, we're not looking at this book from a Western/Greek mindset, but a Hebraic/Eastern mindset. Rather than one long, continuous vision, Revelation is actually a series of visions, with each vision being chronological within itself, but not necessarily chronological as placed in the book.

Review: Principles of Interpretation

- People and 'entities' are given symbolic names in Revelation, and the identity and role of the various characters in the end time story will be revealed through the use of imagery and symbolism. Old Testament *allusions* provide more information and will often tell 'rest of the story'.

- Locations and places in Revelation are also given symbolic names. Jerusalem is called the 'Holy City' before the midpoint/abomination, after which it becomes 'Sodom' and 'Babylon'. Again, Old Testament references help us to identify the meaning of the symbols.

- Spiritual realms are readily identifiable: heaven, New Jerusalem, Mount Zion and the Pit/Abyss.

- Increments of time are to be taken literally: 1,260 days, 42 months, 10 days, 5 months, 1 hour, 3.5 days, 1 day.

- The defining characteristics of the various characters are communicated via symbols. For example: horns=power, wings=speed, crowns=rulership and authority, and so on.

Review: The Watchers

In the apocryphal book of Enoch, and in the Old Testament book of Daniel, we are made aware of a group of angels, also known as the "Watchers". Some of these angels were tasked to watch over humans after God created mankind. Genesis chapter 6 and Jude 6, tell us that some of these angels 'left their first estate' and mated with human women, corrupting the DNA of humanity. The fallen angels were thought to have been particularly attracted to women's long beautiful hair.

According to Enoch, once the Watcher's fell into sin, they made things even worse by proceeding to divulge secret, esoteric knowledge to mankind—knowledge which had been kept from humanity for good reason. The Watchers intended to thoroughly corrupt humanity. These defiled beings imparted the secrets of the biological sciences, technology, warfare, metallurgy and the production of weapons; sorcery, meteorology, astrology, astronomy (movements of the sun and moon in particular), agriculture, methods of seduction (cosmetics) and architecture. The ancient megaliths which appear all over the world, from the pyramids of Egypt to the pyramids of the Mayans, may be attributed to the advanced knowledge mankind gained through the Watchers, and their offspring, the giants.

According to tradition, the Watchers arrived on earth on Mount Hermon, which is part of the present day Golan Heights, lying between Israel and Syria. Mount Hermon has been a place of demon worship from antiquity and at one time there were many altars to demons and pagan deities on the mountain. The transfiguration of Christ took place atop Mount Herman, being the 'high mountain' where Moses and Elijah appeared with Christ in glory. Mount Herman also shows evidence of prior volcanic activity and there is even evidence of a magnetic pole shift which took place at some time in the past. Currently, there is also a UN base at the top of the mountain, adding to the mystery which still shrouds Mount Hermon.

In addition to defiling the DNA of mankind, the forbidden knowledge that the Watchers shared with humanity further corrupted the earth through violence and warfare—*in excess* of what man would have done if he was left to his own devices. The fallen angels added sin to sin, and with additional 'secret' knowledge in man's possession, sin became even more 'sinful'. God saw the accelerating levels of violence and wickedness on the earth. He knew that if left unchecked, the rapid increase in knowledge would lead to the demise of the pinnacle of His creation—

the men and women He created in His image. Instead of retaining the image of God, humanity would be transformed into the likeness of their corrupters. All of this took place prior to, and concurrent with, the days of Noah, and was, I believe, the primary reason for the great flood.

The 'days of Noah' will return during the end times: the Watchers will be released from the pit; violence and corruption will again run rampant, and the DNA of mankind will be altered to create the Image of the Beast in mankind, thereby removing the image of God from humanity—altogether—if possible.

The fallen angels—the Watchers—were imprisoned in the Pit because of their sin, and because of their corrupting influence on humanity. They defiled the DNA of man through having sexual relations with human women, resulting in the hybrid giants or *nephilim*. They also tampered with the DNA of animals and plants. As of now, they are being kept in chains in the darkness of the Pit, to be released during the last days prior to their final judgment. (See 2 Peter 2:4, Jude verse 6)

The demons are the disembodied spirits of the giants, the offspring of the fallen angels. The giants were destroyed in the flood and their spirits were left to wander the earth, seeking a body to inhabit. Because the giants were hybrids, they do not have a 'home' *per se*. The earth was created for people, and the spirit realm was created for spirit beings like angels. The giants were neither totally human nor totally angelic, and so the disembodied spirits of the demons are always seeking a 'home' to inhabit. This home usually takes the form of an earthly body, preferably a human body, but an animal will do in a pinch. Particularly wicked demonic spirits may be sent to the Pit before the time of judgment. When Jesus cast out the Legion of demons from the Gaddarene demoniac, the demons begged Jesus not to send them to the Pit—a place of torture—the place where the Watchers dwell at this time.

The 5th Trumpet: The Release of the 'Locust Army'

Revelation chapter 9 gives an account of the vision of the release of the Watchers ("Locust army") and their king, Apollyon, including the account of how and when the Pit is opened, and the effects this 'army' will have on the world once they are released.

"Then the fifth angel sounded, and I saw a star from heaven which had fallen to the earth."

We already know 'stars' are angels (Revelation 1). In this passage, a 'star'—an angel—is seen falling from heaven...that is, falling from the dwelling place of God (not the starry heavens). Is this angel a holy angel or one of Satan's angels? God's angels are confident, beautiful and strong. This angel appears to have been 'pushed'! Only evil angels are ever said to 'fall', indicating that the angel with the key is one of the Dragon's angels, who will be tasked to unlock the Pit, which, because it's a place of torture, is probably a place he doesn't want to go near! We can also infer that the sounding of the 5th Trumpet must take place BEFORE the midpoint, for we know that *after* the midpoint none of Satan's angels will remain in heaven *to* 'fall'. This 'star' or angel falls to the *earth,* which also lets us know that the Pit is here, somewhere under the earth.

"...and the key of the bottomless pit was given to him."

The fallen angel with the key was commanded to open the Pit. The Pit will NOT be opened until the 5th Trumpet is blown, no matter what people say about the secret purpose of CERN, the 'veil thinning', etc. That's not to say that communication can't take place at a certain level between realms, but only the angel who is given the key to the Pit will be able to open the Abyss at the proper time; and God has already determined when that time will be.

"He opened the bottomless pit, and smoke went up out of the pit, like the smoke of a great furnace; and the sun and the air were darkened by the smoke of the pit."

The result of the Pit being opened will be like the appearance of billows of dark smoke.

"Then out of the smoke came locusts upon the earth, and power was given them, as the scorpions of the earth have power."

These will not be ordinary locusts...in fact, they will not be insects at all. The creatures are represented by locusts because they will have characteristics of locusts and also of scorpions. When locusts invade, they have the appearance of a black cloud darkening the sky. They devour everything in their path and are overwhelmingly destructive. The locusts from the Pit will be 'given' power; that is, the permissive will of God will allow them freedom to act within certain pre-determined, God-ordained parameters. Before they can do *anything*, they must first be released at God's order, and then granted permission from God to carry out their plans once they are liberated from the Pit.

"They were told not to hurt the grass of the earth, nor any green thing, nor any tree, but only the men who do not have the seal of God on their foreheads."

Ordinary locusts eat all vegetation in sight. The creatures that will be released from the Pit, however, will not devour vegetation—they will only be interested in tormenting men! Certain limitations will be placed on them: they will only be permitted to hurt non-believers—people who are not sealed—as those who *are* sealed—new believers sealed with the Holy Spirit—will be off-limits to them.

In Revelation 7, we are informed that the 144K of Israel will be among those who are sealed and we know that Gentile believers will be sealed with the Holy Spirit as well. The seal is the abiding presence of the indwelling Spirit of God which only believers possess. The Spirit will provide protection from the onslaught of the fallen angels/Watchers once they are released from the Pit. Jesus told His disciples that they would have power over serpents and scorpions—both literal and metaphorical.

> " Behold, I give you authority to tread on serpents and scorpions, and over all the power of the enemy. Nothing will in any way hurt you." Luke 10:19

The Watchers/locusts don't have permission to kill anyone. Their job will be to torment and torture people; and their torture will be comparable to a scorpion's sting, which, though extremely painful, usually does not result in death. The pain experienced by those who are stung will be so intense that they would rather die than live, preferring a swift death to the agony of life. The 'locusts' will have permission to torture anyone without the seal for 5 months (150 days).

> "And they were not permitted to kill anyone, but to torment for five months; and their torment was like the torment of a scorpion when it stings a man. And in those days men will seek death and will not find it; they will long to die, and death flees from them."

During the five months that the locusts torment people, death will not be an option for those who are so afflicted. No doubt there will be some who will try to commit suicide because of the horrific pain, but the relief of death will elude them. No matter how terrible their injuries are, *they will not be able to put themselves out of their misery.* They will become the living 'dead'. The big question here is WHY? Why can't they die? The answer to this question lies in Revelation 1:18; where Christ states, "I have the keys to Death and Hades."

> "Don't be afraid. I am the first and the last, 18 and the Living one. I was dead, and behold, I am alive forever and ever. Amen. I have the keys of Death and of Hades." Revelation 1:17b,18

Christ, the One who holds the keys to Death, is also the One who controls access to the realm of the dead, and for five months He will refuse to allow these people to die or have access to Sheol. Those who are stung by the 'locust/scorpions' will be given a small taste of the hopelessness that awaits those who take the mark of the Beast, which, once taken, will sentence that person to an eternity in the Lake of Fire, suffering continuous torture, without even the hope of the release of death. Those who take the mark will suffer in the presence of the Lamb and the holy angels, forever and ever. They will be within sight of heaven, but unable to participate in the glorious fellowship that believers will experience with God around His throne.

What's the purpose? Why would Christ keep these people from dying? The fact is, that unless they come to saving faith in the Lord Jesus, they are ALREADY dead! Their current experience of torment will be their eternal destiny should they refuse Christ and His offer of salvation!

Our God is the God of 'second chances'. During the 5 months of torment, people will have yet another opportunity extended to them to trust in Christ. The excruciating sting which the Watchers will physically inflict on the unsealed, will spill over into emotional and psychological anguish as well. I don't believe the pain these people suffer will be symbolic: the torment will be real. What is not openly stated, but only hinted at in the 5th Trumpet judgment, is that there is a cure for the sting: having the seal of God—accepting Christ as Lord and Savior and being filled with the Spirit.

The Brazen Serpent

When the children of Israel grumbled against Moses in the wilderness, God sent fiery serpents among the people, to sting them, causing some of them to die from the serpent's bite. When the people repented, God told Moses to cast a bronze serpent and put it on a pole. He told Moses to tell the people that whoever was bitten would be healed if they looked at the brazen serpent:

> "They traveled from Mount Hor by the way to the Red Sea, to go around the land of Edom. The soul of the people was very discouraged because of the journey. 5 The people spoke against God and against Moses: 'Why have you brought us up out of Egypt to die in the wilderness? For there is no bread, there is no water, and our soul loathes this disgusting food!'
>
> 6 Yahweh sent venomous snakes among the people, and they bit the people. Many people of Israel died. 7 The people came to Moses, and said, 'We have sinned, because we have spoken against Yahweh and against you. Pray to Yahweh, that he take away the serpents from us.' Moses prayed for the people. 8 Yahweh said to Moses, 'Make a venomous snake, and set it on a pole. It shall happen that everyone who is bitten, when he sees it, shall live.'

9 Moses made a serpent of bronze, and set it on the pole. If a serpent had bitten any man, when he looked at the serpent of bronze, he lived." Numbers 21:4-9

This very strange incident with the Israelites and the brazen serpent prefigured the crucifixion of Christ:

"As Moses lifted up the serpent in the wilderness, even so must the Son of Man be lifted up." John 3:14

There is so much packed into this story: Christ's death on the cross, and how He became a curse for us, the judgment of the serpent—Satan—at the same time the Eternal Son was 'made to be sin for us'; the remedy for the sting of sin and death through the substitutionary sacrifice of the Lamb of God—who was represented by the Serpent on the pole. Anyone who looks to the One who was lifted up, will be forgiven and delivered from the sting of death—and the torment of the Watchers.

Who would have thought that this obscure Biblical allusion would provide the clue to deliverance for those who will be thus tormented? The Watchers will be released at the 5th Trumpet judgment, and, worse than a plague from a horror movie, they will cause a reign of terror that will only affect the unsaved—the unsealed—throughout the earth. How long do you think it will take for those being tormented to come to their senses and look to Christ for healing and deliverance? What about those who are stung—some of whom may have *thought* they were Christians—but when they are stung will realize their own self-deception? Will they not also be provided an opportunity to repent from dead works to receive healing and true salvation? The passage in 1 Corinthians 15:55 proclaims the victory of Christ over the sting of death:

"Oh, Death, where is thy victory? Oh, Death, where is thy sting?" 1 Corinthians 15:55

Chapter 49: Two Great End-Time Revivals

I believe there will be two great revivals during the last days; revivals which will be unparalleled in human history. The first one will take place immediately after the first rapture, after the 'catching away' of the child of Revelation 12:5, on the Day of Atonement, 9/28/20. The 144K of Israel will be the first fruits of that glorious revival, followed by many Gentiles who will also come to faith in Christ at that time. Both groups will be sealed by the Holy Spirit during the Feast of Tabernacles, which will begin on October 3, 2020. Revelation 7:1 tells us that the 144K must be sealed before the judgments can begin:

> "After this, I saw four angels standing at the four corners of the earth, holding the four winds of the earth, so that no wind would blow on the earth, or on the sea, or on any tree. 2 I saw another angel ascend from the sunrise, having the seal of the living God. He cried with a loud voice to the four angels to whom it was given to harm the earth and the sea, 3 saying, 'Don't harm the earth, the sea, or the trees, until we have sealed the bondservants of our God on their foreheads!' 4 I heard the number of those who were sealed, one hundred forty-four thousand, sealed out of every tribe of the children of Israel." Revelation 7:1-4

The four angels who stand at the four corners of the earth hold back the 'wind' of judgment. Before the Lord begins to judge the earth, He will make sure that His people are sealed with the seal of God—the Holy Spirit. The Angel who is seen 'ascending from the east' or from the 'sun', is another appearance of the Angel of the Lord. Christ, represented by the bright Angel, is the One who has the 'seven spirits of God', and from Whom the Spirit is sent out into all the earth. The Spirit proceeds from both the Father and the Son:

> " I saw in the middle of the throne and of the four living creatures, and in the middle of the elders, a Lamb standing, as though it had been slain, having seven horns and seven eyes, which are the seven Spirits of God, sent out into all the earth." Revelation 5:6

The Angel who seals the 144K with the Spirit, *is Christ,* whose glory is like the rising of the sun, as is alluded to in this passage:

> "Arise, shine; for your light has come,
> and Yahweh's glory has risen on you!
> 2 For behold, darkness will cover the earth,
> and thick darkness the peoples;
> but Yahweh will arise on you,

and his glory shall be seen on you.
3 Nations will come to your light,
and kings to the brightness of your rising." Isaiah 60:1-3

And again in this passage:

> "But to you who fear my name shall the sun of righteousness arise with healing in its wings. You will go out and leap like calves of the stall." Malachi 4:2

In the gospel of Luke, Zechariah prophesied about the coming Messiah, calling Him the "Dayspring". Other translations call Him the "Dawn" or the "Sunrise":

> "To give knowledge of salvation to His people
> By the remission of their sins,
> Through the tender mercy of our God,
> With which the *Dayspring from on high* has visited us;
> To *give light to those who sit in darkness and the shadow of death*,
> To guide our feet into the way of peace." Luke 1:76-79

Christ is the One with the face like the Sun. He is the Dayspring, who will shine on His people, Israel, once more. He will bestow the Holy Spirit on all those who place their trust in Him. He is the Angel of the Lord who will protect them as He protected the children of Israel during their wilderness wanderings.

The sealing of God's people before calamity befalls, is also pictured in the book of Ezekiel, where we read that God commissioned an angel to mark those who 'sigh and groan' over the abominations being committed in Jerusalem. Those so marked were spared the destruction which then befell the inhabitants of Jerusalem:

> "The glory of the God of Israel went up from the cherub, whereupon it was, to the threshold of the house; and he called to the man clothed in linen, who had the writer's inkhorn by his side. 4 Yahweh said to him, 'Go through the middle of the city, through the middle of Jerusalem, and set a mark on the foreheads of the men that sigh and that cry over all the abominations that are done within it.'
>
> 5 To the others he said in my hearing, 'Go through the city after him, and strike. Don't let your eye spare, neither have pity. 6 Kill utterly the old man, the young man, the virgin, little children and women; but don't come near any man on whom is the mark. Begin at my sanctuary.' "
> Ezekiel 9:3-6

364

Before God judges, He separates the righteous from the wicked. In Revelation 7, the righteous—new believers from the 12 tribes of Israel as represented by the 144K—are marked with the seal of His Spirit, so that when the 5th angel blows his trumpet, the righteous will not be included in the judgment of 'mercy' which follows when the Pit is opened.

The Watchers—the fallen angels who will be released from the Pit—will have five months during which they have permission to torture unbelievers. The five months will begin sometime after the 144K are sealed, placing the start of the 5th Trumpet after the Feast of Tabernacles in 2020. By the spring of 2021, at the feast of First Fruits, the martyrs and the 144K will be in heaven, having either been killed by the Harlot or raptured before the Harlot's destruction at the 6th Trumpet/midpoint. If we subtract 150 days (5 months) from the feast of First Fruits, March 30, 2021, we arrive at 10/31/20—Halloween night, a fitting time for the Pit to be opened. Halloween in 2020, which falls on a Saturday, will also witness a 'blue moon'—the second full moon of the month.

The second great revival will come on the heels of the first, as multitudes upon multitudes of those tortured by the Watcher's scorpion-like sting look to Christ for salvation and healing. This revival will be world-wide, and so unparalleled in human history, that the powers of evil will be compelled to bring this revival to an end the only way God's enemies know how to do that: they will persecute God's people with a vengeance. This 5 month revival will culminate in the deaths of saints without number, being the greatest persecution of Christians the world has ever seen or will ever see again, with the majority of the bloodshed taking place during the ten days of persecution by the Harlot and the earth dwellers.

By First Fruits of 2021, multitudes of saved martyrs and raptured saints will be standing in God's throne room in heaven! Only a very few believers will remain on earth; some of whom will be martyred by the Beast during his 42 month reign, and some who will 'survive' and remain until the 'Day of the Lord rapture', which will be the 3rd rapture of the priesthood, taking place before the 7 Bowls of Wrath are poured out on the Beast kingdom.

Chapter 50: Back to the "Locust Army"...

The Watchers are not our friends. Because of their illicit relationship with mankind before the flood, God consigned the Watchers to the Pit, where, even now they are chained and subjected to torture. After the flood, the offspring of the Watchers—the demons, the disembodied spirits of the giants—were doomed to wander the earth, seeking a body to inhabit. Once the Pit is opened and the fallen ones are finally released, mankind will become the target of thousands of years of hatred and animosity. The Watchers will seek to be avenged for the destruction of their children during the flood; and avenged for the torture they endured in the Pit.

> "The appearance of the locusts was like horses prepared for battle; and on their heads appeared to be crowns like gold, and their faces were like the faces of men."

The symbols used in this chapter tell us something about the characteristics of these fallen ones. The locusts hoards are like "horses prepared for battle", both terrifying and overwhelming. In warfare, a foot soldier was no match for a soldier mounted on a horse, and the point here is that the Watchers will be a formidable foe. The way the horses are arrayed on the battlefield of the earth is evidence of a 'battle plan'. These beings will have had thousands of years to come up with an action plan—a carefully crafted strategy to bring mankind to its knees.

Each of these entities will be wearing a crown. A crown is a symbol of rulership and authority. These entities were—and still are—rulers: they belong to the hierarchy of principalities, thrones and powers:

> "For by him all things were created in the heavens and on the earth, visible things and invisible things, whether thrones or dominions or principalities or powers. All things have been created through him and for him." Colossians 1:16

The Watchers are the 'elite' of the fallen spiritual realm, hence their crowns of gold. Gold indicates 'divinity' and gold is the precious metal of things pertaining to God and His glory. The fact that these beings are wearing crowns which *appear* to be gold, indicates that they will attempt to imitate God's glory and power in order to deceive people into believing that they are angels of light and goodness.

These 'fallen ones' will also have faces like men, indicating that they may take on human appearance, just as they did in the time preceding the flood. These highly intelligent and malevolent personalities will manifest as 'one of us'—only more dangerous, well-organized and powerful.

"They had hair like the hair of women..."

"Women's hair" is a symbol of beauty, glory and seduction. Perhaps these beings will lure, tempt and seduce people into joining them...followed by the 'sting'.

"...and their teeth were like the teeth of lions."

Lions rip apart their prey and drag it off to their lair. These beings are fierce and exceedingly dangerous.

"They had breastplates like breastplates of iron; and the sound of their wings was like the sound of chariots, of many horses rushing to battle."

Iron is the metal of war and battle, and breastplates defend the wearer from enemy attacks. (See 1 Samuel 13:19-22.) These beings will be indestructible, and more than able to defend themselves against any who come against them. Wings depict swiftness and freedom of movement. The sound of these angels will inspire fear and dread in the hearers.

"They have tails like scorpions, and stings; and in their tails is their power to hurt men for five months."

These angels possess the power to 'sting' people and torment them. A 'tail' is an 'animalistic' appendage. Neither God nor His people are ever represented as having tails. The Dragon is depicted as having a 'tail' with which he enforces his will on his subjects. In Revelation 12, Satan uses his tail to cast a third of his angels to the earth. Both the dragon's tail and the scorpion-like tails of the Watchers communicate the merciless and beast-like nature of their owners.

The following verse is where we are told that the 'locusts' are actually evil, fallen angels who are ruled by an even more wicked and powerful angel: Apollyon, also known as Abaddon, the "Destroyer":

"They have as king over them, the angel of the abyss; his name in Hebrew is 'Abaddon', and in the Greek he has the name 'Apollyon'."

Apollyon is an angel. He is also the entity who will indwell the "Beast who ascends from the bottomless pit", the Beast who makes 'war' on the 2 Witnesses and kills them. The Beast from the Sea is a 'hybrid': a combination of the 7th King —a man—and the 'king' who ascends from the bottomless pit, Apollyon, the Destroyer. This wicked spirit will energize the Beast, indwelling and possessing him. The Scarlet Beast, formerly controlled by the Harlot, will, upon his death and resurrection, be controlled by the spirit of Destruction, the spirit of Apollyon, the 'seed of the serpent'.

Two entities are joined as one in the person of the Antichrst: the Beast who is a man, and Apollyon, who is a spirit. Both the Beast and Apollyon ascend from the bottomless pit. They become 'one' when the Beast is resurrected.

This superimposing of two entities also occurs in Revelation 12, where we are meant to see the 'child' and the 'Man-child' as the same baby. The child represents living present day believers. The Man-child is Christ, the One who rules with a rod of iron. The child is caught up to heaven—a depiction of the rapture— the Man-child is not raptured, but He is the King who will rule on earth.

"The first woe is past; behold, two woes are still coming after these things."

The 5th Trumpet is equated with the 1st Woe, and therefore must take place BE-FORE the midpoint of the 7 years. The Beast must die, resurrect and be possessed by Apollyon before the 'man of sin'—the Antichrist—can be revealed at the time of the abomination of desolation. Any chronology which places the 5th Trumpet AFTER the midpoint will be inaccurate and not consistent with the scriptural context of Revelation. We know that the 2nd Woe/6th Trumpet will take place at the midpoint, therefore Trumpets 1-5 must take place before the middle of the 7 years.

The Watchers will remain on the earth for the rest of the seven years. They will be joined by their 'brethren', the fallen angels when these angels are cast out of heaven. Satan and the rest of his angels will be cast to earth at the midpoint and, from that point on, hell will be on earth. The wicked angels from the Pit will descend upon the earth like a plague of locusts; and Satan and his angels will be cast from heaven to the earth. All the forces of darkness, along with the deceived earth dwellers, will be present on earth in full force during the 42 month reign of the Beast.

Apollyon, (who will indwell the Beast) along with his angels, the Watchers, may give mankind additional forbidden knowledge during their remaining time on earth; knowledge which would then be used in the final battle against the Lord at Armageddon. The knowledge they imparted to men in the past—technology, weaponry, and how to conduct warfare—will continue to be used to further the Beast kingdom. In ways that are currently unimaginable, they may impart new information that will cause the blasphemous transformation of both humanity and the earth. Remember, the 'Beast who ascends from the bottomless pit'

369

Apollyon, the Destroyer, is the KING of the wicked spirits currently being held in the Abyss. No doubt he will continue to be their king while they are on earth, as he is the one who will indwell the Beast. One can only assume that Apollyon and his hoard have been holding back a few 'aces', which they will play during the time of the great deception.

In summary: the 'locusts' symbolize the host of wicked angels who corrupted mankind before the time of the flood. Because of their great wickedness, these angels, (also known as the Watchers) were bound in chains and are currently being held prisoners in the Pit/Abyss. They will be released at the 5th Trumpet/2nd Woe and will be used as God's tools to bring about the last great revival on earth. They will 'sting' and torment men, and all those who are thus afflicted who look to Jesus, will be healed and saved. These fallen entities will be granted permission to torture only the people who do not bear the seal of God. They will torture people for 5 months (150 days). The Watchers will be released from the Pit after the first two groups of new believers—the 144K followed by Gentile believers—are sealed with the Spirit. Afterwards, multitudes of humanity will be saved, threatening the Harlot's very existence and power. In an attempt to squelch the revival, the Harlot, along with the earth dwellers, will conduct a ten day persecution of believers resulting in the deaths of millions of Christians.

Chapter 51: Trumpets and Seals

Earlier in this book I demonstrated that the visions *as they appear in Revelation* are not placed in chronological order. Revelation does not consist of one long vision with events taking place in the order they appear in the book—with a couple of out-of-order 'interludes'. Revelation is actually made up of many smaller visions that over-lay one another in time. Chapter-wise, very little about the book is chronological. For example, all the events of chapter 6 (the opening of the Seals) do not necessarily happen before the events described in chapter 9 (the opening of the Pit at the 5th Trumpet and the fall of Babylon at the 6th Trumpet).

Just because the visions are not laid out in chronological order, chapter by chapter, does not mean that the events described *within each individual vision* are not in chronological order. We know that the events described within each vision will take place in the order that the events appear in the vision. The fact that the seven Seals, seven Trumpets and seven Bowls are numbered in order, from 1 to 7, in each of their respective visions, speaks to a sequential, chronological order of some kind: the first seal (or trumpet or bowl) will be 'opened' before the 2nd is opened; and the 2nd seal will be opened before the 3rd seal and so on. The seals are opened in an orderly sequence, and, once opened, show how the various 'seal' events will unfold over time. The same holds true for the seven Trumpet and Bowl judgments.

If the whole book *were* chronological, the letters to the seven churches in chapters 2 and 3 would form the beginning of the chronology, and what's written in the letters would lay the foundation for the rest of the 'story'. However, a simple reading of the seven letters reveals only a series of commands and commendations given to various churches by Christ, and there is no real chronology or story-line present in those chapters at all. That's one of the reasons why the letters to the seven churches are considered by many to be 'historical', with each of the seven churches representing various 'ages' of Christianity, and thus not really a significant part of the end time story. Because many teachers don't include the letters to the seven churches as being a part of the last days 'timeline', they then begin the 'story' in Revelation 4 and 5, with the Elders appearing in heaven, and with the Lion of the tribe of Judah taking the scroll.

Starting the end time story in chapter 4 makes a little more sense, as there are at least some characters to follow: the Elders, the Lamb and the Almighty, the four Living Creatures, etc; as well as some kind of action taking place: the search for someone who is 'worthy' to take the scroll, the Elders singing and interceding for the saints on earth before the heavenly altar, and so on.

Every vision must be looked at very carefully, paying close attention to the details in the vision. The story contained in the vision of Revelation 5, for example, begins with Christ taking the scroll with the seven seals. Once He takes the scroll the story rapidly moves from Him taking the scroll, to Him being worshiped and adored by ALL creation. If 'all' means 'every single conscious entity', then this group of 'worshippers' must also include every fallen, evil entity and unrepentant person who ever existed. When will every created being worship Christ as King? The fallen angels will *not* worship Christ until at least after His 2nd Coming. The fact that we see *every created being* offering praise and worship to the Lamb indicates that we have already reached the 'end of the story'! We've jumped from the Lamb being worthy to take the scroll, straight to the acknowledgement of *all created beings* that the Lamb has the right to reign; an acknowledgment which won't be given at least until the end of the seven years, after Christ has defeated His enemies at Armageddon:

> "I heard *every created thing which is in heaven, on the earth, under the earth, on the sea, and everything in them*, saying, 'To him who sits on the throne and to the Lamb be the blessing, the honor, the glory, and the dominion, forever and ever! Amen!'[14] The four living creatures said, 'Amen!' Then the elders fell down and worshiped." Revelation 5:13,14

At the end of the 'Scroll' vision, Christ's subjects, both friend and foe alike, acknowledge His Lordship and His right to rule over them. In Revelation 5, we move swiftly from the search for Someone who is worthy to open the scroll, to the 'happy ending' at the triumphant return of Christ; when "every knee will bow and every tongue confess that Jesus Christ is Lord, to the glory of God the Father".

The vision which immediately follows the 'Scroll' vision, is the vision where we see Christ actually opening the seals on the scroll, beginning with the opening of the first Seal in Revelation 6. We have now moved from the Scroll vision to a brand new, but related vision: the 'Seal Vision'.

The Seal vision is a stand-alone, independent vision which has its own timeline, and is not attached chronologically to the events of the Scroll vision. In the Seal vision we are tracing a *theme*—not a chronology—and the theme in this case is the opening of the 'Seals' on the scroll. The theme or topic of 'Seals' is the 'thread' which connects chapter 5 with chapter 6. When viewed in this way, the events associated with the opening of the first seal *do not immediately follow* the worship of all creation; something which we know will not take place until the return of Christ. If the first seal 'event'—the Rider on the White Horse—took place immediately after the worship of all creation at the end of chapter 5, the White Horse Rider would begin his 'ride' *after the return of Christ*—after the 'happy ending'— which makes no sense whatsoever.

The fact is, we have no way of knowing *when any* of the Seal events will take place, or exactly where they fit into the end time story just by reading through chapter 6. What we *do know* is that the Seals are 'sequential'—that is, the first seal will be the first seal to be opened, and the second seal will be opened second, and so on, with the 7th seal being opened last. Just because the Seals will be opened in sequence—1 to 7—does not mean that all the seals which are opened in chapters 6-8 are opened before the Trumpet angels sound their trumpets in chapters 8-11. Or that all the Seals must be opened before the Two Witnesses arrive on the scene in chapter 11. What we are presented with in the Seal vision is a series of events which will take place sequentially, in a prescribed order, within a seven year time frame. The only way we can know *when* a specific Seal will be opened is by looking at the clues in the other visions; and by making sure that the events associated with the opening of each Seal is placed on the timeline in such a way so as to harmonize and avoid contradiction with other events described within the book of Revelation.

We know that Christ must take the scroll with the seals before He can actually break the seals and open the scroll. This means that the 24 Elders must be in heaven before the seals can be opened. That's a timing clue. We've also already associated the 6th Seal with the wrath of God and the 2nd Coming of Christ:

> "I saw when he opened the sixth seal, and there was a great earthquake. The sun became black as sackcloth made of hair, and the whole moon became as blood. 13 The stars of the sky fell to the earth, like a fig tree dropping its unripe figs when it is shaken by a great wind. 14 The sky was removed like a scroll when it is rolled up. Every mountain and island was moved out of its place. 15 The kings of the earth, the princes, the commanding officers, the rich, the strong, and every slave and free person, hid themselves in the caves and in the rocks of the mountains.

> 16 They told the mountains and the rocks, 'Fall on us, and hide us from the face of him who sits on the throne, and from the wrath of the Lamb, 17 for the great day of *his wrath has come*, and who is able to stand?' " Revelation 6:12-17

We've also already associated the 5th Seal martyrs with those who are killed by the Harlot during 10 days of persecution, and event which takes place *before* the midpoint. So here's what we already know about the timing of the Seals:

• The 24 Elders are in heaven *before any seal* is opened, indicating that the resurrection of the dead in Christ and the rapture of the child will have already had to have taken place.

- Christ will have the Scroll in His possession before any Seal is opened.
- The 5th Seal is opened sometime before the midpoint.
- The 6th Seal is opened toward the end of the seven years.
- The 7th Seal is opened after the 6th Seal, meaning that whatever takes place as a result of the opening of the 7th Seal must come *after* the events of the 6th Seal, and the event which the 7th Seal describes must also be associated with the 2nd Coming of Christ/wrath of God. (More on this later.)

Another clue that the judgments associated with the 7 Seals and the 7 Trumpets won't take place until just after the 144K are sealed is found in the following verse:

> "After this I saw four angels standing at the four corners of the earth, holding back its four winds so that no wind would blow on land or sea or on any tree." Revelation 7:1

The four angels who stand on the four corners of the earth holding back the four winds, are holding back the judgments of God. The 'winds' symbolically depict God's judgment; and they are not just holding back the Trumpets, but ALL judgments will be withheld, until after the 144K are 'sealed':

> "Do not harm the land or sea or trees until we have sealed the foreheads of the servants of our God." Revelation 7:3

The following Old Testament allusions depict wind as a symbol of judgment:

> " At that time it will be said to this people and to Jerusalem, 'A hot wind blows from the bare heights in the wilderness toward the daughter of my people, not to winnow, nor to cleanse. 12 A full wind from these will come for me. Now I will also utter judgments against them.' " Jeremiah 4:11,12

> "Upon the wicked He will rain snares; Fire and brimstone and burning wind will be the portion of their cup." Psalm 11:6

The Seventh Seal

Before we look at the 7th Seal—the last seal which will be opened sometime during the end of the seven years—we need to understand how the Bible has been divided into chapters and verses. The verse and chapter numbers that we see in our Bibles are not in the original Greek and Hebrew manuscripts which make up the Bible. Chapter and verse numbers were added long after the books of the Bible were written, as an aid to quickly locate specific scriptures. There is nothing holy or sanctified about the verse numbers, and some translations of the Bible leave them out altogether.

Chapter and verse numbers—when used as an aid to Bible reading—are usually helpful, but they also can artificially break up the train of thought of a passage of scripture. People tend to stop reading at chapter divisions, assuming that they have just completed a section or thought. The verses at the start of a new chapter are usually considered to be the beginning of a new thought. For the most part, this way of reading the Bible does not interfere with the meaning or interpretation of a passage, but, occasionally, the incorrect placement of chapter and verse numbers can form a giant roadblock to truly understanding the meaning of a passage of scripture.

The chapter and verse placement of the 7th Seal is an unfortunate case in point, and is a great example of how Revelation would have been better off not having the chapter and verses listed at all! Because of a wrongly placed chapter division, many Bible teachers misinterpret what is happening in chapter 8 with the 7th Seal. We read about the 7th Seal being opened by the Lamb in Revelation 8:1:

> " 1 When the Lamb opened the seventh seal, there was silence in heaven for about half an hour.   2 And I saw the seven angels who stand before God, and they were given seven trumpets." Revelation 8:1,2

Because the 7th Seal is opened at the beginning of a new chapter, people tend to think that what immediately follows the opening of the 7th Seal, will be the events depicted in the *rest of chapter 8*. Reading chapter 8 in this way would lead one to believe that the 7 Trumpet judgments come after, or 'out' of, the 7th Seal, that is, they happen directly after, or as a result of the silence in heaven. If one were interpreting Revelation chronologically, this is how the chapter would be interpreted; that *all* the Seals must be opened before the first Trumpet angel blows his trumpet.

This interpretation, however, is incorrect. Though we read about the Lord opening the 7th Seal in verse 1 of chapter 8, the 7th Seal does not initiate the Trumpet judgments. Rather the opening of the 7th and last seal tells us that the Seal Vision *is over*. The 6th Seal describes the beginning of the wrath of God, and the 'silence' in heaven (the 7th Seal) must therefore also be associated with the wrath of God, and we know that the wrath of God will take place toward the end of the seven years. Therefore 7th Seal does not initiate the 7 Trumpet judgments and the Trumpets do not come 'out' of the 7th Seal.

The 7th Seal triggers silence in heaven, and *silence precedes judgment*. When Christ opens the 7th and final seal, there is a hush in heaven: all is deathly quiet, no angel sings, the Living Creatures cease their worship among the saints, no praise is lifted towards God. Perhaps for the first time in eternity, heaven is totally silent:

> "Be silent, all flesh, before Yahweh; for he has roused himself from his holy habitation!" Zechariah 2:13

> "Be silent at the presence of the Lord Yahweh, for the day of Yahweh is at hand. For Yahweh has prepared a sacrifice. He has consecrated his guests." Zephaniah 1:7

The silence in heaven is in response to God rousing Himself for the Day of the Lord; the great and fearsome day of His wrath. With the opening of the 7th Seal, the Scroll of judgment is read and the full fury of the wrath of God and the Lamb are about to commence. The 7th Seal is the 'calm before the storm', the reverential hush of creatures in the presence of an angry and just Creator God; the God who has said, "vengeance is mine...I will repay"; the God who has come to the end of His merciful patience and is about to crush His foes in the winepress of His fury.

Looking at the timeline below, the first four Seal judgments and the first four Trumpet judgments will take place after the 144K are sealed, but before the Pit is opened. In a timespan of less than 30 days, the earth will be pummeled from the cosmic impact of the first 4 Trumpet judgements; and the Four Horsemen will begin to ride shortly thereafter, bringing about further devastation on earth:

Many will object to this compression of time, preferring to believe that the Seals and Trumpets will unfold in a leisurely manner over the course of a seven year 'tribulation'. But the events of Revelation will come on the world hard and fast. The very first verse of Revelation emphasizes how quickly the events will unfold once they begin:

> "The revelation of Jesus Christ, which God gave Him to show to His bondservants what things it behooves *to take place in quickness*." Revelation 1:1, Berean Literal Bible

The first four Seals and the first four Trumpets will overlay one another, and, like the contractions of a woman in labor, they will come in enormous waves of ever-increasing sorrow and pain.

Trumpets 1-4, will affect only a third of the earth: the whole earth will not be impacted by these events. It's possible that the first four Trumpet judgments will come upon only the Western hemisphere, which makes up about one-third of the world's landmass. Europe, Asia, Africa and the Middle East will most likely be relatively unaffected by the earth changes, as these places are known 'players' in the end time story:

> "The first sounded, and there followed hail and fire, mixed with blood, and they were thrown to the earth. One third of the earth was burned up, and one third of the trees were burned up, and all green grass was burned up.
>
> 8 The second angel sounded, and something like a great burning mountain was thrown into the sea. One third of the sea became blood, 9 and one third of the living creatures which were in the sea died. One third of the ships were destroyed.
>
> 10 The third angel sounded, and a great star fell from the sky, burning like a torch, and it fell on one third of the rivers, and on the springs of water. 11 The name of the star is "Wormwood." One third of the waters became wormwood. Many people died from the waters, because they were made bitter.
>
> 12 The fourth angel sounded, and one third of the sun was struck, and one third of the moon, and one third of the stars, so that one third of them would be darkened; and the day wouldn't shine for one third of it, and the night in the same way." Revelation 8:7-12

The sounding of the first four Trumpets initiate events that will affect a third of the earth's environment, causing it to become desolate and toxic. With each of these four Trumpet judgments, the same third of the earth will be affected—most likely that part of the earth which has no place in end time prophecy. The kings of the East (China, N. Korea and India in particular), the European nations, the Middle East and parts of northern Africa will be left intact to fulfill their roles in the end time drama.

The earthly and cosmic disturbances of fire and hail mixed with blood; a great 'mountain' (possibly an astroid) thrown into the sea; 'Wormwood' and a third of the light of the sun, moon and stars being removed—will render 1/3 of the earth virtually uninhabitable. Not until the earth is in the process of being impacted by the first four Trumpet judgments, will the Living Creatures call forth the Four Horsemen of the Apocalypse, after the Lamb opens the first four seals in rapid succession:

> "I saw that the Lamb opened one of the seven seals, and I heard one of the four living creatures saying, as with a voice of thunder, 'Come and see!'2 Then a white horse appeared, and he who sat on it had a bow. A crown was given to him, and he came out conquering, and to conquer.

3 When he opened the second seal, I heard the second living creature saying, 'Come!' 4 Another came out, a red horse. To him who sat on it was given power to take peace from the earth, and that they should kill one another. There was given to him a great sword.

5 When he opened the third seal, I heard the third living creature saying, 'Come and see!' And behold, a black horse, and he who sat on it had a balance in his hand. 6 I heard a voice in the middle of the four living creatures saying, "A choenix (*quart*) of wheat for a denarius, and three choenix of barley for a denarius! Don't damage the oil and the wine!"

7 When he opened the fourth seal, I heard the fourth living creature saying, 'Come and see!' 8 And behold, a pale horse, and the name of he who sat on it was Death. Hades⁺ followed with him. Authority over one fourth of the earth, to kill with the sword, with famine, with death, and by the wild animals of the earth was given to him." Revelation 6:1-8

When the four angels sound their Trumpets, they will cause a third of the earth to become a desolate wasteland, and when that happens, the *world's power systems will come crashing down as well*. This will be especially true if the United States is one of the nations that is affected by the cosmic disturbances and the other catastrophes which will rain down on the earth, affecting everything from vegetation, to ready access to fresh drinking water, to the fish in the sea. Ocean going vessels will be pummeled by the wind and waves, their crews and cargo sinking beneath the angry waves. Tsunamis will wipe out the coastlands and major cities will be utterly destroyed. But more important than the climate catastrophes that are sure to take place, will be the chaos in society. As society breaks down, once mighty nations will crumble, leaving a gaping power void. When the first Seal is opened and the Rider on the White Horse is released, that void will be filled. The White Horse rider will be followed immediately by the Red Horse Rider, who will bring war, violence and bloodshed in his wake.

As the remaining nations of the world vie for political dominance; gangs, cartels and other factions will also use violence and bloodshed to control the remaining resources. The Rider of the Black Hose, the third horseman, will usher in famine pestilence and disease. Those in power will initiate price controls, limiting the amount of resources available to the average person. The rich will be unaffected by the famines and food shortages which follow ("do not harm the oil and wine"). One-fourth of the earth's population will be overcome by the violence and social upheaval which will ensue, and many will die. The Pale Horse depicts the sum total of the destruction brought about by the first three horsemen: death, plagues, pestilence, famine, bloodshed, wars. Up to a fourth of the people who remain on the earth may perish.

The first four Trumpets describe the monumental changes which will take place *on the physical earth*, while the first four Seals describe the *societal* changes which will take place, as world rulers battle one another in a desperate attempt to achieve hegemony. A third of the earth will be directly affected by the astroid strike and other cosmic disturbances brought about by the Trumpet judgments; and a fourth of the earth's population will be directly affected by the subsequent social and political upheaval which will spread from nation to nation. The four Trumpets depict the physical destruction of the earth and the annihilation of a third of the vital resources, without which, life, in all its forms: animal, vegetable and human; will be unsustainable. The harmony of society depends upon access to the basics of food, water and shelter. The destruction of a third of the earth's most essential and basic resources, (not to mention the final blow to the once mighty USA), will be like a bomb going off in the world.

All of these events can—and most likely will—take place in *less than a month*, after which the dust will settle and a new world structure will emerge. The Harlot will hold the reins of power whilst sitting astride the Scarlet Beast—the 7th King who remains only "a little while".

After the 144K are sealed, the first four angels will blow the first four Trumpets, one after the other in rapid succession, and then the real trials on the earth will begin. The Trumpet judgments will be followed closely by the Four Horseman, when the first four Seals are opened by Christ. But before the Trumpet angels can begin to blow their trumpets, we must go back in time, back to the throne room of heaven, where all of this began, at the altar of incense before the throne of God.

Chapter 52: The Altar of Incense and the Throne of God

Heaven is a very big place and many spiritual beings inhabit heaven. These beings include the myriads of angels who minister before God, the four Living Creatures who stand before God's throne guarding His glory, the spirits of the dead in Christ, the seven torches of the Holy Spirit and, of course Christ, the Lamb.

God Himself is seated on a glorious, radiant throne, surrounded by an emerald rainbow and a sea of glass. One day soon, believers in Christ—as represented by the 24 Elders—will be seated on thrones in His presence. Not long afterwards, the souls of martyrs will appear under the golden altar of incense which stands before His throne. Symbolized by the ark of the covenant on earth, God's throne is where His glory is manifested. He dwells in the heavenly temple, in absolute holiness.

God's throne in heaven is represented on earth by the ark of the covenant. The ark held the commandments of God: commandments which must be obeyed in order for people to stand in the presence of a holy God. The punishment for violating even one commandment was death: "the soul that sins shall die." While the earthly temple stood, the blood of goats and rams and bulls temporarily covered over the sins of Israel until such a time as the sinless, Eternal Lamb would make complete, everlasting atonement for the sins of the whole world, and especially those who would place their trust in Him.

Above the ark of the covenant was the 'mercy seat', the place where the blood of the Lamb was sprinkled. The blood on the mercy seat reminded God that mankind's debt of sin had been paid through the death of Another. Anyone who violates the commandments must fall under the righteous judgment and wrath of God. Anyone who places their trust in God's provision, will be made clean and pronounced righteous because of the sprinkled blood of the Eternal Lamb on the mercy seat. The requirements of the Law, with its impossible demands, were met in the Perfect Son of God. The throne of God is a place of mercy for those who take refuge in the blood of the Lamb; and it is a place of judgment for those who refuse the sacrifice of His Son.

The New Jerusalem is also present in heaven, but the Holy City is not a part of God's throne room—it is located somewhere else in heaven. One day in the future, after the present earth will have melted away and dissolved into nothingness, God will also do away with His heavenly temple, His current throne room, and He will dwell in the New Jerusalem with the glorified saints. At that time, the Holy City, will become God's new 'throne room', and will descend to the New Earth, where the dwelling place of God will be with man:

"I saw a new heaven and a new earth, for the first heaven and the first earth have passed away, and the sea is no more. 2 I saw the holy city, New Jerusalem, coming down out of heaven from God, prepared like a bride adorned for her husband. 3 I heard a loud voice out of heaven saying, 'Behold, God's dwelling is with people; and he will dwell with them, and they will be his people, and God himself will be with them as their God.' " Revelation 21:1-3

"I saw no temple in it, for the Lord God the Almighty and the Lamb are its temple. 23 The city has no need for the sun or moon to shine, for the very glory of God illuminated it and its lamp is the Lamb. 24 The nations will walk in its light. The kings of the earth bring the glory and honor of the nations into it. 25 Its gates will in no way be shut by day (for there will be no night there), 26 and they shall bring the glory and the honor of the nations into it so that they may enter. 27 There will in no way enter into it anything profane, or one who causes an abomination or a lie, but only those who are written in the Lamb's book of life." Revelation 21:22-27

In the future, the throne of God will be in the New Jerusalem, and from His throne will flow the River of Life:

"Then he showed me a river of the water of life, clear as crystal, coming from the throne of God and of the Lamb." Revelation 22:1

God's throne itself will one day be transformed from a place of impending judgment and doom, to a place of eternal joy and the source of everlasting life. At this present time, however, His throne is the source of 'angst'; the place where His mercy and wrath meet, the place of judgment that is at this present time, being withheld from the world:

"And from the throne proceeded lightnings, thunderings, and voices." Revelation 4:5

The 'lightnings, thunderings, and voices' represent the judgment that is being withheld. The judgments are being held back until the proper time, and they stand in stark contrast to the blessings that will flow from His throne as pictured by the beautiful river life— a picture of the Spirit—that will one day flow from the throne of God.

"The angel took the censer, and he filled it with the fire of the altar, then threw it on the earth. Thunders, sounds, lightnings, and an earthquake followed." Revelation 8:5

"Then the temple of God was opened in heaven, and the ark of His covenant was seen in His temple. And there were lightnings, noises, thunderings, an earthquake, and great hail." Revelation 11:19

"And there were noises and thunderings and lightnings; and there was a great earthquake, such a mighty and great earthquake as had not occurred since men were on the earth." Revelation 16:18

The book of Revelation tells us that the "lightnings, noises, thunderings" which emit from the throne of God are manifested just prior to the start of the Trumpet judgments (Revelation 8), then again at the end of the Bowl judgments (Revelation 16), and at the 7th Trumpet—the trumpet which announces the victory of Christ over His enemies, the end of the 'tribulation' and the destruction of the Beast kingdom.

In front of the rumbling and flashing throne of God stands the golden altar of incense. The presence of this altar is hinted at in Revelation 5, where we see the 24 Elders holding golden bowls of incense, which represent the prayers of the saints on earth:

"Now when he had taken the book, the four living creatures and the twenty-four elders fell down before the Lamb, each one having a harp, and golden bowls full of incense, which are the prayers of the saints." Revelation 5:8

The thematic thread of the altar can be followed throughout the book. The next place we read about the altar is found in the passage relating to the opening of the 5th Seal, where the souls of the martyrs appear underneath the altar:

"When He opened the fifth seal, I saw *under the altar the souls* of those who had been slain for the word of God and for the testimony which they held." Revelation 6: 9

These are the people for whom the Elders have been praying. The souls of the martyrs of the Harlot will gather under the altar upon their death. They will cry out for their blood to be avenged. Soon after, each martyr will be given a 'white robe'—their resurrection body—and told to wait until all their fellow martyrs arrive in heaven. At the end of ten days, when all the believers who are to be killed are finally in heaven, they will have their prayers for vengeance answered. And they will not have long to wait for God's vengeance to come down like a hammer on those who killed them. At the blowing of the 6th Trumpet, Mystery Babylon—the Harlot who, along with the earth dwellers, murdered the saints—will herself be destroyed in one hour.

A 'voice' over the altar then commands the 6th angel to sound his trumpet. The origination point of the 'voice', is the very same place where the martyred souls gathered upon their deaths, the very same place their prayers ascended before God: the golden altar of incense. The voice calls out from between the horns of the golden altar before God's throne. Horns represent power, and in this case, they represent the power of prayer and the answer to the martyrs' pleas for vengeance. Now, instead of voices coming from *beneath* the altar, a voice speaks from *above* the altar:

> "The sixth angel sounded. I heard a voice from the horns of the golden altar which is before God, 14 saying to the sixth angel who had the trumpet, 'Free the four angels who are bound at the great river Euphrates!'
>
> 15 "The four angels were freed who had been prepared for that hour and day and month and year, so that they might kill one third of mankind." Revelation 9:13-15

Prayers and judgment take place at the altar of incense. The prayers of the saints on earth are offered by the 24 Elders in heaven. Their prayers rise like incense from the altar in the presence of God and the Lamb. The plea for vengeance on those who persecuted the saints on earth also originates from the altar; and, after Satan is cast to the earth at the midpoint, praise and worship will erupt from the Elders and the martyrs in front of this same altar, the place where Satan had previously brought his accusations:

> "I heard a loud voice in heaven, saying, 'Now the salvation, the power, and the Kingdom of our God, and the authority of his Christ has come; for the accuser of our brothers has been thrown down, who accuses them before our God day and night. 11 They overcame him because of the Lamb's blood, and because of the word of their testimony. They didn't love their life, even to death.' " Revelation 12:10,11

During the time of the out-pouring of God's wrath—the time when the 3rd Bowl judgment will result in the waters of the Beast kingdom being turned to blood— the souls of those *martyred by the Beast* will affirm the righteousness of God's judgments. This company of martyred souls under the altar, unlike the martyrs of the Harlot, must wait for their resurrection bodies, which they will not receive until *after* the visible return of Christ at His 2nd Coming, when they will be resurrected.

Revelation informs us that there are two different groups of martyrs. Those beheaded by the Beast are not the same group of martyred saints as those who are martyred by the Harlot. The Harlot and the earth dwellers kill Christians before the midpoint, and those who die at that time are given their 'white robes'—their resurrection bodies—in heaven, shortly after their deaths on earth. The resurrected multitude who stand before the throne of God in white robes in Revelation 7, are the newly resurrected martyrs of the Harlot, those who 'keep coming' out of the 'great tribulation'—the tribulation for believers. The martyrs who are killed during the reign of the Beast will also be resurrected and participate in the priestly rotation, but not until the 2nd Coming of Christ, after which they will be resurrected into their glorified bodies and join the rest of the priesthood in heaven where they will minister to God.

Prior to the reign of the Beast, the Spirit will give a word of hope to those believers who will be living during the 42 month reign of the Beast, encouraging them to persevere and to refuse to take the mark or worship the Beast or its image. Even though the believers who are to be martyred by the Beast are not immediately raised from the dead like their brethren who were martyred by the Harlot, they are assured that they will not be forgotten:

> "Here is the perseverance of the saints, those who keep the commandments of God and the faith of Jesus."
>
> 13 I heard a voice from heaven saying, 'Write, "Blessed are the dead who die in the Lord from now on." '
>
> 'Yes,' says the Spirit, 'that they may rest from their labors, for their works follow with them.' " Revelation 14:12-13

Whereas the martyrs of the Harlot received their glorified bodies almost immediately upon their martyrdom, the martyrs of the Beast must wait under the golden altar until the wrath of God is over. At the time of the 3rd Bowl, the 'altar' will speak: it is the voice of the martyred saints who were beheaded during the reign of the Beast:

> "I heard the angel of the waters saying, 'You are righteous, who are and who were, O Holy One, because you have judged these things. 6 For they poured out the blood of saints and prophets, and you have given them blood to drink. They deserve this.'
> 7 I heard the altar saying, 'Yes, Lord God, the Almighty, true and righteous are your judgments.' " Revelation 16:5-7

This group of martyrs (those who will be beheaded by the Beast) will be resurrected at the return of Christ, in what is termed the 'first' or 'premier' resurrection. This is not the first resurrection *in time*, nor is it the general resurrection of all the righteous dead. *The only people who will be raised are the beheaded martyrs*:

> "I saw thrones, and they sat on them, and judgment was given to them. I saw the souls of those who had been beheaded for the testimony of Jesus and for the word of God, and such as didn't worship the beast nor his image, and didn't receive the mark on their forehead and on their hand. They lived and reigned with Christ for a thousand years. 5 The rest of the dead didn't live until the thousand years were finished. This is the first resurrection. 6 Blessed and holy is he who has part in the first resurrection. Over these, the second death has no power, but they will be priests of God and of Christ, and will reign with him one thousand years." Revelation 20:4-6

All the rest of the dead, both good and bad, must wait until the Great White Throne judgment at the end of the Millennium. Only then will they be reunited with their bodies, and enter into the place of their eternal destiny:

> "I saw the dead, the great and the small, standing before the throne, and they opened books. Another book was opened, which is the book of life. The dead were judged out of the things which were written in the books, according to their works. 13 The sea gave up the dead who were in it. Death and Hades gave up the dead who were in them. They were judged, each one according to his works. " Revelation 20:12,13

The altar of incense is the place where prayer and intercession take place in heaven, and the altar is also where the judgments of God originate in answer to prayer. The Lord Jesus stands before this altar in heaven even now, making intercession for us as our great High Priest:

> "Therefore he is also able to save to the uttermost those who draw near to God through him, seeing that he lives forever to make intercession for them." Hebrews 7:25

The 24 Elders will participate in this priestly work of intercession upon their arrival in heaven, where they, too, will offer up the prayers of the saints on earth. Angels also stand before the altar, ready to deliver the answers to the prayers of God's people—including the answer to the prayer of 'vengeance' on behalf of the martyred saints. Angels will initiate God's judgment on the Harlot and the earth dwellers who killed them. The first angel we see 'delivering' an answer to prayer stands at the altar of incense in Revelation chapter 8:

"I saw the seven angels who stand before God, and seven trumpets were given to them.³ Another angel came and stood over the altar, having a golden censer. Much incense was given to him, that he should add it to the prayers of all the saints on the golden altar which was before the throne.

⁴ The smoke of the incense, with the prayers of the saints, went up before God out of the angel's hand. ⁵ The angel took the censer, and he filled it with the fire of the altar, then threw it on the earth. Thunders, sounds, lightnings, and an earthquake followed.

⁶ The seven angels who had the seven trumpets prepared themselves to sound." Revelation 8:2-6

The actions of the angel standing before the altar of incense in Revelation 8, is a continuation of the throne room scene in Revelation 5. In the earlier passage, the Elders were seen holding golden bowls of incense containing the prayers of the saints, and in Revelation 8, the angel takes *those same prayers* and offers them on the golden altar, after adding even more incense to mingle with that of the Elders. Everything in chapters 6 and 7, which depicts the opening of the Seals, the four Horsemen, the sealing of the 144K and the martyrs appearing in heaven etc, is a parenthesis in the story—isolated 'topics—and the actual story line, the chronology, picks up in Revelation 8:2, with the angel at the altar, casting fire to the earth initiating the beginning of the Trumpet judgments.

Fire, like the wind, is also a symbol of judgment. The answer to the prayers of the saints on earth—the 144K of Israel and the new Gentile believers—will be delivered when the fire from the altar is heaved toward the earth, accompanied by noises, thunderings and lightnings, AND an earthquake.

We know that the 144K will be sealed before the Trumpet judgments begin, and the *Trumpet judgments will begin before the Seals are opened*. We can assume that the prayers offered by the 24 Elders, along with the 'much incense' of the angel at the altar of incense, are the prayers of the 144K of Israel, and the new Gentile believers on earth. The 'seven Spirits' will have already been sent out into all the earth, sealing and indwelling believers and empowering their prayers. The earthquake which takes place when the angel casts fire to the earth cannot happen until *after* the feast of Tabernacles, the feast during which believers will be sealed by the Spirit. After the earthquake, the first four angels will sound their trumpets, and a third of the earth will soon be crushed in the four Trumpet judgments, which the four trumpet angels will announce, followed by the violence and turmoil of the first four Seal judgments.

Chapter 53: Building the Bride

The whole of scripture is connected. From Genesis to Revelation there is but one story being told and it's the story of God's desire to have a people to love, who will dwell with Him in holiness. At its heart, the Bible is a love story. This desire for human companionship on the part of the Divine Community caused the Eternal Son to be born as a man, die on a cross and rise again as a glorified Man. The death and resurrection of Christ enabled sinful man to enter into the presence of a holy God. The relationship between God and man, which had been torn apart because of sin, was restored through the blood of the Lamb. Through Christ, the prodigal sons of Adam have been welcomed home by the Father.

In eternity past, when the Divine Community envisioned the creation of man, they also took into account the fall of man and subsequent need of a Savior. The shed blood of the perfect Son of God would be the means of redemption and the only way that could happen was if the Eternal Son entered time and became a man. And once the Son became a man, there would be no going back: He would be a man forever.

Upon His resurrection, Christ became a glorified Man, but He was still a man nonetheless. The Father knew the Son would be all alone in His glorified humanity and so embedded in the plan was a provision for the creation of a Bride for His Son. Believers—the 'called out ones'—are the eternal companion of the Son, the Bride, who was included in the plan from before the foundation of the world.

> "Blessed be the God and Father of our Lord Jesus Christ, who has blessed us with every spiritual blessing in the heavenly places in Christ, 4 even as he chose us in him before the foundation of the world, that we would be holy and without defect before him in love." Ephesians 1:3,4

The book of Genesis tells the story of creation, including the story of how God created men and women as well as animals, plants and so on. The details of the creation of man are expanded upon in Genesis chapter 2. We learn that God formed the man before He created the woman:

> "Yahweh God formed man from the dust of the ground, and breathed into his nostrils the breath of life; and man became a living soul." Genesis 2:7

God 'formed' man of the dust of the ground. The English translation of the Hebrew word, '*yatsar*', is 'formed'. *Yatsar* is a word which also refers to potters and pot-making. God formed man the way a potter would form a vessel of clay.

"But now, Yahweh, you are our Father.
We are the clay and you our potter.
We all are the work of your hand." Isaiah 64:8

Adam was formed of the dust of the earth the way a potter forms a vessel. Then God breathed spirit and life into the man, and the man became a living being, created in the image of God, someone who was capable of having an intimate and personal relationship with His Maker.

God placed the man in a beautiful garden and gave him the job of tending the garden. The Lord had not created the woman yet, and before He would make Eve, God desired to have Adam's cooperation—Adam's 'yes' to God's plan.

First, He wanted Adam to acknowledge his *need* for a helper and friend. The Lord caused the animals to pass before Adam in order for him to name them. As the animals paraded by Adam, he noticed that animals came in pairs—a male and a female—and, of all the creatures who passed before him, there was not one living creature who was in any way like himself. He was alone. Though he was living in the beauty of Eden, in a sinless world, and enjoying fellowship with the Eternal God, the man realized that he was the only one of his kind. That was not good, and no doubt the Lord told Adam that He desired to make a companion for him to fill that need for human love and fellowship. But in order for this new creation to be brought into existence, God would require Adam's cooperation: Adam must fall into a deep sleep and allow God to take a rib from his side. God would make the woman using the rib of the man. Adam consented.

> "Yahweh God caused the man to fall into a deep sleep. As the man slept, he took one of his ribs, and closed up the flesh in its place. 22 Yahweh God *made* a woman from the rib which he had taken from the man, and brought her to the man. 23 The man said, 'This is now bone of my bones, and flesh of my flesh. She will be called 'woman,' because she was taken out of Man.' 24 Therefore a man will leave his father and his mother, and will join with his wife, and they will be one flesh. 25 The man and his wife were both naked, and they were not ashamed." Genesis 2:21-24

God formed the man from the dust of the earth, much as a potter would form a clay vessel; but God did not 'form' the woman: *He 'built' her.*

The scriptures tell us that God "**made** a woman." The Hebrew word translated as 'made' in our English Bibles, is *'banah',* which is a construction term, often used when the Bible speaks of building cities, altars or buildings.

In Revelation, when we see the 'wife of the Lamb', she is described as a city that is *constructed or built*, consisting of 12 foundations, 4 great, high walls and 12 gates. Christ said that He would *"build* His church" (Matthew 16:18). Paul tells us in Ephesians, that the church is *built* on the foundation of the apostles and prophets:

> "So then you are no longer strangers and foreigners, but you are fellow citizens with the saints and of the household of God, 20 being built on the foundation of the apostles and prophets, Christ Jesus himself being the chief cornerstone; 21 in whom the whole building, fitted together, grows into a holy temple in the Lord; 22 in whom you also are built together for a habitation of God in the Spirit. " Ephesians 2:19-22

Peter refers to believers as living stones, connected with each other, and built into one spiritual house, with the cornerstone being Christ:

> "Come to him, a living stone, rejected indeed by men, but chosen by God, precious. 5 You also as living stones are built up as a spiritual house, to be a holy priesthood, to offer up spiritual sacrifices, acceptable to God through Jesus Christ. 6 Because it is contained in Scripture,
>
> 'Behold, I lay in Zion a chief cornerstone, chosen and precious.
> He who believes in him will not be disappointed.' " 1 Peter 2:4-6

No wonder the Bride of Christ, which is also the Body of Christ, is represented as the Holy City, the New Jerusalem in the book of Revelation. Just as God 'built' the woman in the Garden of Eden, the Bride is also built by the Lord, stone by living stone, into a habitation for God.

The story of the creation of the woman in Genesis, prefigures the story of Christ and building of His Bride. We who trust in Christ, are a part of the Body of Christ, the new body which came forth from His wounded side when He entered into the sleep of death, as He hung lifeless on a Roman cross. He is the 'last Adam', the progenitor of a new race of humanity that will one day be like Him.

> "The first man is of the earth, made of dust. The second man is the Lord from heaven. 48 As is the one made of dust, such are those who are also made of dust; and as is the heavenly, such are they also that are heavenly. 49 As we have borne the image of those made of dust, we shall also bear the image of the heavenly." 1 Corinthians 15:47-49

All those who trace their spiritual 'lineage' to the heavenly Man, will become like Him, bearing the image of Christ, no longer merely bearing the image of Adam, the man of dust. They will possess a glorified body like Christ's glorified body, and through the ministry of the Holy Spirit, they will also possess the character and nature of Christ. *The Father has done all this for us so that Christ would not be alone in eternity.*

Just as Adam was alone in the garden before the creation of the woman, even now, Christ is the only One of His kind, the only glorified Man in existence. He is alone in the perfection of heaven and in communion with His Father, but, in all of Heaven, there is no one else like Him. Not until His return, when every believer has been resurrected and raptured and taken into heaven, will Christ finally have obtained His Bride. On that day, He will no longer be alone, but He will rejoice in the fruit of the travail of His soul and be satisfied. (Isaiah 53:11a)

Right now, the dead in Christ dwell in heaven in their spirits, and they must await the resurrection of the dead to receive their glorified bodies. Even Enoch, Elijah and Moses—people who were brought into heaven in mortal bodies, have not yet received glorified, eternal bodies, but are awaiting the day when they will put on their 'white robes'—their glorified, resurrection, immortal bodies.

The Church was taken from the Body of Christ, and she is His Wife, the Bride, who will dwell with the Lamb in the New Jerusalem. When Christ returns to earth and the martyred dead are resurrected on the Day of Atonement in 2024 and they join all the other saints in glory, then at last Christ can say, "This is a last is bone of my bone and flesh of my flesh!"

The New Jerusalem: The Future Home of Believers

In John 14, Jesus told his disciples that He was going to prepare a place for them so that they could be with Him in heaven. Jesus used 'bridegroom language', and His disciples would have recognized the analogy between Jesus leaving to 'prepare a place' and a groom completing a home before taking his betrothed to live with him.

Jesus was the Eternal Son who left His Father, who left heaven, to find a 'wife' and after He paid the bridal price on the cross, He ascended back into heaven to prepare a home for us in His Father's house. When all is ready, He will come and take His Bride, stone by living stone, from the earth to be with Him in heaven. In ancient Israel, the bride was 'purchased' from the bride's father. The higher the bridal price, the more precious the woman was to the man. In this analogy, we are the Bride who was purchased with the priceless blood of our Bridegroom when He died on the cross.

When Christ rose from the dead, He became a New kind of Man, the progenitor of a new race. Paul referred to Christ as the 'last Adam' (1 Corinthians 15). God had already stated in Genesis 2, that it was not good for man to be alone, that He would create a helper suitable for him. Jesus fulfills the type of Adam, who, after His incarnation, was alone until the Lord created the Woman to be 'with' Him. Like Adam, Jesus procured His 'wife' from His wounded side, entering the sleep of death so that the Bride could come forth.

His Wife, the Bride, is still being 'built' as more and more people come to faith in Christ. The Wife of the Lamb will not be complete until the end of the 7 years, when Christ returns to earth and the *very last group of martyrs are resurrected* as priests and kings. The Bride is ready when the Lord God, the Almighty, reigns on earth through His Son:

> "I heard something like the voice of a great multitude, and like the voice of many waters, and like the voice of mighty thunders, saying, 'Hallelujah! For the Lord our God, the Almighty, reigns! 7 Let's rejoice and be exceedingly glad, and let's give the glory to him. *For the wedding of the Lamb has come, and his wife has made herself ready.'* 8 It was given to her that she would array herself in bright, pure, fine linen, for the fine linen is the righteous acts of the saints." Revelation 19:6-8

The marriage of the Lamb to His Bride, the *'ekklesia'*, will take place at *the end* of the 7 years, not at the beginning as many people think. The Bride is not described as being 'ready' until the return of Christ to the earth, at which time He will resurrect the last group of believers: those beheaded by the Beast. Only then will the Bride be declared 'ready' to enter her heavenly home, the New Jerusalem.

The earth was created for men of 'dust' who are descendants of Adam. The heavenly New Jerusalem is being created for those who take after the Man of Heaven, Jesus, the 'last Adam', the progenitor of a new race of people we call the Church, the *'ekklesia'*. The descendants of the 'last Adam'—Christ—are neither solely 'spiritual' beings like the angels nor merely 'physical' beings, like natural men, but are a 'new race' of men in the likeness of Christ. Though they are people who can be equally at home in heaven as they are on the earth, their real home is the New Jerusalem, the city which now exists in heaven, but which will one day come to the earth.

At the end of the Millennium, when the old heavens and the old earth have passed away, the New Jerusalem will survive that final cataclysm. God will create a new heaven and a new earth—but He will not create a 'new' New Jerusalem—for that city will stand in perfect holiness and beauty, with no need to be renovated. At the re-creation of the heavens and the earth, the New Jerusalem will descend from heaven to the New Earth. God will set His throne in the Holy City, and the dwelling place of God will be with men on the earth. God will make His home in the city of the Lamb and His Wife, the New Jerusalem.

The survivors of the Millennium, those whose names are written in the Lamb's book of Life, will enter eternity to dwell on the New Earth as mortal men. The New Heavens will still be inhabited by angelic spirit beings, but the Bride will reside in the New Jerusalem, having descended from heaven to the New Earth. All believers who make up the Bride will live in fellowship with the Father, Christ, their Heavenly Groom and the Spirit, as well as with mortal people who will live on the New Earth.

Chapter 54: The Wrath of God and the Day of the Lord

The story of the judgments we read about in Revelation will culminate in the out-pouring of the wrath of God, a time referred to in other passages of scripture as the Day of the Lord.

Two Phases of Wrath

The wrath of God comes in two phases: first, God 'gives people over' to do as they please, after which God's judgment falls on them. In the first phase, He allows the unrepentant to live without restraint: He "gives them over" to follow their passions and desires. In the second phase, He pours out His wrath on the disobedient. Paul speaks about the two parts of wrath in the book of Romans:

> "The wrath of God is being revealed from heaven against all the godless-ness and wickedness of men who suppress the truth by their wickedness... Therefore God *gave them over* in the desires of their hearts to impurity for the dishonoring of their bodies with one another...For this reason *God gave them over* to dishonorable passions...*He gave them up* to a depraved mind, to do what ought not to be done." Romans 1:18, 24, 26a,28b

The first part of God's wrath is silent: He simply allows people do whatever is in their heart to do. They are free to engage in any, and every, form of wickedness and degradation—without limits of any kind. Whereas God had formerly placed limitations on how far people could go in their rebellion against Him, during the first part of God's wrath, people will no longer have the blessing of God's merciful intervention. God's intervention is intended to bring people back into their right minds and provide an opportunity for repentance before God. Because of God's lack of intervention during the reign of the Beast—because of His silence—fallen mankind will deceive themselves into believing that God doesn't really care about them anymore; that He has walked away from the earth and her inhabitants, and that there won't be any repercussions for their reprehensible behaviors.

After the midpoint of the seven years, at the time of the abomination of desola-tion, after the majority of God's people are present in heaven and only a few saints remain on earth, the reign of the Beast will begin. At that time the first part of God's wrath will be manifested. Mankind will throw off all restraint with re-gard to the laws of God. They will place themselves under the rule of the An-tichrist; taking his mark, and some will even choose to bear his image. The law of the Antichrist will be straightforward, "Do as thou wilt." In other words, "be a rebel" against God. And God will be silent.

For 42 months the earth dwellers will revel in their new found freedom and licentiousness. The Two Witnesses who had tormented the earth dwellers will be gone, having ascended to heaven at the time of the abomination of desolation. The multitudes of believers, with their antiquated ideas of morality will be dead and gone, having been martyred in the 10 day persecution of the Harlot. Even fake Christians who were a part of the Harlot religion are gone, having been annihilated at the 6th Trumpet. There's only the wondrous, resurrected Beast, and the ushering in of his glorious, technologically advanced false millennium which will include incredible advances in technology; advances brought about in part through the expertise of the Watchers working in conjunction with fallen humanity. Then there's the presence of the Dragon—Satan himself—the false angel of light; and the False Prophet, with his amazing spiritual powers and spell-binding orations, regaling the worthiness of the Beast who died a man, and then returned from the grave as a god-man.

The few Christians who are left will find themselves in a world they could never have imagined, something straight out of a science fiction horror movie—now become reality. Many believers will be beheaded by order of the Beast. Those who are not beheaded, will be in desperate straights to acquire food, shelter and most of all, fellowship with other believers. Everything and everyone in the Beast kingdom, will be tracked, chipped and surveilled. Spies will be everywhere. Yet, believers are admonished to overcome, to endure. They are not forgotten. God remembers them. Before His wrath is poured out, they will be removed from the Beast's false millennium, to meet the Lord in the clouds, their lowly bodies changed into glorified bodies. They will be transported into heaven accompanied by all the previously glorified and resurrected saints. This is the third rapture, the rapture that takes place 'like a thief in the night', the rapture of which Christ said "no man knows the day or hour, not even the Son."

> "But no one knows of that day and hour, not even the angels of heaven, but my Father only. 37 As the days of Noah were, so will the coming of the Son of Man be. 38 For as in those days which were before the flood they were eating and drinking, marrying and giving in marriage, until the day that Noah entered into the ship, 39 and they didn't know until the flood came and took them all away, so will the coming of the Son of Man be....

> "Watch therefore, for you don't know in what hour your Lord comes. 43 But know this, that if the master of the house had known in what watch of the night the thief was coming, he would have watched, and would not have allowed his house to be broken into. 44 Therefore also be ready, for in an hour that you don't expect, the Son of Man will come." Matthew 24:36-39, 42-44

The 42 month reign of the Beast will usher in the return of the 'days of Noah'. The Watchers will be on the earth at that time, just as they were during the days of Noah, and the perversion and violence in the world will be as it was when Noah was alive...only worse—much, much worse. One of the difficulties being a believer at that time will be that there is *no appointed time*—no feast day that they can look forward to and know that their redemption is near. They will only know the *window of time* during which they will be raptured. They will be caught up sometime after the Beast's reign began at the abomination/midpoint, and before the 42 month reign of the Beast ends. On the day they leave this world, the wrath of God will begin.

We see these overcoming believers present in heaven, standing before the sea of glass, just as the 7 angels holding the 7 Bowls of God's wrath exit the heavenly temple to begin the out-pouring of the wrath of God:

> "I saw another great and marvelous sign in the sky: seven angels having the seven last plagues, for in them God's wrath is finished.
>
> 2 I saw something like a sea of glass mixed with fire, and those who overcame the beast, his image,* and the number of his name, standing on the sea of glass, having harps of God. 3 They sang the song of Moses, the servant of God, and the song of the Lamb, saying,
>
> 'Great and marvelous are your works, Lord God, the Almighty!
> Righteous and true are your ways, you King of the nations.
> 4 Who wouldn't fear you, Lord,
> and glorify your name?
> For you only are holy.
> For all the nations will come and worship before you.
> For your righteous acts have been revealed.'
>
> 5 After these things I looked, and the temple of the tabernacle of the testimony in heaven was opened. 6 The seven angels who had the seven plagues came out, clothed with pure, bright linen, and wearing golden sashes around their chests.
>
> 7 One of the four living creatures gave to the seven angels seven golden bowls full of the wrath of God, who lives forever and ever. 8 The temple was filled with smoke from the glory of God and from his power. No one was able to enter into the temple until the seven plagues of the seven angels would be finished." Revelation, Chapter 15

When the last group of surviving believers are finally brought into heaven, the Day of the Lord will commence, and the wrath of God will be poured out on the Beast and his kingdom.

The Second Phase of God's Wrath: Vengeance

Paul tells us in the book of Romans that rebellious, unrepentant people are 'storing up wrath for the day of wrath':

> "But according to your hardness and unrepentant heart you are treasuring up for yourself wrath in the day of wrath, revelation, and of the righteous judgment of God." Romans 2:5

The silence of God—expressed as the absence of immediate judgment—does not mean that He has forgotten or that He will leave off judging the wicked who live in active rebellion against Him. God allows people to store up wrath, to fill up their cup of wickedness and evil. God gives people time to repent, or if they will not repent, to suffer the full fury of His indignation.

The Bible has much to say about the coming Day of the Lord, as this Day is one of the most prophesied events in all of scripture. Isaiah, Joel, Amos, Jeremiah, Zephaniah, Jesus, Paul, Peter all had something to say about this most dreadful Day. To the earth dwellers, God's silence will interpreted as though the day of reckoning will never come at all—that they are in the clear with regard to judgment. To the average earth dweller, who lives their life under the rule of the Beast, the prophesied coming Day of the Lord will fade into oblivion, that is, until the day the surviving believers are secretly raptured, followed by God's wrath bursting on the scene quite unexpectedly and without warning.

To the average earth dweller, the reign of the Beast will be marvelous. The Beast will have solutions to pressing world issues and he will bring his own brand of peace and prosperity to the earth. The earth dwellers will heave a sigh of relief: "Peace and safety! All is well—the earth is ours!" and then...sudden destruction will pour down from on high.

Satan knows that his time is short. Unlike the rank and file earth dweller, the Beast and the world leaders will not be so deceived as to think that there will never be a day of reckoning. They know that Christ will return 1260 days after the abomination/midpoint. The Antichrist, the False Prophet, Satan and the Watchers will be feverishly making preparation for the coming Day of the Lord, and the return of Christ. When Christ returns, they must be ready to battle Him for control of the earth and their very existence.

The Divine Community of the Father, Son, and Holy Spirit foresaw everything that would happen during the last days. God's plan for the redemption of mankind, which began in eternity past, took into account all the events of the last days. Satan has *his* plans for mankind as well, and his plan is to rule over fallen men and fallen angels on a fallen earth...forever. Everything Satan has been doing on the earth for at least the last 6,000 years is part of a well-developed, devilishly intricate and orchestrated plan(s) for the enslavement, and eventual annihilation of the image of God within the human race, and complete ownership and control of the earth. Over the course of history, Satan has inspired powerful men, who in turn have conspired together to create a system of enslavement within all human organizations, institutions and cultures, preparing for the day when *Satan's* man —the Antichrist—would rule on the earth.

Tribulation Does Not Equal Wrath

A common error that people make with regard to the 'tribulation', an error that I've already touched on in this book, that they equate 'tribulation' with the 'Day of the Lord/wrath of God'. This error is pervasive among end time Bible teachers, and very dangerous: for how we define 'tribulation' and 'wrath' will greatly influence how a we interpret Revelation and all other end time events found in scripture.

The Biblical definition of 'tribulation' is 'persecution and trials', something believers have endured since the beginning of Christianity. Believers are exempt from the wrath of God, but they are not exempt from tribulation—in fact, Jesus said that believers should *expect* tribulation in this world! Paul told Timothy that all who desire to live a godly life in Christ Jesus will be persecuted. (2 Timothy 3:12) When the book of Revelation uses the word, 'tribulation'—and it does so on several occasions—each time the word is used it *only, ever, means persecution, trial and extreme trouble.*

Believers (and Israel) aren't the only ones who will suffer tribulation during the last days, either. According to Revelation, the Harlot/Jezebel will also be thrown into great tribulation. The Harlot has her own time of trial and persecution which will culminate in her destruction by the Beast and the 10 Kings at the 6th Trumpet.

'Wrath', on the other hand, refers to the righteous out-pouring of the vengeance of God upon the wicked rulers of the world, the Beast and the rebels who make up his kingdom. Many people tend to interpret *all the events* in the book of Revelation as being a part of God's wrath, with all the Seal, Trumpet and Bowl judgments constituting the out-pouring of God's vengeance. They believe that the 144K first fruits of Israel, as well as those who are to be martyred by the Harlot, and the Over-coming believers—will undergo the wrath of God. They do not believe that people who come to Christ during the last days are actually Christians who will be a part of the Body and Bride of Christ. May that never be! No one who trusts in Christ will EVER be subjected to the wrath or judgment of God, not even believers who come to Christ after the first rapture has taken place, believers who will be living during the time of the first Seal and Trumpet judgments.

Paul tells us that the Day of the Lord—which is equated with the wrath of God—will take place sometime *after* the abomination of desolation, an event which occurs at the midpoint of the seven years for believers. The 'man of sin' or lawlessness must be revealed *first* and he will be revealed when he takes his seat in the temple of God:

> "Now, brothers, concerning the coming of our Lord Jesus Christ and our gathering together to him, we ask you 2 not to be quickly shaken in your mind or troubled, either by spirit or by word or by letter as if from us, saying that the day of Christ has already come. 3 Let no one deceive you in any way. For it will not be unless the rebellion comes first, and the man of sin is revealed, the son of destruction. " 2 Thessalonians 2:1-3

Jesus tells us that the signs that accompany the Day of the Lord will take place after the tribulation (read, "persecution") of those days:

> "But immediately after the (*tribulation*) suffering of those days, the sun will be darkened, the moon will not give its light, the stars will fall from the sky, and the powers of the heavens will be shaken;'" Matthew 24:29

The 'tribulation' to which Jesus is referring is the *persecution* of the remnant of Israel and the 'elect'.

> "But woe to those who are with child and to nursing mothers in those days! 20 Pray that your flight will not be in the winter nor on a Sabbath, 21 for then there will be great suffering, such as has not been from the beginning of the world until now, no, nor ever will be. 22 Unless those days had been shortened, no flesh would have been saved. But for the sake of the chosen ones, those days will be shortened." Matthew 24:19-22

Jesus states that the length of time during which God's people will undergo tribulation will be 'cut short'—abbreviated—otherwise no human being would remain. (Possibly referring to the dwindling numbers of actual humans as more and more people choose to abandon their humanity in order to be transformed into the Image of the Beast.) The days are said to be 'cut short', in that, the Day of the Lord will commence *before* the last half of the 7 years is over. The elect—the remaining believers—will not be on earth during the full 42 month reign of the Beast. Jesus will cut that time short at the 3rd rapture, which will initiate the events associated with the Day of the Lord and the wrath of God.

The indication that the coming of the Lord is at hand will be unusual signs in the heavens: the sun will be darkened, the moon will not give her light, the stars will fall from the sky. Revelation also tells us that there will be great hailstones falling from the heavens, earthquakes, thunder and lightenings. These are the phenomena which will be the indicators that the events associated with the Day of the Lord are on their way. The 6th Seal and the 7 Bowls include these devastating cosmic signs:

> "I looked when He broke the sixth seal, and there was a great earthquake; and the sun became black as sackcloth *made* of hair, and the whole moon became like blood; and the stars of the sky fell to the earth, as a fig tree casts its unripe figs when shaken by a great wind. The sky was split apart like a scroll when it is rolled up, and every mountain and island were moved out of their places. Then the kings of the earth and the great men and the commanders and the rich and the strong and every slave and free man hid themselves in the caves and among the rocks of the mountains; and they said to the mountains and to the rocks, "Fall on us and hide us from the presence of Him who sits on the throne, and from the wrath of the Lamb; for *the great day of their wrath has come,* and who is able to stand?" Revelation 6:12-17

> "Then I heard a loud voice from the temple, saying to the seven angels, "Go and pour out on the earth the seven bowls of *the wrath of God.*" Revelation 16:1

The sixth Bowl will cause the Euphrates River to dry up allowing the kings of the East to cross and gather in Israel for the battle of Armegeddon:

> "The sixth poured out his bowl on the great river, the Euphrates. Its water was dried up, that the way might be prepared for the kings that come from the sunrise. 13 I saw coming out of the mouth of the dragon, and out of the mouth of the beast, and out of the mouth of the false prophet, three unclean spirits, something like frogs; 14 for they are spirits of demons, performing signs, which go out to the kings of the whole inhabited earth, to gather them together for the war of that great day of God the Almighty.

> 15 'Behold, I come like a thief. Blessed is he who watches, and keeps his clothes, so that he doesn't walk naked, and they see his shame.' 16 He gathered them

together into the place which is called in Hebrew, 'Harmagedon'." Revelation 16:12-16

Once the enemies of God are gathered on the battlefield, Christ will return as King of Kings and Lord of Lords:

'I saw the heaven opened, and behold, a white horse, and he who sat on it is called Faithful and True. In righteousness he judges and makes war. [12] His eyes are a flame of fire, and on his head are many crowns. He has names written and a name written which no one knows but he himself. [13] He is clothed in a garment sprinkled with blood. His name is called 'The Word of God.' [14] The armies which are in heaven, clothed in white, pure, fine linen, followed him on white horses. [15] Out of his mouth proceeds a sharp, double-edged sword that with it he should strike the nations. He will rule them with an iron rod.✧ He treads the wine press of the fierceness of the wrath of God, the Almighty. [16] He has on his garment and on his thigh a name written, 'KING OF KINGS AND LORD OF LORDS.'

[17] I saw an angel standing in the sun. He cried with a loud voice, saying to all the birds that fly in the sky, 'Come! Be gathered together to the great supper of God,' [18] that you may eat the flesh of kings, the flesh of captains, the flesh of mighty men, and the flesh of horses and of those who sit on them, and the flesh of all men, both free and slave, small and great.' [19] I saw the beast, the kings of the earth, and their armies, gathered together to make war against him who sat on the horse and against his army.

[20] The beast was taken, and with him the false prophet who worked the signs in his sight, with which he deceived those who had received the mark of the beast and those who worshiped his image. These two were thrown alive into the lake of fire that burns with sulfur. [21] The rest were killed with the sword of him who sat on the horse, the sword which came out of his mouth. So all the birds were filled with their flesh." Revelation 19:11-21

Earlier in Revelation we read about the enemies of God who will be cast alive into the 'winepress' of the wrath of God:

"Another angel came out of the temple which is in heaven. He also had a sharp sickle. [18] Another angel came out from the altar, he who has power over fire, and he called with a great voice to him who had the sharp sickle, saying, 'Send your sharp sickle and gather the clusters of the vine of the earth, for the earth's grapes are fully ripe!' [19] The angel thrust his sickle into the earth, and gathered the vintage of the earth and threw it into the great wine press of the wrath of God. [20] The wine press was trodden outside of the city, and blood came out of the wine press, up to the bridles of the horses, as far as one thousand six hundred stadia." Revelation 14:17-20

Since the 'grapes' are gathered in the fall, these passages provide us with another clue that the battle of Armageddon will take place in the fall, with the Lord's return scheduled to take place on the Day of Atonement, September 14, 2024. (Torah Calendar)

In a sort of 'reverse rapture', Christ will cast the Beast and the False Prophet alive into the Lake of Fire apart from dying. The rest of the world's armies will be killed and judged at the Great White Throne judgment a thousand years in the future. Satan will be bound and thrown into the Pit:

> "I saw an angel coming down out of heaven, having the key of the abyss and a great chain in his hand. [2] He seized the dragon, the old serpent, who is the devil and Satan, who deceives the whole inhabited earth, and bound him for a thousand years, [3] and cast him into the abyss, and shut it and sealed it over him, that he should deceive the nations no more until the thousand years were finished. After this, he must be freed for a short time." Revelation 20:1-3

The Old Testament scriptures indicate that Christ will lead the remnant of Israel back to Jerusalem. Believers who were martyred by the Beast will be resurrected and rewarded. Thrones will be set up for judging the nations who survived the reign of the Beast and the wrath of God. Then the glorious Day of the Lord—the thousand year rule of Christ on the earth—will commence.

The Day of the Lord is the 7th Day of this age, the 'sabbath day' after 6,000 years of human history, and will be the true day of rest for the people of God. Though sin will not have been eradicated in the hearts of the remaining mortal people, Satan and his cohorts *will be gone from the face of the earth,* taking with them the rebellion and chaos which invariably accompanied them. The wolf will lie down with the lamb. Christ and His saints will begin their rule and reign on the earth.

At the end of the thousand years, Satan will be released for the last time, and he will be allowed to deceive the nations once more. This final rebellion will end swiftly with fire coming from heaven:

" And after the thousand years, Satan will be released from his prison [8] and he will come out to deceive the nations which are in the four corners of the earth, Gog and Magog, to gather them together to the war, whose number is as the sand of the sea. [9] They went up over the width of the earth and surrounded the camp of the saints and the beloved city. Fire came down out of heaven from God and devoured them. [10] The devil who deceived them was thrown into the lake of fire and sulfur, where the beast and the false prophet are also. They will be tormented day and night forever and ever." Revelation 20:7-10

Satan will finally be gone for good: cast into Lake of Fire, never to deceive mankind again.

Chapter 55: "Like a thief in the night…"

There are several passages in scripture which refer to Jesus coming for His people like a 'thief in the night'. We first encounter this metaphor in the gospels:

> "Watch therefore, for you don't know in what hour your Lord comes. 43 But know this, that if the master of the house had known in what watch of the night the thief was coming, he would have watched, and would not have allowed his house to be broken into. 44 Therefore also be ready, for in an hour that you don't expect, the Son of Man will come." Matthew 24:42-44

Paul refers to this same metaphor in his epistle to the Thessalonians:

> "For when they are saying, 'Peace and safety,' then sudden destruction will come on them, like birth pains on a pregnant woman. Then they will in no way escape. 4 But you, brothers, aren't in darkness, that the day should overtake you like a thief. 5 You are all children of light and children of the day. We don't belong to the night, nor to darkness, 6 so then let's not sleep, as the rest do, but let's watch and be sober." 1 Thessalonians 5:2-6

The phrase, 'coming like a thief' also appears in Revelation:

> "Remember therefore how you have received and heard. Keep it and repent. If therefore you won't watch, I will come as a thief, and you won't know what hour I will come upon you." Revelation 3:3

> "Behold, I come like a thief. Blessed is he who watches, and keeps his clothes, so that he doesn't walk naked, and they see his shame." Revelation 16:15

Jesus describes Himself as a thief. Who is He stealing from, and what is He stealing? Jesus is coming for His people. He is 'stealing' them away from the 'owner' of the house, who is Satan. As long as believers are on the earth, they are held hostage by the prince of this world and his false son, the Antichrist. Satan also knows that the day that Christ comes for this last group of believers, the events associated with the Day of the Lord will be set into motion, including the impending defeat of the Antichrist/Beast at Armageddon, and the collapse of the Beast's rule and kingdom. If Satan can keep believers hostage on the earth, *the Day of the Lord and the judgment of the Beast will not come,* because God would never pour out His wrath on His own people.

If Satan, as the owner of the house, knew when Jesus, the thief, was coming, he would make sure to keep his valuables (believers) in a safe, secure place. He would engage his minions to battle Christ for the possession of the remaining believers, so that they could not be taken into heaven by Christ. Satan and the Beast would do whatever possible to hold on to these believers in order to delay the Day of the Lord.

That is why the Lord has chosen to take this last group of priest/kings into heaven on a day that is not associated with a Feast day. *This is the only time that God's priests will enter the heavenly Holy of Holies in a rapture event on a non-feast day.* Their rapture will be on a day of which 'no man knows the day or hour, not even the Son, but only the Father'—in order to keep Satan in the dark.

In Revelation 14, we see the Son, seated on a cloud with a sharp sickle in His hand, awaiting word from an angel, that the Father is now ready for Christ to gather this last 'crop' of living believers into heaven:

> "I looked, and saw a white cloud, and on the cloud one sitting like a son of man, having on his head a golden crown, and in his hand a sharp sickle. 15 Another angel came out of the temple, crying with a loud voice to him who sat on the cloud, 'Send your sickle and reap, for the hour to reap has come; for the harvest of the earth is ripe!' 16 He who sat on the cloud thrust his sickle on the earth, and the earth was reaped."   Revelation 14:14-16

In this passage, Jesus comes seated on a cloud. This is the same rapture that Paul referred to in 1 Thessalonians:

> "—then we who are alive, who are left, will be caught up together with them in the clouds to meet the Lord in the air. So we will be with the Lord forever. 18 Therefore comfort one another with these words." 1 Thessalonians 4:17, 18

Paul tells the Thessalonian believers that the dead will be raised first. The first group of believers to be resurrected will be the 24 Elders who appear in Revelation 4. Their resurrection will take place when the Mighty Angel of Revelation 10:1 descends from heaven, and, with a mighty roar, raises the dead and changes the living. The first group or division of priest/kings will enter into the heavenly temple on the Feast of Trumpets, followed by glorified, living believers who will be caught up to God and to His throne on the Day of Atonement, as represented by the 24 Elders of Revelation 5.

The saints who 'remain' or 'survive' until the Day of the Lord represent the Overcomers, believers who must endure the reign of the Beast. They will be caught up into the clouds to meet the previously resurrected (and previously raptured) believers who will have accompanied Christ from heaven, a thing which God will allow them to do. Christ must have God's permission to bring the Father's priests with Him to meet this last group of saints. As first fruits, *believers belong to God*, as His priests. The Father will release His priests to go with Christ to meet this last group of raptured saints in the clouds.

Chapter 56: The Great White Throne Judgment

The conclusion of seven thousand years of human history—which began with the creation of man in the Garden of Eden—will come to a close at the end of the Great Week, the week where each day is as a thousand years, at the end of the Millennium. All the prophecies contained in the scriptures will have found their fulfillment by that time. What little is mentioned in the Bible concerning what happens *after* the Millennial Sabbath comes to a close, is contained in the closing chapters of Revelation. We read that God will inaugurate an eternity of joy, peace and love beyond our wildest expectations. No sin, no death, no sadness will be present to mar the glory and beauty of our eternal destiny. As we gaze upon God's enemies in the Lake of Fire, we will wonder how these puny beings ever wielded any power over mankind at all. They will be tormented in the garbage heap, the Lake of Fire, which burns outside of the Holy City:

> "But for the cowardly, unbelieving, sinners, abominable, murderers, sexually immoral, sorcerers, idolaters, and all liars, their part is in the lake that burns with fire and sulfur, which is the second death... 26 and they shall bring the glory and the honor of the nations into it so that they may enter. 27 There will in no way enter into it anything profane, or one who causes an abomination or a lie, but only those who are written in the Lamb's book of life." Revelation 21:8, 26, 27

The final judgement of all humanity will take place at the end of the thousand year reign of Christ, at the Great White Throne judgment:

> "I saw a great white throne and him who sat on it, from whose face the earth and the heaven fled away. There was found no place for them. 12 I saw the dead, the great and the small, standing before the throne, and they opened books. Another book was opened, which is the book of life. The dead were judged out of the things which were written in the books, according to their works. 13 The sea gave up the dead who were in it. Death and Hades gave up the dead who were in them. They were judged, each one according to his works. 14 Death and Hades were thrown into the lake of fire. This is the second death, the lake of fire." Revelation 20:11-14

The Great White Throne judgment will be when the final resurrection takes place, when all the dead will be raised to stand before God. This is the general resurrection of all the dead, who were not a part of the Body of Christ. This resurrection will take place on the very last day of this present age, after the thousand year reign of Christ. All the remaining dead who have ever lived will be raised from their graves at that time. Everyone will go back into their mortal—now become immortal—bodies. The books which recorded the lives of every single person will be opened and examined, and God will know whether people lived according to the light of their consciences or not. There is another book, the Book of Life, which also has names recorded in it. If anyone's name is in the Book of Life, they will live on the New Earth which God will create. If their name is not recorded in the Book of Life, that person will be cast alive, in their eternal, resurrected body, into the Lake of Fire.

Who gets resurrected, when?

The Bible records the stories of a number of people who were raised from the dead, the raising of Lazarus from the grave being an example. Elisha also raised people from the dead, as did Paul—who raised a young man named, Eutychus. All those who died, and were then resurrected, were raised back into their mortal bodies and they would have to die again. The people who rose from the dead at Jesus' resurrection, were also raised back into their mortal bodies. They were witnesses of the victory of Christ in Sheol, over the powers of Death and Hades, and testified to Christ's power which they witnessed while they, themselves, were in Sheol, the place of the dead. These resurrected believing saints would eventually die again to await their final, eternal glorification when they would receive their immortal, glorified bodies along with all the rest of the dead in Christ, on the Feast of Trumpets in 2020.

Christians will be the first to receive their immortal bodies. *Not only will believers be the first to become immortal, they will also be the only people to possess glorified bodies like Christ's body.* Believers will be the 'first fruits' of the larger group of humanity, all of whom will eventually be raised from the dead. The first fruits belong especially to God, and those of us who trust in Him are His priests in heaven and will become co-rulers with Christ on earth. The *resurrection of believers takes place before the resurrection of anyone else*: it is the first or 'premier' resurrection!

> "The rest of the dead didn't live until the thousand years were finished. This is the first resurrection. 6 Blessed and holy is he who has part in the first resurrection. Over these, the second death has no power, but they will be priests of God and of Christ, and will reign with him one thousand years." Revelation 20:5,6

Some teach that only the wicked will be raised at the Great White Throne judgment, all of the rest of the 'righteous' dead having already been resurrected at the 2nd Coming of Christ, but this is not what the Word teaches. The *only people* who will be resurrected at the 2nd Coming are the *dead in Christ*—believers who were beheaded by the Beast. These believers will join the rest of the raptured and resurrected priesthood in heaven. *No other people—good, bad or otherwise—will be raised at the 2nd Coming of Christ!*

This is why the resurrection of dead believers at the return of Christ is called the 'first resurrection'. It is not because it is the first resurrection to take place in *time* —millions of believers will have already been raised from the dead before this final resurrection of believers. Rather this is the first resurrection in the sense that it is the *'premier'* resurrection, the BEST resurrection and the last resurrection of the people of God who belong to Christ. These saints will be the last priests resurrected of the *first cohort* of resurrected people. Paul tells us that everyone will be resurrected in their own order: Christ first, believers next, and finally all the rest of humanity at the end of the Millennium:

> "But each in his own order: Christ the first fruits, then those who are Christ's at his coming.[24] Then the end comes, when he will deliver up the Kingdom to God the Father, when he will have abolished all rule and all authority and power. " 1 Corinthians 15:23, 24

Christ was the first to be raised from the dead, never to die again. The next group are all those who belong to Him, who will be raised on an appointed day during the last 7 years—as in the case of the righteous dead who are a part the 24 Elders, and the martyrs of the Harlot. At His return, the martyrs of the Beast will be resurrected. At the end of His thousand year reign, Christ will hand the kingdom over to His Father, and then *all the rest of humanity will be raised.* This includes people whose names are in the Book of Life, *and* those whose names are not recorded in that book. The righteous and the wicked will go their separate ways at that time: the righteous will live on the New Earth and the wicked will be cast into the Lake of Fire.

Mortal people who live on the New Earth after the Great White Throne judgment are not Christians—not technically. They will not be glorified and they will not be a part of the Bride of Christ, since during their lives they did not walk *by faith* in Christ, and they were never born into the new race of humanity by the Spirit of God. In fact, some of the people whose names are recorded in the Book of Life may have never even heard the name of Jesus, yet they were 'God-fearers'—people who lived according to the light of revelation which they had received during their lifetime. These will be among those whose names are recorded in the Book of Life, whom Christ has saved from all tribes, tongues and nations, because of His mercy and grace.

At the end of the Millennium, there will still be mortal people living on the earth, people who will not need to be resurrected at the Great White Throne judgment because *they never died.* They will go on to live on the New Earth in their mortal bodies. Their sin nature, which was at the root of the cycle of death, will be 'healed'. They will be permitted to eat from the Tree of Life, whose leaves are for the healing of the nations:

> "He showed me a river of water of life, clear as crystal, proceeding out of the throne of God and of the Lamb, 2 in the middle of its street. On this side of the river and on that was the tree of life, bearing twelve kinds of fruits, yielding its fruit every month. The leaves of the tree were for the healing of the nations. " Revelation 22:1,2

The sacrificial blood of Christ which was shed on the cross, will be efficacious for all the inhabitants of the New Earth, and provision will be made for all to receive eternal life from the Tree of Life. Sin, death and the grave will be done away with. The devil will be out of reach in the Lake of Fire. All that is wrong in the world to-day will become a distant memory, and God will wipe away the tears of all mankind:

> "He will wipe away every tear from their eyes. Death will be no more; neither will there be mourning, nor crying, nor pain any more. The first things have passed away." Revelation 21:4

Chapter 57: The Eternal Plan

God's original plan was to have a people with whom He could have loving, unbroken fellowship. When, through the fall of Adam, sin came into the world, God's fellowship with man was broken. Before God could fellowship with man again, mankind's sin debt needed to be paid. God sent His Son, the Lord Jesus, to pay the penalty for mankind's sin. The Eternal Son became a man, taking on a human body, so that He could die for us and take our place as a Perfect Substitute. His blood paid for the sins of the world, especially those who believe:

> "For to this end we both labor and suffer reproach, because we have set our trust in the living God, who is the Savior of all men, especially of those who believe." 1 Timothy 4:10

In eternity past, when Christ said, "Yes" to the plan of God—voluntarily agreeing to become a man who would suffer and die—He knew that He would be forever 'changed'. Once He became a man, there was no going back to His former state. He would always and forever be a man—albeit a glorified Man—after His resurrection. And as a glorified Man, He would be the only one of His kind. And the same God who said,"it is not good for man to be alone", also made provision for a Bride for the Lord Jesus, a 'helpmeet'—the church—the called out ones, the *ekklesia*. They are 'bone of his bone and flesh of his flesh'. Glorified believers will be like Him when they see Him as He is.

At the consummation of all things, at the creation of the New Heaven and the New Earth, when Christ hands the kingdom over to His Father, God will dwell with mankind in true fellowship. Christ will have obtained His Bride. Nothing in all creation can, or ever will, keep Almighty God from achieving His eternal plan for mankind through Christ. Fellowship with you and me and all redeemed humanity is the goal of His eternal plan.

Salvation is a free gift to all who call upon the Lord. Today is the day of salvation. Do not let the offer of God pass by you—receive the salvation that He has made freely available in His love for you since before you were even born.

God loves you. He has done everything He can to bring you home. The rest is up to you.

> *"Lord Jesus—I need you. Forgive my sin. Fill me with your Holy Spirit and grant me entrance into Your eternal kingdom. Amen"*

Chapter 58: Timelines and Other Resources

How I arrived at these dates

1. In 2017, Israel, the 'fig tree' nation celebrated 70 years since receiving statehood by a UN mandate in November of 1947. Jesus said that the generation that sees the 'fig tree budding' (Israel regathered) would also see the return of Christ, including the apocalyptic events of the 7 years preceding His return. (1 generation=70-80 years, Psalm 90:10) If the 'last days' began in 2017, then, we need to add the 80 year limit set by Psalm 90:10 for an average 'generation', to the year 1947, arriving at 2027. Subtracting 7 years ('tribulation') from 2027, we arrive at 2020 being the last possible date for the 7 years to begin. The beginning of the 7 years therefore must begin some time between 2017 and 2020.
2. A series of **astronomical events** directed our attention both to Israel, and to the starry heavens. These events included a 'blood moon' tetrad taking place on Jewish Feast days; a reoccurrence of the 'Star of Bethlehem'; a total solar eclipse over the United States in 2017, with another scheduled to occur 7 years later in 2024; and the 'Great Sign' of Revelation 12 on September 23, 2017.
3. If the years 2017-2024 provide us with the correct timeframe, then the Day of Atonement in 2024 would be the day of the Second Coming of Christ to earth. Using this date as the 'end point'—the Day of Atonement, September 14, 2024—we can subtract 1260 days from the Day of Atonement in 2024 to arrive at the midpoint. Subtracting another 1290 days from the midpoint takes us to the Feast of Trumpets in 2017. The Feast of Trumpets in 2017 is exactly 2550 days before the Day of Atonement, 2024. (Daniel 12:11 tells us there will be 1290 days before the midpoint/abomination.) I checked all other day counts for the 'Trumpets to Atonement' timespan, through the year 2028. No other timeframe except for 2017-2024 'worked', with exactly 2550 days from Trumpets to Atonement, staying within the 80 year upper limit of a generation.
4. Many were expecting the rapture to take place in 2017 (myself included) and when the Revelation 12 Sign came and went and we were all still 'here', I entertained the idea that maybe my understanding of the timing of the rapture, and the nature of the 7 year 'tribulation' was flawed, **not what the Sign itself was telling us.**
5. I also realized that the **book of Revelation probably contained the keys to the chronology of the end times.** Though many dedicated and earnest Bible teachers have expounded profusely on the various aspects of eschatology, I realized that they, and most 'watchman', were using end time passages from the gospels, Daniel and Paul's writings, even extra-biblical books; to try to determine the date of the rapture and other end time events. Rather than being used as the primary 'source' material, the book of Revelation was taught as an 'aside', or as a 'supporting' book to back-up timelines which had already

been pre-determined from the gospels or the Pauline epistles. I decided that Revelation was the 'elephant in the living room'—the book that people kept stepping around—so I decided, to apply myself to understanding the book of Revelation.

6. I deliberately chose to set aside what other people taught about the book, and what I had learned about end times in general. I decided to 'fact check' what I thought I already knew, and I was open to considering an alternative view should my first understanding prove faulty.

7. Crucial to my understanding was the idea that Revelation is not a chronological narrative, but *a series of visions*, with the same characters appearing over and over again within the various visions. Rather than the dramatic events of the Seals, Trumpets or Bowls 'telling' the story. I discovered that the *characters* in the visions were telling the end time story; that the narrative is actually about *people*, not the catastrophic events taking place. Once I realized that the characters were the focal point, instead of the various 'judgments, I decided to follow the narrative *they* were telling, and then the events of Revelation—and the order in which they occurred—became understandable.

8. In addition, I discovered that each vision has its own timeline and the events of the visions often overlay one another. Most of the visions start during the first half of the 7 years, and many of the visions 'end' at the Second Coming of Christ.

9. The story is understood by 'decoding' the symbols and imagery. Though the characters are depicted symbolically, they represent real people and real events that will take place sometime in the future.

10. Revelation is its "own thing", and it's important to interpret Revelation 'using Revelation', as most of the symbols found in Revelation are explained somewhere else in the book (unless the symbols are commonly understood by those literate in the Bible).

11. Understanding the visions in the context of Old Testament references that are *clearly alluded to in Revelation*, was also necessary to get a complete picture of what would be taking place; to 'whom' and 'when'.

12. The 'day counts' and other time references are actual days: 1,260 days, 10 days, 42 months, 'time, time and half a time', 5 months, one hour, etc. They are NOT symbolic.

13. Revelation was written to the Lord's 'servants' who would be living through the events depicted, so that they would KNOW what was about to happen. Once the events begin to take place, they would happen in quick succession. Knowing what would take place in advance would help them not be taken by surprise when the events begin to unfold.

14. 'His servants' are believers, who walk by faith and have the Holy Spirit. They are encouraged to be 'over-comers' and persevere—whether through martyrdom or until Christ comes for them and takes them in a 'rapture' event.

15. For all intents and purposes (and contrary to popular opinion), there is no 'church history' in Revelation and the letters to the 7 churches were written to the people who will come to Christ once the (1st) rapture of the 'child"/24 Elders has taken place, that being the 144,000 of Israel.
16. There are clues in Revelation that help us place events in a timeline with many events taking place very close to the midpoint, which is when the 'Woman flees' and the Beast from the Sea begins to reign for 42 months. The midpoint/ 3.5 year mark is also referred to as the Abomination of Desolation in Matthew, and Daniel; and as the day when 'the man of sin takes his seat in the temple of God' in 2 Thessalonians 2:2.
17. An understanding of the 7 Feasts of the Lord is vital. MANY of the crucial events depicted in the book of Revelation actually take place on one of the Feasts of the Lord!
18. I had to 'unlearn' a lot of stuff....

If you are interested in viewing the timelines and charts you will need to obtain a PDF copy which is available in the PDF version of this book or by emailing me: BrendaWeltner@gmail.com

Explanation of the Timeline for the 'Child'/24 Elders

Scriptural Considerations: Revelation 12:3-5; Revelation 5:6-8; 2 Kings 2

1. The 'child' (Revelation 12:4, 5b) is 'delivered' after the 'travail' of the 'woman' (Revelation 1:2). The 'child' symbolically represents present day believers. The 'woman' is Israel, from whom came the Messiah (also known as the 'Man-child' in this passage). The woman is described as being in 'travail'. In the Old Testament, the 'travail' of childbirth is often used as a metaphor for war or conflict, as when a nation is overtaken by an invading force, or any other grievous calamity, plague or disaster. (Jeremiah 30:6, Psalm 48:6) We can assume a war or other conflict in Israel shortly before believers are 'born' and 'caught up'.
2. The '9th of Av' is associated with the destruction of both the first and second Jewish temples, as well as the expulsion of Jews from various countries, and the day when the Israelites were consigned to wander for 40 years in the wilderness due to unbelief. This is a day of mourning for Jews and a likely day for the 'woman'/Israel to go into 'travail'/war.
3. The 'stars' being cast from heaven indicates that Satan will bring some of his angelic forces here on earth. These 'stars' will possibly be disguised as 'aliens' from another planet or another dimension. 'Disclosure' will take place before the rapture of the child.
4. The resurrection of the dead and the 'change' of the living may take place on the Feast of Trumpets (the 'birth' of the 'child'). The 'child' is then 'caught up' ('raptured') to God and to His throne (room) after a short time of persecution by Satan (the Dragon who seeks to 'devour' the child). The actual day of the rapture will be on the Day of Atonement, 9/28/20.
5. The 24 Elders are seen in heaven's throne room, around the throne of God and in the presence of the 4 Living Creatures. The 24 Elders, who are pictured worshipping before the throne in Revelation 4, represent the *resurrected saints,* who will receive their glorified bodies in heaven. The 24 Elders in Revelation 5—those who are described as singing a 'new song'—represent the glorified and raptured 'child' of Revelation 12:5. The number '24' symbolically represents the 24 divisions of priests who ministered in Solomon's temple. When David set up the administration for the future temple, he established 24 'courses' or 'divisions' of the priesthood. This idea of a 'rotation' of groups of raptured saints entering the Heavenly Holy of Holies to serve God as priests, is embedded in the number '24'. (See 1 Chronicles, chapters 23-27.)
6. The Lamb comes *from the midst* of the Elders to receive the scroll. The Elders worship and act as *priests* by offering 'golden bowls full of incense, which are the prayers of the saints' on earth. (Revelation 5:6-10) Christ's unity with believers is pictured as Christ *'in the midst'* of His people. He is *'in the midst'* of the 24 Elders. In Revelation chapter 1, He is "One like a Son of Man" who

walks *in the midst* of the 7 golden lampstands. He intends for us to rule and reign with Him, and to be joint heirs with Him. Just as we have been qualified to rule as kings, we are also qualified to act on His behalf as priests before God. Once the Lamb has taken the scroll, He will begin to exercise His right to rule. **Someone must take His place before the altar of incense, to offer prayers on behalf of the saints on earth.** That role will be ours, as priests and kings. (Revelation 1:6) *It's conceivable that Christ would not be able to rule as King, without the first division of the priesthood being present in heaven to take His place at the altar.* This may be why Satan casts a third of the 'stars'/angels to earth, and positions himself to 'devour' the child as soon as it is born, in an attempt **to prevent the rapture of the child.** (Revelation 12:4) If believers don't arrive safely in the throne room, Satan would be able to maintain the 'status quo', and the Second Coming of Christ would conceivably be rendered impossible.

7. It's important to understand that the 'Man-child' represents Jesus. The 'child' represents present day believers on earth. The Man-child—Jesus—is the One who will "rule all nations with a rod of iron". He was NOT 'caught up'— forcibly brought to God after His resurrection, but gently ascended into a cloud from the Mount of Olives almost 2000 years ago. Believers, on the other hand, WILL be forcefully taken from the earth, away from the clutches of the Dragon and his angels. The 'Man-child' rules; but the 'child' is 'caught up'.

8. The rapture of the 'child' is forceful. The Greek word 'harpazo', translated as 'caught up' in Revelation 12:5, implies a forceful rescue or removal. There is no mention of clouds or trumpets in this rapture passage. Revelation 12 is also devoid of any kind of 'Jewish wedding' imagery associated with the rapture.

9. The story of Elijah's translation into heaven in a fiery chariot, is the Old Testament type of the 'catching away'. Elijah's servant, Elisha, who watched Elijah depart, received a double portion of Elijah's spirit once Elijah was taken into heaven. When the church leaves, another group of 'witnesses' will take their place, that being the 144K of Israel—a symbolic 12,000 from each of the 12 tribes of Israel. Elisha received assurance that he would receive the 'double portion' which was reserved for the first born, if he SAW Elijah taken into heaven. Elijah, the sons of the prophets and Elisha *all knew* the day that Elijah was going to be taken into heaven.

10. The rapture of present day believers will also take place *on a known date.* There *will be* a secret rapture later on, the rapture where "no man knows the day or hour", but that rapture belongs to believers who endure the reign of the Beast, and it will take place towards the END of the 7 years, in conjunction with the Day of the Lord. In the secret rapture, the Over-coming believers will be taken into heaven before the wrath of God is poured out on the Beast kingdom. The rapture of the present day church will likely take place on the Day of Atonement, September 28, 2020. If Israel goes into 'travail' in the summer of

2020, I would expect to be in God's presence sometime between the Feast of Trumpets and the Day of Atonement, 2020.

11. The 'Mighty Angel' (Christ, symbolized as the Angel of the Lord) announces 'there will be no more delay'. (Revelation 10:5,6) **The 'delay' is because the 'priesthood' has not yet been brought into the throne room, to intercede for the saints on earth before the golden altar of incense.** Christ can take the scroll from His Father and begin to rule *only* when He is 'relieved' by the next division of priests who have received authority to act on His behalf. Once the Elders are in heaven, the rest of the events will follow rapidly from one event to another.

12. The rapture of the 'child'/24 Elders will be preceded by several events which must happen in very quick succession: the 'travail' of Israel, Satan's angels cast to the earth, the resurrection of the dead and the 'change' of the living. If the 9th of Av proves to be the day when the 'travail' of Israel begins, then 60 days later, on the Day of Atonement, the 'child' will be caught up.

13. The Day of Atonement was the one day when the High Priest could enter the Holy of Holies in the earthly temple. God's throne room is the *real* 'Holy of Holies', of which the earthly temple was only a shadow. It is fitting that the 24 Elders—priest/kings—enter the heavenly Holy of Holies on the Day of Atonement.

14. Five days later will be the Feast of Tabernacles, the time when the first fruits of the fall crops are offered to God. The 144K are described as 'first fruits to God' in Revelation 14:4. The 'olive tree' represents spiritual Israel. (Romans 11:24) Since olives are offered as first fruits during the Feast of Tabernacles, the 144K of Israel will be the 'first fruits' of the 'olive' harvest. The 144K will be sealed/offered to God in the fall, at the Feast of Tabernacles, immediately after the rapture of the 'child'/Elders, to complete the 'Elijah/Elisha' type.

15. The main reason for the rapture of the 'child'/24 Elders is not to escape the wrath of God or the rule of the Beast, but to assist Christ in His High Priestly duties so that He can begin to rule and reign.

Explanation of the Timeline for the Two Witnesses, the 144,000 of Israel and the Rebuilt Temple

1. Once the first rapture of the 'child' has taken place, the 'baton' will be passed to the new believers on earth whose job it will be to share the Gospel. The 144,000 of the 12 tribes of Israel, who will be 'sealed' on the Feast of Tabernacles, will be tasked with sharing the good news of salvation. New Gentile converts will join them and they will also be filled with the Spirit on the 8th day of Tabernacles. The Two Witnesses will give accurate 'testimony' to the Savior as well.

2. The 144,000 (144K) of Israel are a special group of believers. They are mentioned by name in Revelation 7 and 14. They will be the very first group of people to believe in Christ after the rapture of the 'child'. They are called 'first fruits to God and to the Lamb'. This indicates they will have a special status similar to that of the 12 disciples. Both the 12 disciples/apostles and the 144K are said to 'follow' the Lord. They both comprise the first of Israel to come to Christ, in two different dispensations.

3. The 144K will be 'sealed' by the Lord, who will appear as the Angel of the Lord in Revelation 7. The seal He places on the foreheads of the 144K is the gift of the Holy Spirit, whose presence in the life of the Christian guarantees them a place in heaven, and in the case of the 144K, protection from the 'locust army'.

4. The 144K are also said to be 'redeemed' from the earth, which alludes to the Old Testament requirement of purchasing the redemption of the first born male, who was to be dedicated to God.

5. The 'first born' was promised a 'double portion' of the inheritance (the birthright), provided he didn't disqualify himself through immorality (as did Reuben, Jacob's oldest son) or by spurning the birthright (as did Esau, who sold his birthright to his brother, Jacob). The double portion for the 144K will be signified by a 'double filling' of the Holy Spirit, which will take place at the Feast of Tabernacles (first day and 8th day), and a place of preeminence in God's kingdom, similar to the 12 Apostles.

6. The seal on the foreheads of these 'servants of God' is replaced by 'writing' on their foreheads after they arrive in heaven in Revelation 14.This indicates that the promise of eternal life, the promise which the seal of the Spirit guaranteed, has been fulfilled.

7. The believers of the church of Philadelphia ("Brotherly Love") also have writing on them. In addition, they are told that the Jews who reviled them will ultimately bow down before them. This seems to indicate that the letter to the church of Philadelphia was written specifically to the 144K. This group will be kept from the 'hour of trial'. (The 'hour of trial' refers to the hour that the Harlot is destroyed at the 6th Trumpet/2nd Woe.) The 144K are told that they will be taken in their own rapture sometime before the midpoint, most likely on the Feast of First Fruits, 3/30/21. (All the letters to the seven churches are

written to the 144K of Israel, the first people who will come to Christ after the rapture of the child.)

8. Those of Israel who are chosen to be a part of the 144K, but who, through *spiritual* immorality disqualify themselves from the birthright, will not be taken in the rapture promised to the 144K. However, if they persevere through the reign of the Beast without taking the mark, worshiping the Beast or its image, they will be taken in the 'secret rapture', which will take place just prior to the Bowl Judgments/Day of the Lord/wrath of God.

9. The exhortations in the letters to the churches are directed to the 144K in particular.

10. The Two Witnesses are identified as Moses and Elijah. They have a specified length of ministry, spanning exactly 1260 days. During that period of time they will be invincible and have the power to destroy anyone who comes against them.

11. At the resurrection of the dead in Christ, which will coincide with the 'change' of believers, Christ (the Mighty Angel of Revelation 10) will also deliver a 'little scroll', the decree from God to rebuild His temple in Jerusalem. One aspect of the ministry of the Two Witnesses will consist of rebuilding the Temple, following the 'type' of Zerubbabel and Joshua the High Priest in Zechariah 4. They will encounter opposition to their temple rebuilding efforts but the opposition will be rebuffed and the temple will be completed by Hanukkah, 2020. The 144K will worship in the newly rebuilt temple.

12. The Two Witnesses will lead many of Israel in repentance toward God, using the rebuilt Temple as an 'object lesson' of the Person and work of Christ.

13. The ministry of the Two Witnesses (specifically the ministry of calling people to repentance) will have begun shortly after the Revelation 12 Sign. These two powerful men must be present on the earth at the time of the resurrection/ change of believers, which could have taken place on the Feast of Trumpets in any year after 2017, the year the Great Sign appeared through the fall of 2020. The Two Witnesses need to be present on earth in order to receive the little scroll authorizing them to begin rebuilding the Temple. The public ministry of the Two Witnesses will not begin until after the resurrection of the dead on the Feast of Trumpets, at which time they will have the little scroll in their possession—the decree from God to rebuild the temple.

14. The visible, active presence of the Two Witnesses is not a 'sign' for believers that the end is near. The visible ministry of the Two Witnesses will over-lap the witness of present day believers by 10 days: from the Feast of Trumpets to the Day of Atonement, at which time the rapture of the 'child' will take place, and the 'baton' of ministry will be passed to the 144K and the Two Witnesses.

15. The Temple will be completed by Hanukkah in 2020, "2300 evenings and mornings" (or 1150 days) from the day the Two Witnesses began their ministry on October 17, 2017.

16. Animosity toward the Two Witnesses on the part of the earth dwellers will be evident once the rapture has taken place, and during the construction of the Temple. The Jews in Israel may not accept the Temple built by the Two Witnesses, though the Antichrist/Beast WILL recognize it as God's temple at the time of the abomination of desolation at the midpoint.

17. The Scarlet Beast—the 7th King—will come against the Two Witnesses, who will kill *the Beast* on Passover. This will be during the ten day persecution of believers at the hands of the earth dwellers encouraged by false religion, as personified by the Harlot. The Scarlet Beast will be killed in a personal conflict between the Two Witnesses.

18. Two days later, the Beast will resurrect into the person we know as the Antichrist or the 'Beast from the Sea/bottomless Pit'. He will imitate the resurrection of Christ on the feast of First Fruits. The newly resurrected '8th King' will be the host body for Apollyon, the 'seed of the serpent', and receive power from his 'father', Satan, who will have been cast to the earth from heaven on the Feast of First Fruits, standing by the 'sea', awaiting the resurrection of the Beast from the sea.

19. The Beast's first act upon being raised from the dead will be to kill the Two Witnesses, which will also take place on First Fruits. This will be the final day of the 10 day persecution of believers, and all who were martyred in the purge will be in heaven in glorified bodies. The 144K of Israel—the first fruits of Israel—will be taken to heaven on that day as well.

20. The bodies of the Two Witnesses will lie in the streets of Jerusalem for 3.5 days. The people on earth who had been tormented by the plagues of the Two Witnesses, who will have also seen the Beast rise from the dead, will follow the Beast, and celebrate his victory over God's people and the Two Witnesses. Gift giving and general merriment will be the order of the day. They will also bestow their worship on the Beast and Satan.

21. The Two Witnesses will resurrect and ascend into heaven 3.5 days after their death, on the same day the Beast defiles the rebuilt Temple at the midpoint.

Explanation of the Timeline for the Spiritual Opposition

1. Satan is the enemy of God, and, by extension, he is the enemy of the people of God. Just as God has been working out His plan for the salvation of mankind since before Adam and Eve ever sinned in the Garden of Eden; Satan has a plan as well, one that he has been working since before the corruption of our first parents.
2. One of the consequences of the fall of man, was that Satan was able to wrest control of the earth from Adam, and in the process Satan became the 'lord of the earth'. His lordship means that he has holds power over God's highest creation—man.
3. Satan, as the prince of this world, desires to maintain control over both mankind, and the earth on which man dwells.
4. Satan uses men to further his plans; sometimes as witting agents, but mostly unwitting, in an effort to maintain control over his domain.
5. Christ's death on the cross and subsequent resurrection, spelled the 'beginning of the end' of Satan's rule over all mankind, and over the earth as well.
6. Those who receive Christ as their Savior, are no longer subject to Satan's lordship; and the penalty for the consequence of sin—eternal separation from God—was paid through the death of Christ.
7. Though Satan has lost control over believers—people who belong to Christ—he still seeks to rule over the earth and the rest of lost humanity.
8. During the last days, the conflict between light and darkness—between the kingdom of Christ and the prince of this world—will come to a head. At that time, God will methodically tear down Satan's kingdom and bring his reign to an end, including the eternal banishment of Satan's presence from heaven, the rescue of believers from the earth, and the judgment of the Antichrist/False Prophet and the Beast kingdom.
9. Satan will attempt to preemptively 'check mate' God's end time plan, by casting a third of his angels to the earth, keeping two-thirds in heaven. Satan knows that he will need to be able to fight on two fronts: one war in heaven, and one on the earth. The war in heaven will be the more dangerous of the two wars for Satan, with Michael leading the hosts of heaven against Satan and his army. Two days before the midpoint, precisely on the feast of First Fruits, Michael and the armies of heaven will succeed in removing Satan's presence from heaven, forever. Satan, along with his angels, will be banished to the earth.
10. About six months before Satan will be cast out of heaven, he will come against the believers on earth—specifically the 'child' who is about to be raptured, believers who will be "caught up to God and to His throne" in heaven. Israel, represented by the 'woman' of Revelation 12, is pictured as being in 'travail', which, symbolically represents a war or invasion. Satan, who is represented by

the 'dragon', will stand before the 'woman', Israel, during her 'travail'. At this point in time, his goal is *not the destruction of the woman/Israel*, but the devouring of the 'child' after it is 'born'.

11. Satan's one-third angelic forces, who will be present on earth, will no doubt assist him in attempting to prevent the rapture of the child.

12. The child—believers—will have already been 'born'—transformed into their glorified bodies—before they will be caught up to God's presence. Once they arrive in the heavenly throne room, they are depicted as 24 Elders—priests and kings. As members of the heavenly priesthood, they have authority to intercede before the throne of God for the new believers on earth. Once the Elders are in heaven and praying before the altar, Christ may, at that time, leave the altar of intercession to take the scroll from His Father and, upon so doing, begin the process of meting out God's judgments on His enemies—Satan included.

13. Once the child is in heaven, Satan will also return to heaven from the earth, in order to accuse the new believers, before the throne of God.

14. Not long after the child is in heaven, the 144,000 of Israel plus multitudes of saved Gentiles will be sealed and baptized in the Holy Spirit. This revival will be followed by the first 4 Trumpet judgements and the opening of the first four Seals. When the angel sounds the 5th Trumpet, the Pit/Abyss will be unlocked, and the fallen angels (the Watchers) and their king, Apollyon, will be released to invade the earth.

15. These angels are depicted as an army of locusts, who have the sting of scorpions. They are allowed to torture anyone who does not have the seal of God—anyone who is not a believer and filled with the Holy Spirit. The torture will be unbearable and men will wish to die, but death will elude them. Christ, who holds the keys to death and Hades, will not permit those who are stung to die. They will be given a taste of the hopelessness that will come to those who take the mark of the Beast and, as a result, suffer eternal punishment in the Lake of Fire. For many, the torture that they will be subjected to during the five months will result in their salvation,

16. Any of those who are stung will have the opportunity of receiving Christ and will then be sealed with the Spirit. If they turn to Christ in faith, they will be healed. (The story of the 'fiery serpents' in the book of Numbers, is a type of the 'sting of rebellion', and gazing at the brazen serpent on a pole is a type of the spiritual healing that will come to those who look to Christ, who was crucified for them.)

17. Rather than being an instrument of Satan, God will turn the sting of the locust army into the instrument whereby salvation will come to millions of people. This will result in another wave of revival on earth.

18. Satan will then use his agent, the Harlot—including false Christianity—to persecute believers. Operating in conjunction with the Scarlet Beast (the 7th King) and the earth dwellers—people whose hearts and affections are set on

things of this world—millions of believers will be imprisoned and martyred for their testimony in a 10 day orgy of bloodshed.

19. While believers are being persecuted on earth, Michael and his angels will be warring with Satan and his angels in heaven. At the end of 10 days, both the war in heaven and the persecution taking place on earth, will be over. Satan will be cast to the earth, and the martyrs will be present in heaven, in their glorified, resurrected bodies.

20. Before the end of the 10 days, the Scarlet Beast (7th King) will make an attempt on the lives of the Two Witnesses. This attempt will backfire, and the Two Witnesses will kill the Beast. This will take place on Passover.

21. The Beast will resurrect two days later, on First Fruits. Apollyon, the king of the angels of the Abyss, will take up residence inside the resurrected Beast, changing him into the 'Beast who ascends from the bottomless Pit'. This resurrected 'seed of the serpent' is also known as the 'Beast from the Sea', the '8th King', and 'the Antichrist'. He will receive the dragon's power, throne and very great authority. (At this point, all those martyred by the Harlot will be in heaven in their resurrection bodies. The 144K of Israel will also be in heaven, having been raptured on the Feast of First Fruits. These two groups of 'priests' will join the 24 Elders already present in heaven.)

22. The feast of First Fruits in 2021 will bring the 1260 day ministry of the Two Witnesses to an end. As of this day, they will no longer be invincible. The newly resurrected and satanically empowered Beast will kill the Two Witnesses as one of his first acts. The bodies of the Two Witnesses will lie unburied in the streets of Jerusalem.

23. With the death of the Two Witnesses, the earth dwellers will have cause to celebrate and hail the resurrected Beast as their king and messiah.

24. Three and a half days later, the Two Witnesses will resurrect, and be called up into heaven. This will coincide with the 'abomination of desolation' which is when the Beast will take his seat in the temple of God, declaring that he, himself is God. At that same hour, the Two Witnesses will resurrect and ascend into heaven, and a great earthquake will split the Mount of Olives. Christ Himself, will appear in a cloud of glory and lead the remnant of Israel into the wilderness. Satan's army will follow the remnant in an attempt to prevent their escape. As his army pursues the remnant through the newly created valley in the Mount of Olives, the mountain will close back up, 'swallowing' the army of the dragon.

25. Meanwhile, the Beast (and 10 Kings who have given their power to him), will take this opportunity to destroy the Harlot—the current reigning world religious system. They will accomplish this in one hour on a single day, with fire, smoke and sulphur. Anyone associated with the Harlot will die, even believers who took 'refuge' in her. One-third of the earth will perish in the judgment of the Harlot.

26. Once the destruction of the Harlot is complete at the midpoint/6th Trumpet, God will sound one last warning to those on earth before the reign of the Beast begins. Three 'gospel' angels will plead with people to worship God, the Creator; they will inform the world that Babylon...the Harlot...has 'fallen'; and warn them not to take the mark of the Beast.
27. Anyone who takes the mark or worships the Beast or the Image of the Beast will be thrown into the Lake of Fire, to suffer in the presence of God and the holy angels, forever and ever.
28. Unlike the martyrs of the Harlot, any believer who dies from this point on, must wait until the return of Christ to be resurrected. Those who are not killed by the Beast during his reign, must remain faithful to the Lord who will come get them in a rapture event before the wrath of God is poured out on the Beast and the Beast kingdom.
29. The Beast, the False Prophet and the Dragon will establish their version of the Millennium over the next 42 months, dwelling in 'peace and safety', with no opposition from God or God's people who still remain on the earth.
30. On an unknown day, the few believers remaining on earth will be taken to heaven by the Lord who will come for them on a cloud. Once these believers are safely in heaven, the wrath of God will begin to fall on the earth. The kings of the earth will be lured to Armageddon to war against Christ. They will be defeated, and the Beast and the False Prophet will be thrown alive into the Lake of Fire. Satan will be bound and thrown into the Pit for a thousand years.
31. The remnant of Israel will return to Jerusalem, and the martyrs of the Beast will be resurrected to join their brethren in heaven.
32. Christ will establish His Millennial kingdom on earth. Believers will live in the New Jerusalem in heaven, minister to God as priests in His temple, and also assist Christ in His earthly rule.
33. At the end of the thousand years, Satan will be released from the pit, and gather to himself a large group of disgruntled people, creating yet another rebellion against the rule of God. This rebellion will be crushed and Satan will be cast into the Lake of Fire.
34. All the remaining dead will then be resurrected at the Great White Throne judgment. The righteous whose names are written in the Lamb's book of Life will go on to live on the New Earth. The wicked will be cast into the Lake of Fire, along with Satan.
35. The New Jerusalem will come to earth and God will dwell with man, forever.

Chapter 59: *Cast of Characters and Symbols used in Revelation:*

The Lord God, the Almighty: Himself

The Throne Room of God: The Heavenly 'Holy of Holies'

The (Divine) Lamb: Jesus. AKA: "King of Kings, Lord of Lords, Alpha and Omega, the Lion of the Tribe of Judah, the Root of David, One like a Son of Man, Faithful and True, Word of God, Faithful Witness, First Born of the Dead, the Ruler of the Kings of the Earth". Jesus is also symbolized by three 'angels' in Revelation: The Angel in the Rising Sun of Revelation 7:1, The "Strong" Angel of Revelation 10:1 and the 'Resplendent Angel' of Revelation 18:1.

Four Living Creatures: Heavenly beings near God's throne who do His bidding and are the guardians of His glory. Probably the same as cherubim in the Old Testament.

24 Elders: The priestly body of Christ in heaven; the 'brethren' of the 'saints'. Occupied with worship and intercession.

The Male child: Christ, Who rules all nations.

The Child: Believers who are taken alive into heaven at the first rapture on the Day of Atonement.

Angels: Messengers of God; spirit beings, both good and evil.

Mighty Angel: The Angel of the Lord, who is Christ, who comes to resurrect the dead and 'change' the living. He also delivers the 'little scroll'. (Revelation 10)

The Angel from the Rising Sun: An appearance of Christ as the Angel of the Lord, sealing the 144K of Israel. (Revelation 7)

The Glorious Angel: Christ as the Angel of the Lord overseeing the destruction of Mystery, Babylon, and leading the remnant into the wilderness. (Revelation 18)

The 144,000 of Israel: Men and women of Israel who worship the Lamb during the time of the end, the first fruits/firstborn of saved Israel.

Virgin: Someone who has not been spiritually corrupted by the Harlot religious system.

The Saints: Believers who live during the time of the end.

Earth Dwellers: AKA: "those who dwell on earth", mankind, man. All those who worship the Beast/Dragon or are a part of the Harlot church.

The Woman in travail: The remnant of Israel; AKA: The "Woman".

The Two Witnesses: Moses and Elijah. They also embody characteristics of Joshua the High Priest and Zerubbabel in Zechariah 4, and John the Baptist, the forerunner of Christ.

Stars: Angels, or literal stars in the sky

Dragon: Satan, the 'ancient serpent', devil.

Harlot/"Mystery"Babylon/the Woman who Rides the Beast: The first of two end-time religious systems. This religion may be based in Rome, but represents an amalgamation of all religions, and is world-wide.

The Scarlet Beast: The 7th end time king. Rules in conjunction with the Harlot before the midpoint.

The Beast from the Sea: The 8th end time king who rules over the 7th kingdom. Rules with the False Prophet (Beast from the Earth) and the 10 Kings. A continuation of the 7th king. AKA: "the Beast who ascends from the bottomless pit"

Beast From the Earth: The False Prophet. Spokesman, miracle worker and 'deceiver in chief' for the 'Beast from the Sea'/8th king/Beast who ascends from the bottomless pit/Apollyon.

Apollyon: Angel from the bottomless pit (Abyss) who manifests in/as the 8th end-time king. Also known as Abaddon, the Destroyer, the king of the 'Watchers'.

Ten Horns: Ten end time kings who rule with the Beast from the Sea.

Frogs: Demonic spirits

Locusts: The 'Watchers' who have been imprisoned in the pit and will be released during the last days.

Bride: The inhabitants of the New Jerusalem.

Churches: The '*ekklesia*' of God; those called *out of* the world and *to* God. In Revelation 2 & 3, the 144K of Israel are the members of the 7 churches.

The Rider on the White Horse: The 7th king as represented by Nimrod. Nimrod was the prototype of the Antichrist mentioned in Genesis; the ruler of Babel, who was transformed into a mighty man, a '*gibborim*'—mighty man.

The Holy City: Jerusalem, both earthly and heavenly.

Sodom and Egypt: Jerusalem under the reign of the 8th king.

Clouds: The manifestation of God's glory; heavenly transportation.

Scroll with 7 Seals: Writ of judgement against the earth and its inhabitants.

Horn: Power and authority.

Eyes: All-seeing, omniscient.

Little scroll: The heavenly authorization to rebuild the temple.

Two Olive Trees and Two Candlesticks: Moses and Elijah as types of Joshua, the High priest and Zerubbabel, who oversaw rebuilding the 2nd Temple (Zechariah 3 and 4).

Grapes: Living people doomed to destruction in the winepress of God's wrath.

Great tribulation: There are three different 'great tribulations': 1) the tribulation which takes place in the first part of the 7 years for the martyrs; 2) at the midpoint/6th Trumpet for the Harlot/'Jezebel' and her followers; and 3) the tribulation which takes place during the 2nd half of the 7 years, for Israel.

Mark of the Beast: irreversible evidence of Beast worship

Image of the Beast: a 'new race' of man 'created' in the Image of the Beast

Fiery red: The color of the Dragon and the 2nd Seal Horse; represents evil, war and destruction.

Scarlet: The color related to blood and religion.

Purple: The color related to royalty and wealth and associated with the Harlot.

Crowns: Rulership and authority.

Altar: The altar of incense in heaven; the place where prayers are received and answered.

Ark of the Covenant: God's throne of judgement and mercy in heaven.

White robe: Glorified body; also represents righteous deeds

Torches of fire: Holy Spirit. Also represented by the 7 'eyes' and 7 'horns' of the Lamb, sent out into all the earth.

The River of Life: A picture of the Holy Spirit in the New Jerusalem.

Gold: Glory, divinity, purification through trial.

Lampstand: That which facilitates the impartation of spiritual light and truth; the 7 churches of Asia Minor are represented by seven lampstands, as are the Two Witnesses.

Trumpet: That which announces something.

Waters: People, multitudes and nations.

The Sea: place of the dead, including the dead Beast.

Tribulation: Persecution and trials

The Land: the place of the living: "the land of the living". Also a reference to the land of Israel.

Jews: People of Israel who follow the traditions of men; in juxtaposition to those 'of Israel', who follow the Lord.

"7": The number of fulness, completion, maturity, totality and divinity.

"24": The number associated with the temple, the priesthood, worshipers, stewards and co-rulers.

"12": The number associated with the 12 tribes of Israel and the Apostles. Twelve is the number associated with government and rulership, both earthly and spiritual.

"1000": Represents the fullest amount possible, therefore: 12 X 1000 equals the fullest representation of each of the tribes of Israel.

"666": The number of the Beast. Six is the number of man. Three '6's'=the full manifestation of man or 'superman'.

"1,260" days: The equivalent of 3 and a half years. Also 42 months and "time, times and half a time".

Chapter 60: Common Objections

The most common objection to this timeline is that it is not 'pre-tribulational', that is, believers will be present on earth during the 7 years commonly known as the 'tribulation. (This timeline is also not mid- or post-tribulational, or 'pre-wrath'.)

> **Objection #1**: *The 'tribulation' is the out-pouring of God's wrath and Paul tells us that believers are not subject to God's wrath. If the entire 7 years are, in fact, the wrath of God, then believers must be raptured prior to the beginning of the 7 years.*

Refutation: There is NO VERSE, anywhere in the Bible which tells us that the 'wrath of God' (also known as the 'Day of the Lord') lasts for 7 years. If the wrath cannot be shown to last 7 years, it is entirely possible for believers to be 'present' on earth anytime during the 7 year period, until the very day that the wrath of God/Day of the Lord begins.

> **Objection #2**: *"The 7 year 'tribulation' is the time when God is dealing solely with Israel. The 'dispensation of grace' has ended and the next dispensation begins. God only deals in one 'dispensation' at a time. Believers who are a part of the 'dispensation of grace' must be in heaven before God will to go back to working with Israel."*

Refutation: The 'end time' events are the culmination and convergence of ALL of God's plans and workings: plans which include EVERY group of people—Jew and Gentile—as well as His plan for spiritual entities like angels. Israel, the church, 'earth dwellers', the Beast, the False Prophet, Satan, fallen angels, the Harlot/corrupt system of religion, the occupants of the Pit/Abyss, and the nations all have a role in the end time story. The *preaching* of the gospel will move from Gentiles back to Israel once believers are removed from the earth in the first rapture. Revelation tells us that there are 3 distinct groups of people who will be raptured at different points in the 7 years.

According to Daniel 12:7, Matthew 24:15, and 2 Thessalonians 2:1-4, there are actually only 3.5 years left of Israel's 7 year timeline. The last 3.5 years will begin at the abomination of desolation. The 3.5 year ministry of Christ has already taken place, and comprised the *first half* of the 70th Week of Daniel, leaving only 3.5 years. (The church, however, DOES have a full 7 year timeline. The timeline for the Jews and the timeline for believers will 'meet up' at the abomination of desolation/'flight of the woman'.)

Objection #3: *Once John was taken to heaven in Revelation 4, the 'church' is not seen again until the end of the book. This indicates that the 'church' is not present during the end time events recorded in Revelation.*

Refutation: 'The Church', as an 'entity', is a Pauline concept which is not expressed in Revelation using the word 'Church'. When the word, church' appears in Revelation, it is only referring to individual assemblies, or groups of believers. There is no singular 'Church', ie: "Body of Christ" to be found in Revelation at all—only assemblies of professing Christians designated symbolically by the names of various 1st century communities. *(This objection is what is known as an "argument from silence", which, like all such proofs, doesn't provide a very compelling argument.)*

Objection #4: *"Your timeline allows for multiple 'rapture' events. There is only one Bride (the 'Church'), therefore there can only be one rapture."*

Refutation: Even though the Jewish wedding analogy is prevalent in modern Christian pre-millennial doctrine, and is a dominant theme in popular eschatology, the typical Jewish 'bridal' imagery is no where to be found in Revelation. In the standard 'bridal scenario', Christ is depicted as the Bridegroom who 'steal's the Bride/Church like a 'thief in the night', followed by a 7 year 'wedding supper' in heaven, while 7 years of wrath takes place on earth. This imagery is not to be found in Revelation.

In Revelation, believers are symbolized as *'priests and kings'* who minister in God's presence. Believers are depicted by the following symbolic representations in Revelation, and all are 'priest/kings', as signified by their presence in God's heavenly temple: the 24 Elders, (also pictured as the 'child' who is 'caught up to God and to *His throne*'); the 144,000 of Israel who appear on Heavenly Mount Zion, and the "Over-comers" of Revelation 15:2, who stand before the sea of glass in God's throne room. As part of their inheritance in Christ, *all* believers have been made into a kingdom of priests, and have confidence to enter the 'sanctuary by the blood of Jesus.' (Hebrews 10:19) The day that the first division of 'priest/kings' will be raptured into the heavenly Holy of Holies will be on the Day of Atonement, 2020.

In addition to using symbols which pertain to the priesthood, God also uses the *feasts of the Lord* and *'harvest' imagery* to depict when He 'gath-

436

ers' His 'harvest' of souls. The pattern of using the Feasts of the Lord was first identified with Christ's death on the cross at Passover. Christ was then raised on First Fruits, the 'feast of the Lord' which followed Passover, at the time when the first fruits of the barley harvest were offered to God. Christ's resurrection indicates that, in addition to fulfilling the Passover, He also fulfilled the type of the 'first fruits' of the 'barley harvest'. (There were also other fulfillments on that day.)

The First Fruits of the 'wheat' harvest were offered next, on Pentecost, when the 120 disciples who gathered together in Jerusalem received the Holy Spirit. (Plus 3,000 more people after them.) Those upon whom the Spirit descended represented the first fruits of the 'wheat Harvest'. (Present day believers are the 'main' harvest of the 'wheat': we are not the first fruits.)

In Revelation 14, the 144K are also called 'first fruits', indicating that they will be 'presented' to God at the *remaining unfulfilled first fruits feast*: the Feast of Tabernacles. The olives, grapes and other fruits are offered to God in the fall, at Tabernacles. The 144K of the 12 tribes of Israel, represent the in-gathering of the 'first fruits' of the 'olive' harvest *of Israel* at the Feast of Tabernacles, which is the only 'first fruits' feast that has yet to be fulfilled. The olive tree is often used as a symbol for spiritual Israel. (The fig tree represents national Israel.)

There is, however, some 'bridal' imagery in Revelation, *but not until the end of the book, which is at the* end *of the story,* in Revelation 19 and 21. The New Jerusalem—the dwelling place of all believers from Old Testament saints through tribulation saints—comes down from heaven as a Bride. The 'Bride' is never depicted as going 'up' or being taken in a rapture. She only *comes down* to earth at the 're-creation', after the Millennial reign of Christ.

All believers will be brought into God's presence in His throne room BEFORE they go to live in the New Jerusalem. The New Jerusalem, the place Christ is preparing for believers, *will not be completed* and occupied until every saint is resurrected or raptured. This includes the so-called 'tribulation saints'—believers who will be beheaded by the Beast during the last 3.5 years. Those thus martyred will be resurrected at the return of Christ, on the Day of Atonement in 2024. The 'Bride' will not be 'made ready' until the last division of the heavenly priesthood—the martyrs of the Beast—are resurrected and presented before God in heaven.

Chapter 61: Potential Significant End Time Dates for 2017-2024

The dates for the Feasts of the Lord are taken from TorahCalendar.com; day intervals from "timeanddate.com". Words in red indicate a significant day, or a known 'holy day', Jewish or otherwise. All dates are plus or minus 24 hours. Obviously, all this has yet to be proven out in real time. I am not a prophet. This is not "thus saith the Lord". This is my best effort to lay out what I have discovered as a result of my personal studies.

September 21, 2017: Feast of Trumpets; beginning of the 7 years for believers; begin 1290 days of Daniel 12:11.

September 23, 2017: Revelation 12 sign in the heavens at the close of the 2nd day of the Feast of Trumpets.

October 17, 2017: The Two Witnesses begin their ministry of 1,260 days, ending on First Fruits, 3/30/21. Begin 2,300 'evenings and mornings' (1150 days) until the temple is cleansed/dedicated on Hanukkah, 12/10/20.

May 14, 2020: Pope's "Global Compact" conference at the Vatican. (Israel's independence day on the Gentile calendar.)

Spring/summer 2020: "Alien" disclosure; arrival of 1/3 of Satan's fallen angels. Collapse of the world's economic, ecological and political systems. Begin devastating famine, pestilence, plagues and natural disasters.

July 30, 2020: 9th of Av. War in Israel, possible Gog/Magog invasion.(At the same time China may invade Taiwan dragging the US into war in the Far East.)

August 20/21, 2020: Elul 1. End of Gog/Magog war. Beginning of Israel's national repentance and cleansing of the land for 7 months, ending on the day before the spring Equinox. (The Equinox is the start of 10 days of persecution for believers by the Harlot and the earth dwellers. Israel's 'covenant with death' exempts them from persecution.)

September 18, 2020: Feast of Trumpets. Mighty Angel (Christ) announces 'no more delay'. The resurrection of the dead and the 'change' of the living. Authorization to rebuild the temple ('little scroll'). Begin ten days of ministry by glorified believers. Satan attempts to 'devour' glorified believers.

September 28, 2020: Day of Atonement. Rapture of the first division of priest/kings (present day believers). Passing of the 'baton' of ministry to the 144,000 of Israel. Revival.

October 3, 2020: First day of Tabernacles. Sealing of 144K in the Holy Spirit. First anointing of the 'double portion' birthright for the 144K.

October 11, 2020: "8th Day" of Tabernacles. Sealing of Gentile believers in the Holy Spirit. Second out-pouring of the Spirit on the 144K. Fulfillment of Joel 2:28,29 and John 7:37-39.

Sometime after the "8th Day" of Tabernacles: A great earthquake will be followed by the first 4 Trumpet and first 4 Seal events, which will take place almost simultaneously. One-third of the earth (western hemisphere?) will be devastated. Fresh water, vegetation, salt water are rendered toxic. One-third of the light of sun and moon no longer shines (due to volcanic activity?). One-quarter of the earth is affected by wars, pestilence, plagues, diseases, wild animals, famine of the first 4 Seals. Many will die.

October 31-November 1, 2020: Halloween/All Saint's Day. The opening of the Abyss. Five months torture ending on First Fruits, 3/30/21. Those stung are not allowed to die. Millions come to faith in Christ. **Final revival on earth before the return of Christ.**

December 9/10, 2020: Hanukkah Eve. Dedication of the Temple, 1150 days since the beginning of the ministry of the Two Witnesses. Seventy days since the first day of **Tabernacles** and the sealing of the 144K, (which took place on 10/3/20).

March 19/20, 2021: Spring Equinox. Israel is 'cleansed' after the war which took place in the summer of 2020. Seven days before **Passover.** Begin 10 days of persecution of the saints by the Harlot and the earth dwellers.

March 28, 2021: Passover (falls on Sunday). The Scarlet Beast (7th King) suffers a mortal wound--most likely at the hands of the Two Witnesses, as a result of coming against them before the end of their 1260 days of ministry.

March 30, 2021: First Fruits. Rapture of the 144K. End 10 days persecution of believers--resurrected martyrs appear in heaven. End 5 months of torture by the 'locust army'. End war in heaven. Satan is cast out of heaven with his angels. Satan, now on earth awaits the 'resurrection' of the Scarlet Beast/Beast from the Sea. Resurrection of the Beast and the 'birth' of the 8th King, now indwelt by Apollyon. Satan gives his 'power, throne and great authority' to the Beast. End

440

1260 days of the ministry of the Two Witnesses. The Beast/antichrist kills the Two Witnesses. Begin 42 month trampling of the Holy City/Jerusalem.

March 30-April 3, 2021: Feast of Unleavened Bread. Two Witnesses lie unburied in Jerusalem. Party time for the earth dwellers including gift exchanges. Earth dwellers 'marvel' at the resurrection and power of the Beast; worship of the Beast and Satan commences. Preparation for the 'coronoation of the king/Antichrist', which will take place in the rebuilt temple of God.

Midpoint, April 3, 2021: *(Sabbath ends at sundown, 7PM).* Midpoint of the 7 years, 1290 days since the Feast of Trumpets, 9/21/17. Abomination of desolation. Fire comes down from heaven, 'authenticating' the legitimacy of the Beast/Antichrist as Israel's messiah. Sixth Trumpet--the destruction of Mystery Babylon by the Beast and the 10 Kings. One third of mankind is killed in one hour by a 200 million man army led by 4 fallen angels, by means of 'fire, smoke and sulphur'. Begin persecution of Israel. Israel's 'covenant with death/Harlot' is annulled. Two Witnesses resurrect and ascend into heaven. Three 'gospel angels' deliver God's final warning before the reign of the Beast begins. Terrified people give glory to God. "Glorious Angel"/Christ appears and declares the fall of Babylon. His feet touch down on the Mount of Olives and split the mountain in two. One tenth of the city falls and 7,000 people are killed.

Begin 42 month reign of the Beast/Antichrist. "Days of Noah"; Golden Age 2.0; the 'Watchers' and fallen angels dwell with man on earth, False Millennial reign of the Antichrist. Persecution and beheading of believers; destruction of the earth by the earth dwellers and fallen spiritual entities.After sunset on 4/3/21: Close of Sabbath. The remnant of Israel flees through the opening in the Mount of Olives and is led into the wilderness by the Angel of the Lord/Christ. "Not in winter, not on the Sabbath." Dragon's army pursues the remnant of Israel. The Mount of Olives closes up, killing the Dragon's army. Call for the endurance of the remaining saints on earth. No more resurrections or raptures until just before the Day of the Lord/Bowl judgments.

Earth dwellers make the Image of the Beast. Mark of the Beast is required to buy or sell.

May 18, 2021: Pentecost. The Image of the Beast receives 'spirit/breath' from the False Prophet/anti-Holy Spirit? Worship of the Image of the Beast is mandatory under penalty of death. (Sixty days between Equinox and Pentecost.)

Unknown Date: Third and final rapture of remaining believers, the day that 'no man knows the day or hour'. Jesus comes on a cloud to collect the saints who 'are alive and remain'. Beginning of the wrath of God/Bowl judgments/Day of the Lord. Heaven is closed.

September 14, 2024: Day of Atonement. Second Coming of Christ. Battle of Armageddon. Beast, False Prophet are captured and thrown alive into the Lake of Fire. Remnant of Israel returns. 1,260 days since April 3, 2021--the day of the Abomination of Desolation/midpoint. 2550 days since the Feast of Trumpets, 9/21/17. Satan bound and thrown into the Pit. The resurrection of the beheaded martyrs of the Beast.

November 27, 2024: Hanukkah eve. End 1335 days since the Abomination of Desolation, 4/3/21. Christ begins His Millennial Reign.

The odds of so many events landing on actual feast days or significant occult days, is astronomical, especially considering the fact that the nature of the event coincides with the significance of the 'holy day'. (For example, the bottomless pit is opened on Halloween, 10/31/20.) *The fact that most events land on significant days cannot be sheer coincidence, but evidence of a Divine plan unfolding before our eyes.*

"Negotiable Dates"

The dates for the war in Israel, the rebuilding of the Temple, the resurrection of the dead and the first rapture of the priesthood of believers are 'negotiable' and are not 'fixed': that is, these events do not have 'day counts' associated with them--but they all must take place during the first half of the 7 years. These events could have taken place in 2018 or 2019--after the Revelation 12 Sign first appeared--and must take place by the fall of 2020. Because these events have not happened as of this writing (winter 2020), these events must take place this year: 2020.

When the Mighty Angel--an appearance of Christ as the Angel of the Lord--declares "there will be no more delay!", the 'change'/resurrection/rapture will finally take place. According to the timeline presented in Revelation 12, the (1st) rapture must take place sometime after the Revelation 12 Sign, but BEFORE the midpoint of the 7 years; and in conjunction with a war in Israel and an 'alien' invasion/disclosure. Some events in Revelation take place on 'non-negotiable' dates: the beginning of the 7 years (Revelation 12 Sign/Feast of Trumpets, 2017), the ministry of the Two Witnesses (10/17/17 to 3/30/21) the day of the 'abomintion of desolation' (4/3/21), the Second Coming of Christ (9/14/24). All these have definite starting and ending dates. (Dates are reckoned from the Feast of Trumpets, 9/21/17.)

Afterward

What I have presented in this book is, I believe, the most accurate of all the interpretations of Revelation that I have come across in over 50 years of being a Christian. Even so, that doesn't mean that I am right about everything I've described in the book—but I've come about as close to telling the story of The End, as has anyone else who has attempted to unravel the mysteries of Revelation. And even if I'm wrong about some things, I pray that God will receive the glory that's due Him, in spite of my weakness and limitations.

If you do not know the Lord, *right now* is the best time to get your heart right with Him. Do not put this off—time is not on your side:

"Dear Jesus: I want to be a part of God's family and I'm sorry for my sinful heart. Please forgive my sins and give me your Holy Spirit so that I can be God's child."

If you prayed this prayer sincerely, you can be assured that God will forgive your sins, no matter what you have done, if you come to Him with a humble heart.

> "If we confess our sins, He is faithful and just to forgive us our sins and to cleanse us from all unrighteousness." 1 John 1:9

If you're a born again, Spirit-filled believer—keep watching, waiting and working for the Lord until He comes!

May God bless you, dear reader. I look forward to meeting you in glory!

Brenda Weltner
February, 2020

Made in the USA
Middletown, DE
12 June 2020